The Scottish Miners, 1874–1939

Volume Two

The Scottish Miners, 1874–1939

Volume Two

Trade Unions and Politics

ALAN CAMPBELL

Ashgate

Aldershot • Burlington USA • Singapore • Sydney

Published by

Ashgate Publishing Ltd
Gower House, Croft Road
Aldershot, Hampshire
GU11 3HR
England

Ashgate Publishing Company
131 Main Street
Burlington
Vermont 05401–5600
USA

Ashgate website: http://www.ashgate.com

ISBN 0 7546 0192 7

British Library Cataloguing in Publication Data
Campbell, Alan, 1949–
      The Scottish Miners, 1874–1939
      Vol. 2: Trade Unions and Politics
      1. Coal miners–Labor unions–Scotland–History–19th century
      2. Coal miners–Labour unions–Scotland–History–20th century
      I. Title
      331. 8' 8122334' 09411

US Library of Congress Card Number: 00–104722

This book is printed on acid free paper

Printed and bound in Great Britain by MPG Books Ltd, Bodmin, Cornwall

Contents

Preface

My interests in trade unions and politics are long-standing. After completing my doctoral and post-doctoral research in labour history at the University of Warwick (later published in 1979 as *The Lanarkshire Miners: a social history of their trade unions, 1775–1874*), I was engaged in trade union education for some fifteen years. As well as teaching shop stewards as part of the TUC's training provision in Manchester and Liverpool, I was later involved in more advanced forms of union education, particularly with lay activists and union officials in Region Six of the Transport and General Workers' Union, covering North West England. Whilst the operation of the TUC's provision taught me more about the laws of oligarchy than Michels' famous study, the enduring neo-syndicalist impulses of the TGWU's Liverpudlian activists provided greater insight into the cut and thrust of workplace conflict and union factionalism than the most sophisticated industrial relations textbook. My first debt in this volume is to the hundreds of shop stewards and officials who educated me in the practical world of industrial politics.

Yet I hope that this volume will not only be read by those with a specialist interest in trade union and labour history, whether as students or activists. For one aim of this and its companion volume, is to pose questions which extend beyond the narrow confines of trade unionism in the coalfields and to expand our knowledge of Scotland's recent past. Volume one, for example, raises issues of religious sectarianism and class conflict which continue to have resonances within contemporary Scottish society, though they are too often politely evaded. This volume addresses Scotland's distinctive political trajectory in the twentieth century, which cannot adequately be treated as merely a regional sub-set of a British 'forward march of labour'. In the coalfields by the 1920s, as in some other parts of Scotland, the social forces existed which might have made for a more radical politics than that represented by the Labour Party, even though these were ultimately contained and distorted by the exigencies of Stalinism. Nevertheless, the political traditions established by the miners during the period covered by this volume had a lasting influence on the Scottish – and ultimately the British – labour movement. For example, Lawrence Daly and Michael McGahey – whose uncle, James McKendrick, figures in these pages – were products of the Communist tradition in Fife and Lanarkshire respectively and played key roles in the critically important British miners' strikes of 1972 and 1984.

These traditions also helped shape contemporary Scottish political and social identities. Although only one deep mine remains in Scotland today, compared with the hundreds of collieries which existed at this study's terminal date, there are tens, perhaps hundreds, of thousands of Scots whose ancestors or relations – Scottish, Irish or Lithuanian, male or female – endured hard and harshly exploited lives in the pits and mining villages. As we stand on the cusp of the millennium, having won the half-loaf of a newly devolved parliament in Edinburgh, Scottish people are freshly contemplating their past as well as re-calculating their future. It is hoped that this and its companion volume may inform, however modestly, such reflections.

* * *

I wish to record my thanks to the staff at the following institutions: the National Library of Scotland, the Scottish Record Office, the Public Record Office, the National Museum of Labour History, the British Library Newspaper Library, The British Library of Political and Economic Science, Manchester Central Reference Library, the University of Glasgow Business Record Centre, Merthil Public Library, the Modern Record Centre, University of Warwick, the Sidney Jones Library, University of Liverpool, the John Rylands Library, University of Manchester, and the William Gallacher Memorial Library, Glasgow Caledonian University.

I also acknowledge the support of the University of Liverpool's Research Development Fund, which allowed me to conduct a preliminary survey of sources during study leave in 1988; the Nuffield Foundation, Grant number: SOC/181 (1838), which permitted field work in 1989; and the Economic and Social Research Council which granted me a Senior Research Fellowship in 1995–6 to complete archival research and write a draft manuscript (Award number: H524427500795). Without this vital financial support, these volumes would not have been written.

Participants at numerous conferences and seminars have offered constructive criticism of the preliminary sketches of the material contained in this volume over the years, but the following deserve special mention: the Second International Mining History Congress, Bochum, 1989, allowed me to present findings on Communist militancy; the Fourth British-Dutch Conference on Labour History, held at Oxford in 1988 on the theme of 'generations in labour hsitory', was valuable in developing my ideas on this concept which inform this volume; the Manchester seminars held in 1995 of contributors to the collection of essays, *Miners, Unions and Politics, 1910–1947*, which I co-edited, helped further to refine my arguments.

I would also like to thank the many individuals who have encouraged or assisted me in my research or discussed aspects of the content of this volume with me, even though some will almost certainly disagree with my interpretations: Tony Adams, Stephen Bird, John Benson, Bill Burrill, Gidon Cohen, Rob Duncan, Nina Fishman, Andy Flinn, David Gilbert, John Halstead, David Howell, Merfyn Jones, Monty Johnstone, Bill Knox, John Laslett, Dave Lyddon, John McIlroy, Arthur McIvor, David Martin, Kevin Morgan, Suzanne Najam, Fred Reid, Martin Sime, Duncan Tanner, Klaus Tenfelde, Chris Wrigley and Matthew Worley. Once again, special thanks to Alec McAulay, formerly of Ashgate Publishing; to the political philosophers of the Cumberland Bar, Edinburgh; to Jenni; and especially to Sheila.

Alan Campbell
Edinburgh
December 1999

List of Tables

List of Figures

List of Maps

List of Abbreviations

AMMW	Amalgamated Miners and Manual Workers
AMU	Ayrshire Miners' Union
BSP	British Socialist Party
CC	Central Committee
CI	Communist International
CP	Communist Party
CPGB	Communist Party of Great Britain
CPSU	Communist Party of the Soviet Union
CPUSA	Communist Party of the United States of America
COF	Committee on Organisation and Finance
Comintern	See CI
DLP	Divisional Labour Party
DPC	District Party Committee
ECCI	Executive Committee of the Communist International
FCKMU	Fife, Clackmannan and Kinross Miners' Union
FCMA	Forth and Clyde Miners' Association
FKCMA	Fife, Kinross and Clackmannan Miners' Association
FKMA	Fife and Kinross Miners' Association
FKMIU	Fife and Kinross Miners' Industrial Trade Union
ILP	Independent Labour Party
ILS	International Lenin School
INL	Irish National League
IWGB	Industrial Workers of Great Britain
IWW	Industrial Workers of the World
JK	James Klugmann Papers
LCMA	Lanarkshire Coal Masters' Association
LMA	Lanarkshire Miners' Association
LMMM	Lanarkshire Miners' Minority Movement

LMU	Lanarkshire Mineworkers' County Union (later the Lanarkshire Mineworkers' Union)
MELMA	Mid and East Lothian Miners' Association
MFGB	Miners' Federation of Great Britain
MM	Minority Movement
MMM	Miners' Minority Movement
MPL	Methil Public Library
MRC	Modern Record Centre, University of Warwick
MRU	Mineworkers' Reform Union of Fife, Kinross andClackmannan
NLS	National Library of Scotland
NLMA	North Lanark Miners' Association
NMLH	National Museum of Labour History, Manchester
NUDAW	National Union of Distributive and Allied Workers
NUSMW	National Union of Scottish Mine Workers
NUWM	National Unemployed Workers' Movement
NWCM	National Workers' Committee Movement
PAC	Public Assistance Committee
PB	Political Bureau
PRO	Public Record Office
Profintern	See RILU
PS	Political Secretariat
RILU	Red International of Labour Unions
SCLP	Scottish Council of the Labour Party
SCMA	Scottish Central Miners' Association
SCFSA	Scottish Colliery Firemen and Shotfirers' Association
SCMIU	Stirling and Clackmannan Miners' Industrial Union
SDF	Social Democratic Federation
SLC	Scottish Labour College
SLLL	Scottish Land and Labour League
SLP	Socialist Labour Party
SLRL	Scottish Land Restoration League
SMF	Scottish Miners' Federation
SMNF	Scottish Miners' National Federation
SNTUA	Scottish National Trade Union Association
SPLP	Scottish Parliamentary Labour Party
SRO	Scottish Record Office

STC	Supply and Transport Committee
SUTCLP	Scottish United Trades Councils' Labour Party
SWMF	South Wales Miners' Federation
SWPEC	Scottish Workers' Parliamentary ElectionCommittee
SWRC	Scottish Workers' Representation Committee
TLC	Trades and Labour Council
UMWA	United Mine Workers of America
UMS	United Mineworkers of Scotland
URC	Unofficial Reform Committee
WIIU	Workers' International Industrial Union

Introduction

Aims and approaches

The aim of this book is deceptively simple: to describe and analyse the development of trade union organisation among the Scottish miners and the patterns of political mobilisation in the coalfields. However, fuller elaboration of these objectives discloses considerable complexity in the many divergences from conventional notions of a 'forward march' of the labour movement's 'archetypal proletarians'.[1] First, the establishment of trade unionism was far from straightforward, its development never unilinear. The early 1870s marked a high point of union organisation among the Scots colliers, unparalleled since the 1820s, which was soon to be dashed in the economic crisis of 1874.[2] The following two decades registered numerous failed attempts to construct stable organisation and a framework of collective bargaining was not achieved until 1900. The continued expansion of the Scottish coal industry until 1920 witnessed the consolidation of trade unionism – symbolised by enthusiastic Scottish participation in the first British miners' strike in 1912. But the miners' defeat in the national lockout of 1921 marked a turning point which was soon followed by the seven-month dispute in 1926. Much of the inter-war period in the Scottish coalfields was characterised by union weakness and the fragmentation of carefully nurtured organisation along fault lines of localism, religion and politics, most notably with the formation of the Communist Party's 'red union', the United Mineworkers of Scotland (UMS), in 1929. Yet in the same period, Scottish miners became the most industrially militant group of workers in Britain.

The UMS was a unique organisation within the British coalfields and points to the distinctive political trajectory of the Scots miners. While Labour became the dominant political party, two out of the three Communist MPs elected in the inter-war period represented seats in the Scottish mining regions. Yet Conservative and Unionist candidates also enjoyed significant success in mining constituencies. This suggests complexities of political development which stereotypical images of an essential class consciousness among miners and the unproblematic solidarity of their communities cannot adequately comprehend, and which are explored further in chapters two and eight of this volume.

The conception of politics adopted in this study is broader than that of party politics, however. A further concern is to analyse competition between factions within the miners' unions, struggles which developed with unprecedented bitterness in the Scottish coalfields by the 1920s. Studies of the government of trade unions have been dominated by the legacy of Robert Michels, who in *Political Parties* (published 1911) postulated his famous 'iron law of oligarchy', whereby trade union officers retained power within formally democratic union structures through organisational expertise, the control of information and resources, and patronage. In addition to such functional sources of power, Michels also noted the shift in lifestyle experienced by union leaders, drawing on the work of the Webbs. They had earlier commented on this sociological process of *embourgeoisement* in a classic description of the emergence of bureaucracies within unions as they moved from the 'primitive democracy' of the workshop and locality to national bodies:

> The former vivid sense of the privations and subjections of the artisan's life gradually fades from his mind; and he begins more and more to regard all complaints as perverse and unreasonable. With this intellectual change may come a more invidious transformation. Nowadays the salaried officer to a great union is courted and flattered by the middle class ... He goes to live in a little villa in a lower middle class suburb ... His manner to his members ... undergoes a change ... A great strike threatens to involve the Society in desperate war. Unconsciously biased by the distaste for the hard and unthankful work which a strike entails, he finds himself in small sympathy with the men's demands, and eventually arranges a compromise, on terms distasteful to a large section of his members.[3]

These ideas were in common currency among union activists in the 1890s and also underpinned later analyses of the trade union bureaucracy.[4] While Michels' views have been subjected to qualification for their 'overdetermination' of oligarchic tendencies – for example, critics have pointed to the constraints placed upon the bureaucracy by normative expectations of democratic practice and the countervailing pressures of membership revolt – we wish to retain the emphasis on material differences of interest between leaders and led as one element in the analysis of the internal dynamics of union government.

More recent historical debate initiated by Zeitlin has questioned allegedly prevalent notions of a homogeneous 'rank and file' having interests in opposition to, and to the left of, established union leaderships.[5] While there is merit in Zeitlin's essentially pluralist argument that some internal conflicts within unions are best conceived as factional struggles between alternative leaderships, to privilege such a 'vertical' cleavage is as one-sided as perceiving only a perpetual dichotomy between a radical rank and file and moderate leadership. As Price notes: 'Tensions within unions can take a variety of forms: between various bodies in the official hierarchy as well as between recognised functionaries and those who are merely members', while Cronin also argues that:

> the fact that officials were sometimes more militant or more politically radical than their members is one of those facts every student of labour history knows but one which, at the same time, hardly disproves the general point that leaders tend over time to become more cautious than those they lead.[6]

In a further contribution to the debate, Leier has suggested that labour bureaucracies cannot be defined by ideologies; but 'what does remain constant for labour bureaucrats is the desire to promote and protect their own self interest ... As leaders the labour bureaucrats have interests that are significantly different from those of the membership, for they wish to maintain their positions.'[7] The adoption of radical or collaborative policies will therefore be conditioned by how leaders perceive their interests.

Any treatment of 'union politics' must therefore embrace both vertical divisions, based on shared ideologies, between contending factions, and also horizontal cleavages, rooted in differing material interests, between leaders and their members. Within such structural intersections, human agency and contingency, individual values, generational experiences, organisational cultures and patterns of political socialisation need to be accommodated. Bureaucratic interests must also be differentiated at the local, regional and national levels, while the 'membership', too, consists of layers of activists as well as the diverse sections of the 'rank and file'.[8]

A further dimension of political analysis centres on the work-place. Worker resistance within the labour process has already been analysed in the preceding volume. Our concern here is with how informal 'pit politics', defined by Gibbon as 'a combative tradition of local pit bargaining over both wages and working arrangements, where withdrawal of labour is used not as a last resort when other processes of negotiation and conciliation have failed but as a pre-condition for negotiation and conciliation ...', were articulated within the formal structures of union organisation and how they might be translated into party political mobilisation.[9]

Organising Concepts

In making sense of such complexities within the following narrative, the consciousness of activists in the Scottish coalfields is explored through a typology of orientations to trade unionism: the indepen-dent collier, the bureaucratic reformist and the militant miner. These ideal types are summarised in Figure I.1.

The writer and others have previously approached the miners' unions in Scotland for the earlier years of the nineteenth century through the work culture of the independent collier.[10] It was this work culture, rooted in the skills and autonomy of the hewers at the coalface, which informed the policies of a succession of unions, focusing particularly on control of the labour and product markets. The failure of such policies to prevent wages being driven down after 1874 led to bureaucratic reformism, with its goal of state reg-ulation of the coal industry dependent upon parliamentary repre-sentation, coming to dominate the miners' unions by 1900. The years immediately preceding the First World War marked the emer-gence of the militant miner.[11] While the imposition of state control during the war could be seen as a partial fulfilment of the aspira-tions of bureaucratic reformism, wartime conditions produced strong oppositional currents within the miners' unions. The cre-ation of a revolutionary-led reform committee movement during the war provided the nucleus of the Communist cadre which mounted a serious challenge to the existing union leadership from 1926, a challenge which was only ultimately successful after more than a decade of bitter factionalism.

Figure I.1 Ideal types of orientation to trade unionism in the Scottish coalfields

	Independent collier	Bureaucratic reformist	Militant miner
Historical period	18th century	1880s --➤	1930s
			c. 1912 ·········➤
Union recruitment	Exclusive	Open	Open (including miners' wives)
Union organisation	Federations of local and district unions	Federations of county unions	One industrial miners' union
Industrial relations methods	Unilateral regulation of recruitment and output	Collective bargaining within context of state regulation of hours and minimum wage	Militant waging of all disputes as an expression of class struggle
Politico-industrial goal	Cooperative production	Nationalisation of the mines	Socialist revolution involving socialisation of the mines
Political affiliation	Liberal	Independent Labour	Communist
Typified by	Alexander Macdonald (1821–81); General Secretary, Scottish Coal and Ironstone Miners' Assoc., 1855–81; Liberal MP for Stafford from 1874	Robert Smillie (1857–1940); SMF/NUSMW President, 1894–1912, 1922–8; MFGB President, 1912–21	Willie Allan (1900–70); LMU President, NUSMW General Secretary elect, 1927–9; UMS General Secretary, 1929–31
'Corresponding' stage of labour process and mine ownership structure	Hand mining Small mining enterprises, local markets	Hand and machine mining Larger mining companies, regional and national markets	Machine mining Monopoly combines, international markets

Note: The "18th century" for Historical period connects via a dashed arrow to "1930s".

These ideal types represent at best a skeletal summary of the attitudes and values of the miners' leaders and their activist opposi-
tions. Their crudity is readily acknowledged: empirical history
rarely fits neatly into a sociological matrix. Bureaucratic reformism,
for example, encompassed not only the anti-war Robert Smillie
(sometimes described by labour historians as exemplifying the 'militant reformism' of the immediate post-war years because of his
temporary use then of the rhetoric of 'direct action') and the con-
servatively respectable James Brown, the Ayrshire miners' leader
who reflected many of the cultural values of the traditional Scots
colliers. Nevertheless, such men and their colleagues shared a commitment to political reformism – both Brown and Smillie became
Labour MPs – coupled with a bureaucratic trade union practice.

It should also be emphasised that the relationship between ideology and the labour process alluded to in Figure I.1 was neither a
simple nor reductionist one. Indeed, the impact of underground
mechanisation in the early decades of the twentieth century initially
evoked a re-affirmation of 'exclusive' policies associated with the
independent collier by adherents of bureaucratic reformism. There
were also some affinities between the work practices of the independent collier and the militant miner. Allan Flanders' observation
that unions simultaneously pursue a number of methods to achieve
what he describes as internal and external job regulation is relevant
here. The former includes unilateral workgroup regulation of
output and apprenticeship controls, and bi-lateral, often informal,
negotiations within the workplace enforced through unofficial sanctions. The latter category includes regulation by unions and employers' associations of their respective members, formal collective
bargaining between unions and employers or their associations, and
state regulation through legislation.[12] Our ideal types suggest an
alignment between processes of internal regulation and both the
independent collier and militant miner, while external regulation
corresponds with bureaucratic reformism. Such a framework permits tentative linkages between the mining labour process, trade
unionism and mineworkers' political behaviour: the industrial policies of the Communist Party were more compatible with the 'pit
politics' of the militant miner, while the Labour Party's promise of
state regulation appealed to the trade union bureaucracy and its
supporters.

Although these ideal types display a chronological sequence in their emergence, they were not historically discrete: all three can be seen as co-existing and competing by the early decades of the century, although by the 1920s the primary antagonism was between bureaucratic reformism and the militant miner. The concept of generation is employed to explain the emergence and sustenance of these competing orientations. Because this concept has been almost unused (other than in the most commonsense way) within British labour historiography, and because it has been much contested by social scientists since Karl Mannheim's pioneering essay in 1928, and by philosophers of history such as Ortega, some discussion of its relevance to this study is required.[13] There has been considerable debate about the 'length' of a generation.[14] Many writers have accepted a span of approximately thirty years, and it can be noted that the dates of birth of the three miners' leaders chosen to exemplify our ideal types are separated by thirty six and forty three years.

The most systematic attempt to formulate a historical theory of generations was developed by Marias from the insights of Ortega. Marias proposes that a generation constitutes a span of fifteen years and suggests that if we consider any single date, 'we see in it several human strata, coexisting, interacting ...'. These strata represent four generations:

Generation A – 'the survivors of previous periods without full historical parts to play any more, but remaining as geological evidence, as it were, pointing unequivocally to the origin of the present situation'.

Generation B – 'those in power, whose aims correspond in general to the prevailing world style'.

Generation C – 'the opposition, fully assertive on the historical scene, but still lacking leadership powers, struggles against the ruling generation ...'.

Generation D – 'youth, which begins a new life feeling and anticipates the eventual overturn of the present situation ...'.

Thus, suggests Marias, 'the year 1800 is not a single date; it is four different dates that exist simultaneously and are mutually involved in an active form'.[15]

It is possible to interpret certain years, say 1921 or 1926, in a similar way for the Scottish coalfields, with Generations A, B, and C plus D corresponding to our three ideal types. However, Spritzer cautions against the danger of a simplistic, 'stages of man' theory inherent in such an approach and suggests that, instead of querying how long a generation 'really' is, or how many usually coexist, it is more fruitful to 'ask whether, and in what respects, age-related differences mattered in a given historical situation'.[16] The need for concrete, empirical studies is also posited by Philip Abrams. He defines a 'sociological generation' as 'that span of time within which identity is assembled on the basis of an unchanged system of meanings and possibilities. A sociological generation can thus encompass many biological generations.'[17]

In analysing the historical emergence of new sociological generations, Abrams argues that 'within any age-set some will experience historical events more acutely than others or be able to respond to them more vigorously', and he follows Mannheim in using 'generation units' to describe such subgroups. But as Abrams points out, an important feature of such generation units is that:

> their location and effectiveness in a social system cannot be explained adequately on the basis of age alone. Age is a necessary but not a sufficient condition of their existence ... all the conventional categories of social-structural analysis must be introduced to explain their unique ability to make something of historical experiences.[18]

This is the approach which we shall attempt to develop in this study, situating generational conflict within the structures already analysed in volume one.

Method and structure

To the complexity of the varied meanings of 'trade unions and politics' and the concepts employed to analyse them must therefore be added the diversity of the social and economic 'terrains' upon which union organisation was constructed and politics conducted. The preceding volume analysed how the four regions of the Scottish coalfields were constituted historically, through a comparison of their varying capital structures, their productive base and organisation of the labour process, their demographic patterns and gender, authority and ethnic relations. While readers will derive greatest benefit from this study through a preliminary reading of volume one, a summary of the defining characteristics of the four regions –

Ayrshire, West Central, Fife and Clackmannan, and Mid and East Lothian – is contained in Figure I.2. (See also Map 1.) Such a schematic representation is inevitably broad and static. In order to accommodate intra-regional diversity and allow analysis at the level of individual communities, ten localities were subjected to particular scrutiny: Annbank and Hurlford in Ayrshire; Blantyre, Larkhall, Craigneuk and Douglas and Coalburn in the West Central region; the Culross and Wemyss districts in Fife; and Newtongrange in Midlothian, Prestonpans in East Lothian. Our narrative in the following chapters draws on these regional and local studies to situate the relative support for the three ideal types within the material conditions and cultural traditions of specific communities.

The structure of this volume is primarily chronological, but with some pairs of chapters providing parallel analyses of trade unionism and politics respectively for a given period. Chapter one charts the slow and fragile construction of union organisation in the two decades after 1874. The bruising Scottish miners' strike of 1894 demonstrated a new found solidarity and inaugurated a separate phase of union development and consolidation. The complex structures of union government, and the emergence of a more extensive, culturally distinct union bureaucracy at local, county and national level are also outlined. Chapter two examines union policy and the gradual adoption of strategies of state regulation and independent labour representation alongside and complementing the traditional policies associated with the independent collier. Chapter three first traces the limited growth of syndicalist and industrial unionist ideas in parts of the coalfields before the First World War, then the expansion of their constituency during and after the war. Chapter four details the fissiparous character of union organisation in the years of growing unemployment after the 1921 lockout, with a breakaway Protestant union being briefly formed in Lanarkshire while in Fife a Reform union was established in opposition to the bureaucratic manipulation of the existing leadership. Chapter five compares the regional responses of activists in the county unions during the 1926 lockout, with Lanarkshire and Fife characterised by 'guerilla warfare' against blacklegs and colliery property while Ayrshire and the Lothians largely displayed passivity. The growth of support for the Communist Party's militants generated during 1926 led to their electoral success in union elections in 1927. The contours of this

Figure I.2 Summary of the defining characteristics of the Scottish coal mining regions

	WEST CENTRAL	AYRSHIRE	FIFE AND CLACKMAN-NAN	MID AND EAST LOTHIAN
Numbers employed, 1920 and as a % of Scottish total	82,690 56.1	16,948 11.5	32,007 21.7	15,678 10.6
Capital structure	Growing concentration of large firms surrounded by many small companies	High degree of concentration; one company employs two-thirds of workforce by 1931	Four companies concentrated in four geographical areas	Several medium-sized companies with interlocking directors and links to other larger companies
Coal markets	Primarily industrial, domestic, some export	Industrial, domestic, export to Ireland	Primarily export to Europe	Divided between export and industrial, domestic and ship bunkering
Size of mines	Wide variation between large and small mines	Generally smaller mines	Generally large mines	Generally large mines
Owners' attitude towards trade unions	Persistently hostile	Persistently hostile	Initially cooperative but growing antagonism by Fife Coal Company	Generally cooperative
Extent of mechanisation	High	Lowest	Highest	High
Level of industrial conflict	Persistently and increasingly the highest	Low	Moves from low to high	Low
Incidence of social disorder during strikes	Persistently high	Generally low	Moves from low to high	Generally low

	WEST CENTRAL	AYRSHIRE	FIFE AND CLACKMAN-NAN	MID AND EAST LOTHIAN
Social structure	'Cosmopolitan' composition; residence often within a semi-urban setting; relatively high rates of mobility	Mainly born in county; often scattered settlements in rural environment	Mainly born in county, though increasingly cosmopolitan; often residential concentrations of miners; initially less mobile than other regions	Mainly born in county; residence in stable mining villages
Extent of employer-owned housing	Relatively low	High	Relatively low	High
Ethnic and religious composition	Highest percentage of Irish and Catholics; highest number of Orange lodges and IRA companies; frequent sectarian clashes; largest concentration of Lithuanians	Second highest concentration of Irish and Catholics; significant number of Orange lodges; limited Irish Republican presence; few sectarian clashes	Irish concentrated in West Fife; Culross district only significant number of Catholics; very limited Orange and Sinn Fein presence; no sectarian clashes	Low Irish and Catholic presence; very few Orange lodges and no sectarian clashes

support and the consequent factionalism which culminated in the formation of the UMS are analysed in chapter six. While the UMS had strong indigenous origins, its subsequent development was subject to close direction by the Communist Party and the Commmunist International. Chapter seven provides the first detailed account of this union and locates its evolution within ongoing debates on the nature of British communism. Chapter eight returns to party politics, highlighting the imperfect domination of the coalfields by the Labour Party as well as the general failure of the Communist Party to translate its industrial influence into electoral success.

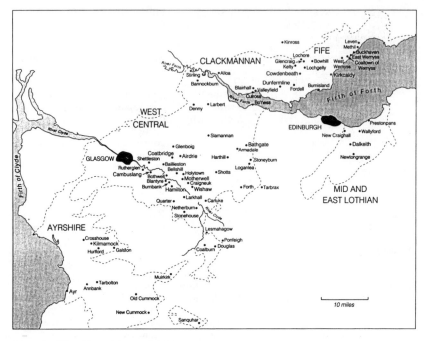

Map 1   The Scottish coalfields

Notes

1.   The only existing study, R. Page Arnot's, *A History of the Scottish Miners* (1955), displays some elements of this approach.

2.   See A.B. Campbell, *The Lanarkshire Miners: a social history of their trade unions, 1775–1874* (Edinburgh, 1979), chs 3 and 9.

3.   Quoted in K. Coates and T. Topham, *Trade Unions in Britain* (Nottingham, 1982), pp. 68–9.

4.   For example, see Fred Knee's references to the processes which rendered union officials 'mentally corpulent' in his article 'The evolution of a trade union official' (*Justice*, 21 November 1896); Richard Hyman provides a concise summary of Marxist analyses of trade union bureaucracy in his *Marxism and the Sociology of Trade Unionism* (1971).

5.   J. Zeitlin, '"Rank and filism" in British labour history: a critique', *International Review of Social History*, 34, 1, 1989; R. Price, '"What's in a name?" Workplace history and "rank and filism"', *ibid.*; J.E.

Cronin, 'The "rank and file" and the social history of the working class', *ibid.*; R. Hyman, 'The sound of one hand clapping: a comment on the "rank and filism" debate', *International Review of Social History*, 34, 2, 1989.

6. Price, 'What's in a name?', p. 70; Cronin, 'The "rank and file"', p. 82. A recent study of contemporary union officials has criticised 'bureaucracy theory' for overgeneralisation and reasonably points to the different pressures on local and national officials; yet its emphasis on the autonomy of union functionaries may be equally criticised for its undue neglect of structures and material interests. See J. Kelly and E. Heery, *Working for the Union: British trade union officers* (Cambridge, 1994) and the perceptive and persuasive review of its arguments in J. McIlroy, 'Still under siege: British trade unions at the turn of the century', *Historical Studies in Industrial Relations*, 3, 1997, pp. 110–20.

7. M. Leier, 'Which side are they on? Some suggestions for the labour bureaucracy debate', *International Review of Social History*, 36, 1991, p. 426. See also M. Leier, *Red Flags and Red Tape: the making of a labour bureaucracy* (Toronto, 1995). In so far as the debate has been empirically situated, British writers have usually focused on the period from the First World War to 1926, particularly on the metalworking industries and to a lesser extent the railways, and attempted to interpret the significance of oppositional movements within already entrenched union structures. For example, see Zeitlin, 'Rank and filism'; R. Hyman, 'Rank-and-file movements and workplace organisation, 1914–39', in C. Wrigley (ed.), *A History of British Industrial Relations, vol. 2: 1914–39* (Brighton, 1987); T. Adams, 'Leadership and oligarchy: British rail unions, 1914–1922', *Studies in History and Politics*, 5, 1986; R. Aris, *Trade Unions and the Management of Industrial Conflict* (1998). Yet what has generally been lacking from the debate are studies of the historical processes by which such bureaucracies develop, their material interests, and the basis of conflicts which emerge within them. The rapid growth of the Scots miners' unions between the 1890s and the First World War, within a complex federal structure, permits such an analysis which will in turn allow an understanding of the nature of the challenges which subsequently developed to the Scottish union leadership.

8. For elaboration of these points, see J. McIlroy and A. Campbell, 'Still setting the pace? Labour history, industrial relations and the history of post-war trade unionism', *Labour History Review*, 64, 2, 1999.

9. P. Gibbon, 'Analysing the British miners' strike of 1984–85', *Economy and Society*, 17, 2, 1988, p. 152.

10. See vol. 1, ch. 2; A. Campbell and F. Reid, 'The independent collier in Scotland', in R. Harrison (ed.), *Independent Collier: the coal miner as archetypal proletarian reconsidered* (Hassocks, 1978); Campbell, *Lanarkshire Miners*, chs 2 and 10.

11. For the development of the new tradition of 'the militant miner', see S. Macintyre, *Little Moscows: communism and working-class militancy in inter-war Britain* (1980), p. 169.

12. For a discussion of Flanders' categories, see D. Lyddon, 'Industrial relations theory and labour history', *International Labor and Working-Class History*, 46, 1994.

13. K. Mannheim, 'The problem of generations', in *Essays in the Sociology of Knowledge* (1952); for Ortega's views, see J. Marias, *Generations: a historical method* (1970). For pioneering attempts by historians to apply the concept in a variety of contexts, see the essays in A. Blok et al. (eds), *Generations in Labour* (Amsterdam, 1989) and M. Roseman (ed.), *Generations in Conflict: youth revolt and generation formation in Germany, 1770–1968* (Cambridge, 1995).

14. For example, B.M. Berger, 'How long is a generation', *British Journal of Sociology*, 11, 1960; P. Abrams, 'Rites de passage: the conflict of generations in industrial society', *Journal of Contemporary History*, 5, 1, 1970; M. Rintala, 'The problem of generations in Finnish communism', *American Slavic and East European Review*, 17, 2, 1958; P.W.M., 'Generation', in M. Mann (ed.) *Student Encyclopedia of Sociology* (1983), p. 145.

15. Marias, *Generations*, pp. 183–4.

16. A.B. Spritzer, 'The historical problem of generations', *American Historical Review*, 78, 5, 1973, p. 1354.

17. P. Abrams, *Historical Sociology* (Shepton Mallet, 1982), p. 256.

18. Ibid., pp. 261–2.

CHAPTER ONE

Trade union organisation and structure, 1874–1918

Introduction

The period 1874–94 was bounded by two mass strikes in the Scots coalfields, both of which resulted in employers successfully imposing wage reductions. During the intervening decades, unions were generally weak and, outside of Fife, ephemeral. The first aim of this chapter is to trace briefly the repeated attempts at organisation and the reasons for their failure. The first national strike of Scottish miners in 1894 can be seen as an important turning point in their organisational fortunes. Although ending in defeat after fourteen weeks, it demonstrated their capacity for national action and a new found integration into the Miners' Federation of Great Britain (MFGB). After the establishment of permanent organisation throughout the Scots coalfields from the mid-1890s, linked within national and British federations, coal owners were forced to recognise the growing power of their miners. By the early years of the twentieth century, unions throughout the Scots coalfields had achieved a significant degree of organisational strength. The latter part of the chapter examines the development of their government and structure in the context of this general process of consolidation.

Trade union organisation

The obstacles to permanent union organisation created by the fissures of sectarianism in Lanarkshire have previously been analysed.[1] Catholic parochial bodies and Orange institutions also competed with trade unions for the miners' limited leisure time. For example, a meeting of Lanarkshire colliers in Hamilton in July 1877, which was addressed by visiting speakers from Staffordshire, Stirling and Fife, was poorly attended 'because so many miners had gone to the Orange Walk'; William Brown, from Staffordshire, 'made it clear how appalled he was by the lack of union in Lanarkshire'.[2] Religious organisations represented only one demand upon miners' finite associational energies. In Burnbank in 1888, a union activist complained that mineworkers in his district were interested only in 'pastimes, excursions and theology to the neglect of politics and trades organisations'.[3] An additional distraction was the growing interest in football as a mass spectator sport. The Larkhall district union had to change temporarily its weekly 'idle day' from Thursday to Saturday in December 1890 by an almost unanimous vote of the membership, 'on account of the great interest which was being taken in the football match' between the Albert and the Celtic. At the same meeting, the chairman urged 'the necessity of more united action' and pointed out to the members 'how foolish it was to have a committee unless the body of the men were going to support them in any action which they might take for the good of the men'.[4]

A further factor militating against union organisation was the high rates of geographical mobility among mineworkers in the western coalfields.[5] The North East Lanark and Airdrie District Miners' Association was registered in August 1894 and wound up ten months later. Its secretary explained its demise to the Registrar of Friendly Societies:

> Owing to members shifting from place to place, leaving no address and not paying arrears and having a radius of six miles and no money coming in it is impossible to have a staff of collectors (even if we could make members recognise this liability) to cover the ground. Again owing to bad trade and disorganisation amongst the men we are not able to comply with the requirements of our certificate. Moreover in our opinion it is a mistake to register a miners' union because of mobility among miners as a class.[6]

Sometimes the movement of miners to new areas debilitated union organisation. It was reported in 1888 that, since the 'invasion' of men from Ayrshire to Bannockburn, Stirlingshire, during a strike the previous year, union organisation in the district had 'gone to the dogs':

The Dalry men will do nothing in the way of union, or anything good regarding it, and the natives who were, and have in times past always been, good union men, cannot even try to do anything while having these 'blacklegging' interlopers working amongst them.[7]

At Slamannan, where 'a very large number of strangers' had arrived six or seven years previously, 'these have not been able to coalesce with the natives and they cannot be got to pull together'.[8]

One of the most important elements in the weakness of the miners' unions in the western counties was the attitude of the employers. The paternalistic relations fostered by small employers in areas such as Larkhall in Lanarkshire undermined collective organisation.[9] One union activist from Motherwell complained in 1881 that it was common to hear men say: 'Union never did any good, we are better without it. If we trust to the honour of our employers, they will do far better for us than any union.'[10] A more significant consideration, however, was the policy of the large mining companies. Throughout the nineteenth century, large coal and ironmasters were implacably opposed to trade union organisation.[11] At a meeting soon after the formation of the Lanarkshire Coal Masters' Association (LCMA), a letter from William Small on behalf of the Lanarkshire union proposing a board of arbitration to settle wage questions was considered by the association's committee: 'it was agreed not to recognise the union in such questions and the secretary was instructed to write Mr Small and inform him that all questions of wages will be settled between the Coal Masters and their workmen direct, in accordance with the rules of the Association'. Thereafter, letters from the union were ignored.[12] In Ayrshire, too, Keir Hardie claimed that 'we have tried to open communications with the employers but they have always refused to meet us'.[13]

There was a similar experience at the local and district level. Robert Smillie, representing the Larkhall miners before the Royal Commission on Labour in 1892, complained that 'the employers will not negotiate':

they have never negotiated with the officials of our association. I have several times made an attempt to open up negotiations about a dispute before it came to an open rupture in order to have it settled; but the answer of the employers invariably is that they want to deal directly with their workmen, not with any association.[14]

The cumbersome form of 'bargaining' which took place over district wage movements is described in the Larkhall union minutes for 1890: pickets were placed at all the pits in the district to convene meetings of the men; deputations appointed from the pit meetings then approached their respective employers for an advance of one shilling a day and subsequently reported the various responses to a general meeting of the association for further consideration.[15]

Both Andrew McCosh of William Baird and Company and Robert Baird, Secretary of the LCMA, claimed to the Royal Commission that their primary objection to trade unions in Lanarkshire was the 'extreme views' of the men's leaders and secondly the lack of organisation. They would not object to an organisation 'on moderate and reasonable' lines, stated McCosh.[16] Other evidence suggests they were antagonistic to the methods and aims of trade unionism and that the weak organisation they complained of was in large part due to their own hostility. Smillie testified that the failure to organise unions in Lanarkshire in the preceding twenty years had 'generally been due to opposition on the part of the employers':

> Sometimes the employers dismissed an individual who [had] taken an active part or a leading part in the union; at other times 20 or 30 men would be told that unless they were prepared to break the rules of the Union, either as to hours of work or the system of working, they would be dismissed. At other times Union men would be unfairly treated as to the distribution of tubs or hutches; in fact every means have been tried to break up and prevent organisation.[17]

He concluded, 'the principal cause of disorganisation in Lanarkshire arises ... from the fact that in the past all men who have taken an active part in organisation have been victimised'.[18] The spread of the contracting system of underground supervision provided a further mechanism for victimisation.[19] In 1912, when the Lanarkshire union was generally well organised, only 200 of the 1,400 men employed at the five pits of Rosehall Colliery were union members: this was 'principally due to the system of contracting which is vogue in these collieries'.[20]

As Baird admitted, strikes in Lanarkshire were countered by the operation of 'the block' by associated masters, whereby no new workman would be employed, whether or not they were strikers.[21] Smillie recalled his own experience when he had been kept out of work 'for a considerable time looking for employment'. When he finally found work at a small colliery at the distant end of the Larkhall district, after four days his new employer told him that he had received four letters requesting his dismissal.[22] Small, on behalf of the Blantyre Miners' Association, also complained that 'the dismissal of delegates has so terrorised the men that union has been crushed out of existence; names of delegates have been passed from colliery to colliery so that they had to change their name or leave the country'. Only a few months previously, an overman had been fined £1 by his employer for taking on a blacklisted activist.[23] Hardie, representing the Ayrshire Miners' Union, spoke of 'systematic persecution' and 'numerous instances of men who have been dismissed for being trade union officials or for going on deputations seeking advances of wages and other matters of that kind, and for appointing a checkweigher'.[24] In the Lothians, Bob Selkirk recalled the older miners' dread of victimisation in the early years of the twentieth century; he was himself blacklisted in 1909 and forced to seek work in Fife.[25]

Although Baird denied the existence of a blacklist and insisted that fears of victimisation were 'to a great extent' groundless, he nevertheless admitted:

> There can be no doubt that men who have made themselves obnoxious to a colliery may have in some instances a difficulty in getting employment there. You can understand that a coalmaster does not want a man of that stamp continually interfering with the working of the colliery.[26]

One source of such 'interference' was from the miners' checkweigher (or 'justiceman') who was legally entitled to verify the accurate weighing of each collier's output. Employers' weighing practices were a constant source of grievance. For example, the Cambuslang union complained that their employers would only weigh to the nearest half hundredweight, so that a miner whose tub weighed 10 tons 55 pounds would only be credited with 10 tons.[27] That such grievances were a stimulus to union organisation is suggested by the first objective of the Mid and West Lothian Miners' Association which was 'the protection of labour and the establishment of checkweighmen to secure actual weights and to resist illegal claims and deductions'.[28]

The Coal Mines Regulation Act of 1872 offered only limited legal protection to checkweighers, and none to men who demanded their election. Small described the case of a Lanarkshire miner who, for having filled a total of fifteen hundredweights of dirt over a three month period, had more than nineteen tons of coal deducted from his output: 'smarting under such deductions, he was urging his fellow workmen to organise so as to check such impositions but as usual he has paid the penalty [and] is now dismissed and will be starved elsewhere into meek submission'.[29] When John Anderson's father organised a meeting of Hamilton Palace miners to demand the election of a checkweigher, the manager and overman 'visited each miner in his working place with a view to intimidating him against the proposal ... in two day's time my father's place was stopped, and there was no more work for him in the colliery. He was served with a notice to leave the house at once.'[30] In Ayrshire, twenty-seven men who had taken part in the election of a checkweigher at Lanemark Colliery in 1890 were dismissed the following day: 'the same thing happened at that colliery in 1887, and a similar thing has occurred at collieries throughout Ayrshire'.[31]

Even where a checkweigher had been lawfully elected under the Act, it was possible to get rid of him by dismissing the entire workforce, and re-employing them all the next day except the checkweigher. However, the Coal Mines Regulation Act, 1887, no longer required the checkweigher to be an employee of the mine at which he was stationed, although masters could still have him removed by court order if he interfered with the management or working of a mine.[32] Nevertheless, Scottish courts upheld the employers' right to dismiss all the men and make a condition of their re-employment that they did not elect a particular individual as a checkweigher. Such cases occurred at Merryton Colliery, Larkhall, Bardykes Colliery, Blantyre, Bellfield Colliery, Lesmahagow and at Kirkwood and Rosehall Collieries in Coatbridge.[33] In the latter instance, the manager allegedly stated that the checkweigher 'has done his work well enough, but he is holding meetings of the workmen and is posting bills up and down throughout the district calling meetings, and we are not going to have a man as check-weigher who is going to do this'. The man had subsequently been blacklisted in the district and could only secure employment four miles away 'on the condition that he will not talk of organisation'.[34] Such managerial influences on the appointment of checkweighers were only legally prohibited by the Coal Mines (Check Weigher) Act, 1894.

The case of William Small exemplified the power of the coal-masters in some communities. The son of a prosperous Dundee merchant, Small 'lost all' after the collapse of the City of Glasgow Bank, and opened a small business as a draper in Cambuslang. An 'earnest radical', a Christian and later a socialist, he 'drifted into work with the miners till he gave it [his business] up altogether to serve them'.[35] In the mid-1880s, he moved from Cambuslang to live in Blantyre, 'the centre of the mining industry':

> The days in Blantyre were even more strenuous, as day and night he was called upon to go and settle disputes in all parts of the country, many nights sleeping out on the lap of mother earth, with the Glasgow Herald and the Scotsman for his blankets ... he often slept thus on summer nights when he was 18 or 20 miles from home addressing the miners at the pit head at night, so that he could picket and speak to them the following mornings at 6 o'clock before beginning their work.[36]

As a result of his efforts on behalf of the miners, he earned the enduring hostility of the coal owners. He was evicted from his home and no local landlord was willing to rent him a house. Although at this point his wife left him and his family, he was undeterred and rented half an acre of land from a local landowner. His daughter recalled:

> Here he placed his furniture and precious books; next he went to the Station Master and borrowed a tarpaulin, with which he covered his furniture, and slept under it until he was able to build a wooden shanty round them. We five children were scattered among neighbours for a few nights. Soon a gypsy fire was fixed on the ground. On this I cooked all the family food, (as I was now little mother) ... My eldest brother went to a pit to become a miner, but on coming up on his first day, was told not to come back, as no son of William Small's would be allowed to work here. Then my father went to work as a Check-Weigh-Man, as his wages allowed, he bought bricks and wood and with the help of his two sons, (none of them knew the building trade) they built 'Olivia Cottage' ...[37]

Although it took five years to complete, the building was described by the County Medical Officer as 'one of the healthiest houses in the district', containing six rooms, a bathroom and a large garden:

> As soon as our own house was completed, they set about and built
> two model miners' houses on the same plot of land. Each house had
> two rooms, kitchen, scullery, bathroom, sun porch and rain water led
> into the scullery for washing the clothes, this together with a garden
> which he rented at 5 shillings per week.

The contrast with housing conditions elsewhere in Blantyre was
striking, and 'while all this work and ground cultivation was in
progress, crowds used to gather each Sunday to watch the
progress'.[38] The vindictiveness of the coal owners further rebounded
when Olivia Cottage became a centre for radical education and culture in the village, accommodating a series of prominent socialists
who visited Blantyre, including Kropotkin, William Morris and
H.M. Hyndman.[39]

Only the most dedicated of men were willing to risk victimisation
in the task of organising the demoralised miners in the western coalfields. Hardie, who had been dismissed as a miner at Quarter for
trade union activities in 1878, before being appointed Hamilton
union secretary, ironically adumbrated the necessary qualities of a
miners' agent in 1882: 'He must be honest, sober, possessed of
neither wife nor family, have no personal feelings, be prepared to
receive kicks from the Pulpit, the Press and, what is worst of all,
from the body he is trying to serve.'[40] A similar weary cynicism permeated a letter of John Wilson, Agent and Secretary of the Mid and
West Lothian Miners' Association, who claimed he attended:

> 360 to 400 meetings per year and travelling about 2,000 miles on foot
> ... No man who spends his life among miners envies their agents ... I
> would stake my life that if you leave your present position and give
> six years to the combining of Tories, Liberals, Catholics and
> Protestants into one body to think and act alike on any one question
> of labour or politics, you will be more sympathetic to those engaged
> at such work, especially if the people you are working amongst are
> much scattered over a wide area.[41]

The rigours and risks of such activity help explain the prominence
of young men in the agitation to build unions in the 1880s and
1890s: Hardie was 22 years old when he was appointed Secretary of
the Hamilton union in 1878; Smillie was 29 when he first became
Secretary of the Larkhall union in 1886; Chisholm Robertson
became Secretary of the Forth and Clyde Association at the age of

25 in that same year; Wilson was described as a 'young and energetic agent' in 1887.[42]

In Fife, which traditionally had enjoyed more amicable industrial
relations and had a permanent union dating from 1870, coalmasters
did not display such hostility towards union activists. John Weir,
Secretary of the Fife and Kinross Miners' Association (FKMA),
claimed in 1891 that 'we have no interference with representative
delegates ... As to the use of the blacklist, I do not know anything
of the kind in our district ...'. He could recall only one case of victimisation in eleven years.[43]

Within the constraints of these obstacles, union organisation followed A.J.Y. Brown's dictum that 'the cycle and the trend were the
master influences ... the ebb and flow of unionism was closely and
clearly related to the ebb and flow of trade'.[44] Wage fluctuations
were the primary focus of union activity and also the main concern
of the masters' associations. Scotland was more prone to such fluctuations than other British mining districts. In some years, the nominal day or 'county' wage might vary almost monthly according to
the state of the coal markets. In the last four months of 1879, for
example, there were five changes in the Lanarkshire rate: from 4
shillings in September up to a maximum of 6s 3d, and down to 4s
9d by December.[45] Such variation was exceptional, but in 1909 it
was claimed by a Lanarkshire miners' agent that there had been 50
alterations in general wage rates in the previous 23 years.[46]

The recurring attempts to organise unions up to 1899 – and their
often brief duration – are summarised in Table 1.1. It should be
emphasised that this table is indicative of their ephemeral nature
rather than a comprehensive listing. The dates of dissolution are
sometimes uncertain because unions often faded from the historical
record. Some did not register with the Registrar of Friendly
Societies – as was the case with the Larkhall union of 1886 which
had 1,500 members but effectively lasted only 12 months.[47] In
Larkhall after 1887, 'we had still a remnant of the Union, but it
could not be called a Union in the true sense of the term of having
any real power. We continued for a considerable time after that.'[48] A
new Larkhall union was formed in 1890 which did not recognise the
debts of any former association in the district but operated under
the rules of debate 'which had guided previous committees'.[49] Given
their precarious nature, unions delayed their formal registration
until confident that they were on a secure footing. This revived

Table 1.1 Duration of some Scottish miners' unions, 1873–99

Date of formation	Title	Date of dissolution	Source
1873	Association of the Confederated Miners of Scotland	Skeletal existence after 1874	*Glasgow Sentinel,* 28 June 1873
1873	Amalgamated Coal Miners' Mutual Protection Society of Wishaw and Surrounding Districts	1875	SRO FS 7/35
1873	Carluke Miners' Association	1874	SRO FS 7/39
1873	Mid and East Lothian Miners' Association	1881	A.S.Cunningham, *Mining in Mid and East Lothian,* p. 93; *Dalkeith Advertiser,* 23 June 1881
1874	Hamilton, Lesmahagow and Stonefield Miners' Protection Association	?	*Glasgow Herald,* 4 September 1874
1874	Larkhall Miners' Mutual Protection, Accident and Funeral Association	1876	SRO FS 7/1
1875	Maryhill Miners' Labour Protection and Benefit Association	1878	SRO FS 7/23
1878	'new Hamilton union'	?	F. Reid, *Keir Hardie,* p. 46
1879	Lanarkshire Miners' Association	1881	SRO FS 7/14; Evidence of R. Smillie before Royal Commission on Labour, Group A, vol. 1, q. 9,940

Table 1.1 Duration of some Scottish miners' unions, 1873–99 (Continued)

Date of formation	Title	Date of dissolution	Source
1879	North Lanarkshire Miners' Association	1880	NLS Dep. 176, vol. 8
1880	Ayrshire Miners' Association	1882?	SRO FS 7/3; R.P. Arnot, *A History of the Scottish Miners*, p. 67; Reid, *Keir Hardie*, pp. 52, 61
1880	Scottish Miners' Association	?	SRO FS 7/2 and 3; Reid, *Keir Hardie*, p. 50; SRO FS 7/3, Introduction, Ayrshire Miners' Association Rules
1886	Ayrshire Miners' Union	1893	SRO FS 7/18
1885/6	Larkhall and Upper Ward of Lanarkshire Miners' Association	1887	R. Smillie, *My Life for Labour*, p. 43; Evidence of R. Smillie before Royal Commission on Labour, Group A, vol. 1, qs 9,851–3
1885	Lanarkshire Miners' Association	1889	Evidence of W. Small before Royal Commission on Labour, Group A, vol. 1, q. 10,158; *Hamilton Advertiser*, 15 December 1888

Table 1.1 Duration of some Scottish miners' unions, 1873–99 (Continued)

Date of formation	Title	Date of dissolution	Source
1886	Forth and Clyde Miners' Association (Stirlingshire)	1898	SRO FS 7/17; see Arnot *History*, p. 90n; PP 1900, LXXXIII, 694–5
1886	Scottish Miners' National Federation	1888?	Arnot, History, p. 70; *Hamilton Advertiser*, 31 March 1888
1886	Mid and East Lothian Association	1888 split between the two counties	*Dalkeith Advertiser*, 2 September 1886, 8 March 1888, 24 January 1889
1886	Mid and West Lothian Miners' Association	1893	It seems likely that this union primarily covered West Lothian, with some membership in the mines over the county border in Midlothian; its Secretary was John Wilson, the West Lothian agent; its President was Thomas Brown of Niddry in Midlothian. In July 1893, Wilson referred to it as 'the late union' and the Registrar of Friendly Societies declared

Table 1.1 Duration of some Scottish miners' unions, 1873–99 (Continued)

Date of formation	Title	Date of dissolution	Source
			it 'irregularly dissolved, April 1893', SRO FS 7/72. However, there were six branches linked in a union of the 'West Lothian Coal District' with Wilson as Agent during the 1894 strike; only two survived the dispute, Harthill and Benhar, and these provided the nucleus of re-organisation in the county in 1898–9. See J. Doonan et al., *A Trades Union Tragedy in Scotland* (1902), pp. 6–7.
1887	Clackmannanshire Miners' Association	Merged again with Fife and Kinross Miners' Association in 1917 to form Fife, Kinross and Clackmannan Miners' Association	Arnot, *History*, p. 70; *Colliery Guardian*, 9 February 1917

Table 1.1 Duration of some Scottish miners' unions, 1873–99 (Continued)

Date of formation	Title	Date of dissolution	Source
1887	Amalgamated Order of the Sons of Labour	1890	SRO FS 7/75; *Miner*, July, August 1887; J.D. Young, 'Changing images of American democracy and the Scottish labour move ment', *Inter-national Review of Social History*, 18, 1, 1973, p. 84
1889	Mid and East Lothian Miners' Association	Permanent	*Dalkeith Advertiser*, 25 July, 8 August 1889
1889	Blantyre Miners' Association	Became branch of LMU, 1896	SRO FS 7/79
1890	Bellshill miners' union	Became branch of LMU, 1897	PP 1900, LXXXIII, 694–5
1890	Cambuslang Miners' Labour Protection Association	1892	SRO FS 7/82
1890	Larkhall and Upper Ward Lanarkshire Miners' Association	Became branch of LMU, 1896	SRO FS of 7/93; NLS Mss. 8023
1893	Baillieston Miners' Association	1895	SRO FS 7/94
1893	Ayrshire Miners' Federal Union	1894	SRO FS 7/18
1893	Lanarkshire Miners' County Federation	Became LMU, 1896	Arnot, *History*, pp. 90–3

Table 1.1 Duration of some Scottish miners' unions, 1873–99 (Continued)

Date of formation	Title	Date of dissolution	Source
1893	Kirkintilloch and Twechar Miners' Association	Permanent until merger with LMU, 1927	PP 1900, LXXXIII, 694–5; Arnot, *History*, p. 184
1894	North East Lanark and Airdrie District Miners' Association	1895	SRO FS 7/97
1894	Scottish Miners' Federation	Permanent: became National Union of Scottish Mine Workers, 1914	Arnot, *History*, pp. 71, 134; Miners' Federation of Scotland (Glasgow, 1894)
1896	Lanarkshire Miners' County Union	Permanent	PP 1900, LXXXIII, 694–5
1897	Scottish Central Miners' Association	1904	PP 1906, CXIII, 94–5
1899	Stirlingshire Miners' Association	Permanent	PP 1900, LXXXIII, 694–5
1899	Amalgamated Miners' and Manual Workers (West Lothian)	Permanent	John Wilson re-organised the defunct branches of the West Lothian miners' union in the latter part of 1898; 'by the end of 1899 the county was in a fair state of organisation' (James Doonan et al., *A Trades Union Tragedy in Scotland* (1902), pp. 6–7). Minutes of delegate

Table 1.1 Duration of some Scottish miners' unions, 1873–99 (Continued)

Date of formation	Title	Date of dissolution	Source
			meetings commence in August 1899 with consideration of the new union's structure (NLS Acc. 4312/1). The Board of Trade appears to have treated the union as a revival of the earlier Mid and West Lothian Miners' Association 'and lists its date of formation as 1886. John Wilson was agent for both organisations.

Larkhall union only officially recorded its establishment in December 1891.[50] Even so, Smillie admitted the following year that 'we have a committee that meet from time to time, but there is really no Union at present amongst the men'.[51] In Blantyre, there was only a minority of unionists among the 2,000 or so mineworkers in the district: 350 in 1890, 129 in 1893, 290 in 1894, and 350 in 1895.[52]

Trade union strength could therefore fluctuate considerably. Estimates of union membership are given in Table 1.2. The figures for 1874 and 1886 (and the bracketed figures for 1893 and 1894) are based on representation claimed at union conferences; for subsequent years the data were compiled by the Chief Labour Correspondent of the Board of Trade. Although not fully comprehensive, the latter are probably more representative of paid up membership. During wage agitations, the membership which conference delegates claimed to represent, often on the basis of mandates from mass meetings, might be considerably higher. For

Table 1.2 Estimated trade union membership in the Scots coalfields, 1874–1912

Year	Trade union membership by county						
	Lanark	Stirling	West Lothian	Dumbarton	Ayrshire	Fife and Clack- mannan	Mid and East Lothian
1874	19,940	5,480	900		9,308	5,800	2,000
1886	16,350	1,300	2,500[1]		1,500	6,000	3,277
1887		2,000	1,577		1,000		
1888		1,200	1,293		500		
1889		929	939		1,100		
1890	420	1,883	674		500		
1892	1,175	1,150	500		500	7,145	3,413
1893	2,529	2,280	3,000	500	3,350	7,050	3,400
	[16,830	10,000		500	8,100		3,000]
1894	2,790	2,762	3,000	500	5,952	8,750	3,670
	[12,883		2,400		4,000	6,500	3,000]
1895	1,550	1,037	1,120	500	3,371	7,800	3,000
1896	3,315	800	600	600	2,332	7,250	2,500
1897	3,200	750	700	600	1,959	7,250	2,500
1898	14,500		1,600	600	2,245	7,250	2,540
1899	26,000	342	2,000	650	3,587	8,875	2,750
1900	30,000	2,100	3,130	900	8,294	12,655	3,250
1901	30,000	2,750	1,200	725	7,337	12,083	3,260
1902	28,000	2,000	1,200	1,200	5,837	11,509	3,300
1903	27,000	3,400	1,800	1,250	5,234	12,527	3,350
1904	25,500	4,000	1,500	1,000	4,700	13,004	3,400
1905	26,000	4,010	1,600	1,500	4,621	13,068	3,850
1906	26,000	4,000	1,600	600	6,281	13,069	4,050
1907	34,000	6,000	3,200	700	9,500	16,683	6,750
1908	33,000	6,000	3,000	540	9,560	19,207	7,500
1909	34,000	6,250	3,050	692	10,568	19,313	8,650
1910	33,000	7,500	3,050	700	10,714	19,238	9,600
1912	30,000	8,000	4,000	750	11,500	20,000	9,700

Sources: Glasgow Sentinel, 11 April 1874; *Hamilton Advertiser*, 14 August 1886, 29 July 1893; *Miners' Federation of Scotland* (Glasgow, 1894); *Glasgow Herald*, 24 February 1912; Annual Reports by the Chief Labour Correspondent of the Board of Trade on Trade Unions.

Notes:
1. This figure is based on the assumption that the published figure of '15,000' for Linlithgowshire is a misprint for 1,500, to which has been added 1,000 members separately listed in the Bathgate district.
2. The table does not include membership of the Scottish Central Miners' Association (1897–1904) which ranged between 3,000 and 5,000 and which recruited in Stirlingshire, West Lothian and Lanarkshire.

example, in July 1893 Lanarkshire delegates purported to represent almost 17,000 miners while the Board of Trade figure for membership in the county was 2,529. However, the fragile vessels of unionism in the western counties all too often foundered on major strikes and here some chronology of union organisation is required.

The boom in coal production in the early 1870s laid the basis for a huge upsurge in membership within the affiliates of the Scottish miners' federation. In Fife, the union was sufficiently strong to impose a 'closed shop' on employers by 1873. The managing partner of the Lochgelly Iron and Coal Company explained that, if he sought to employ any non-union labour, 'we would just have the pit stopped. The men give in their warning in the legal way, and leave the pit altogether. They say "we will leave the pit to your man". I have had that done.'[53] By January 1874, a Scottish union membership of 37,000 was claimed.[54] In that year, a newly formed Larkhall association had six branches covering a large area of the Clyde valley stretching from Blantyre to Douglas and Coalburn.

However, as the market collapsed, a series of wage reductions led to a ragged sequence of strikes from March to July which were conducted against the advice of the veteran miners' leader, Alexander MacDonald. The main focus of strike activity was in the West Central region, where the ironmasters took their furnaces out of blast to impose reductions of up to 40 per cent, but stoppages also occurred in Ayrshire and the Lothians.[55] Although calls were made for a 'general strike' of Scots miners – and were condemned by MacDonald as 'the old and foolish game' – the variable size and tempo of the reductions, and the differing regional markets, prevented any nationally coordinated action.[56] With the increased demand for coal caused by the strikes in the west, the Fife miners did not face such severe reductions and remained at work. After the strikes ended, the Fife and Clackmannan men were locked out in August and September as the masters there imposed a 15 per cent reduction.[57]

The strikes had a disastrous effect on union organisation. The Larkhall association alone spent £3,380 in support of its strikers. This local union, which 'had become strong in numbers, powerful in wealth', was 'torn to pieces, shattered in fragments'.[58] In September, the Larkhall association split into two bodies, the Hamilton, Lesmahagow and Stonefield Miners' Protection Association and the Larkhall Miners' Mutual Protection Association. Neither enjoyed a lengthy existence. The agent of the former resigned the following month while the latter was dissolved by 1876.[59] Similar developments took place elsewhere in the west of Scotland. In Ayrshire, the unions in Dalry, Irvine and Kilwinning had dissolved themselves by August. A Scottish delegate conference in September had a low attendance; when MacDonald addressed a similar meeting in January 1875, he 'expressed regret that so few were present'.[60]

A renewed attempt was made to organise Lanarkshire with the formation of a county union in the summer of 1879. 'It spread with great rapidity', Smillie later recalled: 'Almost every district in Lanarkshire was a member of that county organisation and the union was very strong.' Hardie recounted its growth in similar terms: 'Once the movement proceeded, the thing spread like a plague.' Within six months the union had 15,000 members with an income of £100 per week, and masters were forced to employ only union members.[61] However, after coalowners intimated two reductions of sixpence a day, miners in Hamilton, Larkhall and Motherwell rejected MacDonald's advice and struck work for a month in resistance.[62] While MacDonald urged the avoidance of strikes and a sliding scale, his protege Hardie, Secretary of the Lanarkshire Miners' Association (LMA), supported selective strikes against individual employers, a tactic described as putting the employer 'on the block'. These were ineffective and faced with further reductions, Hardie was reluctantly forced to support a general stoppage in the Hamilton, Larkhall and Motherwell districts.

These differences over tactics split the union. Hardie later admitted 'that the Block was a foolish mistake', but argued 'the General Strike had come to be inevitable'. He claimed that MacDonald had campaigned in the iron company districts of Wishaw, Shotts, Airdrie, Coatbridge, and Baillieston, where trade unionism was weakest, urging the men 'to have nothing to do with the county union'.[63] By the end of the year, a rival North Lanark Miners' Association (NLMA) had been formed in Coatbridge and several other districts, opposed to all 'strikes and blocks'. Insisting he was 'as much opposed to strikes and blocks as any man', Hardie challenged its officials to public debate, but the new organisation was short lived. Hardie claimed 'it struggled on for three weeks and then gave up the ghost'.[64] The LMA was fatally weakened, however, and Hardie was burdened with responsibility for union debts to local traders accumulated during the strike.[65]

Strikes broke out in Lanarkshire in the summer of 1880 to oppose a new round of reductions, and Hardie was despatched to Ayrshire to agitate for support and establish an Ayrshire county union. Some miners there responded to this call and struck work, but they returned in disorder after a week. Consequently, the strike in Lanarkshire crumbled, resulting in the county union 'being broken up'. The Ayrshire county union also appears to have similarly disintegrated after an unsuccessful strike over the winter of 1881–2.[66]

In August 1880, a conference of Scottish delegates had established a committee to formulate rules for a Scottish Miners' Association, within which county unions would retain their 'individuality', the association's National Council 'being more for the purpose of securing united national action during a crisis'.[67] Although the association registered its rules the following year, the weakness of its constituent bodies gave it little scope for developing such a role. In early January 1881 (the year of his death), MacDonald reflected sombrely on the previous decade:

> The strike of 1874 came, and all the work of organisation that had been going on for fifteen years was lost. Wages ran lower than they would have done. What has it been since! You have had strikes in 1878, 1879 and 1880. You have had no general union. Misery has been living with you.[68]

A renewed attempt at national federation was launched in a fresh wave of union organisation five years later. New district and county unions (including a new Ayrshire union and a Lanarkshire association) were united under the umbrella of a Scottish Miners' National Federation (SMNF) with Hardie as Secretary and R. Chisholm Robertson as President in October 1886.[69] The Federation sought to raise wages by restricting output, but there were divisions between regions on the best method to achieve this. In August, Fife argued for a restriction in other districts to the eight hour day (which had been pursued in Fife since 1870) and was supported by the Lothians; Lanarkshire delegates argued for the additional measure of a uniform wage based on a restricted 'darg' (the hewer's daily output). Such divergent strategies were rooted in the workplace practices of the different coalfields, but they evoked the suspicion, long held by the Lanarkshire miners, that Fife benefited from strikes in the West. John Weir, the Fife Secretary, was forced to deny that 'they had watched their west country brethren as a cat watches a mouse, to obtain advantage ...'.[70] In November, a motion to a conference of Scottish delegates to appoint three agents to campaign for restriction throughout Scotland was rejected. The motivation underlying this decision was revealed during a discussion of the issue at a Motherwell meeting where it was agreed to have nothing to do with Fife and Clackmannan, 'having formerly suffered through having been connected with them', an allusion to these counties remaining at work while Lanarkshire struck in 1874.[71]

In December, the willingness of some of the small masters in Lanarkshire to grant a sixpence advance fuelled demands for an all out strike there and men in Glasgow, Cambuslang, Baillieston and Motherwell, 'acting spontaneously of themselves and irrespective of the Central Board', came out on strike.[72] Faced with the fragility of the national federation's commitment to restriction and these local strike calls, Hardie and the federation leaders sought to compromise by calling a week's 'holiday' to further increase demand.[73] By early February, the organised miners throughout the Scots coalfields had suspended work for one week. Before the week was out, however, a mass meeting of 5,000 Lanarkshire miners enthusiastically approved a motion (moved by Smillie, perhaps in response to grass roots pressure) to proclaim an indefinite strike. A motion to adhere to federation policy could not find a seconder and the meeting refused to listen to Small because of his support for the federation strategy.[74]

Although Smillie persuaded the federation to support the strike call, there was considerable disarray. Miners around Coatbridge quickly resumed work on the masters' terms.[75] In Fife, miners lodged their contractually required strike warnings but before these expired an agreement with the Fife masters for an advance of 12 per cent was secured. This was underwritten by the rise in the price of coal caused by the Lanarkshire strikes. At a meeting of Lanarkshire strikers, it was reported that 'on all hands one heard bitter criticism of the "Fife men" who, it was said, had as usual proved themselves too cunning for the Lanarkshire men, at whose expense the "Fifers" had benefitted'.[76]

In Lanarkshire and Ayrshire, police and troops were deployed to protect blacklegs and preserve order. Sensing victory, the LCMA made an offer on 23 February to meet a deputation of *bona fide* miners (though not their union agents or checkweighmen) if the strike was concluded. After five weeks on strike, a meeting of the Lanarkshire miners' County Board accepted the masters' offer 'in view of the inequality in the struggle of starvation against plenty...'.[77] At the conference on 8 March, the Lanarkshire employers offered the carrot of a sixpence advance, conditional on the acceptance of a sliding scale to regulate wages and a six-day working week. The men's representatives refused to accept this offer and no agreement was reached. Thereafter, the employers unilaterally imposed their sliding scale.[78] The SMNF was forced, 'as a matter of expediency ... and in order to preserve unity', to allow its constituents to accept an advance of sixpence conditional on working an eleven-day fortnight.[79] Smillie later claimed that, in Larkhall, this condition proved 'disastrous ... We were never able to organise the men thoroughly after that ... the Union, which had been very strong up to that time, fell through.'[80]

By July, it was reported that in Lanarkshire 'the entire county' was 'out of concord and unity'.[81] At the first annual conference of the SMNF in early August, it was reported that while the organisation had been launched the previous October with 26 districts and 23,750 members, this had been reduced to 15 districts and 13,000 members.[82] Faced with this renewed decline of union organisation, Hardie and Chisholm Robertson supported the launch of a new movement that month, the Sons of Labour, which was modelled on the American Knights of Labour.[83] 'Seeing the want of unanimity among the miners', this secret society was intended to reassure the men of the security of their funds (as the Knights were the largest trade union in the world) and to provide protection from victimisation: 'an oath of obligation is involved in the membership, the leading object being to conceal the movements of the officials and others from the employers and their managers'.[84]

In April 1888, William Bulloch, a miners' agent, was appointed the 'Venerable Sage' of the order and initiated the 'Mother Lodge no. 1' among the miners of the Maryhill district; a second lodge was formed at neighbouring Lambhill.[85] In September, a Lanarkshire delegate conference approved the organisation's constitution with 'hearty commendation', and in Blantyre 'a considerable number' joined the new association. The Blantyre brethren instructed the officials of a new assembly in neighbouring Burnbank; five lodges were formed in the Airdrie district and a total of about twenty such bodies were established in Lanarkshire.[86] Despite being a secret society, the

Knights of Labour had the approval of the Catholic Church; never-theless, controversy dogged the new organisation in Lanarkshire.[87]

In March 1889, a meeting of Motherwell miners opposed any attempt to introduce the Sons of Labour and resolved that 'all miners coming into the district pay into the general union, irrespec-tive of whatever secret society they may be members of'. Two weeks later, the Motherwell union agent challenged the Sons of Labour to demonstrate that 'they are a substance not a shadow'.[88] The hostil-ity of some miners towards the new organisation, which may have been based upon memories of the divisive effects of the secret soci-eties of 'Free Colliers' in the 1860s, led to a form of dual unionism.[89] After a mass meeting of miners near Hamilton, 'there was held in McNish's Hall a general assembly of the Sons of Labour, at which all the local assemblies were represented. The decision of the mass meeting was confirmed and various details relating to rules and organisation were arranged.'[90] At a similar meeting several weeks later, 'considerable differences of opinion were expressed as to whether the future organisation should be carried on secretly by means of the Sons of Labour, or openly in the old fashion', and it was decided to refer the matter to pit meetings. It was later reported that 'very considerable diversity of opinion' existed on the issue.[91]

In Burnbank, an 'open union' was established and it appointed Small, who had severed his connection with the Sons of Labour, as its agent.[92] By June, an open union was reported to have been estab-lished, representing the 'central districts' of Lanarkshire, which 'promises to be more popular than the close [sic] organisation of the Sons of Labour'. A new Larkhall association was also established the following month, and by September Small and Smillie were appointed Secretary and President of a 'Lanarkshire Miners' County Board' which linked these district unions.[93] In the autumn of that year, strikes on a rising market forced the LCMA to grant a series of advances and abandon the sliding scale imposed after the defeat of the 1887 strike.[94]

Attention has so far been concentrated on Lanarkshire and, to a lesser extent, Ayrshire. Conventional historiography has regarded trade unionism in the eastern counties as more robust and durable during this period.[95] However, this requires significant qualification. In Mid and East Lothian, a miners' association had been launched in 1872–3, but the failure of the seven-week strike there in 1874 led to a decline in membership.[96] By 1881, the original membership of over 2,000 had diminished to 510, the great majority of whom voted to dissolve the society and divide the remaining £1,000 of union funds among themselves.[97] Less than two years later, faced with a threatened wage reduction of 15 per cent, the chairman of an informal meeting of delegates ruefully reflected that 'had their organisation been kept up the masters would have hesitated before bringing this reduction upon them'.[98] A three week strike in several of the large collieries failed to prevent its imposition.[99] Further reductions took place in 1885 and 1886. In the latter year, a 'prolonged strike' was reported, as was the formation of a 'County Board' for Midlothian in August and the declared willingness of the East Lothian miners 'to cooperate with those of Mid-Lothian'. By the end of 1886, membership of the newly formed Mid and East Lothian Miners' Association (MELMA) had increased to 1,850.[100] By 1888, however, the association had divided again between the two counties.[101] It was only in 1889 that a permanent association covering Mid and East Lothian was established with a membership of 933.[102] The employers granted recognition and in 1892 a joint conciliation board was established.[103]

Although the Fife union, which appears to have been formed in 1870, was alone among the Scots districts in preserving a permanent organisation, even its existence was precarious.[104] Its membership was reduced by a seventeen-week lockout to impose a ten per cent reduction in 1877.[105] Union funds of £15,000 were dissipated by the dispute, which ended on the masters' terms, and the membership of between 4,000 and 5,000 was drastically reduced: 'only a remnant of the men continued their connection with the Association. During the dull years that followed, membership continued at a low ebb ...'.[106] John Weir, Secretary of the Fife union, admitted that it had been 'very weak', with its membership embracing only a fifth of the miners.[107] By 1886, the eight hour day, famously adopted by the Fife miners in 1870, was under pressure at some collieries where contractors were increasing the hours of labour.[108] Organisation was further weakened when the Clackmannanshire miners split from those in Fife and Kinross to form their own union in 1887. In 1888, the differing market situation of Fife made the association unwilling to cooperate with the other Scots unions in a strike for wage increases, 'as it was felt that mere local action would make matters worse than they were by sending the trade to Northumberland'.[109]

As J.D. Young has pointed out, such evidence undermines the myth of the Fife miners as a bastion of strong unionism created on the principles of collective self-help, a view cultivated by Liberals on the Royal Commission on Labour and subscribed to by Arnot (who describes the outcome of the 1877 lockout as a 'substantial victory of the men').[110] Accused by Commission members of weakening trade unionism and alienating employers by his espousal of social-ism, Hardie perceptively retorted that the more consensual indus-trial relations in Fife were not due to strong union organisation: 'They [the employers] met with them when they [the union] had as small a proportion of the workmen organised as we have today. It is because the employers found it advantageous to do so.'[111] The demands of Fife's export markets and the owners' fear of strikes encouraged a willingness to treat with their workers' representatives.[112]

By the early 1890s, permanent organisations had been estab-lished only in Fife, Clackmannan and the Lothians. In Lanarkshire, a handful of precariously organised local unions recruited a small minority of miners. The estimated total union membership in the county was a mere 2,000 out of a total workforce of 37,000; in Ayrshire, only 10 per cent were organised.[113] It might be concluded from this catalogue of union defeat in the western counties that employer hostility, combined with patterns of mobility and ethnic divisions, rendered organisation there impossible, at least beyond the primitive level of ephemeral district unions. These local unions in part reflected the strength of parochial attitudes in some mining communities. For example, the Ayrshire Miners' Union (AMU) changed to a federal body in 1893: 'in its new form every district gets up and works its own local interests ...'.[114] Similarly, the pre-vious year, Smillie had been unable to foresee any county-wide organisation in Lanarkshire, only district unions 'with separate committees and governing bodies' linked in a federation.[115] Such parochialism could be reinforced by the local mosaic of religious affiliation in the West Central region. In the strongly Protestant Harthill and Benhar district, it was recognised by the union officials that 'the general body of the men were more homogeneous in race, religion and politics' than in any other part of West Lothian. During a revival of union organisation in the county in 1898, the branch displayed 'a very strong determination against them allow-ing their funds to be sent out of their own district ... some of the

Harthill and Benhar officials have been heard to say with vehemence "that their money would never leave Harthill"'.[116]

However, we must remember that so far we have dealt only with unions as formal organisations. As Turner has argued,

> people of the same occupation, who are regularly brought together in the same workplace or town, may acknowledge regular leaders, develop customs of work regulation and systematic 'trade practices', and can produce a disciplined observance of the latter without embedding these procedures in formal records.[117]

It is possible to recognise the recurring attempts at restriction of output and the capacity to organise strikes in the West of Scotland within Turner's formulation. Although the scattered nature of mining settlements in much of Ayrshire tended to limit such informal organisation to individual localities, in Lanarkshire, more widespread, 'spontaneous' union organisation was facilitated by the dense concentration of mining settlements in the Clyde valley and easy communication between them. Small observed in 1892 that, although no county union existed in Lanarkshire, information on the wage rates in the various districts was available 'from coming into contact with the various miners. Also there is a system of check-weighmen through the county, and we know through them.'[118] This explains Small's apparently paradoxical claim that although Lanarkshire was 'the worst organised county in Great Britain', it was also 'the most progressive by means of united and spontaneous action in obtaining advance of wages. Lanark, notwithstanding its being a disorganised county, leads always in the upward movements.'[119]

The mechanism by which restriction was most effectively enforced in Lanarkshire was the five-day week. A collective eight-hour day was more difficult to achieve, as Small remarked, 'because you cannot drag a man out of the pit at eight hours'; however, a five-day policy could be implemented 'by preventing them going to work ... by picketing'.[120] Mass picketing was a habitual weapon in strikes also. It was this pattern of combative struggle and coercive bargaining between masters and miners, the physical force of mass pickets contesting the batons of the state apparatus, through the nineteenth century which helped foster a culture of militancy in the West Central region which persisted into the twentieth.[121] This sharpness of class antagonism towards the large masters helps explain the solidarity which was to be demonstrated in the next phase of union organisation.

By 1893 Lanarkshire was once again reorganising. In June, the LCMA Executive noted that the miners of the county had 'very generally' restricted their work to four days a week and were 'very firm' in adhering to the policy.[122] The Board of a 'Lanarkshire and West of Scotland Miners' Association' met in July and 'the basis of a more comprehensive county union was generally discussed and accepted'. By September, Smillie was chairing a 'Lanarkshire Miners' Federation'.[123] Since the formation of the MFGB in 1889, the AMU and Chisholm Robertson's Forth and Clyde Miners' Association (FCMA) had been its only Scottish affiliates, although MFGB representatives attended Scottish conferences in 1893.[124] The MFGB, which had withstood a lockout in the English 'Midland' coalfields from August to November 1893 and consequently secured a conciliation board to adjust wages, intervened to channel the renewed impetus to organise in Scotland. With the MFGB's encouragement, 'a conference of agents representing the organised miners of Scotland' was held in Glasgow on 26 January 1894. Their organisations included the Lanarkshire federation, which claimed 12,883 members, the FKMA (6,500), the Ayrshire Miners' Federation (4,000), MELMA (3,000) and the 'Coalminers of Mid and West Lothian Federation' (2,400). The conference set about organising a new Scottish Miners' Federation (SMF), with the general objects of securing improved mining legislation and obtaining the eight hour day. The new body immediately affiliated to the MFGB.[125]

The lockout of the English miners in 1893 had forced a rise in the coal markets which Scots miners moved swiftly to take advantage of. In August, nominal wage rates in Lanarkshire increased from four shillings to six shillings a day, while a strike in Fife the following month secured a 12.5 per cent advance.[126] Nevertheless, strikes in the Lothians and Lanarkshire seeking further advances in November were unsuccessful.[127] This reflected a shift in the markets as the English dispute ended. In August 1893, the LCMA Chairman had addressed the question of the best time for the masters to resist the new sense of union confidence:

Shall we give the advance now or shall we refuse and fight now, or fight later on? He thought if we refused the advance now we would have to be prepared to stand now until the English strike were over,

and therefore his opinion was that we should give the advance now
and fight later on when the market was falling.[128]

With the ending of the English lockout, coal prices fell in 1894 and
the Scottish employers moved to test the strength of the new
Scottish Federation. In February, the Lanarkshire federation heard
that victimisation of its activists was taking place 'at many collieries'.[129] A joint meeting of the Scottish coalmasters' associations
in April agreed to implement wage reductions of 25 per cent, or a
shilling a day, which led to a strike in the west of Scotland by 30,000
miners. They returned to work after a week to consult with the
MFGB. After a ballot in support of the withdrawal of labour by
25,617 to 14,490, the MFGB authorised the SMF to strike to resist
the reduction. The Scottish masters viewed this 'importation of
English domination into Scotch trade affairs' with alarm, considering it a 'national danger'. A meeting in June of all the Scottish coal
and ironmasters therefore 'determined to offer uncompromising
resistance to the demands of the men' and by the end of the month
it was estimated that over 70,000 men were on strike throughout
Scotland.[130]

The masters had chosen their time strategically, as demand for
coal was at its lowest over the summer months. Nevertheless, the
Scots miners remained on strike for fifteen weeks (seventeen in Fife
and Clackmannan) until October when they returned on the
masters' terms. The events of this long, bitter dispute are described
elsewhere.[131] Here we can note two points. The first was the unprecedented solidarity of the miners during the first national strike
throughout the Scots coalfields. For example, even though the small
coalmasters in Cambuslang and Coalburn offered to meet their
men's demands, the miners in these districts struck alongside their
fellows.[132] Although the strike began to crumble in Lanarkshire in
mid-September, by virtue of MFGB levies and soup kitchens the
majority of the miners remained out.

Second, this solidarity was maintained despite serious divisions
on strategy which opened up between the Scottish leaders. After a
wage reduction in the English coalfields, the MFGB changed the
strike demands from the restoration of the full shilling reduction to
sixpence plus the establishment of a conciliation board. This retreat
from the initial claim was denounced (as were his fellow leaders) by
Chisholm Robertson, whose views gained majority support both in

Lanarkshire and in his own FCMA in Stirlingshire. Miners in Fife burned Robertson's effigy while his Stirlingshire supporters reciprocated the action with a dummy representing Fife's John Weir. A ballot of over 46,000 strikers indicated a relatively small majority in support of MFGB strategy. In the aftermath of the strike, John Wilson denounced Robertson as 'the Judas Iscariot of the miners' movement'.[133]

The defeat of the strike again seriously weakened union organisation and there was a sharp decline in the official membership figures in all the Scottish coalfields: see Table 1.2. It was claimed that in parts of the west of Scotland, the unions which survived lost up to five-sixths of their members.[134] However, the formation in 1896 of a permanent Lanarkshire Mineworkers' County Union (LMU), as distinct from the previous federation of district unions, signalled a new consolidation of unionism. In 1898, a strike in South Wales drove up demand for coal and renewed agitation for wage increases in the coalfield. Table 1.2 records a dramatic rise in union membership in the county on this rising market. The Chairman of the LMCA urged 'great caution' on his members, 'seeing the difficulty there was in getting a reduction of wages after an advance had been given'. Although the association recommended only an advance of sixpence per day, strikes swiftly forced this up to one shilling.[135] The mutually bruising dispute of 1894 had demonstrated the capacity of Lanarkshire miners to inflict lengthy punishment on the masters and by August 1898 the LCMA was willing to consider, if not yet agree, 'the propriety of meeting the miners' delegates to discuss the wages question'.[136] By the following year, with its membership extended, and the amount of 'idle time' in Lanarkshire causing 'a great deal of irritation' during a period of economic growth, the LCMA agreed with the other masters' associations to meet SMF representatives to discuss the formation of a conciliation board. Had they not done so, the SMF was prepared to call a further national stoppage throughout Scotland on the expiry of contractual notice in Fife.[137]

The inauguration of the conciliation board in 1900 to regulate wages in line with coal prices above a set minimum by no means abolished industrial conflict in the Scots coalfields. While it reduced the threat of widespread disputes over wages, it did not prevent local disputes.[138] Nevertheless, it did afford the unions a degree of recognition. For example, in June 1900, the conciliation board recommended that the Lanarkshire representatives of the owners and miners should confer before the next meeting of the board.[139] In West Lothian, a local conciliation board of employers and union officials was formed 'to settle all differences arising in the county between employers and workmen' except for those matters which fell within the remit of the Scottish conciliation board.[140] In Lanarkshire, a joint disputes committee to resolve local disputes was only established in 1912. Although arbitration was sometimes employed to resolve disputes, industrial relations in the county continued to be combative; for example, the LCMA deployed the 'block' in 1907 and 1908, forcing the LMU to involve the MFGB on the issue.[141]

The extension of union membership in the expanding coal industry in the years preceding 1914 is indicated in the latter part of Table 1.2. Trade union density – the percentage of the workforce in union membership – also increased during these years, as can be seen from Table 1.3. In considering density, it should be borne in mind that union organising efforts were largely directed at underground workers, particularly faceworkers; thus union membership expressed as a percentage of the total workforce will underestimate the 'real' extent of union influence. This explains the discrepancy between the relatively low union density in the West Central region of less than 60 per cent in 1910 recorded in Table 1.3, and the claim by the LMU in 1907 that organisation was 'now practically perfect at nearly all the collieries in the county'.[142] This goal was achieved through a number of strikes over the employment of non-union labour: there were disputes on the issue reported at twelve collieries in

Table 1.3 Trade union density in the Scottish coalfields, 1895, 1905 and 1910

	1895	1905	1910
Ayrshire	25.8	36.7	77.0
West Central	7.1	47.5	59.3
Fife and Clack.	56.2	61.7	66.5
Mid and East Lothian	41.8	37.4	76.3

Source: Calculated from Vol. 1, Table 1.2 and Vol. 2, Table 1.2. The workforce for the calculation for 1910 is taken from the *18th Abstract of Labour Statistics* (Cmd 2740, 1926).

Lanarkshire in 1907 alone.[143] By the First World War, union organ-isation had reached an unprecedented level in all the Scots mining regions, and approximately 80 per cent of Scottish mineworkers were unionised by 1913.[144]

The consolidation of this permanent union structure around the turn of the century was not achieved without inter-union conflict. The miners' strong sense of regional and local identity, county-based unions, their leaders' commitment to the survival and growth of organisations which they had built up with great difficulty and which they regarded as their personal fiefdoms, together with personal antagonisms among these leaders, com-bined to produce a number of bitterly contested 'frontier disputes' between the county unions as they sought to maximise their terri-torial coverage.

The first of these involved Chisholm Robertson, the leader of Stirlingshire's FCMA, who had clashed with his fellow union lead-ers in 1894. In the following two years, despite Robertson's protes-tations, the SMF made detailed enquiries into allegations made by the Redding branch of the FCMA of irregularities over the payment of strike benefit.[145] Robertson thereafter spent some time in South Africa and, on his return to Scotland, was invited to lead the Scottish Central Miners' Association (SCMA) which had been established in Stirlingshire in 1897.[146] In March 1899, Robertson applied to affiliate the SCMA to the SMF but it was agreed by a large majority to adhere to the rule which required affiliation only via county associations.[147] This may have been a bureaucratic device by the SMF leaders to exclude their old adversary, for there does not appear to have been any other viable county organisation in Stirlingshire at that time. In February, the SMF had received a request to assist in organising the dissident Redding and Slamannan districts of Stirlingshire. It was only in May that these districts were admitted to the SMF as constituting the Stirlingshire County Miners' Association. Robertson responded by attempting to recruit members to the SCMA at Bellshill in the LMU heartland.[148]

The following year, after the establishment of the Scottish con-ciliation board, Robertson toured Lanarkshire accusing Smillie of acting in the interests of the coalmasters.[149] After an acrimonious correspondence in the press between the two men, the 'combatants' debated their differences in a series of three lengthy and even more

vituperative meetings before the 'jury' of the Glasgow Trades
Council of which Robertson was President. By the close vote of 41
–40, the council resolved that the work of Robertson in the SCMA
was 'not in accordance with the principles of trades unionism', and
he was subsequently deposed from his presidency of the council.
The SCMA remained outside the SMF and continued to mount
poaching raids on the LMU membership in Lanarkshire – an SMF
conference in 1901 resolved that 'all means should be employed to
stamp out such piracy' – before its dissolution in 1904.[150]

A second cluster of disputes took place between the West
Lothian county union – the Amalgamated Miners and Manual
Workers (AMMW) – and the LMU over six collieries on the West
Lothian-Lanarkshire border. Although five were physically located
in Lanarkshire, they had been organised by the West Lothian union
prior to the formation of the LMU. The Benhar branch, after a dispute with John Wilson, Agent of the AMMW, seceded to the LMU
in 1900.[151] As a consequence, Polkemmet Colliery, although situated
within West Lothian, contained miners some of whom were in the
AMMW and some in the LMU. When the LMU members there
struck against a dirt scale agreed by the AMMW on the county conciliation board, Wilson opposed the LMU policy of arbitration and
the AMMW was subsequently expelled from the SMF.[152] The LMU
sent an agent, Robert Small, to organise a new union in West
Lothian with the support of the SMF; Joseph Sullivan, another
LMU agent attempted unsuccessfully to persuade James Doonan,
the AMMW President, to transfer his allegiance to the new
union.[153] The AMMW published a bitter and lengthy attack on
Smillie and the LMU agents, accusing them of having a 'hungry
eye' for the members in the border pits, of 'robbing' them of the
Harthill and Benhar district, of encouraging 'cut-throats' in West
Lothian, and of 'blackleg and Union-smashing methods'.[154]
Nevertheless, by 1903 the AMMW was forced to cede its
Lanarkshire collieries and also Polkemmet to the LMU and was
only readmitted to the SMF after Wilson had written a humiliating
personal letter of apology on terms dictated by the SMF.[155] Such
cases indicate the ruthlessness with which the emergent bureaucracy
in the Scottish miners' unions were willing to pursue their territorial
interests.

The growth in union membership was reflected in the growing
income and financial reserves of the two largest county unions in

Lanarkshire and Fife. See Table 1.4. The Lanarkshire union was willing where necessary to deploy its carefully nurtured resources in an industrially aggressive manner: between 1901 and 1907, £60,000 was spent on strike pay.[156] By 1912, the Vice-President of the SMF claimed that £100,000 had been spent on local and sectional disputes since 1899. Probably half this sum had been spent compelling employers to pay the nominal day wage set by the Scottish conciliation board:

> there were thousands of cases where the men were underground the full eight hours and either because of abnormal places or some other circumstance over which they had no control they were not able to earn the full wage. Such a state of affairs had given rise to a strong feeling of discontent among the men ...[157]

As a result of such discontents, five-sixths of the Scottish mineworkers who voted in a MFGB ballot were in favour of a general strike to secure a national minimum wage.[158] Scotland solidly joined the other MFGB districts in the first national strike throughout the British coalfields in 1912. After four months on strike, Scotland voted in a second ballot to remain out by 30,000 to 23,000. Support for the strike in England and Wales was reduced, however, and the MFGB agreed to a return to work in exchange for a Minimum Wage Act which required only district minima to be negotiated. In Scotland, a minimum wage of only 5s 10d was secured against union claims for 6s.

However, in the years up to the First World War, union militancy was generally tempered by a willingness to settle disputes through negotiation if at all possible. The numbers of full-time officials increased, their growing workload evidenced by more specialised sub-committees in the county unions: there were legal, medical and political committees in the LMU by the end of the First World War, in addition to the Executive Committee which met several times a week. In 1912, the Lanarkshire union employed six full-time agents, each of whom was responsible for industrial relations in up to fifty collieries. By 1924, there were ten, and since four had been elected to parliament, three temporary agents were appointed to take over their duties.[159] The minutes of the executive committees of the county unions contain abundant evidence of the pressures of routinisation within this evolving bureaucracy as a myriad of sectional grievances and compensation claims were dealt with on a weekly basis.

Table 1.4 Reserve fund of LMU and annual income of FKMA

	Lanarkshire Miners' County Union	Fife and Kinross Miners' Association
	Reserve fund (£)	Annual income (£)
1897	227	4,091
1898	1,685	3,919
1899	6,983	4,186
1900	14,391	5,396
1901	18,693	8,606
1902	28,950	7,783
1903	36,258	8,223
1904	44,973	8,703
1905	52,402	8,555
1906	61,958	
1907	82,556	
1908	72,912	
1909	85,541	

Sources: NLS Dep. 227 (27–32), Annual Reports of Lanarkshire Miners' County Union, 1904–9; Anon., *Mining in the Kingdom of Fife* (Leven, 1907), pp. 19–20.

Note: The reserve fund of the FKMA was £45,900 in 1906; the reserve fund of the Mid and East Lothian Miners' Association in 1912 was £24,000, although this was subsequently depleted by the national strike of that year to £3,112 (A.S. Cunningham, *Mining in Mid and East Lothian*, Edinburgh, 1925, p. 95).

This routinism placed a premium on internal union discipline and a desire to maintain stable bargaining relationships with employers once recognition had been secured. Robert Brown, Secretary of both the MELMA and the SMF's successor, the National Union of Scottish Mine Workers (NUSMW), was reported to 'have always tried to avoid fighting with the employers on the question of wages; he often tried to restrain the demands of the more excitable and less responsible members'.[160] Faced with widespread unofficial strikes in 1919, the Executive Committee of the LMU made every effort to get their members to return to work until negotiations between the MFGB and the Coal Controller were completed. In the aftermath, Smillie proclaimed to the NUSMW conference that 'he was exceedingly anxious to prevent these local outbreaks. He wanted to maintain the power of lightning strikes if necessary, but he wanted to have an organisation which by negotiation would make the local strike impossible.'[161]

Such views led to accusations of collaboration with employers which were not always misplaced. We can note the tone and assumptions in a private letter from Charles Carlow, Managing Director of the Fife Coal Company, to William Adamson, General Secretary of the Fife union. It was prompted by press reports that surface workers at Bowhill had rejected a national agreement on the working week at the end of 1918. 'It is necessary that you should put yourself in communication with the Bowhill men and see that there is no trouble over the adoption of this agreement ...', instructed Carlow. He noted that a national meeting would consider a further reduction of one hour:

> No promise was given that the concession would be made. This information, however, may help you to keep down any trouble arising under the agreement ... I hope you will be able between this and Monday to get the men to resume their work on Monday morning without fail.[162]

These examples of the behaviour of union officials mark an appropriate point at which to direct our analysis towards the nature of trade union government.

Trade union government

The leadership of the early district unions in Lanarkshire was provided by a committee, typically elected at mass meetings of miners. The officers of the district unions were usually elected from and by the committee, often on a quarterly basis.[163] They would organise picketing, general meetings of the membership and send delegates to county conferences. Committee members would often be checkweighers, since they enjoyed a limited legal protection against victimisation and already held the confidence of the men. As the Webbs noted,

> The checkweigher has to be a man of character insensible to the bullying and blandishments of manager or employers. He must be of strictly regular habits, accurate and businesslike in mind, quick at figures. The ranks of the checkweighers serve thus as an admirable

recruiting ground from which a practically inexhaustible supply of efficient Trade Union secretaries or labour representatives are drawn.[164]

The Larkhall association, formed in 1890 with Smillie as Secretary, insisted that all checkweighers in the district attended its committee meetings, subject to the sanction that otherwise 'a meeting of their men would be held for the purpose of the men to appoint a better representative'.[165] In the West Lothian association, also, all checkweighers sat on district committees 'except where they neglect to act as organisers'.[166] As Challinor has observed, against the Webbs' idealised characterisation, there were significant pressures which employers could exert on checkweighers. These might tend towards their adoption of a more conciliatory stance. More importantly, checkweighers automatically received their pay from deductions from the men's wages and hence had a material interest in maintaining their position rather than return to the arduous labour of work underground. They therefore constituted the lowest rung on the ladder of the trade union bureaucracy.[167]

Miners' agents in these district unions, where such posts existed, were employed only for the frequently short duration of the association's existence. The low wages of miners in the 1870s and 1880s meant that union dues to support an agent to organise the district were often grudgingly given and the agent's role subjected to close scrutiny. Even then, since unions typically had built up little or no funds, wages might be inadequate and irregular, and entirely dependent on miners' contributions. Chisholm Robertson resigned as agent of the Slamannan miners in 1886, 'as many of those in the district had failed to keep their pledges to him'. Small complained in 1888 that 'sympathy and promises butter no bread' and threatened to resign as Lanarkshire Secretary 'unless in future more satisfactory financial arrangements can be made'.[168] Two years earlier, at a meeting of the Larkhall miners, 'warm discussion' had taken place as to whether two county agents should be appointed, the men instructing their delegate that 'each district suit themselves in that way'.[169] In 1895, a Blantyre district union meeting closely questioned Small (once again the Secretary of the county federation) about his organisational work since the strike the previous year: 'some very condemnatory remarks were afterwards passed on the waste of money it was to the Federation to keep Mr Small in his position', and the meeting only narrowly voted to retain his services. The following month the Blantyre miners also voted by only a small majority to retain their district agent, Mr Sharp, who thereupon tendered his fortnight's notice.[170]

Before the 1890s, therefore, the Scots miners unions had only the most rudimentary stratum of full-time officials. MacDonald was unique in having amassed sufficient private wealth through speculation in the shares of mining companies to be financially independent.[171] In Fife, the only permanently established union had several long-serving, salaried general secretaries throughout this period. On the death of the first secretary, Richard Penman, Henry Cook succeeded to the post in 1873. On his death in 1880, John Weir, a former president of the Fife union, was appointed Secretary, a position he held until his death in 1908. William Adamson, Vice-President of the association, was appointed Assistant Secretary in 1902 and succeeded Weir as Secretary, holding the post until 1928.[172]

With the establishment of permanent unions throughout the Scots coalfields after 1896, such longevity of office became a common pattern. Some insight into the career trajectories of union officials can be gained from the biographies of LMU agents in 1918–19: see Table 1.5. Five out of seven for whom birth data is available were born in the decade 1857–67. (James Welsh, born in 1880 and newly appointed in 1919, represented a later generation.) As young men they had often experienced victimisation, had almost all been elected checkweighers in their twenties and thirties, and played a leading role in building the union, holding lay posts before full-time appointment.

Such men were also culturally distinct within their communities, being respectable, self-improving and upwardly mobile from the mass of miners. MacDonald epitomised the Scots ideal of the 'lad o' pairts', having attended university in his spare time as a miner before becoming a teacher, business speculator, trade union leader and MP. MacDonald was in many ways a singular case, although there were other examples of miners' children achieving professional status.[173] In Lanarkshire, Hardie, Smillie and John Robertson were also typical of this aspiring minority within the mining population. Hardie was an active temperance reformer in the 1880s and gained employment as a journalist in Ayrshire. Robertson was a 'lifetime abstainer'; as a young man he attended evening classes and then worked several years on the night shift to

Table 1.5 Trade union careers of LMU agents in post 1918–19

Robert SMILLIE (1857–1940): checkweigher 1879; President, Larkhall Miners' Association, 1885; Secretary, Larkhall Miners' Association, 1890–6; President, SMF, 1894–1912; LMU agent and President, 1896–1922; Chairman, STUC Parliamentary Committee, 1897–9; President, MFGB, 1912–21; President, NUSMW, 1922–28; MP for Morpeth 1923–29.

James TONNER (1857–1935): active union member 'since early manhood'; checkweigher and union delegate, Gilbertfield Colliery; one of founders of LMU in 1896; Vice-President, LMU, 1903; LMU agent 1904–35; President, LMU, 1919; Vice-President, NUSMW 1920–21; parish councillor and county councillor; MBE.

Joseph SULLIVAN (1866–1935): checkweigher 1887; LMU agent c.1898; NUSMW Executive Committee, 1921; MFGB Executive Committee, 1921; MP for Bothwell, 1926–31.

James MURDOCH (? -1927): elected as checkweighman and victimised c.1890; LMU agent by 1901; Vice-President, LMU, 1919; NUSMW Executive Committee, 1921.

John ROBERTSON (1867–1926): Holytown district agent, 1893; blacklisted, 1894; checkweigher Hamilton Colliery 1895; LMU agent, 1898; Vice-President, LMU, 1902; Vice-President, SMF, 1894–1914; Vice-President, NUSMW, 1914–18; President, NUSMW, 1919; NUSMW Executive Committee, 1921; MP for Bothwell, 1919–26.

Duncan GRAHAM (1867–1942): checkweigher at Thankerton Colliery 1892, Eddlewood Colliery 1897; member of first LMU Executive Committee, 1896; political agent, LMU, 1908–18; General Secretary, LMU, 1918–23; LMU agent, 1923–42; NUSMW Executive Committee, 1918–30; MFGB Executive Committee, 1920 and 1929; MP for Hamilton, 1918–42.

David GILMOUR (? -1926): checkweigher Firhill and Eddlewood Collieries; miners' agent 1894; General Secretary, LMU, 1896–1918.

James C. WELSH (1880–1954): President, Douglas Castle branch, LMU 1907; checkweigher, Douglas Castle Colliery, 1914; Vice-President, LMU, 1919; LMU agent, 1919–22, 1931–5 ; NUSMW Executive Committee, 1921; MFGB Executive Committee, 1923; MP for Coatbridge, 1922–31; MP for Bothwell, 1935–45.

William B. SMALL (1873–1944): son of William Small (1845–1903); LMU agent from 1903; Assistant General Secretary, LMU, 1919; General Secretary, LMU 1923–27, 1929–37?; NUSMW Executive Committee, from 1921.

Sources:W. Knox, *Scottish Labour Leaders: a biographical dictionary* (Edinburgh, 1984); J. Saville and J. Bellamy, *Dictionary of Labour Biography*, vol. 3 (1976); *Hamilton Advertiser*, 25 August 1917, 1 February 1919, 26 May 1928; *Bellshill Speaker*, 11 July 1919; *Motherwell Times*, 19 February 1926; NLS Dep. 227/85, NUSMW Report of Annual Conference, 1921; Dep. 227/45A, LMU Council, 6 March, 3 April 1935, 7 July 1937; Acc. 3350, Small Papers, 'Note on the story'.

Note: Only the 1921 NUSMW Executive Committee has been systematically searched for membership by these agents. All the LMU agents still in post in 1921 were members of the NUSMW Executive in that year (except Smillie who was MFGB President). Such representation was typical of other years.

permit school attendance during the day. After becoming a union official, he wrote short stories and articles on housing and was offered a job as a journalist. Both Hardie and Smillie received tuition at Olivia Cottage in Blantyre where Small and two of his sons offered free 'talks and lessons' three evening per week, on poetry, literature, social subjects and science; Small's sons – William and Robert – also became union officials. Smillie later recalled devouring books ranging from *The Popular Educator* to the *Encyclopedia Britannica* in his home-made library. James Welsh, appointed LMU agent in 1919, was also a best-selling popular novelist and poet.[174]

Similar men led the other county unions. In Ayrshire, James Brown (1862–1939) was brought up in Annbank and after starting work as a miner there at the age of 12, studied at night school. He became a member of the union branch committee four years later and its Secretary at the age of 18. During the 1894 strike, he was President of the Annbank union branch and was elected President of the Ayrshire union the following year; in 1904, he was appointed the full-time agent for Annbank, and General Secretary of the union in 1908. He became Secretary of the NUSMW in 1917 and served as MP for South Ayrshire from 1918 to 1931. An active Christian since his youth, he joined the Church of Scotland as a young man and was made a kirk elder the same year as he was appointed miners' agent. He taught in the Annbank Sunday School for fifty years and was an active temperance campaigner, serving as Secretary of the Annbank Good Templars.[175]

In the Lothians, Robert Brown (1848–1917) displayed an equally respectable profile. Having started work in Dalkeith Colliery, he then worked in Newbattle Colliery and lived in Newtongrange (after a short spell as a miner in Illinois). He was a master of the Lothian lodge of the Independent Order of Scottish Mechanics and a member of the Newbattle masonic lodge. By the mid-1880s, he was the Newbattle delegate to the MELMA County Board and by 1889 was convenor of its Delegates' Committee. He was elected Agent and Secretary of the MELMA in 1891, a post he held until his death in 1917; he was also a JP, a town councillor and Provost of Dalkeith for three terms.[176] Robert Chisholm Robertson (born 1861), the Stirlingshire union leader, was the son of a mining contractor and manager. After entering the pits at the age of eight, he returned to school following the passage of the 1872 Mines Act, re-entering the mines when he reached 13. He attended evening classes at the mining schools in Coatbridge and Newcastle and obtained his manager's certificate in Glasgow in 1883. Already a union activist – he had been victimised in the early 1880s – he organised the Stirlingshire miners and became Secretary and Agent of the FCMA upon its formation in 1886.[177] Robertson was proud of his professional training, claiming in his debates with Smillie that 'he was to the medical profession as a doctor, having a diploma while these other men [such as Smillie] were to that profession like quacks ...'.[178] Hugh Murnin (1861–1932) was elected checkweigher at Bannockburn Colliery at the age of 30 before becoming one of the first agents of the Stirlingshire union a few years later, a post he held until his death; he was a leading member of the local cooperative movement, a JP and MP, as well as President of the NUSMW.[179]

The classic, labour aristocratic values of temperance and respectability informed the organisational culture of the unions built by such men. The objects of the Mid and West Lothian Miners' Association included 'to improve the moral and social position of all its members.'[180] Reid has demonstrated how Hardie's trade union attitudes in the early 1880s were permeated with a moral elitism and censoriousness derived from evangelical notions of the social residuum: 'a certain class of men would sacrifice anything to get a big fuddle [drink]. The respectable men are rendered helpless by them.'[181] In 1890, the Larkhall committee agreed that any of its members who 'in the opinion of a majority of the committee [was] under the influence of drink and incapable of conducting himself in a proper manner' should be required to withdraw. The rules later specified a fine of sixpence for such an offence and a further similar sum if the miscreant refused to leave.[182] The Maryhill union levied the more severe fine of ten shillings for such an offence while the rules of the AMU prohibited meetings being held in licensed premises.[183]

The clash between such respectable values and those of many miners was epitomised by an exchange between MacDonald and John Crossan, a working collier, during a meeting in Fife in 1874. After MacDonald's advice that the state of the markets required the acceptance of a 15 per cent reduction had been received with 'hissing, howling and prolonged uproar', Crossan clambered on to the platform to the dismay of the chairman who expressed the hope that someone more 'respectable' would have replied to MacDonald.

Crossan's interruption prompted an outburst from MacDonald: 'Sit down, Sir, you are drunk, Sir, Sit down. You shameless dog to attempt to speak to any body of men in that state (uproar)', after which the meeting broke up in disorder.[184] Such differences are visually apparent in contemporary photographs of miners and their leaders. A picture of John Robertson, accompanied by Hardie, Smillie and other union agents, addressing a Lanarkshire demonstration around the turn of the century, shows all the agents wearing bowler hats while the audience of miners are uniformly attired in flat caps.[185]

The structure of the trade union movement built by these leaders was a complex pyramid, constructed on interconnecting layers of lay delegates and full-time agents within an increasingly oligarchic, federal framework. At its base were the branches of the various county unions, based on individual collieries in Lanarkshire and the Lothians, on geographical localities in Fife and Ayrshire. Almost no branch records for this period survive, but minutes of two meetings of the LMU's Viewpark branch in 1920 indicate that the 'monthly committee meeting' took decisions as to the policies and resolutions for which the branch delegate to the union council should cast the branch vote.[186] This supports the claim made in the *Miner* in 1923 that:

> the rank and file in Lanarkshire have no say in the voting which is on the financial basis [i.e. proportional to the size of branch represented by the delegate], and is generally carried out by the local committees, most of whom are pettifogging place seekers themselves whose energies on behalf of the organisation are influenced by smiles and pats on the back from the officials.[187]

Despite such criticisms, Lanarkshire had the most formally democratic constitution. The Council, made up of the branch delegates, met monthly, and oversaw the work of the officers and the Executive Committee which was elected by a membership ballot. This did not make the committee a 'rank and file' body: its 12 members in 1917 consisted of 2 full-time organisers, 6 checkweighmen and only 4 working miners.[188] In Fife and the Lothians, the monthly Executive Board consisted of branch delegates and also officials who were elected by the board.[189] In West Lothian, the Delegate Council met only every six months to hear a report from the monthly Executive, which consisted of officials and the union members of the county conciliation board; the officials were elected (often unopposed 'en block') from the council.[190] When John Wilson, the long serving West Lothian full-time Agent died in 1912, the union's President, James Doonan was formally elected Agent by a ballot of the members; however, the Executive Committee determined that he should be the only candidate permitted to stand in the election.[191] In Ayrshire, in addition to the county union officials, there were full-time local agents 'in almost every branch', who were all members of the county union Executive.[192]

The seven county unions were affiliated to the SMF (from 1914 the NUSMW). Its governing body was the Annual Conference, to which the county unions sent a number of delegates in only approximate proportion to their affiliated membership. Thus in 1909, there were 35 delegates from Lanarkshire, 25 from Fife and Kinross, 11 from Stirlingshire, 9 from Mid and East Lothian, 8 from Ayrshire, 4 from West Lothian, 2 from Clackmannanshire and 1 from Kirkintilloch in Dunbartonshire. Such a pattern of representation tended to favour the smaller coalfields: while Lanarkshire had a ratio of 1 delegate for 971 members and Ayrshire 1 per 1,321, Stirlingshire had 1 per 568, Dunbartonshire 1 per 692, and West Lothian 1 per 762.[193] The Scottish officials were nominated by the county unions and voted on at conference; the membership of the Scottish Executive was constituted by a quota from each county union according to the number of members affiliated. The means by which each county union appointed this quota was left to their own discretion: in Lanarkshire, it was determined by a ballot vote of the members, although in practice there was often a close overlap with the LMU Executive; in Fife, up until 1920, this was decided by the Executive Board – 'the members were not consulted, with the result that the five agents were invariably selected'; in the smaller unions by the executive or by self-selection through 'virtue of office'.[194] The quotas of Executive members again disproportionately favoured the smaller county unions. As a result, the Scottish Executive was dominated by a majority of full-time officials.[195] In response to the unusual presence of a working miner on the Executive in 1923, it was ironically suggested the NUSMW change its name to the 'Scottish National Union of MPs, Miners' Agents, Political Organisers, Checkweighers and One Brusher'.[196]

There were eighteen full-time, 'national' miners' agents in the Scottish county unions by 1918.[197] Their constitutional position was a complex one. They were elected by ballot vote of the members of their respective county unions but were technically employed by the Scottish federation, and held office under the authority of its Executive. In addition, many were also the elected officials, such as general secretary or president, of their county unions and represented these unions on this same Scottish Executive. They were thus commonly employed by the constitutional body on which they sat as influential and voting members. 'At present autocracy rules in the Scottish Miners' Union', noted Welsh in 1918, only a year prior to his own appointment as one of its full-time agents.[198] Long similarly concluded that 'the constitutions of the NUSMW and district unions appear to have ensured that, once elected [these national àgents] were almost impossible to dislodge'.[199]

Holders of positions at each level of this complex structure received financial perquisites which increased over time and as one ascended the union hierarchy. At the level of district unions, and later branches of the county unions, the rates of pay for particular union duties were clearly specified. In Larkhall in 1890, pickets' fees were raised to two shillings each 'which made the remuneration the same as for holding pit meetings'. Office holders received a 'salary' of 35 shillings per quarter, while members of a deputation to London received their rail fare plus 16 shillings per day.[200] In the MELMA, branch officials were paid for conducting ballots at the rate of one shilling per hundred ballot papers. Union collectors were often paid a commission proportional to the dues collected. Branch records for this period are rare, but three balance sheets from branches of the West Lothian association in 1913 indicate the sums spent on payments to this local lay bureaucracy of branch officials, committee men and collectors. In the Bridgeness branch, they accounted for £44 out of members' contributions of £404; in the East Benhar branch, £17 out of £88; and at Loganlea, £10 out of £122, a range of 8–19 per cent of the total branch income.[201]

Similar honorary 'salaries' were paid to the county officials and Scottish federation officials (who might also receive agents' wages). In 1900, the President, Vice-President and Treasurer of the Fife union received payments of £10, £2 and £3 12 shillings respectively; in the West Lothian association that year, the comparable sums were £3, £1 and £4, while the Secretary received £6. In Fife, further sums might be paid to these officials for holding meetings 'in addition to their outlays'.[202] In 1894, the SMF paid the Secretary and

Treasurer £10, the President and Vice-President £2 10 shillings; members of the Executive received an allowance of three shillings per meeting plus their train fare.[203]

Full-time agents' salaries were much higher. John Wilson of West Lothian was paid £3 per week, the same as the highest paid Lanarkshire agent, in 1900.[204] The MELMA Assistant Secretary was paid £2 per week in 1910. These salaries were normally set by the county executive committees (on which some agents often sat) and were also commonly adjusted in line with miners' wage rates.[205] The level of such salaries did not in themselves markedly differentiate union officials from the highest paid miners and contractors; but the regularity of payment and liberation from underground labour did. Miners' agents who were elected MPs (increasingly common after 1922) were paid a salary of £650 from the MFGB, first class rail travel and a retaining fee of £50 from the NUSMW. Should they subsequently lose their seat, they were entitled to resume their agent's duties. Miners' MPs were also entitled to sit on the executives of the county unions.[206]

There were other substantial perquisites for union officials, such as a free house for the Fife Secretary, while Wilson was awarded a grant of £218 in 1900 for past services.[207] National and international travel at union expense was a further advantage of senior office. In 1900, Wilson was granted a fortnight's leave to attend an international conference in Paris, as well as the British TUC.[208] In Fife, the Secretary attended the International Miners' Conferences held in Aix-la-Chapelle in 1896, in London in 1897, in Vienna in 1898 and in Paris in 1900. In the latter year, he stood for election to membership of the MFGB delegation to the 'American Convention of Trade Unionists'.[209] Less senior officers might attend conferences in the British seaside resorts favoured by the MFGB and TUC, representing either their county unions or the SMF.[210]

To catalogue these rewards of union office is not to suggest they were illegitimate or nefarious. But they indicate the vested interest of each overlapping layer of the local, county and national bureaucracy in preserving the existing organisational structure and progressing or exerting patronage within it. The possibility of senior leaders sponsoring promotion within the hierarchy was evidenced by the recommendation of candidates by the SMF Executive to the Stirlingshire union for the post of county agent.[211] To the accusation that this is an unduly cynical or anachronistic interpretation of the normal functioning of trade unions, we should note the carefully constructed mechanisms to allocate membership of delegations to avoid disputes over such 'perks'. These ranged from election at conferences (as in the case of the SMF representatives), by random ballot (as in the Lanarkshire union's delegate council) or rotation (as in the MELMA). A Lanarkshire correspondent in the *Miner*, which purported to be an organ of 'the rank and file', noted sarcastically the complexities of such arrangements in 1923:

> In the Lanarkshire executive committee, the delegates go by turns [to the Scottish executive] and if one of them gets on to the Scottish [executive], he attends the Scottish conferences in virtue of his position on the [Scottish] executive and that does not count as delegation against him for Lanarkshire, with the result that he gets a bigger share of conferences across the Border. Oh! It's a great game getting on to the Scottish executive with its pay of about 17 shillings for a meeting lasting about two hours or thereby. Of course, the Agents don't get 17 shillings, they get a delegation fee and train fare.[212]

That this is how union leaders themselves viewed their remuneration and job conditions is suggested by the bitter comments of John Wilson to a special meeting of West Lothian delegates during a dispute with the other SMF leaders: 'he had opposed these men for years and had at various times exposed their selfishness in keeping all the holidays and dividing them amongst themselves, viz. Smillie, Weir, Brown'.[213] Two years later, the West Lothian union officers (including Wilson) also claimed that:

> Mr Weir, like a number of other Agents in the Committee, was strongly prejudiced against Mr Wilson from the time that Mr Weir and some of his colleagues learned that Mr Wilson had a few shillings per week more salary than they had themselves ... Mr Wilson considers that such a matter is absolutely the business of the miners concerned and the agents that they employ. Mr Weir, however, has taunted Mr Wilson during the last eighteen months with being an exploiter, using other equally repulsive terms in regard to Mr Wilson's salary. In 1896 when Mr Wilson, owing to the disorganised state of his County, was working for much less than Mr Weir and some others, he was then equally insulted by these gentlemen with exactly opposite epithets, the inference being that he was giving his services for less than an agent should do, and was therefore injuring other men in that position. ... During the past three years Mr

Smillie and others, when arguing out questions with Mr Wilson on the Scotch Federation Executive, frequently tried to cut him by references to his salary.[214]

In evaluating such statements, we should bear in mind that there was a bitter inter-union dispute between the West Lothian association and the SMF at this time. However, it was also the case that Wilson was the best paid miners' union official in Scotland: he received not only £3 per week from the West Lothian miners, but also acted as Secretary to the Scottish shale miners, for which he received £4 10s, and the shale oil refinery workers, for which he received £1 5s.[215] That he and four other West Lothian officials (one of whom, James Doonan, was a future President of the NUSMW) should couch their analysis of the motivation of their opponents' hostility in such terms is itself highly revealing of the attitudes of county union officials, whether or not it was true.

The sensitivity of union officials and activists to questions of financial rewards was reinforced by instances of misappropriation of funds and accusations of dishonest claims. Charges by Smillie of financial impropriety figured prominently in his disputes with Robertson and Wilson, while a member of the Wallyford branch committee of the MELMA sued Robert Brown for libel over his claim that the committee had paid themselves more than the usual strike allowance.[216] Such allegations fuelled rank and file demands for financial scrutiny and the full accounting of expenditure. When the newly formed West Lothian board agreed to make the donation of £218 to Wilson, it was reported that 'indignation meetings' were held in West Benhar and the branch subsequently seceded from the union in protest.[217] In 1897, the Buckhaven branch of the FKMA requested that the Board should not vote money for any purpose without first consulting the branches, and also that the union's delegates to the TUC submit a detailed statement of the expenses; the Board rejected the former as impracticable and the latter as a question of confidence in its delegates.[218] During the First World War, these rank and file concerns were to be informed by more politicised opposition to the trade union bureaucracy.

Conclusion

There was slow and uneven progress in the establishment of permanent union organisation in the Scots coalfields up to the 1890s and rapid consolidation thereafter. This pattern of union development can be distinguished from that in the major English coalfields where county unions were often established earlier. The comparatively compressed evolution of union organisation in Scotland after 1894 meant that many of the founding generation of union leaders retained official positions (and a proprietorial attitude) in their county unions up until the 1930s. The position was further complicated by the autonomy enjoyed by these county unions whose affiliation to the MFGB was mediated through the byzantine complexity of the NUSMW constitution. This structure and its ageing personnel were not well equipped to deal with the problems facing the Scottish mining industry during and after the First World War. Before considering these issues, however, we must first turn to the question of the policies which these unions developed in the years after 1874.

Notes

1. See vol. 1, ch. 7.
2. G. Wilson, *Alexander McDonald: leader of the miners* (Aberdeen, 1982), p. 185.
3. *Miner*, August 1888.
4. National Library of Scotland (NLS) Mss. 8023, Larkhall Miners' Association Minutes, Committee Meeting, 25 November, 2 December 1890, General Meeting, 3 December 1890. Note also the exasperated tone of the Lanarkshire miners' leader, William Small, referring to the collapse of terracing at Glasgow Rangers' Ibrox stadium in 1902: 'Such fools are mankind pushing in thousands and tens of thousands to watch twenty two men kicking a ball at one another' (NLS Acc. 3350, William Small Papers, William Small to Belle Small, 6 April 1902). For the often hostile attitude of socialists to popular culture, see C. Waters, *British Socialists and the Politics of Popular Culture, 1884–1914* (Manchester, 1990).
5. See vol. 1, ch. 4.
6. Scottish Record Office (SRO) FS 7/97, James Anderson to Registrar of Friendly Societies, Edinburgh, 11 July 1895.

7.   *Miner*, February 1888.
8.   Ibid., November 1887.
9.   See vol. 1, ch. 6.
10. *Labour Standard*, 30 July 1881.
11. Campbell, *Lanarkshire Miners*, chs 3, 8 and 9; S. and O. Checkland, *Industry and Ethos: Scotland 1832–1914* (1984), pp. 18, 178–81.
12. University of Glasgow, Business Records Centre (UGBRC), UGD 159/1/1, LCMA Committee, 12 January 1887. For examples of the association's refusal to acknowledge the miners' union, see UGD 159/1/1, LCMA Executive, 5 October 1887 and 25 January, 23 May, 5 November 1888, UGD 159/1/2, LCMA Executive, 21 February 1893, UGD 159/1/3, LCMA Executive, 23 March 1898. For the development of the coalmasters' organisations, see vol. 1, ch. 1.
13. Royal Commission on Labour, *Minutes of Evidence taken before Group A, Mining, vol. II*, PP 1892, XXXVI, Pt 1, 195.
14. Ibid., 60.
15. NLS Mss 8023, Larkhall Miners' Association Minutes, 9 September 1890. A similar situation prevailed in Ayrshire: see Royal Commission on Labour, PP 1892, XXXVI, Pt 1, 195.
16. Ibid., 240, 252–5.
17. Ibid., 53.
18. Ibid., 59.
19. For the contracting system, see vol. 1, chs 2 and 3.
20. *Glasgow Herald*, 1 March 1912. See the complaint of the Law miners' agent during the 1894 strike that 'the district of Law was one of the worst in Scotland, and until the cursed system of contracting was done away with, they would never be able to fight with the others' (*Hamilton Advertiser*, 29 September 1894).
21. Royal Commission on Labour, PP 1892, XXXVI, Pt 1, 245. See vol. 1, ch. 1, for discussion of the 'block'.
22. Ibid., 59.
23. Ibid., 85.
24. Ibid., 200, 217.
25. B. Selkirk, *The Life of a Worker* (Dundee, 1967), pp. 7, 9.
26. Royal Commission on Labour, PP 1892, XXXVI, Pt 1, 243.
27. Public Record Office (PRO), POWE 6/61, Matthew Robertson to Secretary of State for Scotland, 15 January 1890.
28. *Statistical Tables and Fourth Report on Trade Unions*, PP 1890–91, XCII, 482–3.
29. PRO POWE 6/63, Enclosure, 20 September 1890.
30. J. Anderson, *Coal! A history of the coal-mining industry in Scotland with special reference to the Cambuslang district of Lanarkshire* (Cambuslang, n.d.), pp. 53–4.

31. Royal Commission on Labour, PP 1892, XXXVI, Pt 1, 200.
32. J.C. Chisholm, *Manual of Coal Mines Regulation Act, 1887* (1888), pp. 28–34.
33. PRO POWE 6/64, Docket notes; Royal Commission on Labour, PP 1892, XXXVI, Pt 1, 67; *Hamilton Advertiser*, 13 May 1893.
34. Royal Commission on Labour, PP 1892, XXXVI, Pt 1, 67–8.
35. NLS Acc 3350, Small Papers, Folder 3, Extract from *Scottish Cooperator*, February 1903; Folder 2, Mss 'Note on this story'.
36. Ibid., Folder 5, 'William Small: Memories, visions and work', pp. 4–5. The 1891 Census Enumerator's Book for Stonefield records Small's youngest son, Gladstone, aged five years, as being born in Cambuslang (Census Enumeration District 624/7, Blantyre Parish); it seems that Small moved to Blantyre in the latter part of 1886. He was described as being from Cambuslang in May of that year (*Hamilton Advertiser*, 1 May 1886). By January 1887, he was resident in Blantyre (SRO HH 55/89, W. Small to Secretary of State for Scotland).
37. Ibid., 'Memories', pp. 6–7. This eviction may have taken place after the unsuccessful Lanarkshire strike of 1887. By 1889 he was resident in Olivia Cottage (W. Small to LCMA, 28 October 1889, reprinted in Royal Commission on Labour, PP 1892, XXXVI, Pt 1, 86). The departure of Small's wife was temporary, as she is recorded as residing with the family in the 1891 census.
38. Ibid., 7–8. For housing conditions in Blantyre and elsewhere in Lanarkshire, see vol. 1, ch. 5.
39. Ibid., p. 8.
40. Quoted in F. Reid, *Keir Hardie: the making of a socialist* (1978), p. 57.
41. SRO FS 7/72, John Wilson to Addison Smith, 18 July 1893.
42. *Miner*, January, March, April 1887.
43. Royal Commission on Labour, *Minutes of Evidence taken before Group A, Mining, vol. I*, PP 1892, XXXIV, 242.
44. A.J.Y. Brown, 'Trade union policy in the Scots coalfields, 1855–1885', *Economic History Review*, 6, 1953, pp. 35, 50.
45. UGD 159/1/2, LCMA Minutes Ledger, 'Nominal wages of miners in the Association' [*sic*].
46. *Justice*, 23 June 1909. For an estimated series of hewers' wage rates in Scotland, see R. Church, *The History of the British Coal Industry, vol. 3, 1830–1913: Victorian pre-eminence* (Oxford, 1986), pp. 641–5.
47. Royal Commission on Labour, PP 1892, XXXVI, Pt 1, 59.
48. Ibid., 71.
49. NLS Mss 8023, Larkhall Miners' Association Minutes, Committee Meeting, 22, 29 April 1890.
50. The registration application stated the union was established on 10 December 1891 and was signed 29 December 1891 (SRO FS 7/93).

51. Royal Commission on Labour, PP 1892, XXXVI, Pt 1, 53.
52. *Statistical Tables*, PP 1890–91, XCII, 492–3; *Report by the Chief Labour Correspondent of the Board of Trade on Trade Unions*, PP 1900, LXXXIII, 694–5.
53. *Report from the Select Committee on the Present Dearness and Scarcity of Coal, Minutes of Evidence*, PP 1873, X, 262.
54. *Glasgow Sentinel*, 10 January 1874.
55. Ibid., 4 March 1874; *Glasgow Herald*, 11 May 1874.
56. *Glasgow Herald*, 14 April, 11 May 1874. See F. Reid, 'Alexander MacDonald and the crisis of the independent collier, 1872–74' in Harrison *Independent Collier*, and Campbell, *Lanarkshire Miners*, ch. 12.
57. *Glasgow Herald*, 21, 28 August, 8, 26 September 1874.
58. Ibid., 31 July 1874; *Glasgow Sentinel*, 12 September 1874.
59. *Glasgow Herald*, 4, 23 September 1874; *Hamilton Advertiser*, 3 October 1874; SRO FS 7/1, Resolution to dissolve the society, 27 December 1876.
60. *Glasgow Herald*, 13, 31 August, 8 September 1874, 6 January 1875.
61. Royal Commission on Labour, PP 1892, XXXVI, Pt 1, 65; NLS Dep. 176, vol. 8, Hardie to Editor, *Labour Tribune*, 31 November 1880.
62. Reid, *Hardie*, pp. 47–50.
63. Reid, *Hardie*, pp. 47–50; NLS Dep. 176, vol. 8, Hardie to A. MacDonald, 11 November 1880. For the weakness of trade unionism in Coatbridge due to the power of the iron companies, see Campbell, *Lanarkshire Miners*, pp. 137–8.
64. NLS Dep. 176, vol. 8, Hardie to Mr Burns, 30 December 1879, Hardie to Mr Panning, 30 December 1879, Hardie to A. MacDonald, 11 November 1880.
65. Reid, *Hardie*, p. 50; NLS Dep. 176, vol. 8, Hardie to A. MacDonald, 11 November 1880. The debt remained a bone of bitter contention between Hardie and MacDonald, who accused Hardie of having 'deceived the miners by making them believe you could get goods enough to support them in the struggle' (Hardie to MacDonald, 11 November 1880). Hardie later informed the creditors that: 'Mr MacDonald has positively refused to render any assistance towards getting the debt paid as long as I am taking anything to do with the miners' affairs of the district'. He appealed to them to relieve him of the responsibility 'so that I may be at liberty to accept of other employment' (Hardie to Alexander Begg, 12 November 1880). This plea was apparently successful (Hardie to Alexander Begg, 18 November 1880) and Hardie moved to Ayrshire the following year.
66. Reid, *Hardie*, pp. 50–3; Arnot, *History*, p. 67; Royal Commission on Labour, PP 1892, XXXVI, Pt 1, 65.

67. SRO FS 7/3, *Rules of the Ayrshire Miners' Association.*
68. *Dalkeith Advertiser*, 6 January 1881.
69. *Miner*, January 1887. This groundswell of organisation in turn stimulated the formation of the Lanarkshire Coal Masters' Association: see vol. 1, ch. 1.
70. *Hamilton Advertiser*, 14 August 1886.
71. Ibid., 27 November 1886.
72. Ibid., 18 December 1886.
73. See Reid, *Hardie*, pp. 88–92.
74. *Glasgow Herald*, 5 February 1887.
75. Ibid., 8 February 1887.
76. Ibid., 18, 21, 23 February 1887.
77. Ibid., 24, 25 February 1887; UGBRC UGD 159/1/1, LCMA Committee, 23 February, 4 March 1887.
78. UGBRC UGD 159/1/1, LCMA Conference with Miners' Representatives, 8, 16 March, 13 April 1887, LCMA General Meeting 20 April 1887; *Glasgow Herald*, 9 March 1887; Reid, *Hardie*, pp. 91–2.
79. *Glasgow Herald*, 21 March 1887.
80. Royal Commission on Labour, PP 1892, XXXVI, Pt 1, 59–60; *Miner*, September 1887.
81. *Miner*, July 1887.
82. Ibid., August 1887.
83. Ibid., July, August 1887. The movement's programme is reprinted in Reid, *Hardie*, pp. 193–5.
84. Ibid., June 1888; *Hamilton Advertiser*, 1 September 1888.
85. *Justice*, 5 May 1888.
86. *Hamilton Advertiser*, 8, 22 September 1888; *Justice*, 29 September 1888; *Miner*, November 1888.
87. J.D. Young, 'Changing images of American democracy and the Scottish labour movement', *International Review of Social History*, 18, 1, 1973, p. 84; H. Pelling, 'The Knights of Labour in Britain, 1880–1901', *Economic History Review*, 9, 2, 1956, p. 327. Why the title Sons of Labour was adopted in Lanarkshire (whereas Knights of Labour was used elsewhere) is unclear. It may have been to avoid confusion with the 'Sir Knights' of the sectarian Royal Black Institution (see vol. 1, ch. 7).
88. *Hamilton Advertiser*, 30 March, 13 April 1889.
89. For the Free Colliers, see Campbell, *Lanarkshire Miners*, ch. 11.
90. *Hamilton Advertiser*, 20 April 1889.
91. Ibid., 11, 18 May 1889.
92. Ibid., 11, 18 May 1889.
93. Ibid., 22 June, 3 August, 14 September, 9 November 1889.
94. Royal Commission on Labour, PP 1892, XXXVI, Pt 1, 86; UGBRC

UGD 159/1/2, LCMA Executive Committee, 4 September, 4 November 1889, General Meeting 11 September, 6 November 1889.

95. Arnot, *History*, pp. 58, 70.
96. A.S. Cunningham, *Mining in Mid and East Lothian* (Edinburgh, 1925), pp. 93–4.
97. *Dalkeith Advertiser*, 2, 23 June 1881.
98. Ibid., 15 March 1883.
99. Ibid., 22, 29 March, 5, 12 April 1883.
100. Ibid., 26 August, 2 September, 4 November 1886; *Hamilton Advertiser*, 14 August 1886.
101. *Dalkeith Advertiser*, 24 January 1889.
102. Ibid., 25 July, 8 August, 3 October 1889.
103. Cunningham, *Mid and East Lothian*, p. 94.
104. There is confusion on the date of its formation. Arnot states ambiguously that the Association was 'definitely formed' in February 1871, implying an earlier possible date (Arnot, *History*, p. 51). It was claimed in a local history, published in 1907, that the association was established in 1869, before the adoption of the eight hour day in 1870, and that its rules were amended then to make this a condition of membership (Anon., *Mining in the Kingdom of Fife*, Leven, 1907, p. 19). There is a press report of a meeting of Fife miners in Dunfermline forming an association in March 1870 (*Glasgow Sentinel*, 12 March 1870) and The Chief Labour Correspondent of the Board of Trade tabulates its formation as 1870 (PP 1900, LXXXIII, 694–5). In January 1871, Richard Penman, represented 8,000 Fife miners at the Miners' National Association conference (*Glasgow Sentinel*, 14 January 1871); the following month a Fife county delegate meeting agreed to adopt a common Labour Fund for the whole county (Ibid., 11 February 1871). This appears the basis of Arnot attributing the 'definite' formation of the union to that date.
105. Royal Commission on Labour, PP 1892, XXXVI, Pt 1, 260.
106. Anon., *Kingdom of Fife*, p. 19.
107. Royal Commission on Labour, PP 1892, XXXIV, 247.
108. J.D. Young, 'Working class and radical movements in Scotland and the revolt from Liberalism, 1866–1900', unpublished PhD thesis, University of Stirling, 1974, p. 256.
109. *Justice*, 15 September 1888.
110. Young, thesis, pp. 255–6; Arnot, *History*, pp. 58–9.
111. Royal Commission on Labour, PP 1892, XXXVI, Pt 1, 203.
112. See vol. 1, ch. 1.
113. Royal Commission on Labour, PP 1892, XXXVI, Pt 1, 64, 78, 200–1.
114. SRO FS 7/18, John Littlejohn to Registrar of Friendly Societies, 9 October 1893.

115. Royal Commission on Labour, PP 1892, XXXVI, Pt 1, 65.
116. J. Doonan et al., *A Trades Union Tragedy in Scotland. Some dark deeds which should be known to all trade unionists and trade union officials. Mr Robert Smillie, Miners' Agent, Larkhall, as a blackleg and would be MP* (n.p., 1902), pp. 74–5. For local religious segregation in the West Central region, see vol. 1, ch. 7.
117. H.A. Turner, *Trade Union Structure and Growth* (1962), p. 51.
118. Royal Commission on Labour, PP 1892, XXXVI, Pt 1, 94.
119. Ibid., 78, 105.
120. Ibid., 88–9.
121. For social disorders associated with industrial disputes in the West Central region, see vol. 1, ch. 6.
122. UGBRC UGD 159/1/2, LCMA Executive Committee, 14 June 1893.
123. *Hamilton Advertiser*, 8 July, 16 September 1893.
124. Ibid., 29 July 1893.
125. *Miners' Federation of Scotland* (Glasgow, 1894); Arnot, *History*, p. 71.
126. UGBRC UGD 159/1/2, LCMA Executive Committee, 5 September 1893.
127. Ibid., LCMA Wages Committee, 8, 27 November 1893; *Hamilton Advertiser*, 16 September, 25 November, 30 December 1893.
128. Ibid., LCMA Executive Committee, 23 August 1893.
129. *Hamilton Advertiser*, 24 February 1894.
130. UGBRC UGD 159/1/2, Meeting of the Trade, 18 April 1894; *Hamilton Advertiser*, 23 February 1895; Arnot, *History*, pp. 74–6.
131. Arnot, *History*, pp. 76–88.
132. *Hamilton Advertiser*, 30 June 1894.
133. *Hamilton Advertiser*, 1 September, 27 October 1894.
134. Doonan et al., *Tragedy*, p. 6.
135. UGBRC UGD 159/1/3, LCMA Executive Committee, 13 and 18 April 1893.
136. Ibid., 17 August 1898.
137. NLS Acc. 4312/19, SMF Conference, 24 February 1899. For the negotiations, see Arnot, *History*, pp. 98–104.
138. See vol. 1, ch. 3.
139. *Colliery Guardian*, 1 June 1900.
140. Ibid., 30 November 1900.
141. Ibid., 24 October 1913; NLS Dep. 227/30 and 31, *Annual Reports for 1907, 1908*.
142. NLS Dep. 227/30, *Annual Report for 1907*. See also ch. 2 of this volume.
143. *Colliery Guardian*, 26 April, 7 June, 16 August, 6 September, 1, 29 November 1907.
144. Church, *History*, p. 693.

145. NLS Acc. 4312/19, SMF Executive, 1, 8, 24 April, 15 October 1895, 5 April 1896.
146. Anon., *The Smillie-Chisholm Robertson Controversy* (Hamilton, 1900), p. 5.
147. NLS Acc. 4312/19, SMF Executive, 7 March 1899, SMF Conference, 23 March 1899.
148. Ibid., SMF Executive, 17 February, 17 April, 2, 5 May 1899.
149. Anon., *Controversy*, p. 5.
150. A transcript of the debates was published (Anon., *Controversy*) and the SMF arranged for 40,000 copies to be circulated (NLS Acc. 4312/20, SMF Conference, 20 August, 27 September, 17 October 1900); *Report on Trade Unions*, PP 1906, CXIII, 94–5.
151. Doonan et al., *Tragedy*, p. 12.
152. Ibid., pp. 15–16; NLS Acc. 4312/20, SMF Conference, 9 July 1900.
153. NLS Acc. 4312/20, SMF Executive, 25 March 1901; NLS Acc. 4312/1, AMMW Executive, 26 November 1901.
154. Doonan et al., *Tragedy*, pp. 14, 15, 83, 94.
155. NLS Acc. 4312/20, SMF Conference, 20, 29 August, 21 November 1902, 23 January, 1 April, 20 April 1903, and Minutes of Meeting between LMU and AMMW delegates re. boundary line, 19 March, 11 April 1903.
156. *Colliery Guardian*, 26 June 1907.
157. *Glasgow Herald*, 16 January 1912.
158. Ibid.
159. *Miner*, 15 September 1923, 30 August 1924; NLS Dep. 227/39, LMU Council, 4 July 1923.
160. *Dalkeith Advertiser*, 27 December 1917.
161. NLS Dep. 227/99, NUSMW, Proceedings of Annual Conference, 1919.
162. NLS Acc. 4311/250, Fife, Clackmannan and Kinross Miners' Union, Miscellaneous Papers, C. Carlow to W. Adamson, 21 December 1918. Abe Moffat, a Communist opponent of Adamson, later recalled that: 'He was very, very close with the coalowners, socially and otherwise. That was the main thing which the miners didn't like about Adamson – his very close association with the coalowners, and particularly the Reids of the Fife Coal Company ... He was always against strike action' (P. Long, 'Abe Moffat, the Fife miners and the United Mineworkers of Scotland', *Scottish Labour History Society Journal*, 17, 1982, p. 13).
163. For example, see NLS Mss. 8023, Larkhall Miners' Association Weekly Committee Meeting, 15 July 1890.
164. Quoted in R. Challinor, 'Alexander MacDonald and the miners', *Our History Pamphlet*, 48, 1967/8, p. 27.

165. NLS Mss. 8023, Larkhall Miners' Association Weekly Committee Meeting, 13 May 1890.
166. NLS Acc. 4312/1, AMMW Executive, 22 August 1899.
167. Challinor, 'MacDonald', pp. 27–9.
168. *Hamilton Advertiser*, 15 May 1886, 15 December 1888. For the Ayrshire miners' failure to pay Hardie his full wages, see Reid, *Hardie*, p. 57.
169. *Hamilton Advertiser*, 9 October 1886.
170. Ibid., 3 August, 7 September 1895.
171. Wilson, *McDonald*, pp. 66–7, 156–8.
172. Arnot, *History*, p. 52; *Miner*, June 1887; W. Knox (ed.), *Scottish Labour Leaders, 1918–1939: a biographical dictionary* (Edinburgh, 1984), p. 58.
173. See R. Haddow, 'The miners of Scotland', *Nineteenth Century*, September 1888, p. 357; Anderson, *Coal!*, p. 45; A. Miller, *Coatbridge: its rise and progress* (Glasgow, 1864), p. 193. Jennie Lee, grand-daughter of a Fife miners' agent, who graduated from Edinburgh University and became a school teacher before being elected an MP, was another example of such upward mobility (J. Lee, *This Great Journey*, 1963). None of Robert Smillie's seven sons remained miners: two became mining engineers, while the others were an electrical engineer (and an officer during the First World War), a professor of agriculture, a market gardener, a carpenter and a bricklayer (J. Saville and J. Bellamy, eds, *Dictionary of Labour Biography*, 3, 1976, p. 171).
174. For Hardie, see Reid, *Hardie*, especially ch. 3; for Robertson, see *Bellshill Speaker*, 11 July 1919; for Smillie, see his *My Life for Labour* (1924), pp. 52–3; Smillie's change of name from 'Smellie' to the more euphonious Smillie in the mid 1890s may have reflected his social aspirations. For Small, see NLS Acc. 3350, Small Papers, folder 8, annotation on ILP Jubilee Souvenir by Belle Small, and folder 5, 'The man and reality', pp. 8–9; for Welsh, see Saville and Bellamy, *Dictionary*, 2 (1974).
175. Saville and Bellamy, *Dictionary*, 1, (1972).
176. *Dalkeith Advertiser*, 21 July 1887, 7 Nov 1889, 26 March 1891, 10 March 1898; *Scotsman*, 21 December 1917. For social relations in Newtongrange, see vol. 1, ch. 6.
177. *Miner*, January 1887.
178. Anon., *Controversy*, p. 50.
179. Knox, *Labour Leaders*, pp. 221–2.
180. SRO FS 7/72, *Rules of the Mid and West Lothian Miners' Association*, Rule 4.
181. Quoted in Reid, *Hardie*, p. 61.
182. NLS Mss. 8023, Larkhall Miners' Association Weekly Committee

Meetings, 29 July 1890; SRO FS 7/93, *Rules of the Larkhall and Upper Ward of Lanarkshire Miners' Association*, Rule 16.

183. SRO FS 7/23, *Rules of the Maryhill Miners' Labour Protection and Benefits Association*, Rule 20; FS 7/18, *Rules of the Ayrshire Miners' Union*, Rule 16.

184. *Glasgow Herald*, 28 August 1874.

185. The photograph is reprinted in Arnot, *History*, opposite p. 96. Pictures of the executives of the FKMA and LMU around the turn of the century, showing the members of both bodies dressed very respectably in suits, starched collars and gold watch chains, are reproduced in I. MacDougall (ed.), *Labour in Scotland: a pictorial history from the eighteenth century to the present* (Edinburgh, 1985), pp. 137, 174.

186. NLS Dep. 227/159, Minutes of the Viewpark branch, LMU, 25 November and 8 December 1920.

187. *Miner*, 13 October 1923.

188. *Hamilton Advertiser*, 4 August 1917.

189. P. Long, 'The economic and social history of the Scottish coal industry 1925–39, with particular reference to industrial relations', unpublished PhD thesis, University of Strathclyde, 1978, p. 345.

190. NLS Acc. 4312/1, AMMW Council, 25 February 1905, 3 March 1907.

191. Ibid., 20 April, 25 May, 1 June 1912.

192. *Miner*, 10 November 1923, 27 September 1924.

193. *Glasgow Herald*, 19 December 1909. Ratios are calculated from the 1909 membership figures in Table 1.2.

194. Anon., *The Fife Miners' Union Split: rank and file versus officialdom* (n.d., 1924?), p. 4; NLS Acc. 4312/1, AMMW, 8 June 1912.

195. J.C. Welsh, 'The Scottish miners and their union', *Socialist Review*, 15, 1918, p. 80.

196. *Miner*, 13 October 1923.

197. NLS Dep. 227/60, LMU Executive Committee, 28 January 1918.

198. Welsh, 'Scottish miners', p. 78.

199. Long, thesis, pp. 345–6; see also *Miner*, 24 November 1923.

200. NLS Mss. 8023, Larkhall Miners' Association Weekly Committee Meetings, 27 May, 15 July 1890, 2 June 1891.

201. NLS Acc. 4312/1, Balance sheets for the Bridgeness, East Benhar and Loganlea branches, AMMW (West Lothian) for 1913.

202. NLS PDL 44/14, FKMA Board, 22 October 1896, 8 March 1900; Acc. 4312/1, AMMW Council, 26 December 1900.

203. NLS Acc. 4312/19, SMF Conference, 27 December 1894.

204. NLS Acc. 4312/1, AMMW Council, 27 August 1900.

205. Doonan et al., *Tragedy*, p. 10; NLS Acc. 4312/7, MELMA Executive

and Financial Committee, 26 November 1910; PDL 44/14, FKMA Board, 20 September 1900.

206. *Miner*, 18 August, 1 September 1923; Long, thesis, p. 346.
207. NLS PDL 44/14, FKMA Board, 8 March 1900; Acc. 4312/1, AMMW Council, 30 January, 27 March 1900.
208. NLS Acc. 4312/1, AMMW Council, 27 March, 22 May 1900.
209. NLS PDL 44/14, FKMA Board, 7 May 1896, 3 June 1897, 2 June 1898, 3 May, 4 August 1900.
210. For a lengthy debate on the numbers of delegates to such conferences, see NLS Acc. 4312/19, SMF Annual Conference, 12 December 1899.
211. NLS Acc. 4312/20, SMF Executive, 29 January 1901.
212. *Miner*, 1 September 1923.
213. NLS Acc. 4312/1, AMMW Special Meeting, 9 October 1900.
214. Doonan et al., *Tragedy*, pp. 48–9, 71.
215. Ibid., p. 72.
216. NLS Acc. 4312/7, MELMA Board, 11 July, 19 December 1912, 23 January, 27 December 1913; for an example of a union treasurer misappropriating funds see SRO FS 7/23, Annual return of Maryhill Miners' Labour Protection Association, 1876. As Eric Hobsbawm pointed out many years ago, trade union historiography has traditionally avoided discussion of 'cavalier' attitudes to union funds (E. Hobsbawm, 'Trade union historiography', *Bulletin of the Society for the Study of Labour History*, 8, 1964, p. 32). For a recent excavation of this hidden 'embarrassment' in labour history, see J. McIlroy, 'Financial malpractice in British trade unions, 1800–1930: the background to, and consequences of, *Hornby v. Close*', *Historical Studies in Industrial Relations*, 6, 1998.
217. NLS Acc. 4312/1, AMMW Council, 27 February 1900.
218. NLS PDL 44/14, FKMA Board, 21 October 1897.

CHAPTER TWO

Trade union policies, socialist politics and labour representation, 1874–1914

Introduction

From the eighteenth century onwards, the policies of successive Scots miners' unions were informed by the values of the work culture of the independent collier. At their heart were attempts to control output (and hence wages). Restriction of output could only be achieved if the unions also limited entry to the trade. This chapter begins by noting the continuing adoption of these strategies by trade unionists until the early years of the twentieth century, even though their implementation was problematic and at best only temporarily successful. This failure, and the enduring weakness of union organisation in the face of employer hostility in the two decades after 1874, forced union activists in the western counties to seek inspiration from the small number of land reformers and socialists propagandising in the Scots coalfields from the 1880s onwards. The increasing acceptance of socialist collectivism within the miners' unions did not displace their traditional policies; rather they were relocated within a framework of state regulation of the industry. Such a strategy in turn was dependent upon parliamentary legislation. Confronted by a Liberal Party less willing than its English counterpart to incorporate working class candidates, the Scottish miners placed themselves in the vanguard of the movement for independent labour representation. After analysing the reasons for the comparative failure of their representatives to secure parliamentary election before the First World War, the chapter concludes by emphasising the continuities apparent in trade union attitudes and policies before 1914.

Trade union policy

The traditional policies of the Scots miners' unions were rooted in the workplace autonomy of the hewers.[1] The notion that individual hewer's control of their daily output or 'darg' could be translated into a collective restriction of production to manipulate the local coal market dated back to at least the eighteenth century. Secret societies known as 'colliery brotherhoods' then enforced a restricted darg so that a scarcity of coal drove up miners' wages.[2] On occasion the brotherhoods temporarily united into wider combinations. This occurred in 1817 throughout Lanarkshire and Ayrshire, and, most notably, in 1825 when the Associated Colliers of Scotland secured huge wage increases through the coordinated control of the Scottish coal markets.[3] Such successes were undermined by improved transport links between coal producing regions, influxes of new labour and the hostility of the increasingly large coal and iron companies.

Nevertheless, in the middle of the nineteenth century restriction of output remained the fundamental element in the wages policy of successive Scots miners' unions by which they sought to moderate cyclical downswings and enhance rises in the coal markets. Indeed, it was regarded as the primary rationale of trade union organisation, as the Holytown union secretary observed in 1846: 'without restriction of labour, the union would be no better than a dead letter: it is to the union what the mainspring is to a watch'.[4] Through restriction, it was hoped that strikes, which threatened to destroy precarious union organisation, might be avoided.[5]

Restriction was pursued within a continuing artisanal view of 'the trade' in which both mineowners and colliers were entitled to a 'fair' return: 'money is the capital of the employer', stated MacDonald in 1867, 'labour is the capital of the workmen. The one capital is dependent upon the other ... The great social problem of the day is to devise the means which shall secure an amicable adjustment – a fair division of profits ...'.[6] Such views did not imply an identity of interests between employer and employed, rather that their interests were distinct but not necessarily antagonistic: the small employers in Larkhall who recognised their obligations to the trade and 'have remained our friends', were contrasted at a miners' meeting in 1872 with those pursuing 'the insane policy' of swingeing waging reductions.[7] Nor did such attitudes imply an ideological surrender to the laws of political economy in which wages automatically followed prices: a national confederation of miners' unions restricting output might instead be conceived of as inversion of the laws of supply and demand, allowing wages to determine prices.[8]

Control of output could only be secured if there were no inputs of new labour into the mines. From the days of the colliery brotherhoods, Scots miners sought to restrict entry to the trade to their sons through formalising the training of colliers by apprenticeship regulations in their union rules and applying the financial disincentive of high entry fees (and often the threat of severe physical violence) to 'neutral' adults seeking to commence work underground.[9] The problems associated with such an exclusive union strategy were enormous in the rapidly expanding western coalfields by the middle years of the nineteenth century. Only the best organised districts at the zenith of the trade cycle might hope to enforce such controls. As a consequence, an additional policy of removing surplus labour through emigration to the coalfields of the United States and Canada was enthusiastically advocated and many Scots miners travelled there, sometimes only temporarily, from the 1860s onwards.[10]

A further union policy which encapsulated many of these aspirations of the independent collier was cooperative production. Alexander Campbell, a former Owenite and close associate of MacDonald, campaigned in the 1850s and 1860s for the Scots miners' unions to form a limited company which would contract with the employers to produce coal at a given price. By this means the miners' union would control production, each man working to produce the 'cooperative darg' while boys in the mine would be 'the apprentices of the cooperative society ... and thus the numbers introduced to the profession would be regulated in proportion to the demand for labour'; cooperative stores would provide 'the best goods' and the same principles would apply to education and health care.[11] This vision of the cooperative commonwealth skilfully addressed many of the immediate grievances of miners and was not wholly implausible given the often small scale of colliery production. Support for cooperative production was widely evidenced at miners meetings in Lanarkshire and Fife in the early 1870s.[12] Yet such support was predicated on the assumption of strong union organisation which, after 1874, was generally lacking.

In the decades after 1874, however, the Scots miners clung tenaciously to output restriction. Large coal heaps, or 'bings', at the pithead were a visible indicator of the balance of forces between miners and their employer. In 1888, stocks of coal in Fife and Clackmannan were at a record 500,000 tons: 'This state of matters places the men completely in the power of the masters'; because of this surplus, work was irregular and 'there is much misery in consequence'.[13] Time after time, the resurgences of trade union organisation in the western counties were based on a restriction policy. In his autobiography published in 1924, Robert Smillie observed:

> Now, it is rather extraordinary that every attempt to organise Lanarkshire miners had invariably been connected with the 'five-day working policy'. Even today it is a difficult task to keep a miners' trade union in Lanarkshire intact unless this policy is part of the movement. The miner regards it as his sheet anchor.[14]

Nearly thirty years previously he had explained to the Royal Commission on Labour that the reasons for this 'weekly holiday' were to regulate output and prevent overproduction, to ensure a good supply of railway wagons and hence five full day's work, and to allow oncost workers to carry out necessary repairs.[15]

In addition to this weekly idle day to limit output (usually a Thursday or Saturday), miners might also shorten their working day to eight hours or restrict the quantity of their darg. Sometimes combinations of these methods were applied, as when a delegate meeting in 1888 resolved that 'in order to improve the miners' conditions and to command the market, the policy of five days and eight hours is essential'.[16] Similarly, William Small explained to the Royal Commission on Labour that 'limiting their output and limiting their days' had 'a commercial aim, namely to regulate the market'.[17] In 1882, a mass meeting of Lanarkshire miners agreed to implement an eight hour day, and dargs of 2.5 tons in the 'fast places' and 3.5 tons at the 'stoops'.[18] This represented a dual check on output, for as one employer complained, 'many a man would put out his quantity in five or six hours or less and he would not be allowed to put out more during the eight hours'.[19]

Although Small claimed that not a single man had worked a Saturday in Blantyre in the previous three years, he stated that 'some of the largest employers in the county give it the most determined opposition, and dismiss men from their collieries if they venture to lay off a day. They do not recognise the five days' policy'.[20] A.K. McCosh of William Baird and Company complained to the

Commission that his company had 'frequently been subjected to these arbitrary limitations of output'.[21]

The restriction policy is a further element in explaining the importance of checkweighmen for the Scots unions. During the SMNF wages agitation in 1886, the Motherwell miners resolved to work only four days a week until they secured an advance and reported that 'justicemen' had recently been appointed 'on all banks' [pitheads].[22] There seems, therefore, to have been some force in the employers' complaint in 1892 that a checkweigher was 'put there simply as an agent of the union ... He was not there with a view to the weighing of the material so much as with a view to carrying out the behests of the Union.'[23] This was a recurring theme of the coalmasters once union organisation had been firmly established in Lanarkshire. In 1904, Robert Baird, LCMA Secretary, complained that checkweighmen were 'invariably union officials' and protested that:

> ... should any workman put out a tub of coal more than what is considered by the union as the number that should be put out from any particular seam, they [the checkweighmen] immediately report this to the union and the erring workman is warned ... If they put out a tub more than the fixed darg they are immediately brought to book for it.

Such practices, he claimed, were 'almost invariably the case in most collieries'.[24]

According to Small, some employers were less hostile to restriction than these representatives of larger companies. They had, he claimed, found it 'a most beneficial policy to themselves. It has advanced the price of coal ... '.[25] This echoed traditional notions of 'the trade', and found similar expression in the dispute of 1879 when the union leaders hoped that by settling with small 'sale' coal masters they might isolate the larger coal and iron companies. As Reid notes, such hopes were 'a survival of the independent collier's dream that big business could be brought to heel by the collaboration of trade unions with small business'.[26] Similar policies were evidenced during the wage agitation of 1886 when Lanarkshire delegates agreed to reward those employers who had granted a sixpence advance by working five days per week but only four days for those companies who had refused.[27] At the commencement of the agitation, a Lanarkshire conference had condemned 'the insane policy of employers underselling and competing against each other, thereby oppressing the worker, robbing capital and wilfully wasting the resources of the country'. To remedy this situation, it had been agreed to keep a weekly idle day, work only eight hours and maintain 'a watchful supervision of bens'.[28]

In the national stoppage of 1894, Smillie had continued to entertain the belief, after thirteen weeks on strike, that the small masters might come to their rescue:

> ... ere long a large number of employers would sign the Federation terms, and then they would only have the iron ring to fight. He wanted to fight the Bairds and the Merry and Cunninghames, and to give the miners of these firms a pound a week to keep their works idle. If they could get the coal masters to take a wise and humane view of matters and to sign the Federation terms, the miners would be able to enter into the contest with the iron ring and would beat them. (Cheers.)[29]

That same week Hardie assured the Ayrshire miners that while 'the big iron masters would not move ... All the small masters would be willing to grant the Federation terms.'[30] These hopes were to prove illusory. Two years later, the Fife union board was forced to recommend acceptance of a wage reduction because of 'the condition of organisation among large bodies of men' in Scotland, but emphasised its belief 'that the only remedy for the present so-called depression in trade is the application of some system of restriction which would be widely applied and have the cooperation of the coalmasters'.[31]

Such aspirations could only be fantasies given the power of the large companies and the competitive nature of their markets, yet they were given a superficial plausibility by the uneven business structure and continuing traditions of paternalism in parts of the Scots coalfields, such as Smillie's own Larkhall district. In addition, restriction might achieve some temporary local success. When wages in Lanarkshire were reduced to three shillings per day in 1886, the bulk of the miners adopted an eight hour day, a five day week, and voluntarily restricted their daily earnings to two shillings. As a consequence, wages were raised temporarily to four shillings a day before the movement was broken in the strikes of 1887.[32]

Union activists continued to look back wistfully to the success of such policies in the early years of the century. This nostalgia was succoured both by an oral tradition – one elderly man who had been a miner for sixty years recalled the combinations of 1817 before a Scottish delegate conference in 1874 – and also by the historical record.[33] In 1888, Hardie's journal, the *Miner*, published lengthy extracts of evidence heard before the 1825 Select Committee on Combination Laws on the efficacy of the colliery brotherhoods.[34] An editorial, redolent with the passing ethos of the independent collier, drew comparisons between the miners' contemporary lot and the situation in 1820s:

> Then the men in Ayrshire had an absolute control of the market ... now unless the miners of the whole of Great Britain cooperate, there is no such power. Then an employer knew every workman under him, and kept up an intimacy with the more respectable of them – sometimes masters and men going on the spree together; now with rare exceptions, the pits are owned by companies ... The whole relations between employer and employed are strictly 'economic' and guided by the rules of exchange ...[35]

The problems of implementing a restriction policy in the coal industry in the last quarter of the nineteenth century were thus beginning to be appreciated, but the proposal for a British restriction – prefigured the previous year in Chisholm Robertson's insistence that 'England and Wales must also be got to restrict' – was wildly impracticable.[36]

Restriction demanded a widespread and disciplined self-sacrifice. After a visit to Ayrshire in 1892, Eleanor Marx lamented that the darg system was being superseded 'by the modern competitive method of the devil taking the hindmost'.[37] During wage agitations, rank and file miners often impatiently disregarded restriction in favour of the mass strike. As a long term strategy, restriction was inevitably ineffective given inter-regional competition for trade, the weakness of union organisation in the 1870s and 1880s, and the fluid labour markets of the western counties. As Hardie noted in 1882, with more than a trace of the Scots miners' ethnic antipathy towards the unskilled Irish:

> Nothing angers the miner so much during a time of restriction than to find a fellow working at a stoop where the requisites are a big shovel, a strong back and a weak brain, said fellow having a few weeks before been busy in a peat bog or a tattie field and who is now producing coal enough for a man and a half, and being remonstrated

with, to hear him say, with a shrug of the shoulders, 'Och, I'll fill as many as I like'.[38]

For such reasons, the traditional methods of limiting entry to the trade continued to appear in miners' union rule books after 1874. The Lanarkshire Miners' Association of 1879 required any man who wished to work as hewer and who had not previously been 'engaged at the face as a collier or miner and wishing to become a member of this association' to serve a 'period of four years as an apprentice'. The Ayrshire Miners Association's rules of 1882 required an apprenticeship for a similar period at less than a full man's pay: two years as a half 'ben' and two years as a three-quarter 'ben'. By 1886, the Ayrshire Miners' Union had reduced this apprenticeship requirement to three years.[39]

Although the entrance fee for young miners who had completed their training was usually a few shillings, much higher premiums were demanded from adult men to deter them from entering the mines. In 1889, the Blantyre Association had a normal entrance fee of two shillings and sixpence but this increased to £1 'for any man who enters the mine for the first time'. The Cambuslang Miners' Protection Society in 1890 required a similar premium from 'any man found entering the mine who has never been a practical bona fide miner'. The Forth and Clyde Miners' Association, the Mid and West Lothian Association and the Motherwell district union all sought to charge such men £5 in 1886: approximately a month's wages.[40] As late as 1906, a Stirlingshire miners' leader claimed that 'they compelled an adult who entered the mine to pay £5 and kept him two years at half a ben'. In 1909, Stirlingshire representatives sought to have a universal adult entry fee of £5 adopted by the SMF conference, their motion being narrowly defeated by 40–31. Two years later, Clackmannanshire delegates secured a conference majority for 'a heavy entrance fee on all unskilled workers', but little action seems to have been taken.[41]

It is significant that these later calls were coming from the still relatively undeveloped counties of Stirling and Clackmannan. Such regulations were proving difficult to enforce in the middle years of the nineteenth century in Lanarkshire and Ayrshire and their persistence should be interpreted as a continuing affirmation by union activists of the skilled status of their occupation rather than an effective barrier to dilution.[42] In so far as they were enforced, they may simply have contributed to union weakness through non-unionism among untrained men who were unwilling to pay high entry fees. The miners' association in Maryhill, on the outskirts of Glasgow, appears to have recognised its vulnerability to inclusion in the metropolitan labour market by requiring an apprenticeship of only 12 months by 'neutrals'.[43]

Reid has persuasively identified the failure of the Scots miners' traditional policies in preventing the large wage reductions in 1874 as constituting 'the crisis of the independent collier'.[44] Yet this crisis should be understood not only as the historical moment of 1874 but also as a longer process of strategic re-evaluation in the following two decades of union weakness and defeat. Young notes that, in the 1880s, 'the new generation of miners' leaders were hectically searching for new ways forward'.[45] Thus we find Small writing in 1889 to the Socialist League in London seeking advice on how to bring trade unionism into 'harmony with the advanced thought of the age'.[46] We can perceive this search for new, or at least supplementary policies, in the Sons of Labour movement launched two years earlier. This equivocal body can be interpreted as a tactical adaptation to victimisation, taking the form of earlier secret societies in the Scots coalfields, such as the Free Colliers some twenty years previously, themselves a revival of the colliery brotherhoods. It is probably no coincidence that Hardie reprinted extracts from the 1825 Commission precisely when the Sons of Labour were organising. However, while the order's rules contained the traditional exclusionary entry fee of £5 for adult men, its programme, which was drafted by Hardie, embodied a radical departure from previous trade union policies. Introduced in an article headed 'Labour Representation', it was largely a political programme, the sixteen points of which included adult suffrage, triennial parliaments, a legal eight hour day, the nationalisation of mines, minerals and railways, a national insurance fund, arbitration by labour tribunals and improved homes. After excoriating the failure of the Liberals and their TUC Lib-Lab supporters to enhance the condition of 'honest, temperate and industrious' working men, Hardie concluded: 'we require, however, a new party to carry it out'.[47] It is the sources of this new strategy in a confluence of elements in the 1880s that we now consider.

The origins of socialist policies

The Scots miners' leaders had already contemplated some state intervention in their industry. In addition to campaigning for stricter mines' inspection, they supported MacDonald in securing the 1872 Mines Regulation Act which limited the working hours of boys underground.[48] Traditional Lib-Lab ideology did not permit the extension of state protection to adults. The Northumberland miners' leader and Lib-Lab MP, Thomas Burt, in an article on 'Self Help' in the first issue of the *Miner*, strongly advised his Scottish readers to 'trust to yourselves rather than to parliament for giving you moderate hours of labour ... to appeal to parliament to fix the hours of adults is to weaken the motives for union and for self reliance'.[49] Although MacDonald had similarly insisted in the House of Commons in 1874 that 'there is no wish on the part of adult men that the government should legislate for them', during the dark days for Scots miners' unionism in 1868, he had commented favourably on the legal eight hour day in Australia and on attempts to introduce an eight hour bill before the United States Congress.[50] Amid the collapse of unionism during the strikes of 1874, the Larkhall agent, Hector McNeil, desperately suggested the miners 'call upon the legislators of Great Britain to take up the question in dispute'.[51] Nothing came of this, but in the ensuing period of union weakness state intervention was reconsidered. Hardie, in 1880, called for a 'fair' sliding scale with a recognised minimum and looked to the Australian example of a government enforced scale and a minister for mines.[52] That same year he also sought Liberal support for legislation to introduce a system of yearly tenure for miners in employers' houses.[53]

In the following decade, a number of influences led to a further shift in attitudes to the state. The first was land reform. Ownership of a small patch of land as a guarantor of 'independence' had figured within the traditional world view of the Scots colliers working small mines in a rural environment before the intensive exploitation of the coalfields.[54] In Cambuslang, for example, the miners had been granted seven acres of land – 'the colliers' acres' – for communal cultivation in 1688 by the Duchess of Hamilton; the amenity was only lost in the 1860s when the Duke of Hamilton sold the colliery and land to the expanding firm of Archibald Russell.[55] This connection with the land persisted vestigially in the pride which many miners took in their vegetable gardens and was one source of the attraction of American emigration: 'go to America, where there was plenty of land', advised MacDonald in 1868.[56] That such aspirations retained their appeal in the 1880s is suggested by the letter from 'A Miner' to the *Hamilton Advertiser* in 1886: 'if one fourth part of the miners of Scotland had an acre or two of land and a house of their own, they could employ themselves on their idle days and during the time they could not find employment in the pits'.[57]

This aspiration to acquire independence through a smallholding was coupled with the anti-landlordism of many Irish miners whose families had been driven from the land. Anti-landlordism was also fuelled by the colliers' antagonistic relations with gamekeepers because of widespread poaching in rural mining areas. Two Lothians miners, hanged in 1884 for fatally shooting two gamekeepers, were reputedly regarded as 'heroes' in their community.[58] It was against this background that the propaganda tours of Henry George, the American land reformer, made a major impact in Scotland in 1882 and 1884–5. Although not a socialist, George contested individualistic explanations of poverty based on thriftlessness and located the cause in unearned income from rent. His solution of a tax on land could act as an easy bridge to the policy of land nationalisation. This was advocated by the popular Irish land reformer, Michael Davitt, who frequently lectured in Scotland in the 1880s.[59]

The Scottish Land Restoration League (SLRL) was formed in February 1884 after George had addressed a meeting in Glasgow, 1800 members of his audience joining on the spot.[60] It put forward a land tax of four shillings in the pound as a first step towards 'taking all ground-rent for public purposes'.[61] Among its propaganda activities, it arranged for speakers to visit the coalfields.[62] By August 1885, Small, acting as a representative of the SLRL, was addressing a meeting of the Blantyre branch of the Irish National League (INL) 'on the suffering of the working class in Ireland and Scotland at the hands of the landlords'.[63] In 1888, the Burnbank Radical Association heard a lecture on the trade depression which argued that its true cause 'was the divorce of the people from the land'.[64]

At the same meeting, Small spoke on the need to nationalise mineral royalties. Small's interest in the subject had been stimulated by researches on early mining legislation in the British Museum library during visits to London.[65] There he discovered a Scottish statute of 1592 which stated that holders of land had no claim to 'metals and minerals' which belonged to the crown. Having secured the advice of the Lord Advocate's office that no later statute existed, he wrote in 1885 to the newly appointed Secretary of State for Scotland pointing out that the nation's minerals were rightfully owned by the crown and triumphantly adverted to a clause by which the sovereign took all miners under 'his special protection declaring that whatsoever wrong or oppression directly or indirectly shall be done to them in their persons or goods shall be severely punished'. The government's reply, based on counsel's advice, was that the Act was obsolete, and in any case had never applied to coal or ironstone.[66]

This rebuff did not deflect Small from his belief that the coal mines of Scotland had once been national property.[67] In 1888, he submitted the draft of a new mines bill 'based upon the law of Scotland of 1592' to a mass meeting of Lanarkshire miners.[68] In 1892, he claimed before the Royal Commission on Labour that

> in the Scotch miners' mind there is a strong conviction that [the mines] should never have been out of the hands of the State. They belonged to the State and it was when the union took place between England and Scotland that our Scotch laws were absorbed in the English and we lost our property in coal, which properly belongs to the State.[69]

That same year he wrote again to the Secretary of State threatening an interdict (the Scottish equivalent of an injunction) against the proposed eviction of the families of thirty striking miners at Carfin on the grounds that it breached the protection guaranteed by the Act of 1592.[70] Although Small's claims appear to have had no firm legal basis, what is significant is his drawing on a 'usable past' to elaborate a myth which presented the nationalisation of minerals as a claim of historical right within a socialism sanctioned by tradition. Thus we find him in 1895 lecturing on 'socialism and miners', quoting from the old Acts of the Scots parliament and tracing 'the condition of miners from the golden age to the present time'.[71]

In 1884, Michael Davitt had toured 'industrial Scotland preaching the nationalisation of the land with a burning eloquence ... And not only land but minerals also he demanded for the nation'.[72] It appears he visited Lanarkshire and was in touch with the miners' leaders there, possibly through men such as Andrew McCowie, a former president of the Cambuslang branch of the INL and a veteran trade unionist.[73] That same year, in a letter to Small, Davitt had recommended that the Scots and English miners should campaign for the nationalisation of mineral royalties and that the monies so acquired should be used to fund a state life insurance scheme for miners.[74]

The demand for the nationalisation of mining royalties was a popular one among the Lanarkshire miners who saw it as a route to secure higher wages. Royalty payments on the tonnage of minerals extracted from under an landowner's property varied within and between coalfields, but was higher in Scotland than in England and Wales, and higher in the west of Scotland than the east.[75] The Motherwell miners' agent stated that when managers refused wage demands, they often professed that it was 'because they were so much handicapped by royalties in meeting competition with other countries'. As a consequence, claimed Smillie, 'the feeling of the miners ... is that the present high lordship charged prevents them often from getting the wages that they would otherwise get ... the general feeling seems to be in favour of nationalising the minerals'.[76]

In 1884, Small convened a conference of union activists and land reformers in Hamilton to discuss Davitt's advice. The trade unionists were unwilling to form a branch of the SLRL, instead agreeing to form a Scottish Miners' Anti-Royalty and Labour League in the coalfield. A branch was established by miners' leaders at Hamilton, trade union organisation being 'deemed useless' at that time, but this organisation does not appear to have developed more widely.[77] The following year, the manifesto of the SLRL included among its demands not only 'the emancipation of the land from the bondage in which it is held for the benefit of a few individuals' but also 'the abolition of cognate private interests such as mining royalties'.[78] Elsewhere in Scotland, miners' leaders were less attracted to nationalisation of royalties in the mid-1880s. Although John Weir, FKMA Secretary, was sympathetic, a majority of his Executive refused to affiliate to Small's organisation and Hardie, still wedded to Lib-Labism in 1884, was ambivalent.[79]

Davitt's writings were radical rather than socialist, but his ambiguous rhetoric of 'bringing about the nationalisation of the mines by the abolition of royalties' – he meant that mining companies would pay rent to the state, not that the state would own and work the mines – provided a point of intellectual access for some of his supporters to the similar phraseology of socialist groups in the coalfields.[80] In Hamilton, a small group of 'social democrats' were in existence in the early 1880s and in 1881 reportedly formed a 'Scottish Labour Party', committed to 'the nationalisation of the means of industrial production'.[81]

Robert Banner, Secretary of this group, had been converted to socialism by Andreas Scheu, an Austrian emigre resident in Edinburgh. His members may have represented the continuation of a republican presence which existed in the Lanarkshire coalfield in the early 1870s.[82] We can discern traces of a similar radicalism in a caricature of a militant Irish union activist published in 1871, based on the family history of the anonymous Scottish author, which contains the following lampoon of a speech by 'Andy McQuirk', an obviously Irish union delegate from Lesmahagow, to a mass meeting:

> 'What made the masters break our wages last week? Was it the fall in the price of coal? No! It was opprission!' (A voice: 'Boul Fellow!') 'What was it made me laive my native land? Wasn't it opprission? ... Where are the opprissors?' ('Hear, Hear') 'No, they aren't "here, here", they are "there, there"', pointing with his hand towards Glasgow. 'It's in the Exchange they are – makin' their fortins by the swate of the poor man's brow, bad luck to them ... Fillow workmen, the pit that your humble sirvint raprisints are willing to strike and stand for six months if yez lack, providing that the boys that are wurking will support them.'[83]

Such sentiments were echoed a decade later when the Motherwell agent referred to the Duke of Hamilton before a mass meeting:

> This honourable gentleman – (laughter) – had 12,000 miners working under the soil owned by him, and received on average 1s per ton from the produce of each miner ... and if his Grace could not live on that, how in the name of Providence could the miner ... live on a paltry 3s 9d or 4s per day (Cheers.)

He was followed by John Dunn, a miner, who in advocating the need for union, 'denounced the heresy of identity between capital and labour'.[84]

The Scottish Labour Party of 1881 appears to have been short-lived. Thereafter, J. Bruce Glasier of Glasgow was described as a 'lone scout' in his advocacy of socialism in the west of Scotland until the formation of a Glasgow branch of the Marxist Social Democratic Federation (SDF) in the summer of 1884.[85] In March 1885, an SDF branch of thirty members was formed in Cambuslang, with Small as Chairman. The following year, the Executive Committee of the Cambuslang miners' union denounced a proposed 'Mines Lease Bill' drafted by Liberal MPs (including the member for Mid-Lanark) as 'one which overlooked the condition of the miners' and characterised it as a 'Capitalist Relief Bill'.[86] The SDF had also established a branch in Coatbridge by 1886, whose members held propaganda meetings in Airdrie, Rutherglen and Hamilton.[87] In April 1887, for example, there was a meeting in Coatbridge of some 2,000 workmen addressed by SDF speakers on 'coercion in Scotland and Ireland', which ended 'with three hearty cheers for the Social Revolution'.[88]

The SDF Edinburgh branch secretary lived in the Midlothian mining village of Loanhead and that same month the branch sent speakers to the mining village of Rosewell (which had a high concentration of Irish). A meeting of 500 miners there unanimously supported resolutions in favour of nationalising the land, mines and machinery and condemning the government over its Coercion Bill.[89] Socialists were also active in Ayrshire. James Patrick, a Cumnock miner, after hearing SDF speakers on a visit to London, converted his friend James Neil, a local union activist, to socialism upon his return. Together they organised the revived Ayrshire union in the district and sold *Justice*, the SDF newspaper; in 1887, the SDF claimed to have 'many sympathisers' among the Ayrshire miners.[90]

The secession from the SDF which led to the formation of the Socialist League in 1885 had the support of a number of Glasgow members, including Glasier. Invited by Small to address a miners' meeting in Hamilton that year, Glasier's 'open advocacy of revolution' received an enthusiastic reception.[91] An early historian of the socialist movement in Scotland observed that, 'between the years 1885 and 1887, the comrades carried on such a vigorous propaganda for socialism in and around the city that branches of the League were started in Paisley, Hamilton, Blantyre, Motherwell, Coatbridge, Rutherglen and other towns'.[92] In 1887, John L. Mahon, 'one of their best agitators', conducted a propaganda tour in eastern Scotland under the auspices of the Scottish Land and Labour League (SLLL) which Scheu had established in Edinburgh and which was affiliated first to the SDF and then to the Socialist

League.[93] Mahon found the miners of Fife 'willing to enrol in tens and twenties at the first or second open air meeting. It was only necessary for him to put round handbills advertising his meetings to get a large and eager audience'. Among the branches he formed were those at Cowdenbeath, Dysart, Gallatown and Lochgelly.[94] Mahon also campaigned in the Ayrshire and Lanarkshire coalfields later that year.[95]

Both the Socialist League and SDF conducted propaganda in support of the striking Scottish miners in the spring of 1887. The Glasgow branch of the League organised a solidarity demonstration attended by 20,000 miners and others.[96] The following week, a mass meeting of miners was held at the same place. According to the *Glasgow Herald*, 'a number of prominent Glasgow socialists' were reported to be in attendance, 'and they took ample advantage of the occasion to propagate their doctrines. They found ready listeners in the starved looking men around them.'[97] A similar demonstration, jointly organised by the SDF and SLLL, took place in Edinburgh. Estimates of the attendance ranged from 4,000 to 12,000 people, who were addressed by Small, Glasier and William Bulloch, soon to be involved in organising the Sons of Labour.[98]

By 1887, support for radical and socialist demands were commonplace at miners' meetings in the western coalfields. At Carluke, a motion was adopted 'that no legislation on the royalties of coal or other mineral or metals be acceptable unless based upon nationalisation without compensation'.[99] At the meeting of the Lanarkshire miners' county board which called off the strike at the end of February, Small moved a motion protesting against 'the iniquitous system of the country which condemned them to a life of privation and pauperism while the middle classes lived in affluence, and that they pledge themselves to agitate and educate until the system be removed'. The motion was supported by Glasier, who attended the meeting, and was passed unanimously.[100] The following week, a large meeting of Larkhall miners approved resolutions calling for the government to set up an independent tribunal to regulate wages and legislation to reduce mineral royalties to a minimum 'with a view to their ultimately becoming state property'.[101] At Bo'ness, R.B. Cunninghame Graham, the radical MP elected the previous year to represent North-West Lanarkshire, urged the miners 'to combine to get legislation passed shortening the hours of labour and ensuring for the workmen a share of the profits accruing from their labour'. At the same meeting, Chisholm Robertson proposed motions supporting the abolition of royalties, a sliding scale, boards of arbitration and an eight hour act: 'the whole of these resolutions were carried by acclamation'.[102] At Broxburn in West Lothian in June similar resolutions at a large miners' demonstration were 'carried enthusiastically and amid frequent cheers'.[103] By then Hardie was campaigning for similar demands in Ayrshire and these were given clear expression in his programme for the Sons of Labour published in July of 1887.[104]

The enduring weakness of trade unionism and the interventionist role of the local state and military forces in protecting blacklegs and breaking mass pickets in the strike of that year had forced a significant section of mining unionists and their leaders to adopt these policies. As Reid observes, the programme was a confused mixture of socialist demands, labour collectivism, republican land radicalism and constitutional reform rather than a coherent vision of socialism.[105] We can see one anonymous writer groping his way from anti-competitive notions of the trade and traditional relations between masters and men towards the abolition of the wages system in an article entitled 'Progress', published in the first issue of the *Miner*:

> Employers are to be sorely blamed for this state of things [low wages]. Taking advantage of the weakness of the men, they have gone on competing one with the other, in a vain endeavour to get the markets to take more coal than there was a demand for, until wages have fallen to the starving point. The whole system on which wages are paid is rotten to the core. Why should the wages of the workmen be at the mercy of the foolishness or avarice of the employer! The labourer and the capitalist are the partners in the working of the concern. Why should all the profits go to one partner while the other starves?[106]

In the same issue, an editorial on the eight hour day argued against securing this goal through the traditional Lib-Lab method of collective self-help in terms which recognised the particular realities of the situation in the west of Scotland: 'we have got to face the fact that all men are not wise ... Thus it is that it has become necessary to protect the men against themselves'.[107]

The demand for state ownership of the mines, the most socialist element in the Sons of Labour programme was also embraced ambiguously. Hardie sought to link it to the older policy of co-operation by referring to it as 'cooperative production under state management' in August 1887.[108] We can recognise a similar ambivalence in the conversations recorded in Fife by Kellog Durland in 1901 with 'Jim ... a typical pitman of the better class', who was hostile to socialist egalitarianism yet favoured the nationalisation of the land; he was firmly of the belief that:

> the workin' men will run a pit for themselves some day. Look at yon cooperative store ... We own the store, and support it and we benefit by it ... there's a difference between lettin' the men run the pit and lettin' the government do it.[109]

Although the six Scots miners' leaders who gave evidence to the Royal Commission on Mineral Royalties in 1890 supported state ownership, they displayed diverse views on what this might mean in practice. Robert Brown of the Mid and East Lothian miners and John Wilson from West Lothian argued for state ownership of minerals which would then be leased out to mining companies 'for the encouragement of enterprise'. Smillie did not wish immediate nationalisation of royalties but contemplated the ultimate nationalisation of both mines and minerals and the mines being worked under state control; similar views were expressed by Robert Steel of Motherwell and Small. Hardie supported state ownership of the mines, but regarded the form of their operation as 'a matter of detail ... the government ... might let them out to a body of miners or work them direct, as in the case of the Post Office'.[110]

Many of the miners' objectives were, in theory, compatible with the radical wing of Liberalism. In practice, they drew a line between the political aspirations of the miners' leaders and the Liberal Party. The relationship between the Scots miners' unions and the Liberals was traditionally less close than in England, because of the hostility of the western employers to trade unionism and the miners' organisational weakness. In the 1868 election, MacDonald had put his name forward as a 'People's Candidate' for Kilmarnock, claiming to be neither a Tory nor a Liberal but 'one of the friends of labour'.[111] In that election, while the Fife miners supported the local Liberal, the miners' leaders in the west of Scotland systematically campaigned against Liberal candidates, in particular James Merry, of the coal and iron firm of Merry and Cunninghame, who was the MP for the Falkirk burghs. In South Lanarkshire, the Liberal

Major Hamilton was related to the mine-owning Lord Belhaven, and MacDonald asked a miners' meeting in Wishaw, 'how many times had that man turned them out of their homes?' MacDonald's lieutenant, James Blee, was imprisoned for three months the following year for bribing electors to vote Tory.[112] Similar sentiments were evidenced at a franchise demonstration in 1884 when Hamilton miners refused to parade behind a huge block of coal donated as an exhibit by a Liberal coalmaster.[113] The following year, under Small's influence, a Lanarkshire miners' meeting agreed to seek to prevent any iron or coalmaster or other employer being elected to parliament.[114]

The failure of the English Lib-Lab MPs to wholeheartedly support a Scottish eight hours amendment to the Coal Mines Regulation Bill in 1887 strengthened this anti-Liberal current. Hardie bitterly asked, 'what difference will it make to me that I have a working man representing me in parliament if he is a dumb dog who dare not bark ...?'[115] Moreover, the Liberal Party in Scotland, suffering from the secession of Liberal-Unionists in 1886, were particularly dependent on middle class candidates with the financial means to mount an effective campaign. Hence it was unwilling to co-opt trade union candidates and made little attempt to prioritise their demands.[116]

Within this context of anti-Liberal feeling, socialists and land reformers increasingly advocated independent labour representation. Members of the Scottish Labour Party of 1881, the formation of which was reported in the *Labour Standard*, were no doubt aware of Engels' call for an independent working men's party in the same journal.[117] During the 1885 election, Small had initially agreed to go forward as the candidate of the SLRL for Mid-Lanark but did not proceed. Nevertheless, the five SLRL candidates who did stand, 'having sought the aid of the more advanced members of the Liberal Party but in vain', as well as an independent candidate who stood for the Falkirk burghs with SLRL support, marked an important point in developing a strategy of independent labour representation.[118] By January 1887, J. McLuckie, a member of the Forth and Clyde Miners' Association was urging readers of the *Miner* to 'set about forming a parliamentary fund so that at the next election we may return as many of our own representatives as there are openings for'.[119] Hardie's first annual report of the SMNF in August confidently predicted the formation of a Labour Party.[120] Two months later, John L. Mahon, an early and creative strategist of the 'labour alliance' of socialists and trade unionists, reported to Glasier on 'a gathering of about a dozen miners' at the home of the Reverend John Glasse of the Edinburgh branch of the Socialist League:

> They were the J.K. Hardie's and Small's lots. They seem an advanced set of fellows but without very definite ideas. I think it would be a good thing if we could help them in forming a Scottish Labour party, and push Socm amongst them. I think such a party, distinct from England, will soon be formed. If they renounced Tory, Liberal and Radical Party Politics and went in for a new departure on Socialist lines, I don't see why we shouldn't help them. Of course always maintaining an advanced Socialist group as well. Had a long talk with R. B. C.[unninghame] G.[raham] He seems to have good stuff in him. I daresay he will lead the new Scotch party.[121]

This was the background to Hardie's well known campaign for the Mid-Lanark constituency in 1888. The details are fully described elsewhere.[122] Here we need only note those features of the campaign which signalled the difficulties Labour candidates were to face in the coalfields in the future. The first concerned policy. Both the Unionist and Liberal candidates ostensibly stressed their commitment to workers' interests. Phillips, the Liberal, whose supporters included Hector· McNeil, the former Larkhall miners' agent, favoured the re-imposition of the four shilling land tax, a legal eight hour day, the abolition of the House of Lords, free education, payment of MPs, an enquiry into mining royalties 'and where these royalties damaged the interests of the miners he would abolish them altogether'.[123] The Unionist candidate spoke in support of action on housing and unemployment, an eight hours bill, a joint conciliation board of masters and men, improved levels of workmen's compensation, increased mines inspection and 'a larger number of inspectors being drawn from the mining classes'. On the question of mineral royalties, he argued that their abolition would not increase wages since at present wage rates might be the same at mines where there no royalties paid as at those where they were heavy. At his Larkhall meeting, he was supported by several local coalmasters, including members of the paternalistic Barr family.[124] Hardie's commitment to socialism was implicit in the subtle distinction of his manifesto's demand for the nationalisation of both royalties and minerals, but his campaign rhetoric echoed that of radical Liberalism.[125]

The contrasting policies of Unionist and Liberal on Irish Home Rule appealed to their respective Orange and Catholic Irish constituencies among the miners. Hardie's candidature appealed to neither. There were an estimated 1,500 Irish voters in Mid-Lanark and although Hardie had the personal support of Davitt and John Ferguson, the leading Glasgow nationalist, a meeting of all the INL branches in constituency 'were unanimous in their disapprobation' of his candidature for fear of splitting the vote.[126] At a campaign meeting in support of Hardie in Wishaw, the audience shouted for the Liberal, Phillips, and Small was forced to sit down amid a chorus of booing. At Hardie's meeting in Blantyre, the audience approved of Phillips by a large majority and the gathering broke up in disorder.[127]

On polling day in late April, Hardie finished an ignominious third with 617 votes out a total of 7,381. His failure indicated the flexibility of his opponents in their cultivation of the mining vote, the political divisions based on ethnicity and religion within the mining population, the low level of enfranchisement, and the lack of electoral organisation among his trade union supporters. 'Outside of Larkhall, there was not a shred of organisation of any kind', he later complained, while even there a local strike had largely occupied the union committee members.[128] It is to the subsequent attempts to address these problems that we now move.

Political organisation, socialist culture and electoral performance

In the immediate aftermath of defeat, Hardie and his supporters agreed to form 'labour electoral associations' as the branches of the Scottish Parliamentary Labour Party (SPLP) throughout Lanarkshire; by early May, branches had been established at Flemington, Cambuslang, Quarter and Larkhall (where Smillie was secretary).[129] In August 1888, a conference in Glasgow formally established the party with Hardie as Secretary and Cunninghame Graham as President. Hardie sought to construct a broad alliance of reformers and trade unionists, independent of the Liberals. Although the party's programme included a commitment to

nationalise land and minerals, Hardie equivocated on a commitment to nationalise the means of production, and this was not proclaimed as an objective until 1893.[130]

The history of the SPLP has been analysed by Reid and Howell,
who both note the twin problems of the ambiguous relationship
between some of its leaders and radical Liberalism, and the weakness of trade union organisation in Scotland. The fragility of its
union base denied it the power to threaten the Liberals and consequently some members drifted back towards the major party. In the
coalfields, although the SPLP could command the support of a
number of miners' leaders – in 1892 Smillie was a vice president
while Small and Andrew McAnulty of Blantyre were executive
members – these leaders were themselves divided by personal antagonisms.[131] Moreover, such men failed to deliver strong support in
their localities: in Larkhall the party branch was described as 'alive
and kicking but the members [sic] not large'.[132] In 1894, the
Dreghorn and Kilwinning miners in Ayrshire, the Forth and Clyde
Miners' Association and the Dalry and Larkhall party branches
were the only bodies from the coalfields to be represented at the
party's annual conference.[133] By then, the organisation which
Hardie had hoped would form a 'federal labour alliance' had
become instead 'a party of labour activists with Christian socialist
leanings'.[134] Howell concisely summarises the vicious circle in which
the SPLP found itself: 'industrial weakness generated an attach-
ment to political initiatives, but the impact of these was damaged by
the same lack of industrial organisation'.[135] At the end of 1894, the
SPLP disbanded to become the Scottish Council of the
Independent Labour Party (ILP), formed in Bradford the previous
year.

ILP organisation in the coalfields in the 1890s reflected the continuing weakness of trade unionism. Although Smillie and Small
had attended the foundation conference of the ILP, and Small was
elected to its National Administrative Council, branches in the
Scottish coalfields rarely sent delegates to the annual conferences.[136]
Branch listings were 'very incomplete' as late as 1899, but after 1900
we can derive a clearer picture of their distribution. Table 2.1 indicates that in 1902 there were only 7 branches within the West
Central field, 5 in the Ayrshire mining region, 3 in Fife and 1 in the
Lothians. This table describes branches situated within the geological boundaries of the coalfields. We do not possess detailed infor-

mation on membership or occupational composition, but from national information on the often petit-bourgeois and skilled nature of much of the ILP's membership, it can be surmised that not all, perhaps only a minority, of the members of these branches were miners.[137]

Fragmentary information on the size of branch membership indicates 33 members in the Rutherglen branch, 10 in Coatbridge and 12 in Dalkeith in 1899; 30 in Kilmarnock and 21 in Motherwell in 1902; in West Lothian, 60 at Armadale in 1906 and 17 at Bo'ness in 1907.[138] From 1906 onwards, there was a marked increase in the number of ILP branches both nationally and in Scotland, where organisers were temporarily employed in Ayrshire, Lanarkshire and on the east coast.[139] The Lanarkshire organiser conducted a flurry of propaganda meetings in the mining towns and villages there, even establishing branches in the outlying Douglas region, at Glespin and Ponfeigh.[140] Thereafter, the ILP in Scotland grew faster than in Britain as a whole and this was reflected in the number of branches within the coalfields by 1909. See Table 2.1

As Hutchison points out, however, the number of branches was an imperfect indicator of the party's vitality, for outside the cities and large towns branches were often only spasmodically active.[141] In 1898, a letter in the *Labour Leader* complained that many branches which were remote from the cities 'have for the most part gone out of existence, or lapsed into a moribund state'.[142] In Larkhall, there was only one meeting (attended by three people) during the 18 months after March 1898, 'the members evidently being more concerned about football and horse racing ...'.[143] Despite the more systematic attempts to strengthen Lanarkshire branch organisation in 1906, the audience at what was advertised as a 'Great Socialist Demonstration' in Hamilton addressed by Smillie and Robert Blatchford was 'not so large as we expected'.[144] Nor should any inevitable 'forward march' be read into the growth of branch numbers, for some were ephemeral.[145]

The comments of ILP propagandists reveal their uphill struggle in establishing branches in Lanarkshire. Glasier reported a meeting in Rutherglen in 1898, where he 'reluctantly went on the stool and spoke for an hour amidst noise and drunken interruption'. He refused to let his wife address the crowd, escorting her to her train before returning to a social, 'which was a miserable little tea party in a miserable little hall'.[146] An ILP organiser remained baffled by the miners' apathy in 1905: 'I don't know what to say about Lanarkshire. There are only five ILP branches in all Lanarkshire and there ought to be fifty-five. I very much believe that there are more socialists in Lanarkshire than in the whole of the rest of Scotland but somehow they have never managed to get themselves thoroughly organised.'[147] In 1908, the Scottish organiser looked forward to a tour of Lanarkshire with unconcealed distaste: 'The Lanarkshire miner is the most disagreeable animal I ever met with. He is dirty, drunken and conceited. It is no use talking to him. The only thing that will do is Prussic Acid.'[148] In contrast, Glasier was more enthusiastic about the prospects for socialism in Fife. After a meeting in Dunfermline in 1895, he recorded in his diary: 'The men here are excellent types of fellows ... fitted to carry on propaganda successfully ... they have won the confidence and respect of [the] outside public to a remarkable degree.'[149]

Table 2.1 also indicates the presence of the ILP's smaller Marxist rival, the SDF. Because of the ILP's significance in Glasgow, where by 1913 half of the party's Scottish membership was concentrated, recent historiography has tended to ignore the SDF in Scotland.[150] Yet, in terms of branches, the SDF was the dominant socialist party in Fife by 1909; it also had 10 branches in the West Central region (against the ILP's 26) that year. At Bo'ness, the first two branch secretaries were both miners.[151] In contrast, there was not a single SDF branch in Ayrshire. SDF branches were often as short-lived and as small as those of the ILP. In 1896, extensive propaganda by the Hamilton branch was 'not resultant in a great influx of members'.[152] In 1900, a branch was opened in Blantyre with a membership of thirty, but it did not survive; that year an Airdrie branch was described as 'small', and the 'war fever' caused by the Boer War made propaganda work 'fearfully stiff'. In 1902, the Secretary of the Kirkcaldy branch admitted 'we have not done much propaganda work this year'.[153]

The SDF in Scotland suffered a secession in 1903 from the 'impossibilists' under the influence of Daniel De Leon and the American Socialist Party. This group formed a new Socialist Labour Party (SLP) which argued against all existing union leaders and for the formation of new unions. The Edinburgh branch of the SLP campaigned in the surrounding towns and succeeded in temporarily establishing a branch at Musselburgh between 1905 and 1909, which in turn conducted propaganda among the local mining villages. However, until after the First World War the SLP had little organisational presence elsewhere in the Scots coalfields.[154]

Through a series of vigorous organising campaigns, the SDF succeeded in extending its network of branches before the First World War, particularly in Fife, where it was claimed that 'the bulk of the membership' consisted of miners. In July 1907, for example, John Maclean of the SDF addressed twenty-one meetings in the Fife coalfield in the course of a week. Maclean's young protege, James D. Macdougall, was temporarily appointed SDF Scottish organiser in 1912 and Maclean claimed that more 'real, good propaganda has been done by us in Lanarkshire' than in the previous five years.[155]

Conventional contrasts between the ethical socialism of a predominantly non-conformist ILP and the economistic Marxism of the atheist SDF should not be overdrawn.[156] Transfer between the two bodies, and even joint membership, in the 1890s was not uncommon. Small, a member of the ILP's National Administrative Council on its formation in 1893, was also a leading member of the Hamilton branch of the SDF formed in 1894 and a member of the SDF's Executive Council in 1896.[157] In 1898, ILP branches even purchased the services of the SDF's Scottish organiser, and ILP speakers on occasion were invited to SDF branches.[158] Although Small was a prominent member of the SDF (and all three of his sons were initially active members), he retained strong Christian beliefs until his death in 1903. Each week in winter his family would transport their piano to the Blantyre village hall where he conducted 'Sunday Communicals'. As his daughter recalled, 'my father always opened the meetings himself by reading from the Bible ...'.[159] It is notable that relatively few townships listed in Table 2.1 contained both ILP and SDF branches. This pattern may simply reflect which party arrived first: when the SDF began campaigning in Cambuslang in 1895, they met opposition from the ILP and ceded the field to them. In Fife, the ILP organiser found that the SDF beat him on a number of occasions to set up a branch first.[160] Sometimes socialists transferred their allegiances. For example, John McMahon, President of the Bo'ness miners' union, also presided over the local branch of the SDF on its formation in 1904, but the branch ceased functioning by 1906; McMahon chaired the founding meeting of the ILP branch in Bo'ness the following year.[161]

Just as all ILP branches aimed at 'making socialists' through propaganda, so 'the work of an SDF branch can be summed up in

Table 2.1 ILP and SDF branches within the Scots coalfields, 1902, 1907 and 1909

Region	Locality	Party	1902	1907	1909
West Central					
	Hamilton/ Burnbank	SDF	+	+	+
	Blantyre	ILP	*	*	*
	Dalserf	ILP	*	-	-
	Larkhall	ILP	-	*	*
	Rutherglen	ILP	*	*	*
	Baillieston	ILP	-	-	*
	Cambuslang	ILP	-	-	*
	Bellshill	ILP	-	*	*
	Uddingston	ILP	-	*	*
	Holytown	ILP	-	*	*
	Coatbridge	ILP	-	*	*
	Harthill	SDF	-	+	+
	"	ILP	-	*	-
	Shotts	ILP	-	*	*
	Newarthill	SDF	-	+	+
	Motherwell	ILP	*	*	*
	Wishaw	ILP	*	*	*
	Cleland	ILP	-	-	*
	Newmains	ILP	-	-	*
	Stonehouse	SDF	-	+	+
	Lesmahagow	ILP	*	*	*
	Kirkmuirhill	SDF	-	+	+
	Douglas Water	ILP	-	*	*
	Douglas	ILP	-	-	*
	Glespin	ILP	-	*	*
	Coalburn	ILP	-	-	*
	Thornliebank	SDF	-	-	+
	Falkirk	SDF	+	+	+
	"	ILP	*	-	-
	Camelon	SDF	-	+	-
	Stenhousemuir	SDF	-	+	+
	Bo'ness	SDF	-	+	+
	"	ILP	-	*	*
	Bathgate	SDF	-	+	+
	Armadale	ILP	-	*	*
	Fauldhouse	ILP	-	-	*
	Kirkintilloch	ILP	-	*	*
	Kilsyth	ILP	-	-	*
	Bannockburn	ILP	-	-	*
	Bonnybridge	ILP	-	-	*

Table 2.1 ILP and SDF branches within the Scots coalfields, 1902, 1907 and 1909 (Continued)

Region	Locality	Party	1902	1907	1909
Ayrshire					
	Ayr	ILP	*	*	*
	Annbank	ILP	-	-	*
	Coylton	ILP	-	-	*
	Kilmarnock	ILP	*	*	*
	Stewarton	ILP	*	-	-
	Hurlford	ILP	-	*	*
	Galston	ILP	-	*	*
	Dalry	ILP	-	*	*
	Kilbirnie	ILP	-	*	*
	Kilwinning	ILP	-	*	-
	Saltcoats	ILP	-	*	*
	Dreghorn	ILP	-	.*	*
	Irvine	ILP	-	-	*
	Newmilns	ILP	-	*	*
	Dalmellington	ILP	*	*	-
	New Cumnock	ILP	*	-	-
	Cumnock	ILP	-	*	*
	Muirkirk	ILP	-	*	*
	Patna	ILP	-	*	*
	Auchinleck	ILP	-	-	*
	Glenbuck	ILP	-	-	*
Fife					
	Kirkcaldy	SDF	+	+	+
	Methil/Buckhaven	SDF	-	+	+
	East Wemyss	SDF	-	+	+
	Leven	SDF	-	+	+
	Dysart	SDF	-	+	+
	Cowdenbeath	SDF	-	+	+
	”	ILP	*	-	-
	Bowhill and Cardenden	SDF	-	+	+
	Lochgelly	ILP	-	*	*
	Kelty	ILP	-	-	*
	Dunfermline	SDF	-	+	+
	”	ILP	*	*	*
	Townhill	SDF	-	-	+
	”	ILP	*	-	-
	Windygates	SDF	-	+	+

Table 2.1 ILP and SDF branches within the Scots coalfields, 1902, 1907 and 1909 (continued)

Region	Locality	Party	1902	1907	1909
Clackmannan					
	Alloa	ILP	-	*	*
	Alva	ILP	-	*	*
	Tillicoultry	ILP	-	*	*
Mid and East Lothian					
	[Edinburgh]	SDF	+	+	+
	Prestonpans	SDF	-	-	+
	Musselburgh	ILP	*	*	*
	Dalkeith	ILP	-	*	*
	Roslin	ILP	-	*	-
	Bonnyrigg	ILP	-	-	*

Key: SDF branch in existence during that year   +
ILP branch in existence during that year   *
No branch in existence during that year   -

Sources: *Justice*, 1902, 1907 and 1909; Independent Labour Party, *Annual Conference Reports*, 1902, 1907 and 1909.

Note: The table lists ILP and SDF branches situated within the geographical boundaries of the coal mining regions. It is not suggested that a majority, or necessarily any, of the members of these branches were miners.

one sentence – propaganda for the purpose of making Social Democrats'.[162] Both parties engaged in similar propaganda activities of street corner meetings in the summer, indoor meetings in the winter, and selling their respective journals and pamphlets. Both displayed elitist attitudes towards the mass of the miners which limited their popular appeal. 'The puritanical and moralistic temperance advocacy' of Scottish socialist miners' leaders, recalled Bob Selkirk, 'antagonised many miners and other workers' while the SDF (and the SLP) demanded a training in Marxist theory from their committed cadre.[163] In Stonehouse, Alexander Anderson, the local schoolmaster and 'a highly cultured man', was the leading member of the SDF branch. He was later described by Macdougall as 'a beacon of light amid the smoky ignorance of the untutored masses in that Lanarkshire coalfield':

... It can be understood therefore how a doctrinaire socialist such as Anderson, who would not deign to compromise his clear cut ideas, was found unsympathetic by the bands of colliers sitting on their hunkers or leaning against the street corners ...[164]

Nevertheless, elements of these attitudes were congenial to the self-improving bureaucratic stratum within the miners' unions; Smillie, for example, declared himself 'deeply sensible of the terrible evils caused by drink' in his 1910 election address.[165] The ILP secured the adherence of a majority of Scots miners' leaders after 1900: many of the Lanarkshire miners' agents listed above in Table 1.5 of this volume were ILP members or supporters; Michael Lee, President and later an agent of the FKMA, was Chairman of the Lochgelly ILP and represented the party on the town council; James Cook, the Clackmannan miners' agent, was an ILP member of Alloa school board; James Brown of Ayrshire joined the ILP about 1899; Thomas McKerrell, his fellow Ayrshire agent and ILPer, was a town councillor and baillie in Kilmarnock.[166] Yet until the First World War there was also a minority of SDF supporters. John Robertson, an LMU agent, was a member of the British Socialist Party (BSP), the successor to the SDF, although he was a pro-war supporter of the party leadership after 1914.[167] William B. Small, eldest son of William Small, was appointed an LMU agent in 1903 and was Secretary of the Lanarkshire District Council of the SDF as late as 1909; his younger brother, Robert, also a Lanarkshire miners' agent until his appointment as Secretary to the small Scottish Shale Miners' Union in 1912, was an SDF member and lecturer.[168] In Fife, Sam Hynds, an SDF member from East Wemyss, unsuccessfully contested the post of FKMA Assistant Secretary in 1909 but was lay President by 1912; in 1914, another Fife official, Robert Robertson was a BSP member.[169]

While both parties engaged in educational and electoral activity, after 1900 the former became more important for the SDF, the latter for the ILP. There were a handful of SDF members on parish councils and school boards in the Scottish coalfields from the 1890s, though their immediate programme had little to distinguish it from the ILP's brand of municipal socialism. When Robert Small stood as a 'social democrat' for Lanarkshire County Council in 1910, his manifesto focused on housing and sanitary conditions and the potential for the council to force landlords to make improvements:

'But, better still', he added with a view to the colliers' traditional concerns, 'the Council can build houses – either tenements or cottages with gardens up to an acre in extent'.[170] His father, William Small, was a long-serving member of the Blantyre School Board; three SDF members were elected to the Hamilton Parish Council and five in Slamannan in 1895. The following year an SDF comrade stood unsuccessfully as a 'progressive' for Hamilton Town Council but secured a respectable 30 per cent of the vote. In 1909, eight SDF candidates stood for the school boards in the mining areas of Buckhaven, Bathgate, Hamilton, Harthill and Stonehouse, winning three seats. Such results were hardly impressive and the scope for socialist interventions was limited: arguing for the withdrawal of non-secular school books or increased tobacco allowances for paupers.[171]

Consequently, the SDF put greater energy into educational and propaganda work in Scotland. Small taught an economics class in his house in 1895 and the Glasgow branches of the SDF regularly organised evening classes.[172] Within this programme, the most well-known SDF educator was John Maclean, who began teaching classes in Marxist economics and industrial history from 1906 onwards. Over the winter of 1908–9, he taught a class in Burnbank and in 1910 in the Renfrewshire mining village of Nitshill. From 1910 onwards, he also taught one night per week in Fife, at Bowhill, Dunfermline, Kirkcaldy or Cowdenbeath.[173]

Although the ILP undertook some systematic educational provision – for example, a class to study trades unionism in Motherwell in 1906 – the party placed increasing stress on electoralism.[174] Their representation on local public bodies within the Scots mining regions in 1907 is summarised in Table 2.2. While they fared significantly better than the SDF, outside of Glasgow their presence could only be described as a toehold in Scottish local government at this time. The total of 47 ILP local representatives compares unfavourably with the 89 in West Yorkshire alone in 1906.[175]

In parliamentary elections in the Scots coalfields, the ILP as such was wholly unsuccessful. Only Smillie, in 1894 as an SPLP candidate for Mid-Lanark, contested a parliamentary seat in the coalfields before 1900. In part this was due to the expense of parliamentary campaigns at a time when both trade unions and the party were weak.[176] In 1900, the ILP and SDF had participated, along with delegates from trade unions, trades councils and the

cooperative movement, in forming the Scottish Workers'
Parliamentary Election Committee (SWPEC). This organisation,
which changed its name to the Scottish Workers' Representation
Committee (SWRC) in 1902, was analogous to the Labour
Representation Committee in England and became the Labour
Party (Scottish Section) in 1907.[177] It was as representatives of this
federal body that miners' officials stood for parliament, although
their membership of the affiliated ILP meant that their campaigns
were effectively conducted by ILP and union branches. The three
Lanarkshire miners' officials who stood in 1906 were described by
the ILP organiser as 'our' candidates, and miners' leaders often
addressed ILP gatherings.[178]

Scots miners' officials' electoral interventions are listed in Table
2.3. In only one instance, William Adamson in West Fife, was a
Scottish miners' leader elected before the First World War. There
are a number of explanations for this in the existing historiography.[179] The first was organisational. The SWRP was inadequately
led and subject to internal divisions. Increasingly, the miners' union
'went their own way' as part of the MFGB's political machine.
Given the pressures of union consolidation during these years, the
miners' unions inevitably treated political activity episodically.
Hardie commented in 1906 that:

> If he were asked to explain why all the miners' candidates in Scotland
> were defeated, he would say that it lay at the door of the Miners'
> Federation. Elections cannot be won with ten minutes' preparation.
> They refused to spend money beforehand in organising the con-
> stituencies which they were to fight ...[180]

This view was supported by a report in the ILP's *Labour Leader*
that in Ayrshire North 'the miners had no political machinery whatever ... '.[181] In an attempt to remedy this, the SMF appointed two
'political agents' as electoral organisers in 1908: William Watson,
who was based in Fife, and Duncan Graham, based in Lanarkshire;
both were ILP members.[182] However, in 1912 the Labour Party continued to express concern at the 'unsatisfactory' state of organisation in the Scots mining constituencies.[183]

A further factor was the electoral inflexibility and the political
resilience of the Liberal Party. In contrast with England, there was
no secret pact in 1903 to permit the development of a 'progressive
alliance' in Scotland.[184] The weakness of Scottish trade unionism

generally meant that the SWRC posed less of a threat to the Liberals. Despite elements within the Liberal leadership being amenable to an accommodation with the miners – as at Lanark North-East in 1901 – local Liberal parties obstructed such moves. Even where union organisation was strong, the Liberals refused to cede seats. Thus when Robert Brown stood for Midlothian in 1912, local Liberals refused to give way (and as a result of the split vote lost the seat to the Conservatives). For their part, miners' leaders remained hostile to the Liberal Party.[185]

The Liberals in Scotland also maintained a tradition of social radicalism from which Labour found it hard to differentiate itself. During the January 1910 contest for Mid-Lanark, Smillie produced a leaflet attacking the parliamentary record of his Liberal opponent, yet his own election address – encompassing amendments to the Workmen's Compensation Act, a reduction in the age limit for old age pensions, rent courts, nationalisation of mineral royalties, temperance reform, Home Rule for Ireland and abolition of the House of Lords – was scarcely distinguishable from 'New Liberal' policies. Only his conclusion hinted at socialism (without actually using the word) in its convoluted prescription of a 'system of production for use and not for mere monetary and individual profit' as the 'only ultimate solution of the Social Problem'. Short of the construction of 'a cooperative commonwealth', he pledged to work 'hand in hand' with all other social reformers (in other words, Liberals). In his attack on the Liberal candidate, he couched his appeal largely in terms of a class-loyal labourism rather than socialism: 'Do not be misled by middle class professional politicians ... let us solidly support one of our own class.'[186]

Such appeals to class solidarity were qualified by only a hint of divisions among workers: 'Let us sink all our petty differences ...', urged Smillie. Yet ethnic and religious fissures ploughed deeply across the Lanarkshire and Ayrshire coalfields.[187] These rivalries, in weakening trade unionism, had stimulated support for the strategy of independent labour representation, yet they simultaneously undermined its efficacy.[188] After the 1911 Kilmarnock Burghs bye-election, it was reported that trade unionists had voted as 'either good nationalists or good orangemen'.[189] John Robertson, elected Labour MP for Bothwell in 1919, later claimed that 'The Irish question has kept me out of Parliament for 20 years – the one side could not vote for me because I was a "home-ruler", and the home-rulers

Table 2.2 Numbers of ILP representatives on local public bodies in the Scottish mining regions, 1907

Region	Parish Councils	School Boards	Town Councils
West Central			
	Bothwell (3)	Bothwell (1)	Armadale (2)
	Carluke (1)	Douglas Water (1)	Kirkintilloch(1)
	Larkhall (1)	Larkhall (1)	Rutherglen (1)
	Rutherglen (3)	Wishaw (1)	
Ayrshire			
	Dalmellington (2)	Dalmellington (1)	Kilmarnock (4)
	Dalry (2)	Dalry (1)	Kilwinning (2)
	Kilwinning (2)	Kilwinning (2)	Saltcoats (1)
	Saltcoats (2)	Muirkirk (1)	
		Cumnock (1)	
Fife and Clackmannan			
	Alloa (1)	Alloa (1)	Lochgelly (1)
		Tillicoultry (1)	
Mid and East Lothian			
	Musselburgh (4)	Musselburgh (1)	Musselburgh (1)

Source: Independent Labour Party, *Annual Conference Report*, 1907

Note: Numbers in brackets refer to the numbers of representatives on the particular body.

could not vote for me because the Irish vote had to go to the Liberal.'[190]

An editorial in the influential *Glasgow Observer and Catholic Herald* in 1898 succinctly summarised the hostility of Irish nationalists to the ILP on the grounds that it sought to 'smash' the Liberal Party: 'To assist in smashing the Liberal Party is to assist in smashing Home Rule ... in practical politics today the ILP is simply a Tory auxiliary.'[191] Table 7.3 in volume 1 noted the varying estimates of the Roman Catholic vote in coalfield constituencies in Lanarkshire, ranging between 10 and 25 per cent. In general, the Irish National League instructed its supporters to vote for the Liberal Party and its promise of Home Rule. (Labour's similar promise carried little conviction given the weakness of its parliamentary party.) Thus when

Smillie contested the 1894 Mid-Lanark by-election, Michael Davitt, who had personally supported Hardie there in 1888, secured for the Liberals 'the solid Irish vote which is all powerful throughout the division. After this it was a mere question of the numbers by which the Liberal candidate was to be returned.' At the religiously divided village of Stane in the constituency, 'the fight was carried on wholly between the Gladstonians and Unionists and the Labour candidate found few supporters'.[192] It seems likely that the Irish vote may have become even more solidly Liberal by 1910 and the prospect of the Third Home Rule Bill; the Labour vote declined by half between 1906 and January 1910 in Lanark North-East and Lanark North-West.[193]

On those rare occasions when the INL supported the Labour candidate – for example, at Lanark North-East in 1901, and at Lanark North-West in 1906, this was not sufficient substantially to increase Labour's vote.[194] Fraser suggests that in the former case, Smillie, as an Ulster Protestant, may have been unacceptable to Irish Catholics. However, in the second example, the Labour candidate, the miners' agent Joseph Sullivan, was a well-known Catholic (and may have been equally unacceptable to Orangemen). A further explanation may lie in the Catholic church's objections to socialism. Although there is some evidence that not all Catholics were unsympathetic to socialism – for example, Andrew McAnulty, a Blantyre miners' union activist and Chairman of the Lanarkshire ILP Federation, described himself as 'a Catholic and a socialist', and John McMahon of Bo'ness was an Irish nationalist – such men were in a minority.[195] Whatever the reason, these examples suggest that INL support was a necessary, but not necessarily sufficient, precondition for a Labour electoral breakthrough.

Religious differences may also have contributed to further divisions evident within the miners' unions on the fundamental issue of whether they should be involved in political activities at all. At a meeting in Lanark during the 1894 strike, Miss Hutton of the Glasgow Trades Council was shouted down when she urged the nationalisation of mines with cries of 'what is she going into politics for?'[196] We can perceive a similar 'non-political' (or anti-Labour) current in the votes in Scotland on the question of MFGB affiliation to the Labour Party. The vote in 1906 was 17,801 in favour of affiliation, 12,376 against; in 1908, there was only a marginally greater majority on a much larger vote: 32,112 to 25,823. This was the lowest ratio in favour in the main British coalfields with the exception of the Midlands.[197] Although all except Fife and the Lothians among the Scottish miners' county unions supported socialism in the form of nationalisation of the mines by 1897, and all endorsed the policy of independent labour representation by 1901, a significant part of their membership supported neither.[198] This is also reflected in the failure of large minorities (and occasionally majorities) of miner voters to support miners' candidates in elections: see Table 2.3.

Finally, there were two related technical, but nevertheless very important, obstacles to securing parliamentary majorities for miners' candidates before 1918. The first concerned the social composition of parliamentary constituencies in the coalfields. It can be seen from Table 2.3 that only in West Fife was there a majority of miner voters in any constituency. This contrasted unfavourably with the classic 'mining seats' found in some English counties: Durham, for example, had four constituencies in which miners formed a majority of voters in 1910.[199]

In addition to this compositional factor, there was also the limited nature of the electoral franchise before 1918. There were a number of franchise categories. The most relevant to our study were the household franchise, which embraced owners or tenants of dwellings, and the lodger franchise, where the lodging was valued at £10 or more. In addition, these qualifications required their continuous possession for twelve months prior to 1 June for inclusion on the electoral roll which came into effect on 1 November; thus permanent residence for 17 months was effectively required. Both householders and lodgers were permitted to change residence within a burgh without losing their voting entitlement, but other changes of residence led to disqualification. There were a number of other grounds for disqualification, including non-payment of rates and receipt of poor relief.[200]

The effect of these franchise qualifications in the specific conditions of the Scottish coalfields was significantly to limit the numbers of miners and their family members eligible to vote. All women were excluded, as were adult sons resident with their families. The considerable geographical mobility among miners affected the residence qualification. Evictions during strikes could also break continuity of residence.[201] The requirement to pay rates had the 'good effect', according to one commentator in 1904, of 'disenfranchising the slums; for casual workers manage to pay their rent, but to the [rates] collector when he pays his quarterly or half-yearly visit they turn a deaf ear'.[202]

It has been suggested that the requirement in Scotland that rates had to be paid personally to qualify for the franchise was more restrictive than English practice. However, the nature of what constituted personal payment requires elaboration. On houses rated at £4 or less, which represented the very poorest dwellings, burgh rates fell to be paid by the owner and thus their inhabitants were automatically disenfranchised; in the counties, occupiers could be excused such rates on the grounds of poverty and if so, they too were ineligible to vote.[203] Although in general rates were collected directly from householders, 'compound householders', who paid both rent and rates to their landlord who then subsequently paid the rates to the local authority, were common in the mining districts. Mining companies usually collected rates along with rent from their employees in company housing and apparently this did not disenfranchise the tenants, provided that the landlord actually paid the rates on their behalf. Thus on one occasion in Hamilton, 'a great number of working men lost their votes because the landlord, who was in difficulties, would not pay the rates he had collected from them'.[204]

The effects of exemption from rates, their non-payment, and the receipt of poor relief on enfranchisement varied considerably, as can be seen from figures relating to the survey districts for 1898. In Wemyss parish, 532 inhabitants were disenfranchised for non-payment of rates, 5 because of exemption from rates on the grounds of poverty and 20 for receipt of poor relief, a total of 557; in Culross the total was 3, in Blantyre 121, Dalserf 136, Dalziel 83, Prestonpans 11, and Newbattle 6. The explanation for such wide variations is unclear (though it may relate to different house letting and rate collection practices).[205] What is apparent is that in some, but by no means all, mining parishes, the numbers excluded from the franchise on these grounds could be a significant proportion of the electorate. Of 5,915 rated inhabitants in the section of Hamilton parish within the constituency of the Falkirk Burghs in 1892, 552 (9.3 per cent) defaulted on paying their rates.[206]

A more generalised source of disenfranchisement in the overcrowded mining settlements was the operation of the lodger franchise. Lodgers were common in mining households. For lodgers to qualify for the vote, the lodging had to be of a yearly rateable value of £10, and this test applied to each lodger if there was more than one in a household. Appeals on the annual registration of lodgers were conducted by the agents of the political parties before the local Sheriff who enjoyed considerable discretion in his application of the franchise legislation. In his authoritative manual on the subject, Whitelaw suggested that a weekly rent of eight shillings (equivalent to £19 per year) was 'usually held to afford a qualification'.[207] However, it is very unlikely that any miners' lodgers would pay such a weekly sum, given that the highest annual rental paid by miners was estimated at £20 for a two roomed house in Lanarkshire in 1907. In Wishaw, for example, in six one-roomed houses occupied by fourteen adult males and ten females, only three men were eligible for registration.[208] Duncan Graham, the SMF political organiser claimed in 1910 that there was not a single lodger vote in any mining village in the Mid and North-East Lanark constituencies.[209] Certainly the numbers of lodgers entitled to vote represented a tiny fraction of the electorate in 1911: 5.1 per cent in Lanark North-East, 4.2 in Mid-Lanark, 4.6 in Lanark South, 1.4 in West Lothian, 3.7 in West Fife, 1.4 in Midlothian.[210] Graham conducted a campaign to abolish the rental requirement by flooding the registration court with appeals and succeeded in getting agreement that two-lodger claims be allowed from two-roomed houses, irrespective of rental. By 1913, there was a thirteen-fold increase in the registration of miners' lodgers in Lanarkshire, and Graham secured a similar agreement in Ayrshire; William Watson also carried out a registration drive in Fife and the Lothians.[211]

The composition of constituencies and the operation of the franchise prevented large numbers of the mining population from voting before the First World War. Many of the disenfranchised miners might have voted for the Liberal or Conservative Parties had they been able to do so. But equally, even if many of those miners who *were* entitled to vote *had* voted Labour, their limited numbers were no automatic guarantee of a Labour victory before 1918.

Socialism and trade union policy before 1914

The espousal of socialism by leading members of the county unions and the commitment of the SMF to state collectivism did not lead

Table 2.3 Miners' candidates for parliamentary seats within the Scots coalfields, 1892–1913

Year	Candidate	Party	Constituency	Miners as % of total vote c.1910	Labour vote as % of miners' vote	Labour vote as % of total vote
1892	R.C. Robertson	SUTCLP	Stirlingshire	20.0		6.3
1894 (b-e)	R. Smillie	SPLP	Mid Lanarkshire	34.0		13.8
1901 (b-e)	R. Smillie	SWPEC	Lanarkshire North-Eastern	34.0		21.7
1904 (b-e)	J. Robertson	SWRC	Lanarkshire North-Eastern	34.0		27.9
1906	J. Brown	SWRC	Ayrshire Northern	12.0		20.8
1906	D. Gilmour	SWRC	Falkirk Burghs	26.0		17.5
1906	J. Robertson	SWRC	Lanarkshire North-Eastern	34.0		29.2
1906	J. Sullivan	SWRC	Lanarkshire North-Western	13.0		23.9
1910 (Jan.)	W. Adamson	Labour	Fife Western	58.0	47.2	36.7
1910 (Jan.)	J. Brown	Labour	Ayrshire Northern	12.0	88.7	12.9
1910 (Jan.)	R. Small	Labour	Lanarkshire North-Western	13.0	64.6	9.7
1910 (Jan.)	R. Smillie	Labour	Mid Lanarkshire	34.0	62.9	25.7
1910 (Jan.)	J. Sullivan	Labour	Lanarkshire North-Eastern	34.0	28.8	11.8
1910 (Dec.)	R. Smillie	Labour	Mid Lanarkshire	34.0	62.7	24.7
1910 (Dec.)	W. Adamson	Labour	Fife Western	58.0	61.0	53.0*
1911 (b-e)	J. Robertson	Labour	Lanarkshire North-Eastern	34.0	38.4	16.3
1911 (b-e)	T. McKerrell	Labour	Kilmarnock Burghs	n/a	n/a	28.5
1912 (b-e)	R. Brown	Labour	Edinburghshire	27.0	52.1	16.7
1913 (b-e)	T. Gibb	Labour	Lanarkshire Southern	21.0	74.0	16.8

Sources: Election results are taken from F.W.S. Craig (ed.) *British Parliamentary Election Results 1885–1918* (Dartmouth, 2nd ed. 1989); miners as a percentage of total voters c.1910 are taken from R. Gregory, *The Miners and British Politics, 1906–1914* (Oxford, 1968), p.96. Gregory's estimates of the constituency mining votes are the basis of the calculation of the Labour vote as a percentage of the mining vote.

Notes:

1. 'Miners' candidates' refers to candidates who were officials in the Scots miners' unions, with the exception of Tom Gibb, who stood with miners' union support in 1913. W. Adamson was General Secretary of the FKMA; James Brown and Thomas McKerrell were General Secretary and agent of the AMU; Robert Brown was General Secretary of the MELMA. The remainder were officials of the LMU.

2. Robert Smillie stood as an ILP candidate for Glasgow Camlachie in 1895 and as an SWRC candidate for Paisley in 1906; in the latter year he also stood as the Labour candidate at a by-election in Cockermouth. John Wilson stood as an independent in Edinburgh in 1892. None of these attempts were successful.

Abbreviations:

SUTCLP	–	Scottish United Trades Councils' Labour Party
SWPEC	–	Scottish Workers' Parliamentary Election Committee
SWRC	–	Scottish Workers' Representation Committee
(b-e)	-	Bye-election
*	–	indicates seat won by Labour candidate

to any abrupt shift in the everyday industrial relations practices of these unions. Socialists continued to advocate traditional policies but now situated them politically within broader strategies of state intervention and rhetorically within a more anti-capitalist discourse. Thus Hardie simultaneously advised Ayrshire miners in 1900 'to beware the big darg; it had proved their ruin a hundred times in the past ...' and also 'to send men to Parliament to look after their interests there'.[212] Restriction policies remained an article of faith. Bob Selkirk, who grew up in East Lothian, recalled a group of miners in the villages around Tranent who combined Blatchfordian socialism with the values of the independent collier:

> [They] would only work four days per week in the pit. They spent most of their time in their large gardens. One of them, nicknamed The Prophet, would only work a 'three day week' in the pit. He had much influence on the younger generation. Despite the 'modern' tendencies militating against a 'four day week', the influence of the Prophet was responsible for many 'accidents' caused by runaway hutches, roof supports collapsing, pumps refusing to pump. Such accidents stopped a section or maybe the whole pit and the drawers enjoyed an 'unexpected' game of football in the open air.

When he did work, the Prophet would accompany each blow of his pick with a didactic refrain illustrating the theory of surplus value: 'one, two, three, four for the company – one, two, three for the laird – one for poor Prophet'. His socialist world view could easily accommodate output restriction: 'if all the miners had been like me they would have been selling coals in the chemist shop by the ounce'.[213]

Less colourfully, Smillie continued to adhere to restriction: 'something must be done to regulate the output of coal to keep up prices', he argued in 1904, and declared his firm belief in a fixed darg in 1910.[214] When faced with a demand for a 25 per cent wage reduction in 1914, Smillie, on behalf of the SMF Executive, stated that 'if the owners could not regulate the prices owing to the insane competition, they would have to attempt it themselves ...'. Rather than take strike action, they instead declared a four day working policy in all Scottish collieries in order to 'stiffen prices and kill mad competition'.[215] As the pro-employer *Colliery Guardian* complained, 'such a policy is but the recrudescence, in a more elaborate form, of the old "ca'canny" policy, which was the primitive device of the workmen to upset the law of supply and demand'.[216] The policy was subsequently abandoned under pressure from the MFGB and the outbreak of the war.

Lanarkshire re-adopted a five-day week after the war and the NUSMW proposed extending it throughout the British coalfields as a solution to the coal crisis of 1921. Unsurprisingly, their representative to the MFGB Executive reported that 'as to the limitation of working days per week, the English and Welsh people held different views from us and did not think that such a proposal would in any way help ... at this present crisis'.[217] However, the Lanarkshire union pursued a five day working policy, with increasingly ragged support until 1925. In that year, the LCMA insisted that the policy would not 'benefit the market or improve the position of the men'. The LMU Executive ascertained by questionnaire that the branches were equally divided on the policy and their recommendation to abandon attempts to re-establish the policy was accepted.[218]

Controlling the entry of the unskilled to the coalface remained a perennial anxiety of the Scots unions in the decade before 1914.[219] In 1908, for example, a motion moved by the Lanarkshire delegates to the SMF annual conference calling on the government to introduce measures to prevent the employment of adult unskilled miners was carried unanimously.[220] In 1910, Michael Lee, a prominent ILP member in Fife, supported by David Gilmour, LMU Secretary, recommended to the conference the establishment of 'a system of bens, whereby all persons starting work at the coal face will only get half a turn for the first two years and a three quarter turn for the second two years'; with strong support from Smillie, the motion was carried unanimously.[221]

Such concerns have to be viewed against the continuing domination of the miners' unions by hewers. This was reflected in Smillie's insistence in 1907 that the LMU's 26,000 members embraced practically all the 'miners' in Lanarkshire; yet there were almost 54,000 underground workers and 4,521 male workers above ground listed for the county in the 1911 Census.[222] Union rules were often silent on the definition of a 'miner', though their emphasis on excluding the unskilled carried the implicit restriction to hewers. Others admitted all underground workers to membership, but distinguished them from 'miners'. Rule 19 of the Baillieston Miners' Association (established in 1893) on 'The admission of special members' was typical: 'Reddsmen, Brushers, Drawers, Bottomers and other workmen employed in or about a colliery will be admitted members of this association on the same conditions as the miner – that is in their own department of workmanship'.[223] The unions made sporadic attempts to recruit oncost workers, particularly during wage agitations, when they might form a nucleus of strikebreakers.[224] However, oncost workers' daily wages were normally adjusted in line with increases or decreases in the hewers' nominal day wage, and thus there was less incentive for them to be union members.

With the consolidation of trade unionism after 1900, these attempts became a little more systematic. In that year, the Fife union board viewed with satisfaction the growth of interest in the union on the part of pithead workers and emphasised that the union's rules clearly provided for this. Despite this attempt at clarification, a ballot was necessary before male pithead workers were admitted to the union. A further ballot was necessary on the question of admitting female pithead workers and it was agreed to exclude females from membership.[225] This vote reflected a more generalised hostility to female pithead labour based on the alleged threat of undercutting male wages and its implicit challenge to the highly gendered world view of the miners. The legislative abolition of female labour at pitheads was frequently supported by SMF conferences. The Lanarkshire Secretary complained in 1904 that 'schoolboys at fourteen could not be got for anything like the wages that the employers could get female labour for. The moral aspect he did not touch on but it was not of secondary importance.'[226]

Attempts at a more inclusive recruitment strategy were thus limited. Despite their commitment to state collectivism, the exclusive culture of the hewers remained the dominant ethos of the Scots miners' unions until at least 1914: 'as miners they agreed that theirs was a trade skilled, intricate and dangerous ...' stated one Ayrshire delegate in 1910: 'If the trade were a trade, intricate and dangerous, a full apprenticeship should be served.'[227] Elements of the hewers' traditional attitudes persisted even into the inter-war period. When the LMU revised its rules in 1919, miners' sons were exempted from any entrance fee but 'adults entering the mines for the first time' were subject to a charge of £2; two years later, the Larkhall branch of the LMU expressed its concern at 'outsiders entering the mines'.[228] Face-workers remained the dominant group within the miners' unions. Confronted with a drastically reduced membership, one Lanarkshire agent suggested in 1933 that 'an endeavour should be made to enrol the surface workers into the union, and consideration might be given to the amount of contribution payable', a clear indication this was not normal practice, however formally open the rules. Lanarkshire's General Secretary, William B. Small, replied that:

> the collier [i.e. the hewer] was the best trade unionist: surface workers, oncost and brushers were more difficult to organise. That may be accounted for by the reason of the fact that their wages were more stabilised and the Executive Committee would require to concentrate their activities to make these classes more union minded.[229]

However, such traditional attitudes and the policies which they underpinned were increasingly challenged by changes in the structure of the industry – 'today the miners' employers were scattered everywhere under heaven', complained one delegate in 1908 – and the labour process.[230] In 1906, a Lanarkshire activist noted 'the enormous increase in the production of coal' which coalcutting machinery had brought about and this had obvious implications for any restriction policy. The threat to skill posed by machinery was clearly recognised by Gilmour of Lanarkshire in 1906 when he dismissed the efficacy of high entry fees, 'especially in machine working'.[231] We can discern the differing ways in which socialists attempted to adapt traditional policies within a proposed framework of state regulation by the comparison of two documents published in 1906 and 1911.

The first, on 'Coal cutting machinery in Lanarkshire mines', was written by William Gallacher, a Larkhall union activist, and published, uniquely, within the LMU Annual Report for 1906.[232] The article began by expressing fears about the hazards associated with machinery, in particular the risks of explosion or shock through electrical faults, and argued for one of the machine operators to be a skilled electrician: 'state legislation seems to be absolutely necessary to guard against the new dangers to the miners' safety'. Smillie, at that time a member of the Royal Commission on Mines, pursued this proposal and a Departmental Committee appointed to draft special rules for the use of electricity in mines made specific provisions concerning the duties of 'the person authorised to work an electrically driven coal cutter'.[233]

The 'greatest danger' from coal-cutting machinery, claimed Gallacher, was the opportunities it afforded for the introduction of unskilled workers. He observed that 'the law as it presently stands is useless, and the prohibitive tariff put upon the entrance of unskilled workers into the mines by some of the miners' unions has proved a comparative failure'. He continued, 'some form of state legislation seems to be necessary' and advocated the official issue of 'certificates of competency' to be granted after an apprenticeship under the supervision of a skilled miner.[234] Against the other 'evils' associated with mechanisation, Gallacher relied on the traditional defence of collective organisation exercised through the vigilance of the union branch committees in local negotiations:

> With regard to wages, hours of working, and other conditions, it lies with the miners and their organisation to see to it that the introduction of coal cutting machinery is not made a means of still further exploitation of the miner by his employer.

The second document was written by Robert Small, second son of William Small, a Lanarkshire union agent and a member of the SDF which published his pamphlet, *The Cry from the Mine and the Claim of the Miner*, in 1911.[235] Small advocated that daily inspections of workplaces should be carried out by 'practical men selected by the miners and paid by the government' and that there should be a 'higher grade of working men inspectors' to examine larger districts. Like Gallacher, Small noted the increased productivity brought about by 'the rapid strides' made by coal-cutting machinery, but instead of the former's commitment to the traditional demand for an eight hour day, he argued for a restriction to six hours, the abolition of piecework and a minimum day wage of eight shillings. He also noted the tendency towards industrial concentration in the Scots coalfields:

> the mines are getting into the hands of fewer wealthy magnates ... soon these few companies will combine into one huge monopoly. The power over the men will be absolute. If a man grumbles or displeases the powers that be, he will be marked. Once out of work his chance of another employer is gone. For there will be only one – the monopoly combine.[236]

While Small was obviously drawing on the Marxism of the SDF for his prognosis of this inexorable tendency towards monopolisation, such an analysis was not wholly inappropriate to sections of the Scottish coal industry at this time. Indeed, in 1893, Sir George

Elliot, a well-known mining entrepreneur, had sent out 2,000 circulars seriously advocating a 'gigantic plan for converting the whole [British coal] industry into a large trust'.[237]

Against the by now ritualised resolutions for the nationalisation of the mines which were carried unanimously at the annual conferences of the SMF, Small argued for their 'socialisation' in a prescient critique of state ownership which also accommodated the concerns which were voiced by men such as 'Jim', the Fife collier cited earlier:

> National property offers the best scope for working economically but unless the economics thus effected are given to the people then we should simply have state capitalism: and the workers know this is not socialism. Therefore the cry from the miner demands more than the mere nationalisation of the mines. The miners insist that the mines be socialised.[238]

The mechanism to achieve this transition was in subtle yet significant contrast to the electoralism of both the ILP and of the SDF in earlier years. After noting the growing industrial strength of the MFGB, and in a call which reflected the growing influence of syndicalist and industrial unionist strategies upon a section of the Scottish SDF, Small advocated a general strike to complement parliamentarianism:

> Prepare to lay down the tools of labour and vote for the social ownership of the tools of capitalism till the right to live as men should live is secured to everyone. Inspired by the ideal that labour which produces all should therefore enjoy all, this mighty federation is marching to the promised land. This promised land means social democracy.[239]

Conclusion

Before proceeding to consider the more systematic elaboration of this strategy, we can briefly recapitulate how this and the preceding chapter have accounted for the painstaking, irregular and uneven growth of trade union organisation before 1914. The swiftness of trade union consolidation in the years after 1900 meant that the men who had suffered victimisation in its bleak years were also the generation who constructed, and benefited from, the edifice of the county unions and their complex inter-relations within the SMF. It is for this reason that we have characterised their approach to trade unionism as *bureaucratic* reformism. The ideology which unified the majority of this bureaucratic stratum was the labourist state collectivism of the ILP. Such views were to remain the dominant and pervasive political orientation of this founding cohort of union leaders. Jennie Lee reflected critically on this outlook of her grandfather, Michael Lee: 'All his life, in the disputes between colliers and coalowners, [he] had been familiar with lies, double-dealing and crude victimisation ... [he had seen] policemen's batons used against his workmates.' But despite state repression and employer victimisation,

> He was still at bottom a gentle, civilized nineteenth century radical who believed that socialism would be brought about mainly by Acts of Parliament and would come in gradual, inevitable stages ... It was not so much what he said as what he assumed. He took it for granted that whenever the public should choose to return a majority Labour Government, large chunks of socialist legislation would be passed through the House of Commons ... It is remarkable how many socialists of that generation, even those whose industrial experience should have protected them against such lavish assumptions, clung to this simple faith.[240]

Yet the repeated efforts of Scots miners' leaders in securing a parliamentary platform to implement such policies were, with one exception, unsuccessful: before 1918, bureaucratic *reformism* as an electoral strategy was largely a failure. This in part accounts for the continued adherence of the miners' unions to their traditional policies developed from the eighteenth century onwards. The relatively unchanged nature of the labour process before 1900 and the uneven progress of mechanisation thereafter were further elements in sustaining long established attitudes.

We should also note the ways in which miners' leaders consciously sought to emphasise continuities from the earlier tradition of the independent collier 'to mould a complex matrix of pre-existing identities and aspirations behind a common programme'.[241] The irony was that such policies had already been found wanting. This was the context in which an alternative conception of trade unionism, opposed to both bureaucratic practice and parliamentary reformism, began to develop. The emergence of this 'new tradition' of the militant miner in the years before, during and after the First World War is the subject of the next chapter.

Notes

1. For the colliers' job control, see vol. 1, ch. 2.
2. For industrial relations in the Scots coalfields in the seventeenth and eighteenth centuries, see R. Houston, 'Coal, class and culture: labour relations in a Scottish mining community, 1650–1750', *Social History*, 8, 1, 1983; C. Whatley, '"The fettering bonds of brotherhood": combination and labour relations in the Scottish coal-mining industry, c. 1690–1775', *Social History*, 12, 2, 1987, and 'A caste apart? Scottish colliers, work, community and culture in the era of "serfdom"', *Scottish Labour History Society Journal*, 26, 1991.
3. Campbell, *Lanarkshire Miners*, ch. 3.
4. W. Cloughan, *A Series of Letters on the Restriction of Labour* (Coatbridge, 1846), p. 10.
5. Campbell, *Lanarkshire Miners*, pp. 265–6.
6. *Glasgow Herald*, 16 March 1867.
7. Cited in Reid, 'Crisis', p. 169.
8. For a further discussion on MacDonald's views on political economy and restriction, see C. Fisher and J. Smethurst, '"War on the law of supply and demand": the Amalgamated Association of Miners and the Forest of Dean colliers, 1869–1875', in Harrison, *Independent Collier*.
9. Campbell, *Lanarkshire Miners*, pp. 50–83, 268; Campbell and Reid, 'Independent collier', pp. 63–4.
10. Campbell, *Lanarkshire Miners*, pp. 268–9.
11. *Glasgow Sentinel*, 20 June 1863.
12. For example, see ibid., 7 December 1872, 25 January, 22 March, 14 June 1873.
13. *Justice*, 30 June, 25 August 1888.
14. Smillie, *Life*, pp. 39–40.
15. Royal Commission on Labour, PP 1892, XXXVI, Pt 1, 57.
16. *Hamilton Advertiser*, 11 February 1888.
17. Royal Commission on Labour, PP 1892, XXXVI, Pt 1, 78.
18. *North British Daily Mail*, 13 October 1882. 'Stoops' were pillars of coal initially left unworked; see vol. 1, ch. 2.
19. Royal Commission on Labour, PP 1892, XXXVI, Pt 1, 251.
20. Ibid., 79. Despite this widespread adherence to the five day week, a minority of Blantyre miners were union members during this period (see ch. 1 in this volume).

21. Ibid., 250–1.
22. *Hamilton Advertiser*, 16 October 1886.
23. Royal Commission on Labour, PP 1892, XXXVI, Pt 1, 254.
24. *Report of the Royal Commission on Trade Disputes and Trades Combinations, Minutes of Evidence*, PP 1906, LVI, 265.
25. Royal Commission on Labour, PP 1892, XXXVI, Pt 1, 79.
26. Reid, *Hardie*, p. 48.
27. *Hamilton Advertiser*, 23 October 1886.
28. Ibid., 9 January 1886. 'Bens' referred to the practice of each fully-fledged collier being able to claim an equal number of hutches in which to load his hewn coal; see vol. 1, ch. 2.
29. Ibid., 29 September 1894.
30. Ibid.
31. NLS PDL 44/14, FKMA Executive Board, 12 March 1896.
32. *First Report of the Royal Commission on Mineral Royalties, Minutes of Evidence*, PP 1890–91, XLI, 503.
33. *Glasgow Sentinel*, 21 February 1874.
34. *Miner*, June, November and December, 1888.
35. Ibid., December 1888.
36. Ibid., January 1887.
37. C. Tsuzuki, *The Life of Eleanor Marx, 1855–1898* (Oxford, 1967), pp. 219–20.
38. *Ardrossan and Saltcoats Herald*, 24 June 1882, cited in F. Reid, 'The early life and political development of James Keir Hardie, 1856–92', unpublished DPhil Thesis, University of Oxford, 1968, p. 76.
39. SRO FS 7/14, *Lanarkshire Miners' Association Rules*, Rule 17; FS 7/3, *Ayrshire Miners' Association Rules*, Rule 21; FS 7/18, *Ayrshire Miners' Union Rules*, Rule 5.
40. SRO FS 7/79, *Blantyre Miners' Association Rules*, Rule 29; FS 7/82, *Cambuslang Miners' Labour Protection Association Rules*, Rule 10; FS 7/17, *Forth and Clyde Valley Miners' Association Rules*, Rule 27; FS 7/72, *Mid and West Lothian Miners' Association Rules*, Rule 32; *Hamilton Advertiser*, 25 September 1886.
41. *Glasgow Herald*, 29 December 1906, 30 December 1909, 18 August 1911.
42. Campbell, *Lanarkshire Miners*, p. 268.
43. SRO FS 7/23, *Maryhill Miners Labour Protection and Benefit Association Rules*, Rule 11.
44. Reid, 'Crisis'.
45. J.D. Young, *The Rousing of the Scottish Working Class* (1979), p. 153.
46. Ibid.
47. SRO FS 7/75, *Amalgamated Order of the Sons of Labour Rules*, Rule 27; *Miner*, July 1887.

48. Wilson, *McDonald*, p. 141; Campbell, *Lanarkshire Miners*, p. 290.
49. *Miner*, January 1887.
50. Wilson, *McDonald*, p. 162; *Glasgow Herald*, 2 July 1868.
51. Reid, 'Crisis', p. 176.
52. Reid, *Hardie*, pp. 51–2.
53. Young, thesis, p. 128.
54. Campbell and Reid, 'Independent collier', p. 65.
55. Anderson, *Coal!*, pp. 17, 21. Memories of the link between mining and the independence bestowed by small scale cultivation were supported by an oral tradition. Anderson recalled his grandfather, born in Cambuslang in 1806, telling him: 'The most of them kept a pig and some hens, and grew their own potatoes' (Ibid., p. 17).
56. *Glasgow Sentinel*, 18 January 1868; Campbell and Reid, 'Independent collier', pp. 66–7; Campbell, *Lanarkshire Miners*, pp. 37, 269.
57. *Hamilton Advertiser*, 18 September 1886.
58. J.D. Young, 'Totalitarianism, democracy and the British labour movement before 1917', *Survey*, 20, 1, 1974, pp. 149–50. See also R. Selkirk, *The Life of a Worker* (Dundee, 1967), p. 7.
59. E.E. Barry, *Nationalisation in British Politics: the historical background* (1965), p. 61. See also Young, *Rousing*, p. 148; Young, thesis, pp. 136–9; Reid, *Hardie*, pp. 82–4; David Howell, *British Workers and the Independent Labour Party, 1893–1906* (Manchester, 1988), pp. 36, 136; E.P. Lawrence, *Henry George in the British Isles* (East Lansing, 1957), pp. 55–8; J. Saville, 'Henry George and the British Labour Movement', *Science and Society*, 24, 4, 1960; T.W. Moody, 'Michael Davitt and the British labour movement, 1882–1906', *Transactions of the Royal Historical Society*, 5th series, 3, 1953, pp. 59–64.
60. Lawrence, *Henry George*, p. 37.
61. Barry, *Nationalisation*, p. 74n.
62. Young, *Rousing*, pp. 149–51.
63. *Glasgow Observer*, 29 August 1885.
64. *Hamilton Advertiser*, 5 May 1888.
65. Smillie, *Life*, p. 42.
66. SRO HH 55/90, Small to the Duke of Richmond and Gordon, 29 October 1885; Donald Beith to the Lord Advocate, 28 November 1885, and docket note, 12 December 1885. See Acta Parliamentorum Jacobi VI, AD 1592 at para. 31, 'For furthering of the kingis comoditie be the mynes and mettallis', in *Acts of the Parliament of Scotland, vol. 111, 1567–1593* (London, 1814). The act does not mention coal although 'mynes of gould/silver/copper leid tin and vther quhatsumeur mettallis or minerallis ...' are referred to.
67. See his evidence to the Royal Commission on Mineral Royalties (PP

1890–91, XLI, 497–500). The Permanent Under-Secretary at the Scottish Office testified before the Commission that the 1592 Act did not apply to coal mines and had been largely replaced in 1649 (Ibid., 516). The Permanent Under-Secretary, R.W. Cochran Patrick, was an expert on early Scots mining law, and the author of *Early Records Relating to Mining in Scotland* (Edinburgh, 1878).

68. *Justice*, 28 July 1888.
69. Royal Commission on Labour, PP 1892, XXXVI, Pt 1, 91.
70. SRO HH 55/90, Small to Secretary of State for Scotland, 22 May 1892.
71. *Justice*, 5 January 1895.
72. T. Johnston, *A History of the Working Classes in Scotland* (Glasgow, 1920), p. 393.
73. Barry, *Nationalisation*, p. 114. McCowie represented the INL on the Cambuslang parish council in 1885; victimised as a checkweigher in Hamilton in 1868, he was later a delegate of the Cambuslang miners (Wilson, *McDonald*, p. 137; *Glasgow Observer*, 27 February 1885, 11 September 1886; Young, thesis, p. 253).
74. Barry, *Nationalisation*, p. 114.
75. *Fourth report of the Royal Commission on Mineral Royalties, Minutes of Evidence*, PP 1893–94, XLI, 353.
76. *Second Report of the Royal Commission on Mineral Royalties, Minutes of Evidence*, PP 1890–91, XLI, 465, 491.
77. Reid, *Hardie*, pp. 80–2; Young, thesis, pp. 139–41.
78. *Glasgow Observer*, 21 November 1885.
79. Young, thesis, p. 140; Reid, *Hardie*, pp. 82–3.
80. Barry, *Nationalisation*, pp. 114–15. By 1886, Davitt was reported as describing himself as a 'Christian socialist' (Moody, 'Davitt', p. 65).
81. C. Tsuzuki, *H.M. Hyndman and British Socialism* (Oxford, 1961), p. 43.
82. Reid, 'Crisis', p. 164, and *Hardie*, p. 23.
83. *Hamilton Advertiser*, 20 May 1871.
84. *North British Daily Mail*, 13 October 1882. Dunn was a contributor to the *Labour Standard*, and almost certainly associated with the 'Scottish Labour Party' (Young, thesis, p. 132).
85. W.M. Haddow, *Socialism in Scotland: its rise and progress* (Glasgow, n.d., 1920?), p. 10.
86. Young, thesis, p. 143; *Glasgow Observer*, 13 March 1886.
87. For examples, see *Justice*, 23 October, 13 November, 4 December 1886, 16 April 1887.
88. Ibid., 23 April 1887.
89. Ibid.
90. D. Lowe, *Souvenirs of Scottish Labour* (Glasgow, 1919), pp. 142–5; Reid, *Hardie*, p. 87; *Justice*, 6 August 1887.

91. L. Thompson, *The Enthusiasts: a biography of John and Katherine Bruce Glasier* (1971), p. 53.
92. Haddow, *Socialism*, p. 14. For William Morris's visit to Coatbridge in 1887, see J.B. Glasier, *William Morris and the Early Days of the Socialist Movement* (1921), pp. 72–83.
93. M. Crick, *The History of the Social-Democratic Federation* (Keele, 1994), p. 36.
94. E.P. Thompson, *William Morris: romantic to revolutionary* (1977), pp. 473–4.
95. Ibid., p. 477; Sydney Jones Library, University of Liverpool (SJL), Glasier Papers, GP/1/1/30, J.L. Mahon to J.B. Glasier, 14 October 1887.
96. Thompson, *Morris*, p. 437; Thompson, *Enthusiasts*, p. 53; *Glasgow Herald*, 14 February 1887.
97. *Glasgow Herald*, 23 February 1887.
98. Ibid., 28 February 1887; Thompson, *Morris*, p. 437. For an account of SDF activities during the strike, see *Justice*, 6 August 1887.
99. *Glasgow Herald*, 20 January 1887.
100. Ibid., 25 February 1887.
101. Ibid., 4 March 1887.
102. Ibid., 16 March 1887.
103. *Miner*, June 1887.
104. For the Sons of Labour, see ch. 1 of this volume.
105. Reid, *Hardie*, pp. 93–6.
106. *Miner*, January 1887.
107. Ibid.
108. Ibid., August 1887.
109. K. Durland, *Among the Fife Miners* (1904), pp. 22, 43–5, 72, 74.
110. Royal Commission on Mineral Royalties, PP 1890–91, XLI, 463–5, 469, 473, 491, 498, 509.
111. W.H. Fraser, 'Trade unions, reform and the election of 1868 in Scotland', *Scottish Historical Review*, 50, 150, 1971, p. 154.
112. See Young, thesis, pp. 74–93, for the campaign in the coalfields.
113. Reid, *Hardie*, p. 77.
114. Young, thesis, p. 149.
115. *Miner*, July 1887.
116. Reid, *Hardie*, p. 79; I.G.C. Hutchison, *A Political History of Scotland, 1832–1924: parties, elections and issues* (Edinburgh, 1886), pp. 169, 180.
117. Tzusuki, *Hyndman*, p. 43.
118. *Glasgow Observer*, 21, 28 November 1885. For the Falkirk Burghs campaign, see Young, thesis, pp. 153–4.
119. *Miner*, January 1887.

120. Ibid., August 1887.
121. SJL Glasier Papers, GP/1/1/30, J.L. Mahon to J.B. Glasier, 14 October 1887. For Mahon's contribution to the labour alliance strategy, and his debt to Engels, see Thompson, *Morris*, pp. 472–3, 525.
122. Reid, *Hardie*, pp. 102–116; J.G. Kellas, 'The Mid-Lanark By-Election (1888) and the Scottish Labour Party (1888–1894)', *Parliamentary Affairs*, 18, 1964–5.
123. *Hamilton Advertiser*, 7 April 1888.
124. Ibid., 21 April 1888. See vol. 1, ch. 6, for the Barr family.
125. Reid, *Hardie*, p. 113.
126. *Hamilton Advertiser*, 24 March 1888; *Miner*, May 1888.
127. *Hamilton Advertiser*, 28 April 1888.
128. *Miner*, May 1888.
129. Ibid.
130. Ibid., September 1888; Reid, *Hardie*, p. 117; Howell, *British Workers*, p. 148.
131. Lowe, *Souvenirs*, p. 82; Reid, *Hardie*, pp. 120–1.
132. *Miner*, September 1888.
133. Lowe, *Souvenirs*, pp. 160–6.
134. Reid, *Hardie*, pp. 145–6.
135. Howell, *British Workers*, p. 155.
136. For example, see *ILP Annual Conference Reports, 1896, 1897, 1899*.
137. Howell, *British Workers*, pp. 330–5; D. Hopkin, 'The membership of the Independent Labour Party, 1904–10: a spatial and occupational analysis', *International Review of Social History*, 1975. In Bo'ness, it was claimed that the early ILP membership consisted not only of miners but ironmoulders, patternmakers, engravers and railway clerks (NLS Acc. 9629, James Livingstone, 'Some events in the early days of the socialist movement in Bo'ness', unpublished typescript, p. 7).
138. *ILP Annual Conference Reports, 1899, 1902*; Livingstone, 'Bo'ness', p. 4.
139. National Advisory Committee Report, *ILP Annual Conference Report, 1907*.
140. *Labour Leader*, 13 April, 22 May 1906.
141. Hutchison, *Political History*, p. 246.
142. *Labour Leader*, 23 April 1898.
143. Howell, *British Workers*, p. 37.
144. *Labour Leader*, 6 April 1906.
145. Howell, *British Workers*, pp. 247–8. See also Table 2.1.
146. SJL GP/2/1/4, Glasier Diary, 9 May 1898.
147. *Labour Leader*, 6 January 1905.
148. Hutchison, *Political History*, p. 247.

149. SJL GP/2/1/2, Glasier Diary, 27 May 1895.
150. Hutchison, *Political History*, p. 248. For the ILP in Glasgow, see A. McKinlay and R.J. Morris (eds), *The ILP on Clydeside, 1893–1932: from foundation to disintegration* (Manchester, 1991). Crick's valuable study of the SDF has little on the party in Scotland.
151. Livingstone, 'Bo'ness', pp. 1–3.
152. *Justice*, 27 June 1896.
153. Ibid., 14 July 1900; 20 September 1902.
154. C. Tsuzuki, 'The "impossibilist revolt" in Britain: the origins of the SLP and SPGB', *International Review of Social History*, 1, 1956; Crick, *SDF*, p. 99; D.M. Chewter, 'The history of the Socialist Labour Party of Great Britain from 1902–1921 with special reference to the development of its ideas', unpublished BLitt thesis, University of Oxford, 1966, Appendix B; Selkirk, *Life*, p. 6.
155. *Justice*, 10, 24 August 1907; 20 July 1912.
156. Cf H. Collins, 'The Marxism of the Social Democratic Federation', in A. Briggs and J. Saville (eds), *Essays in Labour History 1886–1923* (1976), and the more recent work of Crick which points to examples of local collaboration between ILP and SDF members (Crick, *SDF*, pp. 118, 196).
157. *Justice*, 2 February 1895, 15 August 1896. Small may have switched allegiance to the SDF because of differences with Smillie and Hardie. Belle Small's hand-written comments on documents in the Small papers suggest considerable bitterness on her part towards Hardie and Smillie. Scrawled on the cover of the *ILP Jubilee Souvenir 1893–1943* are the words 'Hardie Smillie taught at our home by Papa. Papa was not even mentioned because of jealousy and greed. See page 26. 1893 Conference. Smellie [*sic*] took & read papas amendment as his own' (NLS Acc. 3350, Folder 8, underlining in original). Belle Small later referred to 'younger men ambitious for self' sweeping her father aside (*Hamilton Advertiser*, 30 January 1943). It is not known whether Small himself shared these feelings.
158. *Labour Leader*, 7 May, 25 June 1898; *Justice*, 2 February 1895, 20 July 1907. See also Howell, *British Workers*, p. 389.
159. NLS Acc. 3350, Small Papers, Folder 5, 'The man and reality', pp. 8–9.
160. *Justice*, 30 November 1895; W.H. Fraser, 'The Labour Party in Scotland', in K.D. Brown (ed.), *The First Labour Party, 1906–1914* (1985), p. 48.
161. Livingstone, 'Bo'ness', pp. 1, 4.
162. Howell, *British Workers*, p. 336; *Justice*, 19 October 1895.
163. Young, 'Totalitarianism', pp. 137, 141.
164. NLS Acc. 4251, John Maclean Papers, Box 2, File 9, 'The

Progressive Union'.
165. NLS 6.2057, Robert Smillie Election Address.
166. *ILP Annual Conference Report, 1907*; Knox, *Labour Leaders*, p. 70; *Labour Leader*, 16 November 1906; Fraser, 'Labour Party', p. 54.
167. Arnot, *History*, p. 141.
168. NLS Acc. 3350, Small Papers, Folder 2, Mss 'Note on this story'; *Justice*, 2 January 1909, 8 June 1912.
169. *Justice*, 30 January 1909, 20 July 1912. Maclean referred to Hynds and Robert Robertson as 'our good comrades' (*Justice*, 7 August 1914).
170. NLS Acc. 3350, Small Papers, Folder 7, Candidature of Robert Small.
171. *Justice*, 13 April, 14 May 1895, 27 June, 21 November 1896, 8 May 1909.
172. Ibid., 30 November 1895. For reports of other SDF classes, see ibid., 3 October 1896, 8 September 1900. Small's youngest son, Gladstone, later lectured in economics and industrial history in Govan (Ibid., 28 September 1912).
173. N. Milton, *John Maclean* (1973), pp. 31, 49, 66, 68.
174. *Labour Leader*, 9 March 1906. See Howell, *British Workers*, pp. 337–42.
175. K. Laybourn, 'Recent writing on the history of the ILP, 1893–1932', in D. James, T. Jowitt and K. Laybourn (eds), *The Centennial History of the Independent Labour Party* (Keele, 1994) p. 328.
176. William Adamson spent £824 contesting the West Fife constituency and Smillie £1,058 in Mid Lanark in December 1910 (*Return of charges made to candidates at the General election of December 1910*, PP 1911, LXII, 738–9).
177. See Fraser, 'Labour Party'.
178. *Labour Leader*, 2 February, 23 March, 21 September 1906.
179. See Hutchison, *Political History*, pp. 249–65; Fraser, 'Labour Party', pp. 52–60; Howell, *British Workers*, pp. 37–8.
180. Quoted in Hutchison, *Political History*, p. 255.
181. *Labour Leader*, 2 February 1906.
182. Knox, *Labour Leaders*, pp. 127, 266.
183. Hutchison, *Political History*, p. 255.
184. Ibid., p. 259. See D.M. Tanner, *Political Change and the Labour Party, 1900–1918* (Cambridge, 1990), parts 1 and 2, for the evolution of this 'progressive alliance' in England before 1914.
185. Fraser, 'Labour Party', pp. 42, 45, 55; Hutchison, *Political History*, p. 263.
186. NLS 1974.192, Mr Whitehouse's Parliamentary Record; NLS 6.2057, Robert Smillie Election Address.

187. See vol. 1, ch. 7.
188. Howell, *British Workers*, pp. 38–9.
189. Quoted in Fraser, 'Labour Party', p. 54.
190. *Coatbridge Express*, 7 January 1922, quoted in J. McLean, 'The 1926 general strike in Lanarkshire', *Our History*, 65, 1976, p. 5.
191. *Glasgow Observer*, 26 March, 9 April 1898; Hutchison, *Political History*, p. 260.
192. *Hamilton Advertiser*, 7 April 1894.
193. Hutchison, *Political History*, pp. 258, 260; F.W.S. Craig, *British Parliamentary Elections, 1885–1918* (Dartmouth, 1989), pp. 548–9.
194. Fraser, 'Labour Party', p. 42; *Labour Leader*, 5 January 1906.
195. *Justice*, 13 July 1895; Livingstone, 'Bo'ness', p. 2.
196. *Hamilton Advertiser*, 14 July 1894.
197. R.G. Gregory, *The Miners and British Politics, 1906–1914* (Oxford, 1968), pp. 94, 185.
198. NLS Acc. 4312/19, SMF Conference 1897. For Fife, see NLS PDL 44/14, FKMA Executive Board, 5 July 1900; for Mid and East Lothian, see NLS Acc. 4312/6, MELMA Board, 28 July 1900, 6 July 1901.
199. Gregory, *Miners*, p. 96.
200. J.W. Whitelaw, *Manual of the Qualifications and Registration of Voters in Parliamentary, Municipal and Local Government Elections* (Edinburgh, 1904); N. Blewett, 'The franchise in the United Kingdom, 1885–1918', *Past and Present*, 32, 1965; Tanner, *Political Change*, Appendix 1; M. Dyer, *Capable Citizens and Improvident Democrats: the Scottish electoral system, 1884–1929* (Aberdeen, 1996), pp. 18–21.
201. Whitelaw, *Manual*, p. 38.
202. M. Atkinson, *Local Government in Scotland* (Edinburgh and London, 1904), p. 35.
203. *Report of the Departmental Committee on House Letting in Scotland, vol. II, Minutes of Evidence*, PP 1908, XLVII, 121; J. McCaffrey, 'The Irish vote in Glasgow in the later nineteenth century: a preliminary survey', *Innes Review*, 21, 1970, p. 33; S.H. Turner, *The History of Local Taxation in Scotland* (Edinburgh, 1908), p. 245.
204. Report of the Departmental Committee on House Letting, PP 1908, XLVII, 122. The claim that rates had to be paid personally in Scotland appears to based on the assertion by the Harvard political scientist, A.L. Lowell, that in the Scotland 'the practice of compounding does not exist. The result is that many occupiers are omitted from the parliamentary register every year on account of their failure to pay rates' (A.L. Lowell, *The Government of England, vol. 1*, New York, 1908, pp. 212–13). Cf Atkinson's more qualified assertion

that 'in Scotland the compound householder is rarely found. *With occasional exceptions*, rates are collected directly from the owner and from the occupier ...' (my emphasis. Atkinson, *Local Government*, p. 318). Whitelaw merely states that to succeed in a claim for registration, an occupier had to prove that he had paid poor rates (*Manual*, p. 57). Lowell's authority was followed by Blewett, and in turn by others. However, see the evidence to the Committee on House Letting in Scotland of Keith (qs 4636–7) and Smillie, Gilmour and Murdoch (qs 4795, 4826). It is significant that the latter three witnesses – all miners' leaders – paid little attention to the franchise question; this is unlikely if the large number of miners in employers' houses who paid by compound payment had been disenfranchised.

205. *Return of the number of rated inhabitants in each parish in Scotland whose names were omitted from the Parliamentary Register in respect of non-payment of rates*, PP 1898, LXXX, 755. Dyer suggests that fishermen often deferred paying rates until the end of the summer fishing season and were disenfranchised. This may explain the high rate of disenfranchisement in Wemyss parish (Dyer, *Capable Citizens*, p. 23).

206. *Return of the number of rated inhabitants in each parliamentary division of each county and burgh in Scotland*, PP 1893–94, LXXVII, 1,205.

207. Whitelaw, *Manual*, pp. 39–40. This figure is broadly in line with the £18 per year regarded as the necessary rental in Mid Lanark (Fraser, 'Labour Party', p. 58). For overcrowding, see vol. 1, ch. 5.

208. 'There is not a very large number of our people living in houses of £20', stated Smillie before the Committee on House Letting (PP 1908, XLVII, 127); Dyer, *Capable Citizens*, p. 25.

209. Quoted in Fraser, 'Labour Party', p. 58.

210. Calculated from the *Return showing with regard to each parliamentary constituency in the United Kingdom, the total number, and, as far as possible, the number in each class, of electors in the register now in force*, PP 1911, LXII, 691–3.

211. Fraser, 'Labour Party', p. 58.

212. *Labour Leader*, 27 October 1900.

213. Selkirk, *Life*, pp. 6–7.

214. *Glasgow Herald*, 30 December 1904; *Proceedings of the Seventeenth Annual Conference of the SMF*, 1910, p. 8.

215. *Colliery Guardian*, 17 July 1914.

216. Ibid., 31 July 1914. See also the *Glasgow Herald*'s editorial condemning the miners' 'limitation of individual labour so as to compel ... the employment of a larger number of workers at a higher rate of wages (*Glasgow Herald*, 1 January 1907).

217. NLS Dep. 227/37, LMU Council, 27 December 1919, 3 May, 27 November 1920; Dep. 227/37A, LMU Council, 10, 26 February 1921.

218. NLS Dep. 227/41, LMU Council, 4, 18 February 1925.

219. For examples, see the SMF conference reports in the *Glasgow Herald*, 31 December 1903, 29 December 1906 and the *SMF Conference*, 1910, p. 8.

220. *Glasgow Herald*, 30 December 1908.

221. *SMF Conference*, 1910, p. 8; *Glasgow Herald*, 29 December 1910. A 'half turn' refers here to half the number of hutches claimed by a skilled collier or 'full man', and hence half the normal coal output and so wages.

222. Departmental Committee on House Letting, PP 1908, XLVII, 125; *Census of Scotland, 1911, vol. II*, Table 36.

223. SRO FS 7/94, *Baillieston Miners' Association Rules*.

224. For examples, see *Hamilton Advertiser*, 21 August 1886, 22 September 1894.

225. NLS PDL 44/14, FKMA Executive Board, 8 March, 20 September, 18 October, 14 November 1900.

226. *Glasgow Herald*, 30 December 1904. See also *Justice*, 9 January 1909.

227. *SMF Conference*, 1910, p. 8.

228. NLS Dep. 227/36, LMU Special Meeting, 30 August 1919; Dep. 227/37A, LMU Council, 26 March 1921.

229. NLS Dep. 277/45A, LMU Council, 13 December 1933.

230. *Glasgow Herald*, 31 December 1908. See vol. 1, chs 1 and 3.

231. Ibid., 29 December 1906.

232. NLS Dep. 227/29, LMU Report for year ending 31 December 1906, 'Coal cutting machinery in Lanarkshire mines', pp. 14–19.

233. *Report of the Departmental Committee appointed to consider the working of the existing special rules for the use of electricity in coal mines*, PP 1911, XXXVII, 15, 221.

234. There was a tradition of Scots miners' unions issuing 'diplomas' and certificates to their skilled members from the beginning of the nineteenth century until the early years of the twentieth (Campbell, *Lanarkshire Miners*, pp. 57–8, 61, 68–9, 140; *Glasgow Herald*, 31 December 1903).

235. R. Small, *The Cry from the Mine and the Claim of the Miner*, reprinted in SDF and BSP Pamphlets and Leaflets, Harvester Microfilm, 3, 19. Undated, it was advertised as a 'new pamphlet' in *Justice*, 15 April 1911.

236. Ibid., pp. 10, 11, 14, 15–16.

237. H.W. Macrosty, *The Trust Movement in British Industry: a study of business organisation* (1907), p. 86. For Elliot, see Church, *History*, pp. 57, 444.

238. Small, *Cry of the Mine*, p. 16.
239. Ibid., p. 20.
240. Lee, *Great Journey*, p. 94.
241. The phrase is from Jon Lawrence's article highlighting the continuities with radicalism in the 'socialist revival' of the 1880s (J. Lawrence, 'Popular radicalism and the socialist revival in Britain', *Journal of British Studies*, 31, 1, 1992, p. 86).

CHAPTER THREE

The emergence of the militant miner, 1900–1921

Introduction

In charting the rise of the militant miner, this chapter follows a two part chronology. The years before 1914 saw the spread of syndicalist, dual unionist and industrial unionist ideas in small pockets of the Scottish coalfields. Although the numbers of active adherents of such ideas remained small, they constituted a critical irritant to the existing union leaderships in their demands for greater accountability and the more militant exertion of the industrial strength of the newly consolidated unions. The discontents of wartime – such as increased overcrowding, a rising cost of living and the threat of conscription – provided this nucleus of activists with a new and more substantial platform on which to mount their critique of the older generation of trade union leaders. Their relative but variable success was reflected in the growth of reform committees in the main county unions during and immediately after the war.

In the final section, the extent and bases of support for this reform movement are analysed and the political strategy of the militants evaluated. In the 1980s, a 'new orthodoxy' treated the Clydeside revolutionaries as hopeless, and largely irrelevant, romantics who were marginalised in the inevitable rise of the Labour Party.[1] Although this consensus has recently been effectively challenged by the work of McKinlay and Morris and their colleagues on the ILP, their analysis, like that of the main revisionist Iain Mclean, effectively equates 'Clydeside' with metropolitan Glasgow.[2] Only John Foster, in a further persuasive attack on the orthodoxy, has sought to locate the rising trajectory of class consciousness up to 1919 within a regional framework. This chapter develops these challenges within the wider perspectives of the Scots coalfields.[3]

1900–1914

The significant, if uneven, levels of industrial conflict in the Scots coalfields in the years prior to the First World War were described in chapter three of the companion volume. We need only note here that strikes in Lanarkshire increased sharply after 1910: the LCMA reported 'numerous disputes' in 1911, 'numerous labour troubles' in 1912 and 'numerous disputes and stoppages' in 1914.[4] The disturbances and violent disorders associated with the larger strikes in the period 1893–1921 were also previously reviewed.[5] During the period under discussion here, the national strike of 1912 was accompanied by outbreaks of looting and disorder by strikers. On the Lanarkshire-Midlothian border, a large crowd at Tarbrax attempted 'in a most systematic manner ... to try and destroy the pithead'; hutches and weights were hurled down the shaft and the pithead buildings were set on fire, 'the flames lighting up the countryside for miles around'.[6] In West Fife, crowds of up to 8,000 besieged pits, stoning the police and in one instance smashing a thousand windows in the pithead buildings as well as destroying machinery. When Michael Lee, a miners' agent despatched to the scene to restore calm, described the perpetrators as hooligans, 'great disorder' ensued and he required police protection from the angry crowd. The Chief Constable of Fife learned from an informant 'in close touch with the militant strikers' that the destruction of the pumping apparatus at all the pits in the district was contemplated, which, he suggested, 'clearly shows the malicious and depraved spirit of a large section of the miners'.[7]

The achievement of the statutory eight hour day in coal mines in 1908 and the government's acceptance of the principle of a legal minimum wage during the 1912 strike can be seen as significant fulfilments of the aspirations of bureaucratic reformism. Nevertheless, dissatisfaction at union tactics and the inadequacies of the resulting legislation fuelled oppositional currents within the miners' unions. The decision of the MFGB Executive to call off the strike, although a majority had balloted for its continuation, was a particular source of discontent in Scotland where the question of 'deficient places' (where the hewer was unable for geological reasons to make the nominal county wage) was causing an increasing number of disputes. In the initial strike ballot, five-sixths of the Scottish miners who voted were in favour of a national strike on the issue.[8]

In a second ballot during the strike, there was a higher than average vote to remain out in Scotland. The FKMA, which voted by
9,567 to 3,132 to maintain the strike, 'emphatically protested'
against the MFGB policy of resuming work. Lee was unable to
address a meeting of Fife strikers in the Opera House, Lochgelly, on
the MFGB's decision because of constant heckling; a large section of
his audience were opposed to any return to work and the meeting
broke up in disorder. The normally moderate MELMA also insisted
that the ballot decision be upheld.[9] In the east end of Glasgow, a procession of striking miners carried effigies of coal owners and miners'
leaders bearing the inscription that they would be 'buried via
Parkhead and Shettleston'.[10] The eventual imposition of district
minima rather than a national minimum added further to this sense
of grievance. Despite Smillie's hope that the Minimum Wage Act
would 'largely prevent the employment of unskilled and dangerous
labour underground ... because it could not be got cheaply', the low
level of the award negotiated in Scotland – 5s 10d – 'completely
failed to secure an effective minimum wage'. The disappointment of
the Scots miners at falling short of their desired minimum of six
shillings a day was 'undoubtedly great', observed John Maclean.[11]

These discontents were given an added political dimension by the
agitational activities of the SLP and SDF (later the BSP), as well as
more disparate groups of syndicalists and industrial unionists. The
increasing use of a discourse of direct action by such propagandists
spoke clearly to the already established tradition of the use of
massed physical force. Here we must delineate more fully the industrial politics of these groups before considering their impact in specific localities.

In her analysis of the ILP in Glasgow before 1914, Joan Smith
has argued forcefully that the party's commitment to the Irish and
trade union struggles was as 'profound' as that of 'the avowedly revolutionary' SDF or SLP:

> The lack of a clear distinction between 'revolutionary' and
> 'reformist' before the First World War throughout the British move-
> ment meant that the parliamentary socialism of the ILP leadership
> was not in strong contrast to the Marxist tradition of the SDF and
> the BSP which also accepted a parliamentary road, whereas the anti-
> electoral approach of the SLP and the syndicalists appeared as one-
> sided socialism compared with the ILP's involvement in industry and
> electoralism.[12]

The SDF's 'gradualist Marxism' left little to choose between it and the ILP in electoral practice, while the SDF's internal regime was deeply sectarian and lacking any coherent orientation to trade union activity. Any demarcation between revolutionary and reformist strategies was therefore 'between a tiny group of industrial syndicalists and the rest'.[13] In addition, the standard history of syndicalism in Britain by Holton suggests that the movement was largely absent from the Scots coalfields which were under the 'almost total dominance' of Labour leaders.[14]

Smith helpfully draws our attention to the similarities between the socialist groupings in contrast to the overly formalised distinctions in much labour historiography. In similar vein, and in a companion essay on Glasgow, Alan McKinlay describes the ILP as 'the organisational intersection of a series of progressive social networks':

> The openness of the ILP and the commonalities of thought evident among Clydeside's socialist community make the mutually exclusive categories of 'revisionist' and 'revolutionary' inappropriate to capture the fluidity of left-wing opinion during this period. The Glasgow ILP of the Great War is best understood not as a conventional political party but a loosely organised democratic movement whose primary political terrain was the factory floor and the street corner.[15]

This view of the ILP's 'ideological eclecticism' can be supported by the recollection of a Glasgow ILP member of his branch during the pre-war years: 'its membership represented an extraordinary diversity of ideas. Atheists, Marxists and anarchists rubbed shoulders with Christian socialists like Hardie himself'.[16] Similarly, the young John McArthur from Buckhaven joined the ILP in 1915 but, as there was no branch in the vicinity, he remained a 'paper member'. He subsequently joined the BSP branch in Kirkcaldy, although meetings were concluded by songs from the American syndicalist Industrial Workers of the World (IWW) songbook: 'there appeared to be more meat in these songs than in the socialist hymn book, and we became more susceptible to the stuff contained in the IWW book'. In addition to the BSP's *Call*, he also regularly bought the SLP's *Socialist* as well as the ILP's *Labour Leader* and *Forward*.[17]

Nevertheless, through their understandable failure to accord the SDF/BSP the same detailed attention as the ILP (in a collection concerned with the latter), the arguments of Smith and her fellow contributors tend to obscure significant differences between the industrial politics of the two groups which were of particular relevance to the coalfields. While Smith is correct to indicate the presence of ILP members at all levels in the trade union movement, these members often differentiated their 'trade union' and 'political' activities in the classic labourist bifurcation between the 'two wings of the labour movement'.[18] This certainly appears to have been the case at the level of formal institutions. Records of ILP branches in the Scots coalfields for this period are generally lacking, but those for the Shettleston branch, on the eastern boundary of Glasgow and on the edge of the Lanarkshire coalfield, have survived. During the years from 1905 to 1916 there is no indication that the branch discussed any industrial questions.[19] Nor is there evidence that industrial issues were discussed by the Scottish Advisory Committee of the Labour Party formed in 1915, which Smillie chaired and on to which the two NUSMW political organisers were co-opted.[20] Equally, there was only the most perfunctory discussion of political campaigning during election periods in the minutes of the miners' unions. The miners' leaders awareness of the anti-Labour sentiments of a significant proportion of their members may also have reinforced this division.[21]

Recent scholarship on the SDF suggests it displayed a changing and more complex attitude towards trade unionism than hitherto recognised.[22] The SDF was initially hostile to trade unionism and this antagonism was maintained by elements of its leadership, notably H.M. Hyndman. However, there was increasing coverage of industrial news in *Justice* and a 'centrist' or orthodox Marxist grouping, led by men such as Harry Quelch, viewed unions as useful arenas for propaganda though of limited value in the struggle for socialism. An editorial in *Justice* in 1907 noted that while the SDF had always advocated that every social democrat participate in their union, 'we have persistently preached to the trade unions the growing impotence of the strike and the necessity for them to use political means to secure the objects for which they are organised'.[23] A third, 'pro-union' current emerged which saw unions as a primary focus of activity. This tendency was strengthened by the re-examination of SDF strategy brought about by its poor electoral showing in 1910 and the growth of interest in syndicalist and industrial unionist ideas.

The SLP had been formed as a split from the SDF in 1903 by members influenced by the ideas of Daniel De Leon, the leader of the American SLP. The Marxism of De Leon posited the need both for political activity by the revolutionary party and the simultaneous organisation of new industrial unions. The achievement of a majority vote for revolutionary socialism would signal the dissolution of the political state which would be replaced by a socialist society organised and administered by these industrial unions. The SLP had only a handful of members – no more than 200 by 1910 and perhaps 300 by 1914 – the majority of whom were skilled workers in Glasgow and its environs.[24] In the coalfields, its primary significance at this time was the circulation of industrial unionist propaganda. In 1906, a group of Scottish SLP members had initiated an organisation called the Advocates of Industrial Unionism, intended to parallel the American IWW, which attracted a number of sympathisers from the SDF and ILP. Its first conference in 1907 decided it was inopportune to launch new unions and concentrated on spreading industrial unionist ideas on Clydeside and elsewhere.[25] By 1917, it was claimed that 'large numbers of the pamphlets of the late Daniel De Leon' had been circulated among Lanarkshire miners 'for a considerable time'.[26]

The one area of the Scots coalfields where this tendency had an organisational presence was in East Lothian, where a branch of the SLP existed in Musselburgh from 1905. By 1906, it was organising courses of lectures in De Leonite Marxism for its members and holding more popular propaganda meetings in the locality.[27] Bob Selkirk, who came into contact with this group about that time, recalled its members as being 'sectarian, dogmatic, anti-parliament, anti-trade union, but they were enthusiastic and they formed branches of the Industrial Workers of the World in Ormiston, Wallyford, Dalkeith and Musselburgh'.[28] These branches were short-lived but appear to have stimulated an anti-bureaucratic movement within the moderate ranks of the MELMA. About 1908, Selkirk recalled, a telegram 'came into the hands of the militants' from the MELMA Secretary, Robert Brown, to the manager of Prestonlinks pit, advising him not to give work to Arthur Quinn, who had been victimised in Lanarkshire, 'as he was an agitator'. After the militants launched a campaign against Brown, he responded by holding meetings and touring union branches urging support for his 'sane line of not wanting trouble'. One of Brown's leading antagonists, a 'militant justiceman' at Wallyford called Russell, was ultimately blacklisted by the employers and forced to leave the Lothians.[29]

According to James Macdougall, as a result of their dispute with Brown, the 'syndicalist miners of Wallyford ... broke away from the Mid and East Lothian Miners' Association and successfully maintained their own pit union for years'.[30] There is no corroboration of this and, if such a breakaway took place, it seems ephemeral. In 1910 (the first year for which MELMA records are available for this period) the Wallyford branch was active within the Lothians' union, but, significantly, was a constant source of militant opposition to the leadership. In October, a motion from the branch argued that local efforts against non-unionism be discontinued and that the question should be dealt with by a national coal strike; it was defeated 17–2. A few months later, the branch unsuccessfully sought to have the newly-created post of assistant secretary subject to re-election after one year. The branch's attempts to secure greater accountability of officials met with more success later in 1911 when its motion that all union expenditure be reported monthly was approved, although it failed in an attempt to force Brown to resign as Secretary of the SMF.[31] In 1912, the Wallyford delegate to the MELMA Board was involved in an acrimonious discussion with the union's Vice-President on the expenses of SMF conference delegates during which he accused the Vice-President of representing only himself on the grounds that he was not a pit delegate (being elected by general ballot); as a result, the Wallyford delegate was suspended from the Board. In retaliation, a meeting of Wallyford colliers supported their delegate and threatened to send neither contributions nor a delegate until the branch could scrutinise the SMF balance sheet.[32]

New ideas on the organisation and purpose of trade unionism also came from syndicalist propagandists who emphasised the need to transform the existing organisations into industrial unions through amalgamation. A process of industrial struggle involving violent, direct action would educate workers into the need for a revolutionary general strike to overthrow capitalism and replace it by a society organised on the basis of industrial unions. These ideas were preached by men such as Lawrence Storione, a French-born anarchist who had worked in the Belgian mines and had been involved in several strikes 'where the miners derailed engines and severed the cage ropes and flung cages down the pit'.[33] His son was appropriately called 'Germinal'. Forced to leave Belgium, he had arrived in Muirkirk in Ayrshire in 1897, before moving to Hamilton where he married. He later settled in Fife in 1908, working as a miner in Lumphinnans until incapacitated by an accident in 1917. He soon established an Anarchist-Communist League in Cowdenbeath which ran a bookshop, while his eldest daughter organised a Proletarian Sunday School for local children.[34].

A further source of syndicalist ideas came from South Wales. The bitter Cambrian Combine dispute of 1910–11 witnessed the involvement of a cohort of Marxist, industrial unionist and syndicalist miners who had been educated at Ruskin College and the Central Labour College and who had created the Unofficial Reform Committee (URC) to campaign for the reorganisation of the South Wales Miners' Federation. The leaders of the Cambrian Strike Committee were 'almost to a man' members of the URC.[35] Maclean had links with these militants and in 1911 conducted a week's propaganda tour in South Wales during the dispute, 'at the invitation of the strikers'.[36] During the strike, 'missionaries' were despatched to other British coalfields to agitate for support and Macdougall later claimed that he had been 'indoctrinated' in the URC's ideas by one of its founders, 'Jack Hay', when he was in Fife in 1910. This was most probably, W.F. Hay, a one-time Rhondda miner, a member of the Industrial Syndicalist League, and a joint author of the URC's famous pamphlet, *The Miners' Next Step*.[37]

In July 1912, Hay was among the speakers at a demonstration in Hamilton organised by a 'Miners' Indignation and Reform Committee' as the culmination of a series of campaigning meetings in the district. The chairman stated that the purpose of the meeting was to demand that the rules of the LMU be reconstituted 'in order that the miners of the county might have more say in their own affairs', while James Gray of Lanarkshire asserted that 'there was not a more autocratic organisation' than the LMU: 'democracy was entirely absent in its administration'. A series of resolutions were unanimously approved, demanding reconstruction 'on real, true and unselfish principles', the resignation and re-election of all agents who would not be permitted to sit on the union Executive, and condemning the actions of the leaders over the Minimum Wage Bill.[38]

A third strand of industrial unionist ideas came from the move-

ment of miners between Scotland and the United States and
Canada. For example, Johnny O'Neil, a Buckhaven militant and
member of the Kirkcaldy BSP branch, originally came from
Lanarkshire but had worked in the United States; Bob Lamb,
Chairman of the branch, was a miner from Gallatown who had
worked for two years in the United States before returning to Fife
in 1910.[39] Men like these had experience of the industrial unions
there, such as the United Mine Workers of America (UMWA) and
the IWW. Robert Small, the Lanarkshire miners' agent and BSP
member, drew on the practice of the Western Federation of Miners
(a founding constituent of the IWW) in his pamphlet, *The Cry of
the Mine*.[40] One of Maclean's 'principal assistants' in his propaganda during the war was George Pettigrew, a former UMWA
organiser who played a leading role in the lengthy miners' strike on
Vancouver Island from 1912 to 1914.[41]

By the formation of the BSP in 1911, there was a broadly 'syndicalist wing' within the party. This ranged from uncompromising
syndicalists to those who emphasised the importance of industrial
unionism but did not reject political activity.[42] In 1912, an article in
Justice exemplified the central tenet of the latter group: 'Militant
industrial action by the workers operating in the labour market, and
militant political action by the workers operating through the ballot
box are as necessary to each other as are the two blades of a pair of
scissors.'[43] In Scotland, the leading advocates of such a strategy
were Maclean and Macdougall. After visiting Belfast during the
1907 dock strike, Maclean had 'made more space in his Marxism to
accommodate the reality of industrial militancy than most of his
social democratic contemporaries'.[44] By 1911, in an evaluation of
the unsuccessful strike at the Singer Sewing Machine Company at
Clydebank where the SLP organised a branch of the Industrial
Workers of Great Britain (IWGB), Maclean emphasised that 'all
social democrats are industrial unionists':

> We differ from others in that we insist that real industrial organisa-
> tion must arise out of the fusion and federation of already existing
> unions ... And furthermore we rightly insist that economic organisa-
> tion is subsidiary to political organisation ... [45]

In line with this analysis, a recurring theme in Maclean's propaganda
was his urging the formation of 'one miners' union for Britain, ready
to strike a blow at any time and with paralysing suddenness, and the

best way to get this one union is to force the officials of the various unions to fuse their respective toy organisations'.[46]

Maclean was thus a Marxist and industrial unionist but not a syndicalist, and he did not support the Miners' Indignation and Reform Committee demonstration in 1912. While respecting 'the honest efforts' of W.H. Hay, whom he characterised as a 'sincere and vigorous syndicalist', Maclean complained that James Gray, the son of a Lanarkshire activist formerly associated with Chisholm Robertson, was 'not a syndicalist, and knows not a tittle about Marx or Marxism. His whole rant is bitter personal attacks on Smillie and the other officials and the desire for a new union.' Instead, Maclean organised a BSP rally in Carluke on the same day as the Hamilton demonstration, with the aim of forcing on the LMU 'a policy of revolutionary socialism instead of the timid Labourism of today'.[47]

Maclean's commitment to reforming the existing unions and his receptive audience among sections of the Lanarkshire miners was evidenced in 1913 at Coalburn. A secession from the LMU was threatened that year after those directors of the Coalburn Cooperative Society who were miners came into conflict with the striking employees of the society. The National Union of Distributive and Allied Workers (NUDAW), to which the employees belonged, accused the directors of blacklegging and demanded that the LMU expel them (which would have led to their exclusion from the mines). Maclean and Macdougall, who had campaigned in the district the previous year, attended a mass meeting of 2,000 miners where Maclean defended the directors against Smillie, who upheld the action of the LMU Executive in acceding to the request of the NUDAW officials. Macdougall recalled:

> When Maclean explained that this was not an ordinary strike, namely a conflict between capital and labour but internecine strife between two sections of the working class itself, and therefore was not to be judged by ordinary rules, there was an immense shout of applause from the crowd ... Had Maclean given his assent the Coalburn miners would there and then have separated from the Lanarkshire Union, formed a definitely socialist miners' union, and appointed Macdougall as their secretary.[48]

Macdougall may have been exaggerating in this assessment, although the terse minutes of the LMU Executive provide some support for his account. In August, the LMU Secretary was empowered to suspend the seventeen cooperative members accused of blacklegging, and also the entire Auchenbegg branch to which they belonged if it refused to accept the Executive's ruling. The branch's refusal and subsequent suspension led it to picket out the entire district. It was reported that an unofficial or 'informal' meeting of the district's miners had been addressed by Maclean and Macdougall but that the following week its decisions had been rescinded after Smillie and David Gilmour, the LMU Secretary, had addressed the men. However, the suspension of the cooperative directors was subsequently lifted.[49] What is clear is that Maclean and Macdougall, to the irritation of the LMU officials, who described them as 'outside speakers', were able to provide leadership in the district against the union Executive. We can also note that upon Maclean's release from prison in 1915 after serving his first sentence for anti-war speeches, a large delegation of Coalburn miners struck work, entrained for Glasgow and marched through the city streets – 'in their working garb with their lamps lit' – to Maclean's house to welcome him home.[50]

A variety of competing and overlapping ideas on industrial unionism, stemming from a number of sources, were in circulation among a minority of trade union activists in the Scots coalfields before the outbreak of war. This suggests greater complexity in terms of ideology and of practice than can be accommodated by a simple demarcation between 'syndicalists and the rest'. Rather, it may be more helpful to conceive of a spectrum of connected networks, including dual unionists, syndicalists, industrial unionists, members of the SLP, BSP and ILP, to the polar points of which the labels 'revolutionary' and 'reformist' still had some adhesion.

1914–21

The war transformed the Scottish coal industry and the politics of a significant section of the miners. The most immediate problem for the government was the number of miners who volunteered for the armed forces. By 1915, while 17 per cent of Britain's miners had enrolled, the figure for Scotland was 21.3 per cent. This concealed a range of 30.9 per cent in East Lothian, 27.1 in Midlothian, 24.4 in Fife, 19.3 in Lanarkshire and 16.6 in Ayrshire.[51] The higher percentage in the eastern coalfields was partly due to the collapse of the European and Baltic export markets; Scotland's martial tradition may have been a further ancillary factor. Whatever the reasons, over one fifth of Scotland's miners – and in Fife and the Lothians a quarter or more – joined the military within the first year of the war.

This caused a major manpower problem for the government, since the response of substitution and dilution employed in other industries was not available in mining. As Sir Richard Redmayne, the Coal Controller and historian of the industry during the war noted: 'as far as coal hewers are concerned, the occupation is one requiring experience and skill which can only be acquired by actual work at the face, for which untrained men would not, even had they been available, have been suitable'.[52] Accordingly, by November 1915 mining was defined as a reserved occupation. There was clearly some movement of adult labour into the less skilled mining occupations, as well as continued recruitment of school-leavers: by 1917, the reduction of mining manpower in Scotland compared with 1913 was only 7.9 per cent.[53] One may speculate that the motivation of many of the men who took up mining work was to avoid military service and this should be borne in mind when resistance to conscription is later considered.

Local tribunals were set up in the coalfields, consisting of the Inspector of Mines plus representatives of the employers and unions, to grant exemptions and to ascertain which workmen might be spared from the pits. After the introduction of conscription in 1916, these tribunals became Colliery Recruiting Courts under the Military Service Act; there were four courts covering Scotland, on each of which sat two union officials.[54] Although miners had been exempted from conscription in 1916, this was later removed and, in January 1917, the War Office initiated a 'comb-out' of the unskilled and those who had entered the mines since the outbreak of war. That month, the LMU Chairman complained the military authorities, accompanied by the Mines' Inspectors and doctors, were taking 'many properly exempted men':

> The treatment was scandalous, in many cases calling men out of the mine, at any time and in any condition, withdrawing the exemption papers and substituting an enlistment form in its place. Also the arbitrary manner in which some managers were defining absenteeism in the case of many workmen.[55]

In the summer of 1917, a further 21,000 men were drawn by ballot from single miners aged between 18 and 25 years, 2,600 coming from Scotland; in January 1918 the War Office announced that a further 50,000 miners would be conscripted.[56]

As was the case across Europe, the war presented the socialists in the leadership of the Scots miners' unions with an enormous political dilemma. The majority of the Scots miners' leaders supported the war effort including a number who were at least nominal members of the ILP and the BSP. John Robertson, whose four sons enlisted in the army, adopted a pro-war position and launched a campaign to supply enlisted miners with tobacco, 'one of the many patriotic causes' which led to the award of an MBE.[57] Robertson was a member of the Colliery Recruiting Court covering Lanarkshire, as was the strongly pro-war Gilmour. Smillie was an exception to this trend and he found himself 'in a very small minority' on the issue in the MFGB and NUSMW executives.[58] Smillie's adherence to the pacifist principles of the ILP – he was President of the National Council Against Conscription – and his desire for peace by negotiation did not, however, lead to a sharp break with his colleagues. As Royden Harrison observes,

> it is difficult to find examples of Smillie talking out against the war or threatening to do anything to stop it ... He showed courage, but it was the courage of a stubborn bargainer who was not going to allow himself to be deflected by chauvinistic appeals, rather than the courage of a strenuous and dedicated political fighter.[59]

While he refused to participate in the machinery of recruitment, he was closely involved in the maintenance of coal output: he represented the MFGB on the tri-partite Coal Trade Organisation Committee in 1915. Smillie's claim at the MFGB conference in 1918 that divisions over the war had not been allowed 'to interfere with our carrying on the business of the Executive Committee of this Federation in a friendly spirit' appears largely accurate.[60] Such differences were submerged in a concern to defend miners' trade union interests.

Divisions over the war were also apparent within the wider mining workforce. At a meeting in Blantyre over food prices in 1917, Robertson emphasised they were not there 'to discuss the rights and wrongs of the war':

> There were many in that meeting who were favourable to an imme-
> diate peace by negotiation. There were others who believed that
> peace ought not to be concluded until the Central Powers were
> beaten into submission. They met on neutral ground to protest
> against profiteering in the food supply.[61]

Such conflicting views were evidenced when Kazis Yanga, a
Lithuanian miner employed at Orbiston Colliery, Bellshill, made
statements in 1918 'likely to cause disaffection to His Majesty and
to prejudice the recruiting and discipline of HM forces'; he was not
only convicted and fined £5 at Hamilton Sheriff Court, he was dismissed from the colliery 'at the request of the men'.[62] At a meeting
of miners employed at Coltness Collieries, Gilmour expressed his
hope 'that the Germans would be made to pay in full for the hor-
rors they had perpetrated on mankind'; the meeting unanimously
approved his views.[63]

These incidents can be contrasted with the 'socialist village' of
Douglas Water where there was a vigorous ILP branch and whose
miners were strongly anti-militarist. James Welsh described how
sixty police made a pre-dawn raid on the village in July 1918.
Accompanied by the local constable, they went along the miners'
rows:

> They came for 26 of our young miners who had been turned down
> by the Tribunals. Of these they secured 11, two of whom were carried
> to the motors from sick beds. The village turned out en masse and
> men, women and children told the bluecoats something to their
> advantage. A cordon of police was drawn across the road near the
> motor transport and the lads' relations were not allowed near them.
> The 'Red Flag' was sung by the COs [conscientious objectors] and
> the crowd, and in the grey dawn the spectacle was so impressive and
> inspiring that it will be imprinted indelibly in the minds of all in
> the village. We have to thank the militarists for thus converting the
> remaining 25 per cent of the population of Douglas Water to
> socialism.[64]

Later that day, all the miners of the district stopped work in protest.
This was merely the latest strike in a series of unofficial disputes in
the Douglas and Coalburn districts. The LCMA had complained in
March that 'frequent idle days were being taken at Bellfield and
other collieries in the Coalburn district over trivial matters, and that
the men appeared to be under no restraint'. In June, the Coal

Controller complained that 'a number of the younger men' at Auchlochan Colliery, Coalburn, had adopted a four day week 'without the sanction of either the local or county executive'; such a restriction policy may have been motivated by a desire to maintain the demand for manpower and the Controller threatened to cancel the exemption certificates of such workers.[65] Even those miners exempt from conscription were likely to resent the increasing police surveillance of their daily lives after 1916; for example, police would raid Lanarkshire dance halls 'searching for shirkers' and force young men to show their exemption papers.[66]

Resistance to conscription was amplified because the initial high rate of enlistment among the Scots miners meant that, as the war progressed, every mining village had experienced the death of some of its young men and had heard the harrowing experiences of survivors. For example, Rab Smith, a young Lumphinnans miner, recalled his arrival in Arras in 1918:

> Well, the furst thing, when ah was in tha' place ge'in' drilled afore we went intae the front, there was a fella, 'n' ah can picture him yet, he put the rifle in between his feet ... 'n' put the muzzle in his mouth 'n' pulled the trigger, right up. 'N' the sergeant tha' was givin' us drill tha' day he says, 'Oh, tha's nothin ... Ye'll see a lot mair than tha' yet, a helluva lot mair than tha'.[67]

As a result of such accounts, some miners and their families colluded in hiding deserters from arrest. Hugh Duffy, from Blantyre, recalled that his miner father had volunteered for military service in 1915. After returning home on leave in 1917, he deserted and went to the Bannockburn district:

> That was to avoid the police. He worked in Fallin Pit. I think there was some enquiries made, which was covered up by the neebours: they had wonderful people that lived at Fallin. And there was a cover-up at Blantyre as well: they would say no to everything here.[68]

Tony Brown, from the mining village of Auchentibber near Blantyre, remembered a neighbour who had deserted while on leave in the village:

> He was a married man. He lived in the glen at Auchentibber, just up on the tap side o' the rows. It was thick wi' sma' trees. He had a hut and he lived in the hut. He was there for aboot eichteen month. Ma

mother and the man's wife used tae gie us soup for him and we used tae cairry his soup up in a can, and his tea ... They kep' him goin' wi' cigarettes. And we used tae watch for the polis. There were two polis, well, they used tae sift aboot and sift aboot but he was aye on his gaird. The miners kept the secret, naebody betrayed him ... He used tae come tae his ain hoose if it were a cauld night. And that's when they got him ... near the end o' the war.[69]

In addition to the resentment of conscription by some miners, the war generated more widespread grievances. Housing conditions in the Scots coalfields were often notoriously bad.[70] The expansion of the steel and munitions industries during the war in the central Clyde valley further exacerbated this problem. But the 'chief and fundamental cause of the existing unrest', noted the Commission of Inquiry into Industrial Unrest in 1917, was the increased cost of living.[71] In August 1917, the cost of living index stood at 80 per cent above the figure at the outbreak of war, whereas Scottish miners' wages had been advanced by only 43 per cent. This factor (coupled with some workers being brought within the threshold of income tax) was to be a continuing source of grievance even after the war and was a recurring theme in military intelligence reports on the attitudes of the local population into 1919.[72] This rise in the cost of living may partly explain the increase in the strike rate from 1917 onwards, particularly in the West Central field.[73] By 1918, the LMCA complained of 'a considerable number of disputes and strikes', and the amount paid in strike compensation to its affiliates increased from £2,000 in 1917 to £7,000 in 1918.[74] The number of stoppages in Lanarkshire was of particular concern to the Coal Controller, who wrote to the LMU on several occasions in 1918.[75]

How did the socialist political parties fare during the war and how did their activists in the coalfields address these burgeoning grievances? In the early years of the war, patriotic fervour and state repression adversely affected the support for socialist groupings. The affiliation fees paid by the Scottish division of the ILP indicated a drop in affiliated membership from 2,820 in 1913–14 to 2,100 in 1914–15.[76] Nevertheless, before the end of the war, the ILP in Scotland enjoyed a marked revival, its membership tripling between early 1917 and September 1918 to over 9,000. Similar expansion was not witnessed elsewhere in Britain, and much of the increase must have come from workers in reserved occupations such as mining, and from women.[77] Certainly many of the new ILP branches established in 1917–18 were in mining areas: 9 in Ayrshire, 4 in Mid and East Lothian, 5 in Fife, at Airdrie and Baillieston in the Glasgow ILP Federation, 13 elsewhere in Lanarkshire, 10 in Stirlingshire and 8 in West Lothian.[78] This new influx also moved the Scottish ILP leftwards: in defiance of its leadership, the Scottish ILP voted for affiliation to the Communist Third International in 1919 and 1920.[79]

As the socialist organisation with the largest number of branches, the ILP was well placed to channel rising discontent over wartime conditions. The ILP's moral opposition to the war and its militant resistance to conscription helped extend its pre-war base. For example, an ILP peace demonstration at Motherwell Cross in April 1916 attracted nearly 300 people, after ILP sympathisers had supported conscientious objectors, including young miners, who appeared before the local tribunal the previous month by singing the 'Red Flag'.[80]

Housing reform was also vigorously pursued by the ILP and the NUSMW leadership. The Glasgow rent strikes of 1915, generally regarded as having contributed to the ILP's political dominance of the city, had relevance also to miners living in the east end. The proposed eviction of the family of an enlisted Shettleston miner in June 1915 attracted the denunciation of John Wheatley who organised a meeting of 3,000–4,000 people, mainly women, outside the family's house: at the end of the meeting 500 women volunteered at the local ILP rooms as pickets, and ultimately the eviction proceedings were abandoned.[81] There were also reports of rent strikes in a number of mining localities in 1915 in which ILP participation was likely: at Cambuslang, Hamilton, West Calder, Fife and Mid-Lanark.[82] At Dreghorn, the North Ayrshire Labour Party voiced its concern at the threat of 'serious trouble' over the eviction of two miners from company houses, and William Baird and Company subsequently reconsidered their action.[83] The Royal Commission on the Housing of the Industrial Population of Scotland, set up after pressure from the SMF and on which Gilmour sat as a member, reported in 1917 with detailed recommendations for the improvement of miners' houses. The following year, the LMU protested to the War cabinet 'against the delay in providing houses for the working class' and at the high rents of houses built at the instigation of the Ministry of Munitions.[84] The Scottish Labour Housing Association, which was established to campaign on the issue, had John Wheatley as its

President and Joseph Sullivan, President of both the LMU and NUSMW, as Vice-President. Its call for a 24 hour strike against rent increases in 1920 was supported by the LMU. There were also rent strikes in Hamilton, Burnbank, Motherwell, and at Craigneuk, where it was reported that not a single person had paid the increase. In Motherwell, the ILP played a prominent role in the local Rent Strike Committee.[85]

The ideological eclecticism and organisational flexibility of the ILP allowed it to attract a significant number of industrial militants during the expansion from 1917. It was claimed by the LCMA that the ILP 'were particularly strong' in Coalburn 'and were causing a considerable amount of idle time'. The willingness of sections of the miners to exploit their enhanced bargaining position by the end of the war can be detected in the confident tone of a letter from the Secretary of the Coalburn LMU district to Caprington and Auchlochan Collieries: in the event of any underground emergency during a miners' idle day, it stated, 'application must be made to the pit representative by the oversman, otherwise idle time will assuredly accrue'.[86] Many meetings addressed by Maclean in the coalfields in 1918–19 were often organised under the auspices of ILP branches: for example, at Cambuslang, Harthill and Shettleston in February 1918. At the last meeting, he allegedly advised his audience 'to seize the coal mines and the ships and stores'.[87] When the ILP Scottish Division held a conference in January 1918, a motion from the Wishaw branch supporting the propagation of industrial unionism led to a heated debate but was eventually carried.[88]

The BSP fared less well organisationally during the war, in part because of the renewed vitality of a Marxist wing in the ILP. What little research has been carried out on the BSP in Scotland suggests a number of branches in Clydeside were only intermittently active during the war.[89] The party also suffered internal division. Tensions between the BSP leadership and the anti-militarist faction, of which Maclean was the best known member, became increasingly vituperative after 1914 and culminated in the 'old guard' under Hyndman leaving to form the National Socialist Party.[90] The BSP's involvement in the formation of the Communist Party of Great Britain (CPGB) in 1920 led to a further split between the majority and Maclean and his supporters to which we return in the following chapter.

In contrast to the pacifism of many in the ILP, Maclean came closest to the position of 'revolutionary defeatism' of the Russian Bolsheviks, advocating that resistance to the war effort should be transformed into a revolutionary struggle against British capitalism. Maclean was well informed on the Bolshevik attitude to the war from his Russian comrade, Peter Petroff, who was appointed BSP Political Organiser in Glasgow in 1915. A further link with the Bolsheviks was via Lanarkshire's Lithuanian community.[91] Vincas Mickevicius-Kapsukas, the leader of the radical wing of the Lithuanian Social Democratic Party, a friend of Lenin and the President of the Lithuanian Soviet Republic in 1918, lived in Bellshill during 1915–16, where he gave *Rankpelnis*, the party journal, an internationalist, anti-war position; his successor as editor translated the Bolshevik Alexandra Kollontai's pamphlet, *Who needs war?*[92] In 1917, the Glasgow BSP and the Glasgow branch of the Lithuanian Socialist Federation of Great Britain merged to form an internationalist grouping.[93] Scottish military intelligence sources expressed recurring concern at 'the presence of a strong alien element among the miners of Lanarkshire in particular, and to whom these agitators and their Bolshevik associations appeal ...'.[94]

In comparison with the ILP, the BSP's Scottish leaders were subject to greater persecution by the state for their anti-war stance and industrial agitation: Petroff's internment in 1916 and subsequent deportation, and Macdougall's and, especially, Maclean's spells in prison did not assist in strengthening the organisation. Nevertheless, military intelligence sources – whose judgements were generally more cautious and judicious than the better known assessments of Basil Thompson's Directorate of Intelligence at the Home Office – were in little doubt that Maclean and Macdougall were the individuals who represented the greatest threat to political stability in central Scotland.[95] In 1918, Scottish Command's assessment of the leading 'Red Clydeside' agitators – which included Arthur MacManus, David Kirkwood and Willie Gallacher – concluded that 'the most virulent and noticeable are John Maclean and J.D. Macdougall'.[96] Macdougall was regarded as an even 'more dangerous man than Maclean, and though disapproved of by the more responsible section of the Miners' Agents, has a bad influence among the Lanarkshire miners'; he was a 'clever speaker and may yet cause trouble among the more irresponsible and ignorant element in the community to which he addresses himself'.[97]

Such prescient evaluations are to anticipate our narrative, however. In the early years of the war, Maclean and Macdougall appear to have concentrated their energies in the rents and munitions struggles in Glasgow. Maclean held several meetings in the Lanarkshire mining areas in January 1916 aimed at 'arousing the miners to resist conscription', but little came of them.[98] Ironically, it was Macdougall's imprisonment in 1916 which redirected his efforts towards the miners. 'From the pressure of the Iron Heel', he suffered a 'severe nervous breakdown' before his release in February 1917.[99] On the advice of Maclean, he intended to refrain from politics until his health improved. He found work as a pithead labourer at Bardykes Colliery in Blantyre, where he lived with George Russell, a 30 year old miner and member of Maclean's Glasgow economics classes.[100] As a new wave of agitation swept through the Lanarkshire coalfield, he quickly resumed his political activities among the miners.

George Pollock of the Glasgow BSP had recently taught an economics class in south Lanarkshire, continuing the previous propaganda work in the area by Maclean and Macdougall, and the fruits of this agitation were seen in the formation of a South Lanark Miners' Reform Committee by July 1917. According to Maclean, this body represented 'a link up of all the socialist forces' in the area. The Secretary of this committee was James Hogg, Coalburn delegate to the LMU Council, and the committee succeeded in getting its recommendation to resist conscription adopted by that branch in early August.[101] Some ten days later, a meeting of 3,000 miners in Blantyre was organised by 'a group of rank and file miners'; after speeches by Macdougall and Russell among others, it was unanimously decided to follow the lead of the Coalburn district.[102] Later that month, these two groups came together when about a hundred miners met in Hamilton to form the Lanarkshire Miners' Reform Committee. This meeting, claimed Macdougall, was a result of dissatisfaction with the 'undemocratic methods' of the LMU and 'the propaganda of the ILP and BSP branches in the coalfield'. It represented a broad alliance of socialists and industrial unionists, but its policies were very much derived from the teaching of Maclean.[103]

The committee's four page manifesto, of which 50,000 were circulated, included a repudiation of nationalisation and the demand for 'an industrial democracy in which the means of production shall be owned by the community and largely controlled by the workers

...'; the union 'to be based on the principle of class struggle'; the abandonment of the conciliation board agreements and procedures: 'leave the striking arm free to deliver a swinging blow whenever an opportunity is given!'; the annual election of agents and officials who would attend the Executive Committee in a purely consultative capacity; the establishment of pit committees to handle local disputes; the organisation of all men and women working in the coal industry within one union; and that the union purchase a building 'for the purpose of educating trade unionists in Social Science'.[104]

This last point indicates the influence of Maclean and Macdougall. Over the winter of 1917–18, Maclean taught weekly classes in the Fife coalfield at Leven, Kirkcaldy, Cowdenbeath and Bowhill: in the last village, at least a hundred miners were enrolled. Macdougall taught classes in Lanarkshire at Bargeddie, near Baillieston, Blantyre, Lesmahagow, Kirkmuirhill, Hamilton and Motherwell. In addition, George Russell, Treasurer of the Lanarkshire Reform Committee, taught a course on industrial history in Hamilton, and James Ferguson, a fellow committee member, was tutor of a course in industrial history at Blantyre.[105]

The Lanarkshire Reform Committee, under the guidance of such teachers and their students, drew upon Marxism to make sense of the changes taking place within their industry and union. The committee's manifesto noted changes in technology and the growing industrial concentration within the Scots coalfields:

> ... the constant rivalry between the employers, a continual struggle to reduce the time taken to produce coal in order to lower its price. This is accomplished by the introduction of new machinery ... when one employer lays down a new coal washing plant, or introduces coal-cutting machinery or conveyor pans ... all have to follow suit ... The centralisation of control has, however, reached a far higher degree of control than is apparent on the surface. These seemingly independent companies are in reality related to one another by strong though hidden chains of connection.

It went on to argue that while the formation of the LMU had been a 'progressive step' in the 1890s, 'nothing can cope with the highly trustified condition of the British mining industry' but an amalgamation of all existing unions into one industrial union.

At least twenty four branches of the LMU affiliated to the committee (out of a total of 127) and it was claimed that active minorities existed in the majority of branches; an unofficial Blantyre District Committee also coordinated policy between colliery branches in that area. Neither of these bodies was recognised by the LMU. By October 1917, a Fife Miners' Reform Committee had been formed and a similar body was established in the Lothians in early 1919; there is also evidence of reform activity in Ayrshire.[106] One former member recalled the Fife committee as being 'a fairly loose organisation' of activists which met monthly to coordinate support for militant policies among the FKCMA branches.[107] In Lanarkshire, the committee played a more interventionist role in campaigns against rising food prices and conscription.

In June 1917, Manus Duddy, LMU Council delegate from Blantyre, Secretary of the unofficial Blantyre District Committee and a prominent member of the Reform Committee, had won the Council's support for a one day strike against food profiteering.[108] In August, 50,000 Lanarkshire miners struck work and attended thirteen mass meetings which condemned the high cost of provisions. Because of its political aim, the strike was, claimed Maclean with some exaggeration, 'the most important in the whole history of the working class in Scotland'.[109] The following year, the Reform Committee organised unofficial strikes in the Blantyre district demanding 'a more equitable distribution of the food supplies'; unofficial strikes also took place on this issue in the Blackridge district of West Lothian where a reform committee was being formed.[110]

At the August mass meetings at Blantyre and Coalburn, several thousand miners had also passed resolutions threatening strike action against the government's withdrawal of the exemption from conscription of younger miners.[111] In January 1918, the Coalburn branch reiterated its 'down tool' policy against the Government's proposals to conscript a further 50,000 men from the mines, and demanded that the government enter peace negotiations at the invitation of the Russian government as well as conscript wealth to make adequate provision for the war's victims.[112] Meetings in Shettleston and at Dunfermline against the Manpower Bill were attended by 1,000 and 700 young miners respectively; in Hamilton, 3,000 young mineworkers demonstrated their opposition outside the LMU offices, 'where the socialists harangued the crowd'.[113] In February, a ballot of LMU members on the manpower proposals showed a large majority against assisting the government: 15,283 to

10,866. It was probable, concluded Scottish Command's intelligence evaluation of the vote, 'that many of these miners have been influenced by James Macdougall who has recently been very active in that part of the country'.[114]

Nationally, however, there was confusion on the question: a majority of MFGB votes were cast against such assistance but, anomalously, a majority vote favoured branch committees assisting in the selection of men.[115] At a subsequent conference of LMU branches, 23 delegates voted for resistance to the manpower proposals by strike action while 68 were in favour of the union participating in their local implementation. Accordingly, union committees of 'middle aged or elderly miners' were established 'at the vast majority of collieries' to select by ballot the five and half thousand miners aged between 18 and 31 who were required as the coalfield's allocation. Smillie admitted to a meeting of Coalburn, Douglas and Lesmahagow miners that 'this was not a popular job', but nevertheless preferable to allowing the military authorities to select the men.[116]

The hostility of a significant proportion of the Lanarkshire miners to the war effort was also evidenced by their attitude to the long-serving LMU Secretary, David Gilmour, taking up a post on the government's Labour Advisory Committee. Gilmour claimed that his appointment had been approved by the executive committees of the NUSMW and the LMU, and the LMU Council. When the move was challenged at a subsequent Council meeting, it was agreed by 63 votes to 23 that the appointment should stand; in a further vote at the next meeting, a larger minority, 35 branches, opposed him. A membership ballot was agreed upon and voted narrowly, by 17,099 to 16,270, that he should give up the post. When he refused, he was forced to resign his union position, claiming that he was the victim of 'Bolsheviks'. At a meeting in Burnbank, Gilmour insisted these elements had opposed him since the dispute at the Coalburn Cooperative Society and he denied 'the right of men like Maclean and Macdougall ... to interfere with the internal affairs of the Lanarkshire Miners' Association [sic]. (Cries of "Yes!" and "No!")'.[117]

Similar divisions were evidenced at the height of the Reform Committee's activities in the early months of 1919. In mid-January, 2,000 miners in the Holytown district struck unofficially on a Friday over the alleged victimisation and eviction of William Hughes, a popular under-manager who was a prominent ILP member associated with the Reform Committee. After being addressed by Hughes and Macdougall, the men agreed to remain out.[118] On the following Monday, the strike was joined by a further 4,000 miners in Bellshill and Rosehall. A mass meeting of the strikers refused to accept guarantees from an LMU agent that no action would be taken against Hughes in the meantime, and voted to continue the strike. Members of the Bellshill branch refused to accept this decision and summoned John Robertson, NUSMW Vice-President, to address them later in the day. Although subject to frequent interruption, Robertson pleaded with the strikers to abide by constitutional methods of negotiation, which if necessary could involve 'the miners of all Britain (Loud cheering)', and reiterated that sufficient guarantees had been given ('Applause and cries of "No!"'). Subsequently a majority voted to return.[119]

At the end of January, against the background of a general strike of shipbuilding and engineering workers in central Scotland for a forty hour week and the MFGB demanding that the government introduce a thirty hour week, full nationalisation of the mines and standard wages for demobilised miners until they were re-employed, a widespread unofficial strike by Fife miners' broke out over surface workers' hours.[120] The Fife Reform Committee broadened it into a demand for the Miners' Federation claim. The news from Fife was sufficient for the Lanarkshire committee to initiate an unofficial strike in support of the MFGB's demands. Several collieries in Lanarkshire struck as the NUSMW Executive discussed the situation. The Executive urged all miners to remain at work while negotiations continued between the MFGB and the government and condemned the unauthorised pickets and unconstitutional stoppages which, it claimed, were being 'engineered by irresponsible persons outside the miners and against the express decisions of county conferences of delegates'.[121] This appeal had little effect and the following day all the collieries in the Shotts, Cambuslang, Coalburn, Blantyre and Burnbank districts, as well as some in Uddingston and Hamilton, struck work. In Blantyre, a ballot of the district's miners voted 650 to 330 in favour of the action. Mass pickets brought out a number of pits which had not responded to the committee's strike call in the Hamilton and Holytown districts. According to the *Hamilton Advertiser*, it was alleged that 'in some cases the picketing amounted practically to terrorism'.[122] The events which took place at Hamilton Palace

Colliery on the night of 30–31 January suggested that this was no exaggeration.

Although the colliery was the third largest in Lanarkshire and employed a number of militant Lithuanians, it had an anti-union and paternalistic management, enjoyed relatively good wages and had a high percentage of its workers living in colliery housing in the adjacent village of Bothwellhaugh where there was soon to be a flourishing Orange lodge.[123] At 4.30am on 30 January, the colliery was stopped by 'a massed picket' which was addressed by Macdougall. During that day, all the LMU branches in the Bellshill district met and agreed not to associate themselves with the strike movement; they recommended that their members proceed past any pickets and a meeting of the Hamilton Palace miners agreed to follow this advice.[124]

That evening, a crowd of 50 to 80 'mostly young men' assembled at Tollcross in the east end of Glasgow. According to one police witness, their leader was Charles Hendren, an older miner from Parkhead. Shortly after midnight, the commands 'Fall in!', 'Form fours!', 'March!' were given and the group marched via Cambuslang to the ILP Hall in Blantyre which they reached at 2.15am; by then one of the crowd was playing a melodeon and many carried sticks. They were greeted by a large number of miners already in the hall with 'a ringing cheer'. About 200 men issued forth an hour later and on reaching Craighead Colliery, Blantyre, broke into the lamp cabin and damaged some lamps and the oil tank.[125]

The crowd proceeded to Hamilton Palace Colliery, marching along the rows there, 'crying to inmates to keep indoors as there was to be no work, and they would make sure there would be no work today. They were shouting and blaspheming.'[126] At the pithead, they found seven fireman ready to descend the shaft for their early morning inspection. One later testified that the crowd shouted: 'You –, if you go down the pit we will smash the engines and burn the pithead and you will not get up.' He claimed that had it been an ordinary picket, he would have discussed the situation with them, 'but this was no picket but a mob of Bolshevists and hooligans and roughs ready for any sort of mischief'. He therefore made his escape over the fields.[127] The crowd then forced their way into the lamp cabin and destroyed the safety lamps to prevent any miners descending. The colliery clerk, who had remained in the pit office overnight to guard £5,000 held in the safe to pay the workforce the following day, managed to escape before the crowd ransacked the office and unsuccessfully attempted to force the safe.[128]

To the crowd's confusion, a police sergeant then burst upon the scene. He lived in a house near the colliery and such was the confidence of the marchers that they had done a 'break-down dance' outside his house, to the accompaniment of a melodeon and mouth harps, while shouting 'to hell with the fucking police'. Sergeant Cameron, displaying either considerable courage or stupidity, single-handedly charged into the group in the office wielding his baton; he apprehended one of them, drove the others outside and locked the door. His prisoner, who had suffered serious head injuries while a soldier in France, struggled to get free and, recalled Cameron, 'I had to use my baton to make him quiet'. On realising that the sergeant was alone, the crowd regrouped and forced open the office door. Cameron fought off his assailants until they hurled volleys of brass safety lamps which rendered him bloodied and unconscious.[129] The crowd then set off for Rosehall Colliery, the second largest in Lanarkshire, led by Hendren 'who shouted commands as if trying to keep the crowd in military order, such as "keep your ranks, boys"'. The crowd were met by a detachment of police in Bellshill and, despite Hendren's unmilitary injunction to 'rush the cunts!', were dispersed by baton charges.[130]

Two nights prior to these wild scenes, several thousand miners, mainly from the Shettleston, Cambuslang and Blantyre districts, had demonstrated outside the LMU offices in Hamilton demanding the strike be made official. The telephone lines were severed and a 'score of young men' forced their way into the offices, informing the officials that henceforth they were going to 'run the show'. According to Robertson, 'the officials of the union had been intimidated and terrorised by firearms into handing over the keys of the office to the rioters'.[131] Under this duress, 'and to prevent loss of life and further damage to the property', the union leaders called for an official strike to commence the following day. Reform Committee members addressed the crowd from the building's balcony, hung with scarlet banners; their supporters below sang the 'Red Flag' and blocked the passage of traffic through the town centre for several hours. The union leadership, once safely ensconced in an office in Edinburgh, condemned the committee and demanded the strike end immediately.

They were soon assisted by developments in Fife. A ballot of the Fife miners voted by a majority of only 724 out of a total of over 13,000 to return to work. The results displayed geographical unevenness. In east Fife, in the extreme west of the county, and in Clackmannanshire, there was an overwhelming majority against continuation, while at Cowdenbeath and Lumphinnans in central Fife there was 'a preponderating number of men who were prepared to take drastic action'. Several thousand militants demonstrated outside the union offices in Dunfermline and voted unanimously to maintain the strike. However, despite the presence of large numbers of unofficial pickets, work resumed and after a week the strike movement in Fife and Lanarkshire collapsed.[132]

The Scottish militants had been under no illusion that they could achieve anything in isolation from the rest of the British coalfields. 'The general strike cannot last very long', wrote Macdougall in the *Call*: 'That is its very nature. Either the strike will rapidly extend over the whole of Britain or it must be terminated.' Although the reform committees had links with South Wales miners and the Clyde strike committee, these were too embryonic to achieve such coordinated action. Macdougall visited South Wales at the end of 1918 and A.J. Cook had completed a propaganda tour in Lanarkshire in January, but no preparation had been made to spread the strikes to Wales, perhaps because of their spontaneous origin.[133] When unofficial strikes broke out in South Wales at the end of March over the 'vagueness' of the government's assurances on the Miners' Federation's claim, there was little echo of them in Scotland.[134] The Ministry of Labour reported to the Cabinet that the Scottish miners were 'satisfied in general with the recommendations of the Sankey Report, though in Lanarkshire some efforts have been made to organise an opposition to its acceptance'.[135] Although Maclean and the reform movement campaigned against Sankey's large pay award and the inadequacy of the government's commitment to honour its recommendations, the vote in Scotland followed the advice of the MFGB and Scottish officials and was overwhelmingly in favour of acceptance: over 75,000 to less than 13,000 against.[136]

The interim Sankey report successfully defused the threat of a national miners' strike which the government's later rejection of the Commission's recommendation in favour of nationalisation did not re-ignite. Macdougall conceded that 'there was a slackening of energies' after the Sankey award; demobilisation and the dilution of wartime grievances presented less fertile ground for the reform movement's activists.[137]

Nevertheless, the movement continued under a variety of titles. Maclean had launched a 'One Union Movement' in January 1919 at his first public appearance after release from prison the previous month, and announced that he was now 'the appointed spokesman of the unofficial miners' movement ... an appointment which he was as proud of as he was of the position of [Soviet] Consul for Glasgow'.[138] The 'One Union Movement' was effectively another name for the reform committees and the terms were sometimes used interchangeably, but it also reflected attempts at greater coordination between the various reform groups in the Scots coalfields. The first of several national conferences of the 'Scottish Mineworkers' One Union Movement' was held in April and Macdougall was appointed Secretary-Treasurer. In the following months, the movement conducted propaganda meetings and demonstrations but appears to have been most active in Lanarkshire.[139]

The continued influence of the reform movement over a significant minority in Lanarkshire was demonstrated the following year during the negotiations over the MFGB's national pay claim. In September, Manus Duddy, supported by another Blantyre delegate, moved a motion of censure at the LMU Council on the MFGB Executive for continuing negotiations after a national ballot had authorised strike action; it was lost by 74 votes to 20. A week later, unofficial picketing in Lanarkshire brought 18,000 miners on strike for three days.[140] Once more the LMU officials denounced the 'action of a number of outsiders who by intimidatory methods were causing considerable sections of our members to be idle' and took the precaution of postponing a delegate conference, out of fear 'that the premises would be subject to attack by the people responsible for the unofficial picketing'. Such anxieties were fulfilled the following month. Duddy failed to secure the Council's rejection of the terms negotiated by the MFGB during the official national strike by 101–21. On the penultimate day of the stoppage, 'a number of young men entered the offices unauthorised' and noisily remonstrated with the agents and Executive.[141]

The outcome of the strike stimulated renewed efforts at organising the militants. A meeting 'of all rebel members' of the LMU was convened in Blantyre in November and a committee appointed to draw up a manifesto. About a hundred miners attended a further meeting in Blantyre, the majority of whom were from the district, although there was also representation from Douglas Water, Shotts, Tollcross, Holytown, Tollcross, Shettleston, Cambuslang, Hamilton, Burnbank and Bothwell. Considerable discussion took place on the wisdom of 'boring from within' the existing union, a Tollcross miner arguing that 'trade unionism and capitalism would fall together', but the majority accepted working inside the LMU as the best policy and the committee's recommendation of 'the effective control of their officials, with the power to recall any paid official at any time, and the election of agents every three years'. As a result of the conference, a 'Lanarkshire Miners' Rebel Movement' was established; the central theme of its manifesto was the need for a unified Scottish miners' union in the sharpening struggle between capital and labour: 'the war has ... taught many lessons. It has enlarged the vision of the workers and a more aggressive note has been sounded.' A conference of 'all rebel miners in Scotland' was held the following January in the SLP Hall, Glasgow, attended by some 300 delegates from throughout the Scots coalfields. Scotland was divided into 10 divisions and two delegates from each would constitute a 'central board'. James Jardine of Blantyre was elected Chairman and Willie Kirker, a Bowhill miner and a member of the Fife Communist Group, was appointed Secretary of a 'revived' Scottish Miners' Reform Committee. The formation of a Stirlingshire Miners' Reform Committee was reported in April.[142]

Reform movement 'rebels' played a prominent role in the national dispute of 1921 when government decontrol was followed by a thirteen week lockout to enforce large wage cuts. The aggressive mass picketing, looting and sabotage which accompanied the lockout was as violent as in any previous strike and more widespread.[143] A conference of ministers discussing the crisis received a report from two Scottish coalowners, J.T. Forgie and Sir Adam Nimmo, that 'the miners were going about in gangs of 2,000 strong, some crowds with women, dashing towards the pits and frightening the men at the pumps', and a request from the Chief Constable of Fife that 'only naval or military assistance would be effective'.[144] The growing links between militant groups throughout Scotland, particularly in Lanarkshire and Fife may partly explain the scale and character of the disturbances. Basil Thompson was insistent that the disorders in Scotland and South Wales could 'be traced in practically every case to the influence of the Unofficial Reform Movements'.[145]

Such views by the authorities and the very real problem of public order encouraged repressive policing. At the end of April, Willie Kirker sent a report to the Scottish Organiser of the newly-formed Communist Party: 'most of the best men in Bowhill have been laid by the heels. Already 32 of our chaps have been arrested.'[146] Repressive police tactics in turn fuelled resentment and retaliation. For example, Mary Docherty of Cowdenbeath recalled her father making a baton from the shaft of his pit axe, saying: 'If the police use their batons on me I will use this one on them.' Jas Miller, who later joined the CPGB, witnessed a police baton charge in Cowdenbeath after which 'the street literally ran with blood ... that made a profound impression on me'.[147]

Resentment at state violence must also be viewed against the background of the miners' recent war record. In a speech on the coal crisis, the moderate James Brown of the AMU pointedly noted that 'the flower of the manhood of the mining villages' had volunteered for service on the outbreak of war. He also claimed that the Scottish mine owners had intimated that 'this was not the end but the beginning of reductions'.[148] The miners, urged on by the militant minority, therefore felt their backs were to wall. They were correct. Nominal wages in Scotland had stood at 18s 6d per day in January 1921. In the months following their defeated return to work at 15s per day on 1 July, wages were reduced a further four times to 9s 5d before the end of the year. The 'inter-war' depression in the Scots coal industry had now begun.

Analysis and evaluation

We can discern a number of sources of support for the reform movement. One was clearly based on generation. There is overwhelming evidence that the reform committees drew their primary strength from younger miners: the Manpower Bill in 1918 aroused 'an element of opposition among the younger men affected' according to a Scottish military intelligence summary; 'the tendency of the younger generation amongst the Lanarkshire miners ... is more and more towards socialism', reported a similar source in June 1919.[149] In 1918, detectives and others testified that at meetings addressed by Maclean in Shettleston, 'there was a large proportion of youths' and 'it was mostly young men of military age'; at Cambuslang, 'the greater proportion' were men of military age; at Harthill, 500 people 'chiefly men of 17 to 25 years of age' listened to Maclean speak for two hours on the Russian revolution. John Ford, a Fife Coal Company employee, claimed that 'respectable, orderly and elderly men here are against the extremists. But the extremists are organised and persistent men, mostly young men who might be called up for military service.' James Forrest, a shorthand writer, similarly noticed that at Cambuslang, 'the young men applauded Mr Maclean when he made strong and violent statements but the older men seemed to treat the violent ideas towards the close of his speech more as a joke and laughed heartily'.[150]

Although police witnesses and intelligence agents might have had a vested interest in emphasising that the audiences of the revolutionaries were of military age to secure convictions for sedition, other sources point incontrovertibly to the youth of their supporters. Macdougall referred to the 'young men associated with the reform agitation'; James C. Welsh claimed that in Lanarkshire, 'the young men believe, rightly or wrongly, that wars are the concerns of Capital'; the jury in the trial of the Hamilton Palace rioters recommended leniency 'on account of their youth'.[151] In Ian MacDougall's *Militant Miners*, age is indicated in the biographical notes on 43 left-wing union activists in Fife during the inter-war period: 18 were under 30 in 1920.[152]

Many young miners had been radicalised by the threat of conscription or their experiences in the trenches. Rab Smith from Lumphinnans, whose recollection of Arras was noted above, became a Communist after he returned to Fife: 'the experiences o' the war was the furst thing tha' made me think in a real way tha' something had got tae be done'. Similar traumas, he claimed, made many militant miners in the 1920s.[153] David Proudfoot saw active service as a machine gunner; he joined the BSP after being invalided out of the army and later became a founder member of the Communist Party.[154] Abe Moffat, who joined the CP in 1922 aged 26, also claimed that his radicalism was shaped by his experiences after he volunteered for service in France: 'we were told that we were fighting to make this a country fit for heroes to live in, but we discovered after the war that we had to be heroes to live in it!'.[155] A minority of other ex-servicemen shared his views. The Home Office

Director of Intelligence reported the formation of the International Union of Ex-Servicemen in Glasgow in May 1919 as a breakaway from the larger Federation of Discharged and Demobilised Sailors and Soldiers. This new body was 'frankly a revolutionary organisation', with a reported membership of 'over 7,000'; as well as four branches in Glasgow, there were others elsewhere in Scotland, including Blantyre, Kirkcaldy, Leven, Lochore, Bowhill, Dunfermline, Broxburn and Kilbirnie.[156] While the numerical estimate should be treated with caution, the location of these branches in centres of agitation in the coalfields suggests one explanation for the military-style of picketing in the post-war period.[157]

Within this generational cohort, we can discern three further, overlapping axes defining support for the committees. First, the militants were aligned with the more rebellious youth of the mining communities, who were at this time increasingly involved in gang activities.[158] Jas Miller recalled that, without his involvement in political activities in the 1920s, he 'would have been a rebel without a cause. They saved me. I was angry ... out of my mother's control, organising a gang of little thieves ...'.[159] A number of militants had criminal records for petty crime and public order offences. Of the ten arrested for the attack on Craighead and Hamilton Palace Collieries in 1919, Charles Hendren, 'the leader of the mob', had three convictions for breach of the peace and one for assault between 1900 and 1909; Michael McCue, a 21 year old Burnbank miner, had two convictions for theft, one for malicious mischief and one for theft and malicious mischief; Thomas Hanson, a 19 year old Blantyre miner had been found guilty of housebreaking a year before; Hugh Higgins, a 27 year old miner from Mount Vernon had been convicted of breach of the peace two years previously. James Ferguson, a member of the Lanarkshire Reform Committee, had served two sentences for theft; four other defence witnesses in the trial of those arrested for the attacks on Lanarkshire collieries in 1919 had one or more convictions for breach of the peace. One of these was Patrick Berry, a 24 year old Blantyre miner and a member of the Reform Committee, who had two convictions for breach of the peace in 1916 and 'who escaped from his house when the police went to apprehend him for Military Service in July 1918 and could not be got'.[160]

In contrast to the repeated condemnations of 'hooliganism' by union officials, the revolutionary leaders of these often disorderly elements tended to minimise the violence with which they were associated. Maclean described the wrecking of Woolford's Pit in 1912 as 'the trifling incident at Tarbrax, where some excited miners burned down the engine house of a tiny pit', which had been seized on by the 'yellow press'.[161] Recalling the events of 1919, Macdougall admitted that it was 'action of a fairly rough character – it could scarcely have been called peaceful picketing'.[162] Macdougall himself was convicted in 1921 for encouraging a crowd demonstrating against the recent imprisonment of Maclean to break shop windows, although by that year both he and Maclean were increasingly cautioning the miners against *agents provocateurs* and 'futile and childish acts of destruction'.[163]

A second set of parameters of support relate to geography and scale of mine. The strength of the reform committees was based in particular localities in Lanarkshire and Fife. Although on certain issues, such as the forced resignation of Gilmour, a broad alliance of all left-wing and anti-war miners (including Smillie and his supporters) were able to mobilise a majority of the Lanarkshire miners, this majority was a small one. The core support of the Reform Committee militants was more restricted and probably never more than approximately a quarter of the union membership. At least 24 branches of the LMU affiliated to the committee. That this was probably the maximum number is suggested by Macdougall's later recollection that 'about twenty' branches were formally affiliated and from votes at the LMU council: the council voted by 75 to 24 to delete Macdougall's name from a ballot for additional agents in 1919; later that year, 25 branches voted against Smillie's recommendation to accept the Coal Controller's demand for an end to a militant-led strike in the Coalburn district.[164]

In the absence of Reform Committee records, we cannot be certain which union branches were affiliated. However, some indication of LMU branches which supported policies advocated by the committee can be gained from the views of branch delegates at LMU Council meetings. Twenty two branches have been identified in this way as probable affiliates.[165] These display geographical concentration in the Blantyre/Burnbank/Hamilton district, in the triangle of south Lanarkshire centred on Stonehouse, Coalburn and Douglas, at Shotts, and on the fringes of Glasgow at Baillieston and at Giffnock (near Maclean's home in Pollokshaws). Further evidence of such 'localisation' of protest is contained in a memorandum of a meeting held by the Director of National Service in

Glasgow in April 1918 where it was reported that the young miners who demonstrated at the LMU offices against conscription 'were mostly from the disaffected areas of Coalburn and Blantyre'.[166] In Fife, support was concentrated in the centre of the coalfield around Cowdenbeath and Lumphinnans.[167]

Many of the collieries covered by the branches associated with the Lanarkshire Reform Committee were among the largest in the county, and almost all were mechanised by 1919. The 'central nerve' of the reform movement in Fife, according to Macdougall, was at Bowhill where the largest pit in the county was situated.[168] Two points flow from this. First, the crude number of delegates supporting the reform movement at the LMU council underestimates its influence, since many non-militant delegates represented small, sometimes very small, collieries. Second, the Reform Committee's analysis of industrial concentration and mechanisation was highly relevant to miners in these larger collieries. But the technical and economic development of the Scots coalfields was extremely uneven and this assisted in circumscribing the areas of militant support.[169]

A final element was the association between the Reform Committee militants and Irish republicanism (which was also geographically differentiated in areas of Irish settlement).[170] In 1919, military intelligence noted that 'since the advent of Bolshevism, the Sinn Fein party has gained the goodwill and support of the extreme socialists in the Clyde district'.[171] Basil Thompson claimed during the 1921 lock-out that 'Sinn Feiners are prominent in the rioting in Lanarkshire'. In Fife, three Sinn Fein miners, allegedly members of the Lochgelly detachment of the IRA, were arrested in connection with malicious fire raising on eight farms; one was in possession of a revolver.[172]

Thompson's reports must be viewed with great caution, not least because of his expansionist ambitions for his department within the intelligence community. But other evidence supports his views on the links between the Reform Committee militants and Irish republicanism. Such connections were personified by Andrew Fagan, a Blantyre miner, a Reform Committee supporter, an SLP member, and a graduate of Maclean's Scottish Labour College who taught an economics class of forty-four miners in Burnbank in 1921. He was also the quartermaster of the IRA's Scottish brigade and was arrested that same year in connection with the murder of a police inspector during an attempt to free an Irish prisoner from a 'Black

Maria' in Glasgow.[173] Fagan was not wholly atypical. Johnny O'Neil, a Buckhaven miner, originally from Lanarkshire and a BSP member, 'was also closely linked with Irish militants'. McArthur recalled that: 'We took a close interest in the Irish struggle. There were quite a number of Irish militants with whom we had the closest association ... Without exception all of them that I knew were militant left trade unionists and politicians.'[174]

In Lanarkshire, Reform Committee militants sought to develop union support for Irish independence. Manus Duddy moved a motion at the LMU Council in 1920 that a one-day strike be organised against government policy in Ireland and Russia; it was indicative of the divisions on the issue that 'after several attempts to secure order the chairman adjourned the conference'. Later that year, a motion from the Greenfield, Burnbank, branch urging the LMU Executive to 'take up the question of "Hands Off Ireland"' was agreed to by 70 votes to 52. The following month, the Coalburn branch advocated the continuation of the national coal strike 'until the military regime is withdrawn from Ireland', although this motion was later dropped. In January 1921, the Giffnock branch struck for a day in protest against British 'atrocities' in Ireland, the 400 strikers being addressed on the subject by Macdougall. A month later the branch (narrowly and on a small vote) secured LMU Council support for a motion calling for a 48-hour strike against the government's Irish policy by 38 votes to 29, although this action appears to have been overtaken by the subsequent national lockout.[175]

Support for the Irish republican cause by these branches reflected a persistent theme in Maclean's propaganda. He and Macdougall organised 'Hands Off Ireland' demonstrations in Motherwell in 1920, where they called for strike action by miners in pursuit of this policy. At one meeting, bodies of Orangemen in the audience of 2,000–3,000 attempted to rush the platform, which was eventually smashed and the meeting broken up. Later that year in Motherwell, Maclean was protected from hostile Orangemen by Irishmen 'from all over Lanarkshire' who 'put up a solid phalanx round the platform', shouting 'Up Dublin!'. The adoption of the 'rebel' nomenclature by the reform movement in 1921 may also reflect the Irish republican sympathies of its activists.[176]

A further militaristic element was the link between Sinn Finn supporters and a shadowy body known as the 'Red Army', which was associated with the fledgling Communist Party. Martin

Durham has reviewed reports of attempts by the Communist International (CI) to establish a Red Army officer corps in Britain in 1920–21.[177] Such attempts were in line with the exaggerated optimism of the CI concerning revolutionary possibilities in Western Europe before 1921. A resolution of the Third Congress of the CI in June of that year, 'On the combination of legal and illegal work', noted that:

> Legal Communist Parties in capitalist countries, have as a whole, not grasped fully how seriously they must work to prepare the Party for the revolutionary insurrection, the armed struggle and the illegal struggle ... The legal mass Party must prepare thoroughly to meet the unexpected, to arm itself and adapt itself to illegal work ... Every Communist Party needs some secret preparations, if only on a small scale.[178]

Although Durham concludes that any military activity was never officially authorised by the CPGB, the control exercised by the party in its early years was haphazard and there is evidence of such activities in Scotland. Two leading Scottish Communists, J.R. Campbell and James Messer, publicly declared in 1920 that they were involved in 'the secret arming and drilling of groups of carefully selected workers'.[179] Bob Selkirk recalled that 'a retired army captain came over from Ireland to drill the Workers' Army formed by Jack Leckie'. Leckie was a Glaswegian former anarchist of Irish extraction who joined the CPGB in 1921. MacArthur similarly remembered Leckie's propaganda tours in East Fife, when 'he tried to link up the Sinn Fein development in Ireland with the situation in Britain. And he would tell the miners that they had to practice marching and drill ... he was always on the fringe of illegality ...'.[180] This opinion was borne out by the police seizure of documents and explosives from the house of a Glasgow Communist in 1921. Among the documents was a copy of the 'Oath of the Red Guard – Scots Section', which the authorities claimed had been made by Leckie, and contained the vow to combine 'with my kindred on a military basis for the purpose of establishing economic and social freedom through working class dictatorship'.[181] Such activities led to the Scottish Section of the Communist-led National Workers' Committee publishing a pamphlet entitled *Bombs or Brains? Dynamite or Organisation?* in 1921, which opposed the adventurism of the 'Red Army gospellers'.[182] The SLP, by then supported by

Maclean and Macdougall, was also highly critical of the 'many fools' who had been 'so carried away by the "will to power" philosophy' of some CPGB members.[183]

While it is appropriate to share this scepticism with regard to such military posturing when evaluating the political strategy pursued by the militants, it is important to do so without 'the enormous condescension of posterity' sometimes displayed by the revisionists of the 'new orthodoxy'. If it is widely accepted by social historians that the actions of, say, Luddite stockingers in 1812, should be judged within their contemporary context rather than with patronising and anachronistic hindsight, the same historical courtesy should be extended to the Scottish miners in the early twentieth century.[184] Assessment of the militant miner should be undertaken within the discipline of contemporary context and not from the teleological standpoint of the Labour Party's breakthrough in 1922. There are several important circumstances which require to be borne in mind.

The first is that the growth of class consciousness among British workers during and after the war, which was noted by contemporary observers as well as by later historians, was evident in the Scots coalfields.[185] In addition to a quantitative increase in industrial disputes, a number of strikes demonstrated a greater sense of occupational and gender solidarity. For example, all the miners at three collieries in Bellshill owned by the Wilsons and Clyde Coal Company came out in sympathy with striking surface workers who complained that some pithead women were being overworked. At Valleyfield, the miners struck work over extra-duties which were placed on an ex-soldier working at the pithead. A dispute at one of the collieries of John Watson and Company led to the formation of a combine committee representing miners at all the company's Lanarkshire collieries which was committed to taking joint industrial action.[186] A similar extension of organisational inclusiveness was displayed in the Shotts area where (as at Blantyre) an unofficial district committee was established shortly after the war, consisting of delegates from all the pits in the locality, to challenge the growing power of the Shotts Iron Company.[187]

A second was the continuing failure of bureaucratic reformism's parliamentarianism until 1922. In 1918, Scottish miners' candidates won only two new seats in addition to West Fife: South Ayrshire and Hamilton, though John Robertson also won Bothwell at a by-election in July 1919. Moreover, in the changed political context brought about by the war, parliamentarianism did not necessarily negate left-wing policies: Maclean, standing as a Labour candidate in Glasgow's Gorbals a week after his release from prison in 1918, secured a respectable 7,436 votes against more than 14,000 for the sitting ex-Labour MP, George Barnes.[188] In Motherwell, Walton Newbold, a leading ILP Marxist, won 23 per cent of the vote.

The relative failure of the Labour Party to win more seats in the Scots coalfields also reinforced the militant rhetoric of 'direct action' increasingly employed by miners' leaders; for example, in relation to declarations of solidarity action from the 'triple alliance' of mining, transport workers and railwaymen.[189] As McArthur later recalled, until the disintegration of the 'triple alliance' following the start of the 1921 lockout, 'the miners were looking forward with tremendous enthusiasm to this new weapon that was being forged ... There was the keenest anticipation of what was likely to eventuate from the calling into action of the Triple Alliance.'[190] A similar anticipatory tone pervades Johnny Boyle's recollection of working as a young drawer in Wellesley Colliery, Methil, as the lockout started, and before the leaders of the triple alliance had announced their retreat from solidarity with the miners:

> We were harum-scarum ... this road, they used tae cry it 'penal servitude' ... you were drawin' the tubs, and you were continually on the move, and on the Friday when we were supposed to come on strike ... we rammed the tubs aff the road, an' knocked trees [pit props] an' everythin' tae hell, you know, we were goin' tae close the bloody pit ... (laughs) We thought, we were on strike an' that wis the bloody last o' it.[191]

This point highlights the reform movement's dual strategy of 'legitimate agitation' within the union structures and 'illegitimate action ... which would set the masses in motion, to take early and energetic action on the wages question'.[192] This optimistic policy had more in common with Rosa Luxembourg than Lenin. Maclean and his followers (along with the rest of the revolutionary left in Britain) failed to implement the latter's views on the importance of disciplined political organisation.[193] The reform movement was at best a loose coalition. Greater emphasis was placed on the efficacy of Marxist classes in creating a politicised vanguard among the turbulent youth of the mining villages: 'mass education means mass action', stated

Maclean.[194] The unofficial triggering of a mass strike of miners in 1919, it was hoped, might lead in turn to a general strike.[195] This strategy proved a failure. The reform committees were unable to transcend the divisions in the mining workforce and their unions. The violence associated with mass picketing in 1919 alienated older miners and reinforced the position of the LMU leadership rather than detonating mass support.[196] The more widespread displays of physical force during the 1921 lockout were to prove ineffective against a government which had spent the previous two years planning for precisely such a contingency.[197]

Yet the more cautious strategy of Smillie and the MFGB leadership must equally be judged a failure. No matter how dazzling Smillie's demolition of the coalowners nor the eloquence of his arguments for nationalisation before the Sankey Commission, he was outfoxed by Lloyd George in precisely the manner predicted by the reform movement activists.[198] The militant argument that strike action would have been a more effective tactic to pressurise the government in early 1919 can be evaluated within the contexts both of the attitudes of elements within the government and of contemporary official assessments of the maintenance of social order. Lloyd George recognised that public opinion considered private ownership of the industry discredited, a view shared privately by many coalowners, some of whom reluctantly accepted the prospect of nationalisation with generous compensation.[199] While many owners were 'violently opposed to any "participation in management" by the men', Tom Jones, the Cabinet Secretary, informed the Prime Minister in April that:

> on the other hand some of the more enlightened owners like our friend D.D. [David Davies] will welcome any scheme of genuine cooperation. Some of us are working out schemes of socialisation as distinct from nationalisation with representatives of the miners, consumers and owners on the Board. The crucial matters are (1) to preserve the initiative and responsibility of the technical experts, (2) secure the goodwill and energy of the miners as producers ...[200]

While far from meeting the demands of the reform committees, such a project, with its guild socialist undertones, might have appealed to miners as the compromise outcome of industrial action and a limited accretion of power, had the Miners' Federation been capable of exercising the pressure of a united strike. However, as

Wrigley notes, 'the tide began to turn against the MFGB' after the publication of the Interim Sankey Report in late March and the opportunity to maximise pressure on the government was lost.[201]

Such a possibility must be viewed against post-war instability. There were mutinies in the British army in France in January 1919.[202] Though the weekly intelligence reports of Scottish Command were almost uniformly confident of the loyalty of their troops in 1919, one admitted 'in the event of a miners' strike the position may conceivably slightly alter because the miners on the whole have been a patriotic body of men ... There is also the additional factor that on the whole public sympathy is generally in favour of the miners' case.' In June, loyalty was regarded as conditional on the cause of any industrial unrest: 'circumstances can be foreseen where the attitude of the troops might be sympathetic'.[203] That such fears had some substance was demonstrated by instances of fraternisation during the 1921 lock-out. Abe Moffat claimed that 'the miners and their wives were successful in establishing friendly relations with the troops, who were sons of the British working class', while Mary Docherty recalled that soldiers guarding collieries in Cowdenbeath said 'they would not use their arms against the miners as many of them were themselves from mining families' and passed pit props to villagers to use as fuel. Such recollections by Communists must be treated with caution, but they are supported by the near contemporary plea of a Fife Sheriff to the Scottish Office in 1925: 'I would beg that no such force be sent as was raised in 1921. They themselves were a danger as at Lower Valleyfield they revolted and handed their rifles to the miners to help them rush the guard.'[204] Against this background, the threat of a national mining strike weighed heavily with the government; its implementation, as in 1912, might well have yielded more lasting results than the ephemeral monetary gains of the Sankey award.

Nevertheless, the government and military authorities had a sensitive grasp of the role of the union bureaucracy in generally opposing the militants – 'the vested interests of the unions will be too strong for this movement' – and in defusing any insurgent opposition to the Sankey recommendations: 'the official miners' leaders will explore every avenue of escape before they are compelled to accede to a strike', a Scottish Command intelligence report observed in March 1919.[205] Robert Munro, the Secretary for Scotland, reported to a meeting of ministers during the coal crisis of 1921 'that the three storm centres were Fife, Lanark and Ayr ... Ayrshire was restive, but Mr James Brown, MP, a miners' agent had gone north to try and maintain law and order and secure that the pits should be pumped. Brown was a good moderate man.'[206] Lloyd George clearly perceived the hollow kernel in the MFGB leaders' rhetoric of 'direct action'. He patiently outmanoeuvred them in the two years after 1919 and exploited divisions between moderates and militants within the trade union movement with great skill and a degree of good fortune.[207] Tom Jones recorded in his diary in April 1921:

> The opinion is general that the owners ought never to have put forward such a big cut in wages and that some scheme for graduating the fall should have been devised concurrently with decontrol ... Luckily for the government the miners confused the issue by flooding the mines and clamouring for a subsidy. The PM fastened on this and rode off on the back of the poor pit pony and pulled round.[208]

In addition to the bulwark of the union bureaucracy, the government carefully deployed the power of the state to target the reform movement's leaders; but it could also revoke it with similar calculation in the face of protest.[209] In March 1918, a meeting took place between the Secretary of State for Scotland, the Lord Advocate, the Permanent Secretary at the Scottish Office and the Chief General Staff Officer: they agreed that Maclean and Macdougall should be prosecuted and Louis Shammes, Maclean's Russian personal assistant, be deported.[210] Accordingly, that same month Shammes was repatriated. Evidence was duly collected against Maclean by detectives and shorthand writers, mainly at meetings of miners.[211] He was arrested in mid-April, charged with sedition and sentenced to five years penal servitude the following month.[212] Following 'a growing agitation in Glasgow and in Independent Labour Party circles for his release', and after George Barnes sent a note to the War Cabinet urging this course 'before the agitation assumes larger and more dangerous dimensions', Maclean was freed in December 1918, although the military authorities expressed concern at the potential consequences of 'this sudden yielding to extremist clamour'.[213]

Subsequently, the government made more thorough contingency preparations for industrial unrest by 'extremists', including the use of troops and the establishment of its Supply and Transport Committee (STC).[214] When the promised solidarity action by the railwaymen and transport workers failed to be delivered to the

Miners' Federation in April 1921, the Cabinet Secretary observed mockingly:

> Then came the collapse of the Triple Alliance and the Red Revolution was postponed once more ... The Strike Committee [i.e. the STC] very sick. They had been waiting for two years to press the button. They had pressed it. The Strike Books had been issued from the secret banks where they had been concealed; the milk cans were rolling down to Devon and could not be stopped, the troops were steaming in ship and train from Ireland, from Malta, from Silesia to defend us from the men of Fife.[215]

Conclusion

By 1921, the upward movement of union organisation in the Scots coalfields which had developed from the 1890s had been checked. Within the unions, there was now established a militant minority of young activists who would soon establish themselves as an alternative union leadership. But the effective intervention of this minority was largely confined to the Fife and West Central coalfields, and even within these regions support was constrained by generation, ethnicity and the technological development of the industry. Nevertheless, five years later the British state was to be forced once again to confront the miners of Fife and militants elsewhere in Scotland.

Notes

1. I. McLean, *The Legend of Red Clydeside* (Edinburgh, 1983) is the pioneering work of this revisionist trend. For a perceptive review of this 'new orthodoxy', see T. Brotherstone, 'Does Red Clydeside really matter any more?' in R. Duncan and A. McIvor (eds), *Militant Workers: labour and class conflict on the Clyde, 1900–1950* (Edinburgh, 1992), pp. 52–80.
2. McKinlay and Morris, *ILP on Clydeside*.
3. J. Foster, 'Strike action and working class politics on Clydeside, 1914–19', *International Review of Social History*, 35, 1, 1990, pp. 33–70. Neither Foster nor this chapter suggest that a 'pre-revolutionary situation' occurred in Clydeside or elsewhere in Scotland in the post-war years.

4. SRO CB 8/3, LCMA *Annual Reports*, 1911, 1912, 1914. For an analysis of disputes in Lanarkshire, see S. Renfrew, 'Militant miners? Strike activity and industrial relations in the Lanarkshire coalfield, 1910–1914', in W. Kenefick and A. McIvor (eds), *Roots of Red Clydeside 1910–1914? Labour unrest and industrial relations in West Scotland* (Edinburgh, 1996), pp. 153–74.

5. See vol. 1, ch. 6.

6. SRO HH 55/338, Chief Constable of Lanarkshire to Sheriff of Lanarkshire, 8 March 1912; *Glasgow Herald*, 8 March 1912.

7. SRO HH 55/341, Chief Constable of Fife to Standing Joint Committee of Fife, May 1912; *Scotsman*, 6 April 1912.

8. *Glasgow Herald*, 6 January, 8 March 1912.

9. Arnot, *History*, p. 129; *Glasgow Herald*, 6, 9 April 1912; *Morning Post*, 6 April 1912.

10. B. Holton, *British Syndicalism, 1900–14* (1976), p. 116.

11. *Glasgow Herald*, 6 June, 8 August 1912; Church, *History*, p. 744; *Justice*, 15 June 1912. See also J.D. Macdougall, 'The Scottish coalminer', *Nineteenth Century*, December 1927, p. 766.

12. J. Smith, 'Taking the leadership of the labour movement: the ILP in Glasgow, 1906–1914', in McKinlay and Morris, *ILP on Clydeside*, pp. 58–9.

13. Ibid., pp. 67–8, 79.

14. Holton, *Syndicalism*, p. 170.

15. A. McKinlay, '"Doubtful wisdom and uncertain promise": strategy, ideology and organisation, 1918–22', in McKinlay and Morris, *ILP on Clydeside*, p. 123; see also J. Melling, 'Work, culture and politics on "Red Clydeside": the ILP during the First World War', in ibid., pp. 93, 107, 115. Note the emphasis on the ILP as a 'network' in R. Morris, 'The ILP, 1893–1932: introduction', in ibid., p. 5.

16. Quoted in J. Quail, *The Slow Burning Fuse: the lost history of the British anarchists* (1978), p. 272.

17. I. MacDougall (ed.), *Militant Miners* (Edinburgh, 1981), pp. 11–12. William Gallacher (later the Communist MP for West Fife) was a member of both the SDF and the Glasgow Anarchist Group in 1911 (Quail, *Slow Burning Fuse*, p. 273).

18. See J. Saville, 'The ideology of labourism' in R. Benewick, R.N. Berki and B. Parekh (eds), *Knowledge and Belief in Politics* (1973), and J. Saville, *The Labour Movement in Britain* (1988), pp. 14–22.

19. ILP Branch Records, Harvester Press Microfiche, Item 72, Cards 73–5, Shettleston Branch Minutes, 1905–16.

20. National Museum of Labour History, Manchester (NMLH), Labour Party Archives, Scottish Advisory Committee Minutes, 15 July 1916 and *passim*.

21. See ch. 2 in this volume.
22. Crick, *SDF*, pp. 74–8. See also G. Johnson, 'Social democratic politics in Britain, 1881–1911: the Marxism of the Social Democratic Federation, unpublished PhD thesis, University of Hull, 1989, an abstract of which appeared in *Labour History Review*, 55, 2, pp. 64–5.
23. *Justice*, 10 August 1907.
24. Chewter, thesis, pp. 38, 46; H. Vernon, 'The Socialist Labour Party and the working class movement on the Clyde, 1903–21', unpublished MPhil thesis, University of Leeds, 1967, p. 29; R. Challinor, *The Origins of British Bolshevism* (1977), p. 121.
25. This body became the Industrial Workers of Great Britain (IWGB) in 1909; Vernon, thesis, pp. 83, 112; Holton, *Syndicalism*, p. 41.
26. *Call*, 6 September 1917. For SLP propaganda among miners in Britain before the First World War, see E. Burdick, 'Syndicalism and industrial unionism in England until 1918', unpublished DPhil thesis, University of Oxford, 1950, p. 254.
27. Chewter, thesis, p. 66.
28. Selkirk, *Life*, p. 6. More correctly, these would be branches of the IWGB; see Chewter, thesis, p. 85, for a reference to an industrial unionist group affiliated to the IWGB in Ormiston by 1909.
29. Selkirk, *Life*, p. 8.
30. Macdougall, 'Scottish coalminer', p. 765.
31. NLS Acc. 4312/7, MELMA Board and Financial Meeting, 22 October 1910, 28 February, 21 October, 30 December 1911, 3 February 1912.
32. Ibid., 11 July 1912, Wages Committee, 26 July 1912. The threat was not carried out as the branch was represented at MELMA board meetings later that year, although this does not discount the possibility that some branch members may have seceded. It is possible that this incident was the basis of Macdougall's recollection.
33. *Miner*, 6 January 1923
34. For Storione's biography, see the *Miner*, 6 January 1923; interview with Mary Docherty, Cowdenbeath, 21 August, 1989; Macintyre, *Little Moscows*, p. 54.
35. D. Egan, '"A cult of their own": syndicalism and *The Miners' Next Step*, in A. Campbell, N. Fishman and D. Howell (eds), *Miners, Unions and Politics, 1910–1947* (Aldershot, 1996), p. 21 and *passim*.
36. NLS Acc. 4251, box 2, file 9, Maclean papers, 'Clydeside in wartime'. For Maclean's analysis of the strike, see *Justice*, 29 July 1911.
37. *Justice*, 15 April 1911; Macdougall, 'Scottish Coalminer', p. 767. For Hay, see D. Egan, 'The Unofficial Reform Committee and *The*

Miners' Next Step', Llafur, 2, 3, 1978, p. 79. Macdougall's failure accurately to recall Hay's first name is curious. It is possible, but highly unlikely, that Macdougall was referring to Jack Hughes, another leading member of the Cambrian Combine committee (ibid., p. 78). Hay was funded as a syndicalist lecturer on 'a lengthy propaganda tour of the Northern coalfields' by George Davison, a wealthy anarchist who also financed an anarcho-syndicalist weekly newspaper, the *Anarchist*, in Glasgow in 1912–13. This paper included a contribution from A.J. Cook, another Rhondda miner associated with the militants of the URC (H.W. Lee and E.A. Archbold, *Social Democracy in Britain*, 1935, p. 183; Quail, *Slow Burning Fuse*, pp. 275–6).

38. *Hamilton Advertiser*, 3 August 1912. Among the other speakers were J. Dougherty, of Northumberland, and J. Thornhill, from Derbyshire, both of whom were sympathisers with the South Wales Unofficial Reform Committee (Egan, 'Unofficial Reform Committee', pp. 76–7).

39. MacDougall, *Militant Miners*, pp. 11, 17, 168.

40. Small, *Cry of the Mine*, p. 11.

41. NLS Acc. 4251, box 2, file 9, Maclean Papers, 'The Bath Street Meeting'; *Justice*, 13 April, 11 May 1912, 15 March 1913. Maclean published letters from Pettigrew in *Justice* in 1912, as well as warnings to British miners to avoid Vancouver Island. Pettigrew was the International Board Member for District 28 of the UMWA (I am grateful to Bill Burrill, Victoria, British Columbia, for this information). For traditions of militancy of British miners in Vancouver Island, see J.D. Belshaw, 'The British collier in British Columbia: another archetype reconsidered', *Labour/Le Travail*, 34, Fall 1994, pp. 11–36. During the early years of the First World War, 171 British miners working in British Columbia were recruited to return to the British coalfields (*Departmental Committee appointed to inquire into the conditions prevailing in the coalmining industry due to the war, Third General Report*, PP 1916, VI, 477).

42. Lee and Archbold, *Social-Democracy*, pp. 183–4; Quail, *Slow Burning Fuse*, p. 271; Crick, *SDF*, pp. 229–50.

43. *Justice*, 24 February 1912,

44. B.J. Ripley and J. McHugh, *John Maclean* (Manchester, 1989), p. 32.

45. *Justice*, 2 March 1912.

46. Ibid., 20 July 1912. See also the BSP Executive's manifesto during the national miners' strike of that year urging them to 'stand firm and make ready for the great final struggle for the cooperative ownership of the coal mines and other means of making wealth' (ibid., 2 March 1912).

47. Ibid., 20 July 1912. For James Gray's father, John, see the *Hamilton Advertiser*, 5 January, 6 February 1895. For Maclean's attitudes to trade unionism, see Ripley and McHugh, *Maclean*, pp. 30–3, 57–8, and D. Howell, *A Lost Left* (Manchester, 1986), pp. 162–6.
48. NLS Acc. 4251, box 2, file 9, Maclean Papers, 'The Progressive Union', p. 9.
49. NLS Dep. 227/54, LMU Executive, 13, 16, 20, 23, 27 August, 27 September 1913.
50. NLS Acc. 4251, Box 2, File 9, 'The Progressive Union', p. 9; T. Bell, *John Maclean: a fighter for freedom* (Glasgow, 1944), p. 48; N. Milton, *John Maclean* (1973), p. 104.
51. *Departmental Committee appointed to inquire into the conditions prevailing in the coal mining industry due to the War, First Report*, PP 1914–16, XXVIII, 7; Arnot, *History*, p. 142. For the mining industry during the war, see R. Redmayne, *The British Coal-Mining Industry during the War* (Oxford, 1923); R.P. Arnot, *The Miners: years of struggle* (1953), pp. 153–81, and *History*, pp. 139–45; B. Supple, *The History of the British Coal Industry, vol. 4, 1913–46: the political economy of decline* (Oxford, 1987), pp. 43–111.
52. Redmayne, *Coal-Mining Industry*, p. 50.
53. *Hamilton Advertiser*, 29 November 1919.
54. Redmayne, *Coal-Mining Industry*, pp. 50–3; Departmental Committee, PP 1916, VI, 480.
55. NLS Dep. 227/35, LMU Council, 19 January 1917.
56. M. Woodhouse, 'Rank and file movements among the miners of South Wales', unpublished DPhil thesis, University of Oxford, 1970, pp. 138–42; *Bellshill Speaker*, 3 August 1917; *Hamilton Advertiser*, 4 August 1917.
57. *Motherwell Times*, 19 February 1926.
58. Arnot, *History*, p. 141.
59. R. Harrison, 'The War Emergency Workers' National Committee', in A. Briggs and J. Saville (eds), *Essays in Labour History 1886–1923* (1971), p. 223.
60. Quoted in Woodhouse, thesis, p. 113. For Smillie, see Saville and Bellamy, *Dictionary*, 3, pp. 168–9, and Smillie, *Life*, pp. 231, 244–52.
61. *Hamilton Advertiser*, 4 August 1917.
62. PRO AIR 1/558, Scottish Command Weekly Intelligence Summary, 12–18 February 1918.
63. *Hamilton Advertiser*, 1 September 1917.
64. *Forward*, 6 July 1918.
65. UGBRC, UGD 159/1/11, LCMA Advisory Committee, 15 March 1918; NLS Dep. 227/60, LMU Executive, 15 June 1918.
66. *Motherwell Times*, 15 September 1916.

67. Interview with Rab Smith by Suzanne Najam, 24 February 1984. I am grateful to Dr Najam for making her transcript available to me.
68. I. MacDougall, *Voices from the Hunger Marches, vol. 2* (Edinburgh, 1991), p. 347.
69. Ibid., pp. 363–4.
70. See vol. 1, ch. 5.
71. *Commission of Inquiry in to Industrial Unrest, Report on No. 8 Division, Scotland,* PP 1917–18, XV, 135. See also *The History of the Ministry of Munitions*, vol. 5, part 5, pp. 54–7, for evidence of overcrowding in Mid-Lanarkshire.
72. PRO AIR 1/554, Scottish Command Weekly Intelligence Summary, 27 April–3 May, 11–17 May, 22–28 June 1919. High prices and bad housing were also listed as the two most important 'causes which contribute to revolutionary feeling' in Britain by the Home Office's Directorate of Intelligence (PRO CAB 24/96, CP 462, 'A survey of revolutionary feeling during the year 1919').
73. See vol. 1, Table 3.4.
74. SRO CB 8/3, LCMA *Annual Reports,* 1917, 1918.
75. NLS Dep. 227/60, LMU Executive, 27 March, 24, 29 April 1918.
76. ILP, *Annual Conference Report*, April 1915.
77. C. Harvie, 'Before the breakthrough, 1888–1922', in I. Donnachie, C. Harvie and I.S. Wood (eds), *Forward!: Labour politics in Scotland 1888–1988* (Edinburgh, 1989), p. 24.
78. ILP, *Annual Conference Report,* 1918.
79. Foster, 'Strike action', p. 58.
80. Harvie, 'Breakthrough', p. 23; *Motherwell Times*, 24 March, 28 April 1916.
81. D. Englander, *Landlord and Tenant in Urban Britain, 1838–1918* (Oxford, 1983), p. 219.
82. A. and V. Flynn, 'We shall not be moved', in L. Flynn (ed.), *'We shall be all': recent chapters in the history of working class struggle in Scotland* (Glasgow and London, 1978), p. 33.
83. Englander, *Landlord and Tenant*, p. 219.
84. PRO CAB 24/70, GT 6348, Duncan Graham, General Secretary LMU, to Secretary, War Cabinet.
85. Englander, *Landlord and Tenant*, p. 309; *Motherwell Times*, 2 July, 6, 13 August, 17 September 1920.
86. UGBRC, UGD 159/1/11, LCMA Lanarkshire District Committee, 23 May 1918, Executive Committee, 3 July 1918.
87. SRO AD 15/18/19, Precognitions of Detective Sergeant A. Gordon and J.S. Forest.
88. *Motherwell Times*, 11 January 1918. For the radicalisation of ILP members in South Wales and elsewhere in Britain, see J. Hinton,

Labour and Socialism: a history of the British labour movement, 1867–1974 (Brighton, 1983), p. 104.

89. Foster, 'Strike action', p. 70.

90. See 'Peter Petroff' and 'John Maclean' in Knox, *Labour Leaders*.

91. See vol. 1, ch. 7.

92. J.D. White, 'Scottish Lithuanians and the Russian Revolution', *Journal of Baltic Studies*, 6, 1, 1975, p. 5.

93. *Call*, 10 May 1917,

94. PRO AIR 1/560, 'General survey for the past month', 6 March 1918; see also Weekly Intelligence Report, 12–18 February 1918.

95. D. Englander, 'Military intelligence and the defence of the realm: the surveillance of soldiers and civilians in Britain during the First World War', *Bulletin of the Society for the Study of Labour History*, 52, 1, 1987, pp. 24–31. For the general development of intelligence gathering on socialists and labour movement activists, see C. Andrew, *Secret Service: the making of the British intelligence community* (1985), chs 5, 7 and 10, and B. Weinberger, *Keeping the Peace: policing strikes in Britain, 1906–1926* (New York and Oxford, 1991), pp. 138–42.

96. PRO CAB 24/44, GT 3838, Appendix 2, Memorandum from GOC in C, Scottish Command, to Secretary, War Office, 27 February 1918.

97. PRO AIR 1/560, Scottish Command Weekly Intelligence Reports, 9–15, 16–22 April 1918; cf Harry McShane's recollection of Macdougall as 'the best orator in Scotland', cited in Knox, *Labour Leaders*, p. 172.

98. *Call*, 9 August 1917.

99. Ibid., 15 February 1917.

100. Milton, *Maclean*, pp. 142–3.

101. *Call*, 9 August 1917; *Hamilton Advertiser*, 4 August 1917; PRO WO 32/9577, Document 47A, War Cabinet Memorandum, GT 4119, 'Secret: Anti-recruiting strikes. Memorandum by the Minister for National Service'.

102. *Call*, 23 August 1917.

103. J.D. Macdougall, 'Miners' reform movement in Lanarkshire', *Plebs*, 9, 9, 1917, pp. 208–9; *Call*, 6 September 1917. For the conditional support of James C. Welsh, then a Ponfeigh checkweigher and leading ILP activist, see his 'The Scottish miners and their union', *Socialist Review*, 15, 1918, where he argues for industrial unionism but 'not a bastard syndicalism'(p. 79). Welsh appears to have severed his links with the reform committee before his appointment as a LMU agent in 1919, the commencement of a steady rightward shift during his political career (Knox, *Scottish Labour Leaders*, pp. 271–3).

104. NLS 7.57, *Manifesto of the Lanarkshire Miners' Reform Committee*; Macdougall, 'Scottish coalminer', p. 767. The qualification of 'largely controlled' distinguished this programme from syndicalism and reflected the influence of Maclean and Macdougall; it is likely that both had a hand in drafting it. For further discussion of its ideas, see B. Pribicevic, 'Demand for workers' control in the railway, mining and engineering industries, 1910–22', unpublished DPhil thesis, University of Oxford, 1957, pp. 305, 313–34, 319–20.

105. *Call*, 4, 11 October 1917; *Plebs*, 9, 11, 1917, p. 261. For Marxist education classes in Scotland, see R. Duncan, 'Independent working class education and the formation of the labour college movement in Glasgow and the West of Scotland, 1915–22', in Duncan and McIvor, *Militant Workers*, pp. 106–28.

106. Macdougall, 'Scottish coalminer', pp. 767–73; *Call*, 11 April 1918; NLS Dep. 227/59, LMU Executive, 28, 30 March, 6 October 1917; *Plebs*, 9, 9, 1917, p. 208. It was reported that attempts were also being made to set up reform committees in Stirlingshire and West Lothian (*Plebs*, 9, 9, 1917, p. 209; *Call*, 15 August 1918). See also NLS 6.1484 (11), *Manifesto of the Fife Miners' Reform Committee* and Methil Public Library (MPL) K033, *Manifesto of the Lothian Miners' Reform Committee*. John McArthur, a member of the Fife committee recalled having meetings with Dan Sim of the 'Ayrshire Reform Committee' during the war, although little is known of this body or its supporters (MacDougall, *Militant Miners*, p. 121). An undated typescript constitution of a 'Kilmarnock District United Mine Workers' Committee' which sought to secure 'a form of organisation within and around the mines, in keeping with the aspirations of the rank and file and in accordance with the economic development of the times' may have originated during the war (NLS Dep. 258/5). It was signed by E. Sim, Crosshouse, and William Minford, Hurlford. It is not known if the former was related to Dan Sim. William Minford was later the Hurlford branch Secretary of the Ayrshire Miners' Union (NLS Dep. 258/5, AMU Report and Balance Sheet for year ending 15 May 1931). Despite its title, it is clear that this committee was not connected to the later United Mineworkers of Scotland, since its membership was restricted to branches and members of the AMU.

107. MacDougall, *Militant Miners*, pp. 18–19.

108. NLS Dep. 227/35, LMU Council, 30 June, 12 August 1917.

109. *Hamilton Advertiser*, 4 August 1917; *Call*, 9 August 1917.

110. *Bellshill Speaker*, 11 October 1918; *Call*, 15 August 1918.

111. *Call*, 9, 23 August 1917; *Hamilton Advertiser*, 4 August 1917.

112. *Hamilton Advertiser*, 26 January 1918.

113. *Bellshill Speaker*, 8 February 1918; PRO AIR 1/560, Scottish Command Weekly Intelligence Summary, 5–11 February 1918.
114. *Hamilton Advertiser*, 2 March 1918; PRO AIR 1/560, Scottish Command Weekly Intelligence Summary, 19–25 February 1918.
115. *Hamilton Advertiser*, 23 March 1918.
116. *Hamilton Advertiser*, 6, 20 April 1918; *Bellshill Speaker*, 19 April 1918; Departmental Committee, PP 1916, VI, 480.
117. *Hamilton Advertiser*, 23 February, 6 July 1918.
118. *Motherwell Times*, 17 January 1919.
119. *Bellshill Speaker*, 17 January 1919.
120. For the Fife dispute, see the *Dunfermline Press*, 25 January 1919. For contrasting interpretations of the Forty Hours strike, see McLean, *Legend*, and Foster, 'Strike action'. McLean's conclusions concerning the strike are facilitated by him almost totally ignoring the simultaneous events in the coalfields.
121. *Hamilton Advertiser*, 1 February 1919.
122. Ibid.
123. See vol. 1, chs 6 and 7, and Macdougall, 'Scottish coalminer', p. 772.
124. *Hamilton Advertiser*, 1 February 1919; SRO AD 15/19/54, Precognitions of Police Sergeant D. Cameron and J. McDonald, surface foreman, Hamilton Palace Colliery.
125. Ibid., Indictment against Charles Hendren and others, and W. Thomson, Procurator Fiscal, Hamilton, to W.J.D. Dundas, Crown Agent, Edinburgh, 21 April 1919; *Hamilton Advertiser*, 3 May 1919.
126. Ibid., Precognition of W. McCombe, fireman.
127. Ibid., Precognition of John Russell, fireman.
128. Ibid., Precognitions of J. McDonald, surface foreman, and I. McCully, colliery clerk.
129. *Ibid.*, Precognition of Police Sergeant D. Cameron.
130. *Ibid.*, Precognition of Police Sergeant A. Peden.
131. *Hamilton Advertiser*, 1 February 1919; *Colliery Guardian*, 7 February 1919.
132. *Glasgow Herald*, 27 January–5 February 1919; *The Times*, 31 January 1919; *Hamilton Advertiser*, 1, 8 February 1919; *Colliery Guardian*, 7 February 1919; *Dunfermline Press*, 25 January, 1 February 1919; *Bellshill Speaker*, 31 January 1919; NLS Dep. 227/61, LMU Executive, 29 January 1919.
133. *Call*, 23, 30 January 1919. A further link with South Wales was via John Bird, a Bowhill militant and protégé of Maclean who worked during the war as a miner in the Rhondda, where he lodged with A.J. Cook (MacDougall, *Militant Miners*, p. 37). Miners' delegates from Cambuslang, Shettleston and Blantyre were reported as being among those attending a special conference in Glasgow in support of

the Forty Hours strike. Patrick Murty, a Shettleston miner 'of Bolshevist tendencies' and a leader of the Lanarkshire reform committee – he led the procession to the LMU offices – was also the treasurer of the Clyde Workers' Defence Committee which raised funds on behalf of those arrested in Glasgow during the strike (*Worker*, 1 February, 18 October 1919; SRO AD 15/19/54, Unsigned note on Patrick Murty in 'Precognitions of Exculpatory Witnesses').

134. Woodhouse, thesis, pp. 163 *et seq*.
135. PRO CAB 24/77, GT 7043, 'The labour situation. Report from the Ministry of Labour for the week ending 26 March 1919'.
136. PRO CAB 24/77, GT 7091, 'Report on Revolutionary Organisations in the United Kingdom', 7 April 1919; *Hamilton Advertiser*, 19 April 1919. For the events surrounding the Sankey Commission, see C. Wrigley, *Lloyd George and the Challenge of Labour: the post-war coalition, 1918–1922* (Hemel Hempstead, 1990), chs 5–7.
137. Macdougall, 'Scottish coalminer', p. 773.
138. *Motherwell Times*, 31 January 1919.
139. *Worker*, 24 May 1919, 13 March 1920. Attempts to extend the 'One Union Movement' into the shipbuilding and engineering industries do not appear to have met with any success (*Socialist*, 26 June 1919).
140. NLS Dep. 227/37, LMU Council, 25 September 1920; SRO CB 7/5/37, LCMA, 'List of collieries idle on 4, 5, 6 October 1920 ...'.
141. NLS Dep. 227/37, LMU Council, 7, 28 October, 27 November 1920.
142. *Worker*, 27 November, 11, 25 December 1920, 9 April 1921; *Forward*, 13 November 1920; *Socialist*, 13 January, 10 February 1921; PRO CAB 24/118, CP 2452, 'Report on Revolutionary Organisations in the United Kingdom', no. 88, 13 January 1921.
143. See vol. 1, ch. 6.
144. T. Jones, *Whitehall Diary, vol. 1, 1916–25* (edited by K. Middlemas, 1969), p. 136.
145. PRO CAB 24/122, CP 2838, 'Report on Revolutionary Organisations in the United Kingdom', no. 101, 14 April 1921.
146. PRO CAB 24/123, CP 2916, 'Report on Revolutionary Organisations in the United Kingdom', no. 104, 5 May 1921. For an account of policing in South Wales during the dispute, see Weinberger, *Keeping the Peace*, pp. 181–7.
147. M. Docherty, *A Miner's Lass* (Cowdenbeath, 1992), p. 37; transcript of BBC Scotland interview with Jimmy Miller by Billy Kay for the series, 'Miners', broadcast 1989 (hereafter Kay interviews).
148. *Ayr Advertiser*, 7 April 1921. Lloyd George was moved to remark to the Cabinet Secretary at the height of the negotiations on the coal crisis: 'I'm sorry for the miners – they're a patriotic lot. I'm not heartless enough for this sort of thing' (Jones, *Whitehall Diary*, p. 151).

149. PRO AIR 1/556, Scottish Command Weekly Intelligence Reports, 5–11 February 1918, 1–7 June 1919.
150. SRO AD 15/18/19, Precognitions of Detective Sergeant A. Gordon, PC W. McQuaker, J.S. Forest, shorthand writer, Superintendent A. Taylor, Detective Inspector J. Syme, J. Ford, Fife Coal Company. The Fife militants never forgave Ford for 'acting as a spy against Maclean' and in later years, as Communist trade union leaders, 'always went to town on him' (MacDougall, *Militant Miners*, pp. 44–5).
151. Macdougall, 'Scottish coal miner', p. 768; Welsh, 'Scottish miners', p. 79; *Bellshill Speaker*, 3 May 1919.
152. Calculated from footnotes of MacDougall, *Militant Miners*.
153. Smith interview by S. Najam.
154. Knox, *Labour Leaders*, p. 233.
155. Long, 'Abe Moffat', p. 7; A. Moffat, *My Life with the Miners* (1965), p. 26.
156. PRO CAB 24/92, CP 70, 'Report on Revolutionary Organisations in the United Kingdom', no. 28, 6 November 1919.
157. For the involvement of ex-servicemen in the Forty Hours strike in Glasgow, see Foster, 'Strike action', p. 55.
158. See vol. 1, ch. 6.
159. Kay interview, Jimmy Miller.
160. SRO AD 15/19/54, W. Thomson, Procurator Fiscal, Hamilton, to W.J.D. Dundas, Crown Agent, Edinburgh, 6 February 1919, and 'List of witnesses for defence'.
161. *Justice*, 16 March 1912. Cf John Robertson's condemnation of the incident (*Glasgow Herald*, 9 March 1912).
162. Macdougall, 'Scottish coal miner', p. 772.
163. Knox, *Labour Leaders*, p. 173; Ripley and McHugh, *Maclean*, p. 144; *Socialist*, 7 April 1921.
164. Macdougall, 'Scottish coal miner', p. 768; NLS Dep. 227/36, LMU Council, 26 April, 27 September 1919.
165. The following LMU branches have been identified as supporting Reform Committee policies between 1917 and 1921: Giffnock, Auchengeich, Kirkwood, Barrachnie, Blantyreferme, Auchenraith, Dixon's Blantyre, Bardykes, Priory, Greenfield, Quarter, Earnock, Canderigg, Carluke, Law, Coalburn District, Douglas Castle, Ponfeigh, Douglas, Kepplehill, Shotts, Hamilton Palace (*Call*, 23 August 1917; Macdougall, 'Scottish coalminer'; LMU Council and Executive Committee, 1917–20).
166. SRO AD 15/18/19, 'Memorandum of meeting held by Director of National Service with other government departments, Glasgow, 5 April 1918'.

167. *Dunfermline Press*, 1 February 1919.
168. Macdougall, 'Scottish coal miner', p. 769.
169. See vol. 1, chs 1 and 3.
170. For Sinn Fein support in the West Central coalfield, see vol. 1, ch. 7.
171. PRO AIR 1/ 553, Scottish Command Weekly Intelligence Report, 9–15 March 1919. There were also strong links between Sinn Fein and the International Union of Ex-Servicemen in Scotland; see K. Morgan and T. Saarela, 'Northern underground revisited: Finnish reds and the origins of British communism', *European History Quarterly*, 29, 2, 1999, p. 201.
172. PRO CAB 24/122, CP 2811, 'Report on Revolutionary Organisations in the United Kingdom', no. 100, 7 April 1921; CAB 24/123, CP 2952, 'Report on Revolutionary Organisations in the United Kingdom', no. 106, 19 May 1921; *Ayr Advertiser*, 19 May 1921.
173. MacDougall, *Militant Miners*, pp. 35–6; *Worker*, 10 December 1921; I.D. Patterson, 'The activities of Irish republican physical force organisations in Scotland, 1919–21', *Scottish Historical Review*, 72, 193, 1993, p. 58.
174. MacDougall, *Militant Miners*, p. 18.
175. *Socialist*, 27 January 1921; NLS Dep. 227/37, LMU Council, 29 May, 15 June, 25 September, 28 October, 8 December 1920, 26 February, 26 March 1921.
176. *Motherwell Times*, 2 July 1920; MacDougall, *Militant Miners*, p. 44; Milton, *John Maclean*, pp. 236–41; Howell, *Lost Left*, pp. 211–12. British Communists generally supported the 'rebels' who rejected the peace terms during the Irish Civil War.
177. M. Durham, 'The origins and early years of British communism, 1914–24', unpublished PhD thesis, University of Birmingham, 1982, pp. 75–80.
178. A. Adler (ed.), *Theses, Resolutions and Manifestos of the First Four Congresses of the Third International* (1980), pp. 258–61.
179. Durham, thesis, p. 77.
180. Selkirk, *Life*, p. 12; MacDougall, *Militant Miners*, pp. 22–3. Willie Gallacher recalled his 'old Comrade Jack, from Glasgow', almost certainly Leckie, lambasting two plainclothes policemen at a meeting in Birmingham in 1921, urging his audience 'to copy the IRA; two or three lads on the roof with rifles would put an end to these snoopers' (W. Gallacher, *Last Memoirs*, 1966, p. 186).
181. PRO CAB 24/122, CP 2891, 'Report on Revolutionary Organisations in the United Kingdom', 103, 28 April 1921. A similar oath of the Red Officer Corps was among papers seized on the CI emissary, Veltheim, in London in 1920; see W. Kendall, *The Revolutionary Movement in Britain, 1900–21* (1969), pp. 246–8. For a recent examination of the attempts by Velteim and his associate Salme Pekkala

to construct the nucleus of a 'Red Army' from indigenous elements already engaged in revolutionary, military activities in Scotland and elsewhere, see Morgan and Saarela, 'Northern underground', pp. 198–210.

182. Durham, thesis, p. 77.

183. *Socialist*, 1 September 1921.

184. E.P. Thompson, *The Making of the English Working Class* (1964), pp. 12–13.

185. For contemporary observers in Britain, see J. Cronin, *Labour and Society in Britain 1918–1979* (1984), pp. 23–30; for the 'significant radicalisation' in the specific circumstances of Clydeside, see Foster, 'Strike action'.

186. *Bellshill Speaker*, 22 March 1918; *Colliery Guardian*, 9 February, 7 September 1917.

187. R. Duncan, *Shotts Miners: conflicts and struggles, 1919–1960* (Motherwell, 1982), p. 4.

188. Milton, *Maclean*, p. 83.

189. Hinton, *Labour and Socialism*, pp. 110–14. Smillie spoke in near revolutionary tones when presiding over the Leeds Soviet Convention in June 1917 which advocated the setting up of 'Councils of Workmen's and Soldiers' Delegates' in every town in Britain (Kendall, *Revolutionary Movement*, pp. 174–5). However, Smillie and his fellow union agents were also skilled at using the language of 'direct action' to stifle unofficial strikes; for example, when supporting a return to work during a dispute in Coalburn, he urged that 'direct action must not be taken by Counties but by all the miners' (NLS Dep. 227/36, LMU Council, 27 September 1919). Note the similar comments, quoted above, of John Robertson when recommending an end to the unofficial strikes in January 1919.

190. MacDougall, *Militant Miners*, p. 51.

191. Interview with Johnny Boyle, Methil, 8 August 1986.

192. Macdougall, 'Scottish coalminer', p. 768.

193. See Ripley and McHugh, *Maclean*, pp. 134–6, 176–7.

194. *Call*, 4 October 1917.

195. Ripley and McHugh, *Maclean*, pp. 116–17.

196. Note the vote of confidence by the LMU Council in favour of the Executive's actions in February 1919, of 93 votes to 7 (NLS Dep. 227/36, LMU Council, 10 February 1919).

197. R.H. Desmarais, 'The British government's strikebreaking organisation and Black Friday', *Journal of Contemporary History*, 6, 2, 1971; K. Jeffery and P. Hennessy, *States of Emergency: British governments and strikebreaking since 1919* (1983), chs 1–3.

198. Cf Macdougall's perceptive comment: 'How calculated to appeal to

human weakness of the leaders was this proposal of a Commission' (*Worker*, 31 May 1919).

199. Wrigley, *Challenge of Labour*, p. 190.
200. Jones, *Whitehall Diary*, p. 84.
201. Wrigley, *Challenge of Labour*, pp. 190, 207–8.
202. See Wrigley, *Challenge of Labour*, ch. 3; A. Rothstein, *The Soldiers' Strikes of 1919* (1980). A participant later claimed that one reason the mutinies were abandoned 'was the collapse of the expected general strike which had begun on the Clyde on the same day as our own and to which our eyes were anxiously turned' (*Workers' Life*, 5 April 1929). Foster notes Emmanuel Shinwell's suggestion that Scottish troops had played a prominent part in the demobilisation mutinies of December 1918 (Foster, 'Strike action', p. 55).
203. PRO AIR 1/553 and 556, Scottish Command Weekly Intelligence Reports, 4–10, 9–15, 16–22 March, 15–22 June 1919.
204. A. Moffat, *My Life with the Miners* (1965), p. 27; Docherty, *Miner's Lass*, pp. 35–6; SRO HH 56/14, Sheriff Fleming to Sir John Gilmour, 13 July 1925. The incident described by the Sheriff is obscure – there are no files on the 1921 lockout in the Civil Emergencies series (HH 56) – but the term 'raised' suggests members of the volunteer Citizens' Defence Force were involved. The Cabinet had been informed on 13 April that 'Sinn Feiners, strikers and Communist were enlisting [in the Defence Force] with a view to levanting with their arms' (Jeffery and Hennessy, *States of Emergency*, p. 64).
205. PRO AIR 1/553 and 554, Scottish Command Weekly Intelligence Reports, 16–22 March, 25–31 May 1919.
206. Jones, *Whitehall Diary*, p. 138.
207. Wrigley, *Challenge of Labour*, ch. 8, provides a full analysis of this process; see also Jones, *Whitehall Diary*, pp. 132–54. Jones, the Cabinet Secretary, was the son of a company storekeeper in the Rhymney valley in South Wales and a lifelong Labour Party member. While a student at Glasgow University he joined the ILP's Partick branch in 1895 and came to know Smillie and other labour leaders (*Whitehall Diary*, pp. xii, xxi–xxii). That he did not share the wilder anti-Communist prejudices of the likes of Basil Thompson but rather displayed shrewd insight into the dynamics of the miners' and other unions was demonstrated in his memorandum to the Prime Minister on industrial unrest after the 1919 strikes in the west of Scotland:

> Much of the present difficulty springs from the mutiny of the rank and file against the old established leaders and there seems to be no machinery for bringing about a quick change of leaders. Working men are notoriously tender towards a man in office and most unwilling to sack him, however incompetent or out of touch. The

> Government's decision to stand by the accredited leaders is the
> only possible policy but it does not get over the fact that the lead-
> ers no longer represent the more active and agitating minds in the
> labour movement (Ibid., p. 73).

208. Jones, *Whitehall Diary, vol. 2*, p. 153.
209. See Weinberger, *Keeping the Peace*, pp. 146–7, for a similar analysis.
210. PRO CAB 24/44, GT 3838, 'Revolutionary agitation in Glasgow and
     Clydeside with special reference to the cases of John Maclean and
     others'.
211. SRO AD 15/18/19, 'Indictment against John Maclean'.
212. Milton, *Maclean*, pp. 164–80.
213. PRO CAB 24/66, GT 5923, 'Fortnightly Report on Pacifism and
     Revolutionary Organisations in the United Kingdom', 23, 7 October
     1918; CAB 24/70, GT 6379, 'War Cabinet. Imprisonment of John
     Maclean. Note by Mr C.N. Barnes, 26 November 1918'; AIR 1/553,
     Scottish Command Intelligence Report, November 1918. As
     Maclean's parliamentary opponent in the forthcoming general elec-
     tion, Barnes had a vested interested in checking any groundswell of
     support for him.
214. Jeffrey and Hennessy, *States of Emergency*, chs 2, 3; Desmarais,
     'Strikebreaking organisation'; Wrigley, *Challenge of Labour*,
     pp. 265–6.
215. Jones, *Whitehall Diary*, p. 153.

CHAPTER FOUR

Decline and division, 1921–26

Following the return of the miners on the employers' terms after the lockout of 1921, significant unemployment was experienced in parts of the Scottish coalfields, particularly the West Central region. In Fife and the Lothians, employment marginally increased between 1921 and 1925.[1] Nevertheless, short time working was prevalent throughout the Scots mining districts and all regions were affected by unemployment in the summer and autumn of 1921, though to widely varying degrees. In Mid and East Lothian, only 7 per cent of the MELMA membership was unemployed whereas in West Lothian about 50 per cent of the miners remained out of work. In Ayrshire, the figure was 23 per cent, in Lanarkshire about 20 per cent, although the latter figure concealed local variations. Blantyre was 'an especially black spot', with less than two-thirds of its pre-lockout labour force in work; in Coalburn's mines, the number employed more than halved; in Larkhall, the decline was only 18 per cent. In parts of central Fife, such as Lochore and Glencraig, only about 50 per cent were working but in Lumphinnans this dropped as low as 5 per cent.[2]

With savings and credit exhausted by the lockout, and with the wage rates of those able to secure work tumbling, hardship was widespread. The LMU Branch Secretary at Shields Colliery, near Craigneuk, stated that his members were 'in very distressful circumstances. These men were getting grocers to stand by them to the extent of bread and margarine and the Wishaw Cooperative were giving to their members relief in kind.'[3] Wages rates continued to decline in the following years. For most of 1922 the nominal wage in Lanarkshire was 8s 5d per day, and for 1923 and 1924 increased to an average of 9s 9d. The latter figure was still only half what it had been at the start of 1921 and these rates take no account of the diminution in weekly earnings through short time working.[4]

A report on unemployment by the Scottish Board of Health in October 1921 concluded distress was especially marked in coal and steel areas and warned:

> ... in Fifeshire, Lanarkshire and Glasgow there are very inflammable elements, which, while subjected during ordinary times to damping down by the saner and much larger section of the community, will not improbably be fanned into activity as the endurance of the more sober section is broken by the continued tightening of waist belts round empty bellies.[5]

However, the immediate prospects for the left were bleak in the wake of the lockout, for this hardship inevitably took a heavy toll on union membership. In November 1921, it was reported that in Lanarkshire 'a large percentage of miners are not paying union dues, one reason advanced being the great disparity in the number of shifts wrought by the various collieries'. The following year the LMU reduced its affiliation to the NUSMW from 47,000 to 25,000 members.[6] In Buckhaven, a member of the local union branch committee complained that 'since the defeat of the miners last year it has been impossible to get them to turn out to meetings of any kind ... half of them have left their trade union and are just drifting along, showing no fighting spirit'.[7] Data on union membership and estimates of union density in the total workforce for the years 1921–6 are given in Table 4.1. These figures are based on county unions' affiliations to the NUSMW and may well differ from the actual membership; they provide only an approximate indication of trends. Nevertheless, the sharp drop in membership after 1921 is marked in all the coalfields and this adversely affected union finances. In 1922, the LMU and the FKCMA were both £7,000 in arrears to the NUSMW, and the LMU in 1925 remained solvent only through a loan from the Scottish Horse and Motormen's Association.[8]

In addition to structural and economic factors, unions were affected by internal splits. In the aftermath of the lockout, there was pronounced criticism of the LMU leadership. Blantyre was 'in the forefront of the new agitation' to re-elect officials, and the withholding of union dues until this was achieved was widely canvassed.[9] In Ayrshire, it was reported that the Hurlford, Dreghorn, Irvine and Kilwinning branches, which had accumulated heavy

Table 4.1 Affiliated memberships of the constituent county unions of the National Union of Scottish Mine Workers, 1921–6, and as a percentage of the total number employed

	Lanark	Fife	Ayr	Stirling	West Lothian	Mid and East Lothian	NUSMW
1921	47,000	25,000	13,000	9,000	4,000	3,500	101,500
	79.5	88.9	91.8	76.4	40.8	23.0	72.6
1922	25,000	12,500	8,000	4,000	4,000	2,500	56,000
	43.5	42.6	56.5	35.2	39.1	15.3	39.8
1926	32,000	12,500	9,500	6,000	2,500	7,500	70,000
	75.6	66.2	83.7	85.0	31.4	58.2	68.0

Source: Calculated from P. Long, 'The economic and social history of the Scottish coal industry, 1925–39, with particular reference to industrial relations', unpublished PhD thesis, University of Strathclyde, 1978, Tables 26 and 31.

Note: The county unions' membership is based on the numbers on which they affiliated to the NUSMW; they may have inflated or deflated their affiliated membership in order to increase representation on the Executive or to reduce affiliation fees. It is not suggested that they are accurate figures; they are suspiciously round. However, they may be taken as an approximate indicator of membership trends.

debts during the lockout, seceded from the AMU in 1921 and operated as district unions, 'only combining when attacked by the county union'. The cause of this secession was 'the superfluity of officials' in the Ayrshire union, which 'necessitated heavy contributions which in the end became intolerable'.[10] At Stoneyburn, West Lothian, it was reported that 'keen trade unionists' had formed a local union in preference to the county association 'as there is nobody left in it besides officials'.[11]

Religious divisions led to the most important schism in Lanarkshire. In July 1921, 'Brother Nicol', stated before a demonstration in Holytown that he had been an Orangeman for thirty-seven years and a trade unionist for thirty-three. From his experiences on Motherwell and Wishaw Trades Council, of which he had been a founder member, he claimed that 'if you were a member of a trade union today ... you need not expect to hold office unless you were a Sinn Feiner or a Socialist'. William Knox, from Holytown, declared that 'the time had come ... when they should take a stand for independence as regards the trade union movement'.[12]

A few weeks later, Lanarkshire miners from Bellshill, Harthill, Larkhall, Coatbridge, Motherwell, Wishaw, Newmains, Airdrie, Greengairs and Bargeddie met to discuss the inadequacies of the Lanarkshire union.[13] A 'Sinn Fein Miner' from Blantyre wrote to the local press describing his surprise, on reading a newspaper report of this meeting, that no representatives from Blantyre, Cambuslang or Hamilton were present,

> but on making enquiries I find that there is a feeling at the present time for two unions – that the Orangemen are determined to withdraw from the present union and take their Protestant friends with them, as they maintain that the present Lanarkshire union has turned into a certain political class under Sinn Fein management.

He went on to admit that he had worked beside Protestants who were good trade unionists, 'but when a position came to be filled they were practically ignored, not because they had not the ability, but through religion ...'.[14] Nevertheless, he urged his Orange and Protestant fellow unionists to remain in the one union.

His plea fell on deaf ears. At a meeting in the Masonic Hall, Holytown, a new body – the Scottish National Trade Union Association (SNTUA) – was set up. The President and Secretary were both from Stonehouse, four miles south of Larkhall. The chairman of the meeting was William Knox, the Holytown Orangeman. The constitution was read over and it was noted that all meetings of the Executive Council were to be opened and closed with a prayer. One questioner, who asked whether it was to be a Protestant or Catholic prayer, received the evasive reply that the House of Commons was opened with a prayer. The speeches of the President and Secretary displayed elements of Orange ideology as well as traces of the class collaborationism of the independent collier. The former spoke against the payment of the political levy to the Labour Party – 'who aim at the destruction of the Empire' – by the county union and its members; the latter complained that 'the strike weapon was a disastrous failure ... he believed that there was as much humanity even in the capitalists as would enable them to get down to the bedrock of reason with the men, and allow an amicable settlement of all disputes (Applause)'. [15]

The SNTUA made only limited progress in establishing a presence. In September, branches were being set up at Holytown, Bellshill, Airdrie, Coatbridge and Wishaw, and Haywood in south-east Lanarkshire. It was reported to have 'a large following amongst the miners of Holytown', where Knox was its Branch Chairman, and it temporarily ousted the LMU from the union collector's office at Holytown's Thankerton Colliery.[16] The union's adherents were termed 'the praying colliers' and at a meeting in Holytown the following month, the LMU leadership mocked the SNTUA's willingness 'to organise everybody, men and masters (laughter)'.[17] In the industrially concentrated and strike-prone coal industry of Lanarkshire, such policies held a diminishing plausibility and nothing more was heard of the SNTUA after 1921.[18] Nevertheless, its formation indicated the brittleness of union loyalty in Lanarkshire when under pressure from competing sectarian affiliations in the aftermath of the lockout. Although the SNTUA did not have a lengthy existence, its former members may not have rejoined the LMU: Thankerton Colliery was regarded by LMU officials 'as the weak part of their chain of solidarity' in 1926.[19]

The most significant split occurred within the FKCMA.[20] This requires detailed consideration because the events in Fife in 1921–2 had a profound impact upon the Scots miners' unions in the following two decades. William Adamson, the long-serving FKCMA General Secretary and MP, stood well to the right of the LMU leadership on the Labour spectrum, and had been vociferous in denouncing the Fife Reform Committee.[21] The militants in turn repeatedly pointed to the rewards of his bureaucratic and parliamentary status: 'for thirty years he has been a full-time official of the Fife miners, and at no time during that period did a "cleek", black damp, bad air, or shortage of wagons ever endanger his bread and butter'. While he labelled his opponents 'place hunters' and claimed their agitation was 'simply to secure official positions for one or two leading lights of Communism', they in turn insisted that he feared 'rank and file control' because he knew it meant 'a diminution of his salary'.[22]

The uneven development of the industry in Fife meant there was considerable divergence in the size of the FKCMA branches (which were based on residence rather than individual collieries as was the case in Lanarkshire). Some branches had as few as sixty members, others had 2,000, but all sent one delegate to the county union's Board. Rule Six of the FKCMA constitution existed to remedy the inherently unrepresentative composition of the Board. Where a question had been discussed by members at local meetings, a 'financial vote', proportional to the membership in each branch, could be invoked to more fairly represent the views of the majority.[23]

Prior to 1920, the five Fife representatives to the NUSMW had been appointed by the Board and these were invariably full-time agents. That year, a financial vote called for by Reform Committee supporters decided that in future these representatives would be elected by a ballot of the membership. However, delaying tactics by the officials did not allow sufficient time for a ballot before the NUSMW Annual Conference and the Board made the appointments as before. In 1921, a ballot was taken and the five top names included Willie Kirker, a Bowhill militant and Secretary of the Scottish reform movement, in third place. The Board decided that a second ballot be taken. In this ballot, held during the lockout, reform movement candidates took the top three places. However, the Board agreed that both votes be abandoned, allegedly because of a low turnout in the second, and the sitting five representatives were re-appointed to attend the NUSMW conference held a few days later. At the following Board meeting, a financial vote protesting against this decision was claimed by the reformers. The officials stated that the failure of forty-seven branches to send in their contributions during the twelve days which had elapsed since the termination of the lockout disenfranchised these branches from any financial vote, and only seven branches were allowed to participate. Whereas a normal financial vote represented contributions of some £4,000, this amounted to £50 6s 6d, equivalent to 1.25 per cent of the membership. Even so, this vote only approved the Board's action because the Denbeath delegate defied his branch mandate. One Fife miner wrote presciently that:

> Unless there is a great reform carried out, there is going to be a split up in the ranks in Fife. This is to be regretted, but we cannot shut our eyes to the fact. In this district we have got a large percentage of refusals to contribute to the union and at a meeting Adamson was present at, a resolution was carried that no more money should be sent to Dunfermline until there was a drastic clearout of officials and a reformed constitution.[24]

The following year, such tensions were exacerbated. Because of the need for economy after the lockout, a branch vote rather than a membership ballot for the Fife representatives to the NUSMW Executive was agreed, each branch submitting five names. On the numerical vote, the top five names included Kirker plus four of the sitting officials. A financial vote was then called for, which would have had the effect of electing another reformer, John Bird, also from Bowhill. Unprecedently, the chairman refused, his ruling supported by a majority of the delegates. In the following months, 'rebel' branches withheld their contributions and Philip Hodge, the only FKCMA official to support them, was suspended. Adamson launched a vitriolic 'manifesto', condemning 'a section of malcontents' who were 'the leadership of the Communist Party in the county', dismissing the issue of the financial vote as 'merely the pretext' for their 'policy of disintegration'.[25] The dissident branches constituted themselves the 'Emergency Committee of the Fife Miners' Association', insisting there was 'no suggestion of forming a new union; the fight is being carried on inside the existing one'. The committee denounced 'the trickery' which had 'maintained the old school in office' and denied they were 'out to burst up the Association':

> We desire to make the Association stronger than ever it has been by giving the members full control over the policy and the officials. Rank and file control will mean that we have an organisation in real truth and not an Adamson Admiration Society as at present.[26]

However, the tenacious grip of Adamson and his supporters on the FKCMA Board led to the conviction that reform of the union was impossible since democratic decisions would be flouted. The belief that the growing number of non-unionists might be attracted to a radical, democratic alternative was a further impetus towards the creation of a new organisation. In December 1922, representatives of the dissident branches met and decided to form a new union, the Mineworkers' Reform Union of Fife, Kinross and Clackmannan (MRU). Hodge was subsequently elected its General Secretary. McArthur recalled that 'everyone associated with the movement was brimful of confidence and enthusiasm, was enthusiastic for this inter-union fight, and drove ahead to build up the Reform Union'.[27]

The constitution of the new union sought to put into effect the industrial unionist policies long advocated by the reformers. The General Secretary was elected annually and full-time officials could be removed by a membership ballot called by branches representing a fifth of the members. The union's long term objective was 'to organise and educate the workers with a view to complete workers' control of industry' while its immediate aims included the promotion of 'independent working class education' by forming 'classes in social science'.[28]

The MRU was probably larger than the FKCMA (or 'the old union' as it soon became known), perhaps since indignation at bureaucratic manipulation had centred on the disenfranchised larger branches. Yet in the post-lockout years even the combined membership of the two unions probably represented only about half of the mining workforce.[29] In October 1922, prior to the formation of the MRU, the FKCMA had reduced its affiliation to the NUSMW to 12,500. An auditor's report confirmed the MRU membership as being 7,366 by March 1924 and claimed 'a considerable increase' had taken place since then.[30] Although the MRU's thirty-nine branches were spread throughout the Fife coalfield, the ten largest were at Lochgelly, Kelty, Bowhill, Lumphinnans, Glencraig and Cowdenbeath in central Fife; at Methil and Buckhaven in east Fife; and at Valleyfield and Townhill in west Fife. These branches accounted for over two-thirds of the MRU's contributions in 1923–4.[31]

Colliery managers often refused to recognise MRU delegates and McArthur recalled that it was 'an exceptionally difficult period to deal with individual, sectional or pit grievances unless one had to resort to strike action'.[32] Nevertheless, the MRU's influence beyond the workplace was developed by a number of methods, including door-to-door canvassing and propaganda meetings 'by a team of speakers who went out almost every weekend'.[33] More innovatively, the union published a fortnightly newspaper, the *Miner*, a self-styled 'organ of the rank and file', edited by Hodge. In contrast to the turgid or declamatory prose of other left-wing newspapers, this was a lively journal which was also more readable than the couthy parochialism of much of the contemporary Scottish provincial press. It circulated widely in Fife – McArthur claimed over 700 per issue were sold in Buckhaven alone – and also among militants elsewhere, particularly Lanarkshire.[34] Through its pages, the Fife militants issued a steady stream of propaganda against bureaucratic reformism: for example, in mocking accounts of the convoluted structures of the NUSMW and the perquisites of its agents.[35] In an implicit recognition of the generational cleavage between left and right and the persistence of company paternalism in parts of the coalfield, they also attacked class collaboration and deference within the tradition of the independent collier. An article entitled 'Independence' used the satirical convention of dialect to scorn those 'who still believe in the old order of things' and:

the guid auld days o' auld lang syne. To draw parish relief or unemployment dole is to earn from them the look of bitter contempt. They are of the richt auld Scottish breed, work awa' and say naething; a hauf loaf is better than nae breid; keep in wi' the gaffer ... lift aff yir bannet and laugh bags when the Laird passes ye by in his braw new motor ... and, whatever ye dae, hae naething tae dae wi' the new Bolshevick Union.[36]

The *Miner* also contained regular articles on Marxist education by James Clunie, an SLP tutor and associate of John Maclean. In line with its constitution, the union's branches also unanimously agreed to affiliate to the Scottish Labour College (SLC).[37] In 1925, free tuition was given to any MRU member attending the ten classes organised by the college in Fife, covering economics, industrial history and sociology. Tutors included Clunie and also McArthur, by then a graduate of Maclean's full-time SLC course.[38] The following year, the Fife Local Committee of the SLC reported:

In many places the classes are composed entirely of youthful and ardent members of the Reform Union. It is an inspiring sight to see, in a remote mining village, 30 or 40 young miners sitting down to discuss the problems of the coal industry, of finance and combines and monopolies and their effects on the worker.[39]

Relations between the MRU and FKCMA remained strained, not least because of the pre-existing personal antagonism between Hodge and Adamson. Such was their mutual dislike, the two men had rarely met or spoken to each other when Hodge was employed by the FKCMA, and Adamson and two other 'old union' officials successfully sued Hodge for libel over an article in the *Miner* in 1923.[40] The MRU also remained outside the federal structure of the NUSMW and the MFGB, which weakened the forces of the left within them. It was for this reason that McArthur later considered that the militants had been 'outmanoeuvred' by Adamson 'and forced into forming a rival organisation'.[41] However, any evaluation of the MRU's origins must also consider the ideological divisions within the reform movement.

By early 1921, the Scottish Miners' Reform Committee was made up of 'rebels drawn from all sections of the socialist movement'.[42] Its leaders were usually associated with one of several political parties – the left wing of the ILP, the SLP, or the Communist Party of Great Britain (CPGB), newly formed from elements of the BSP, SLP and ILP.[43] In April of that year, the committee transformed itself into the Scottish Miners' Section of the National Workers' Committee Movement (NWCM), the successor to the war-time shop stewards' movement.[44] Although the NWCM supported, and its leadership was drawn from, the CPGB, the position in the Scottish coalfields displayed considerable complexity.[45]

In Fife, many members of the BSP and the majority of the Fife Communist League had merged into the Communist Party, although McArthur pertinently recalled that many of his comrades in the new party retained 'a syndicalist approach to trade unions'.[46] Many of the leading militants in the Fife union were members of the CP, including the three elected in the second FKCMA ballot in 1921, and the party in Fife was 'mostly composed of miners'.[47] CP industrial policy, as expressed through the NWCM, was to work within the existing trade unions and the party leadership bluntly opposed the establishment of the MRU in which many of its Fife cadre took leading positions: 'the Communist Party cannot welcome the creation of the new union. We would urge the members of the Reform Union to start at once to work for fusion [with the FKCMA].' Communist members of the FKCMA in Clackmannanshire were instructed not to join the MRU while the CP Central Committee sent a 'special organiser' to Fife in 1924 'to demand that the comrades work for unity'.[48]

The CP attitude to the MRU caused difficulties for Fife Communists. Proudfoot, Communist checkweigher at Wellesley Colliery, Methil, who according to Hodge had 'played a great part in building up' the organisation, resigned from the MRU Executive in July 1924, urging a ballot on unification.[49] Proudfoot admitted his views were 'decidedly unpopular' among CP members in Fife and many, such as the MRU Chairman, Tommy Smith, remained active in the union's leadership.[50] Other Communists, such as McArthur, temporarily abandoned the party, declaring that the MRU was 'of more consequence to him than the Communist Party'.[51] When the leading Communist, Harry Pollitt, attacked Hodge for encouraging Fife miners to vote for the Conservative candidate against Adamson in the 1924 general election, and called for the liquidation of the MRU in an article published in both the *Worker* and the *Workers' Weekly*, under the headline 'The Fife Blunder', he was denounced by a member of the Fife District Party Committee. Even Proudfoot thought Pollitt's advocacy of liquidation 'badly advised'.[52] It was indicative of support for the union among CP activists that the party's Political Bureau subsequently issued a statement attempting to clarify 'misunderstandings' of its policy, opposing any of its members advocating the immediate liquidation of the union but reiterating its view that the split was 'a calamity' and urging a unity conference.[53] Proudfoot represented only 'a small section' of CP members in Fife and the majority of Communists remained in the MRU until its fusion with the FKCMA early in 1927.[54]

The dispute also caused tension with the militants organised in the CP-led Miners' Minority Movement (MMM) elsewhere in the Scots coalfields. A meeting of the Scottish Executive of the MMM heard complaints from MRU representatives that 'they were annoyed because they never got support from the Scottish Miners' Minority Movement'; the Executive for its part viewed the split as 'a positive menace to successful resistance to the coalowners' onslaught' and called for the immediate healing of the breach.[55] Divisions over the issue continued within the party until an eventual merger was brokered between the MRU and FKCMA over the summer and autumn of 1926 although it was not implemented until early 1927.[56]

In Lanarkshire in 1921, a number of reform movement activists remained outside the CP. Maclean's refusal to join the CPGB, the party's 'wrecking' tactics towards his activities, and his brief membership of the SLP in 1921 influenced a number of his followers there.[57] William Allan, the 21 year old Blantyre miner who was Secretary of the Lanarkshire Miners' Section of the NWCM and a graduate of Maclean's SLC, was a member of the SLP, as was Andrew Fagan, another Blantyre activist and SLC student.[58] While Allan was critical of the 'harum scarum tactics of the Communists' during the lockout, he also opposed the revival of the SLP's De Leonite strategy of setting up branches of a new Workers' International Industrial Union (WIIU): 'to try and build up a legal, safe, Industrial Union outside of, and hostile to, the existing unions is to attempt the impossible ... The NWC policy is practicable. The WIIU is impossible.'[59]

It was ironic, although in keeping with their mentor Maclean's, views, that SLP members such as Allan, unlike their CP counterparts in Fife, supported the NWCM strategy of fighting within the existing unions. When candidates from the Miners' Section of the NWCM contested all the offices of the LMU in 1921, Allan argued against the views of some of his SLP comrades:

> Quite apart from what any of the 'pure' Socialists may say, we think that the presence of a number of comrades working within the union in an official capacity (even if it is a 'county' union) should give us more material assistance and opportunity for educating the mass of workers than ever we have had before.[60]

Divisions over strategy remained, however, and calls for the setting up of new unions remained a persistent feature of left-wing debate in the Scots coalfields in the following years. In East Lothian, where there had been some SLP presence before the war, the NWCM was forced to reach an 'arrangement' with the WIIU to coordinate efforts inside the unions.[61] At a Scottish Miners' Section, NWCM, conference in January 1922, a proposal was made by West Lothian delegates to set up a 'National Union in Scotland, for all colliery workers outside of the existing county unions'. Although there was sympathy with this suggestion from Bird, another SLC graduate, he felt that the appropriate time for such a move had been after the lockout. The main argument in support of the proposal was that 'it was next to impossible to shift the present officials as they controlled the whole machinery of the county unions and would refuse to recognise even a definite vote of their members', as had been the case in Fife the previous summer.[62]

Although the conference voted to continue working within the existing unions, the following year William Pearson, a Lanarkshire miner and SLP member, vociferously criticised the RILU slogan of 'Go back to the unions': 'never was there such a cowardly policy as this and never more reactionary'. He announced that 'rebel' miners from the outlying villages of Coalburn and Douglas had formed a 'Workers Industrial Union (Miners' section)' which repudiated 'leadership and officialdom'. The aims of the new body included 'the emancipation of the workers from economic slavery' and 'educating the members in classes'. Copies of its constitution were circulated in Lanarkshire in the hope that 'the miners will get into the new organisation and bury the old'.[63] This Lanarkshire Miners'

Industrial Union (as it became known) continued in existence until 1924, although its influence appears to have been confined to the Douglas and Coalburn district.[64]

Such initiatives were encouraged by the MRU which organised a Scottish conference of 'Reform elements' in November 1923. In its report, the MRU's organ the *Miner* optimistically claimed that 'its influence is spreading throughout Scotland – district unions may swing right over to the Reform movement, and out of the crash, officialdom being doomed, will arise a reformed organisation'.[65] In 1924, a correspondent from Ayrshire looked forward to the formation of 'a Scottish Miners' Reform Union', while 'A Lanark Lad', the *Miner*'s regular Lanarkshire columnist, was critical of the Minority Movement's approach of working inside the county unions: 'it must strike out for itself and form a movement separate and apart from the official majority movement'.[66]

These impulses towards the establishment of new unions in the west were reduced, at least temporarily, by the effective demise of the SLP after the cessation of publication of its journal, the *Socialist*, in 1924, and the incorporation of some of its militants into the CPGB. The CP's William Gallacher had conducted an intensive campaign in the Lanarkshire coalfield in favour of establishing a Minority Movement in August and September 1923 and at a conference in January 1924, the Scottish Miners' Section of the NWC reconstituted itself as the Scottish affiliate to the CP-led Miners' Minority Movement.[67] The election of the Welsh miners' leader, A.J. Cook, to the Secretaryship of the MFGB with Minority Movement support in 1924 also indicated the potential of the CP's trade union strategy. Finally, the death of the increasingly isolated Maclean in November 1923 removed a further barrier to the cohort of young Lanarkshire militants whom he had cultivated over the previous decade from entering the CP, which now largely occupied the political space to the left of the Labour Party. Allan, who had been an SLP member in 1923, was a member of the CP's Executive Committee by 1926; the following year, William Pearson, Secretary of the Lanarkshire Miners' Industrial Union in 1924, was a Minority Movement candidate for the NUSMW Executive; even James Macdougall, Maclean's 'first lieutenant', briefly joined the CP in 1925.[68]

The policies advocated by these militants were a combination of the more aggressive waging of industrial disputes, structural reform of the county unions and the MFGB, and demands for a six hour day.[69] We can gauge the tenor of their criticisms of existing union policy from an article by Allan in 1925. He claimed that there were 'literally hundreds' of cases of sackings and victimisation in Blantyre and the surrounding districts. While the LMU officials were 'attempting to grapple with the multitudinous grievances', he asserted that:

> They have frittered away the strength and morale of the men by their prehistoric policy of petty sectional fights and strikes; they have been more intent on getting differences 'amicably adjusted' instead of wading in and walloping the managers into submission; and they have been more concerned with petty intrigues, petty scandals, petty manoeuvring for positions and petty 'plums' than they have about the welfare of the men ... Men held for weeks and months on strike with all the other pits working away now refuse to fight even when they have sufficient cause to fight.[70]

That there was some validity in such charges is suggested by a lengthy dispute at Douglas Castle Colliery where the men were on strike for twelve months from April 1925 over a wage reduction.[71] Despite Allan successfully moving a motion at the LMU Council that they be assisted, the NUSMW Executive strongly recommended a return to work.[72]

The debate over the long-running question of a single union for the Scottish miners also provided some support for Allan's views. Although the militants in Lanarkshire were anxious to press for such a re-organisation, as was Smillie, the proposals ultimately produced by the NUSMW Executive in 1925 were unacceptable both to the militants and to the county unions in Ayrshire, Mid and East Lothian and Dunbartonshire, which were anxious to preserve their regional autonomy.[73] As Long notes, the officials who had built up the Scots miners' unions in the years prior to 1914 were ill-equipped to deal with the wholly different situation presented by the crisis in the industry after 1921, which exacerbated the inherent structural weaknesses of the NUSMW. Contrasting generational experiences further heightened the tensions between the militants and the leadership, as Smillie's presidential address to the NUSMW conference in 1924 testified:

> Personally ... he was not against the ideas and idealism of the young miners. He did not for a moment imagine that he and the older men

knew all about everything and that they should have the last word ... But he did object to the younger people who had not sacrificed a great deal in work or improving their class in unmercifully condemning others who had spent their lives in the movement.[74]

The plausibility of more militant and centralised policies ultimately depended upon increasing union membership. There were campaigns against non-unionism, and several official strikes over the issue. Table 4.1 indicates a revival in union numbers and density in Lanarkshire, Ayrshire, Stirling and Mid and East Lothian by 1926.[75] Militants supported these drives enthusiastically. In Hurlford, MM supporters secured the return of the local union branch to the AMU 'to carry on their fight inside the union'.[76] By 1925, Communist pit groups in Lanarkshire were also organising 'Back to the Union' campaigns and claimed some successes.[77]

Like their counterparts in Fife, Lanarkshire militants sought to extend their influence by maintaining Marxist education classes. Over the winter of 1921–2, Allan conducted a class in economics at Stonehouse while a class of forty-four miners from five collieries in the Burnbank district was taught by Andrew Fagan.[78] In 1922–3, 16 classes with 500 students were held in the coalfield. The following winter, 17 classes in history and economics were organised throughout Lanarkshire. Macdougall taught 5, Alexander Anderson, the local Marxist schoolmaster, taught 2 at Stonehouse and Lesmahagow, James Jardine, a Blantyre militant took classes at Uddingston and Bellshill, while Allan was the tutor for the Blantyre class. In 1924, the number of classes in Lanarkshire increased to 25: Macdougall taught 6, Allan, 2, Anderson 1, Jardine 1, as did James McKendrick, the Bothwell Castle checkweigher and delegate to the LMU council who was also Secretary of the Blantyre branch of the CP; a further 6 classes were taught by George Aitken, a Communist and Lanarkshire Labour College organiser.[79]

In addition to such educational propaganda and their agitation within the LMU, Lanarkshire Communists were active in their communities in the Communist-led National Unemployed Workers' Committee Movement (NUWM). Allan was the NUWM Lanarkshire District Organiser in 1925, when there were fourteen local NUWM committees in the county handling a total of 300–600 cases per week. His claim that there was a NUWM membership in Lanarkshire of 8,000–10,000 is probably an exaggeration, but we can note the high rate of turnover of members through the organisation which amplified its influence, and the widespread industrial distress in the county, described by Allan as 'a welter of misery and sorrow'.[80]

These activities assisted the CP in building up support in the more militant branches of the LMU, although its accretion was uneven. In March 1924, it was claimed that in the Shotts district branch, the largest in the union, 'party members were elected to every position', and similar victories occurred in half a dozen other LMU branches, as well as at Loganlea (near Stoneyburn) in the West Lothian union.[81] That same year, Allan was elected as a Lanarkshire representative to the NUSMW Executive. A further notable success for the party in 1925 was the recruitment of Andrew McAnulty, checkweigher at Dixon's Blantyre Colliery, and an ILP and union activist since the 1890s. He had been elected LMU President the previous year and won the post again in 1925 as MM candidate.[82] Two MM members were also elected to the LMU Executive that year and it was claimed that the audience of a Lanarkshire MM conference early in 1926 contained 'branch presidents, secretaries and pit committeemen galore'.[83]

Some insight into the distribution and trajectory of Communist support in Lanarkshire in the years prior to 1926 can be gained by a comparison of the LMU elections of 1921 and 1925. In the former year, the NWCM put up a slate of seven candidates to contest the posts of officers, lay auditor and finance committee. For the presidency, the militant candidate came third out of eight candidates, but with only 7.8 per cent of the votes he was far behind the victorious Smillie with 66.6 per cent; for the vice-presidency, the militant was second out of seven, but again with only 12 per cent of the vote compared to the winner's 54.7 per cent; for general secretary, the militant came third out of nine, with 9.1 per cent compared to the 44.1 per cent gained by the winning candidate. The lay auditor and finance committee membership were decided by branches casting their financial vote, and this less participatory method may have worked to the militants' advantage. For lay auditor, the militant came second out of twenty-six candidates, but with approximately half of the winner's financial total. For the finance committee, the militants came fourth, fifth and eighth. A comparison of the branch voting patterns in these financial votes shows that only five branches voted uniformly for the four militant candidates: four were attached to collieries in Blantyre; the fifth was Douglas.[84]

The growth of support for the militants by 1925 was indicated when Allan stood for LMU General Secretary in a straight contest with the long-serving incumbent, William B. Small: he secured 5,535 votes (42.4 per cent) against Small's 7,529. Allan's support had extended beyond Blantyre, although it remained concentrated in the large pits of the central Clyde valley. Of the seventeen pits where he received 60 per cent or more of the vote, sixteen were within a circle with a radius of three miles; the seventeenth was Douglas. Significant though the growing influence of this militant minority was, we should not exaggerate its extent or scale. The combined votes for the MM candidates for the posts of General Secretary, President and Vice-President amounted to 28.3 per cent of the total votes cast.[85] Moreover, they secured 40 per cent or more of the vote in only a dozen branches. The Minority Movement had thus captured more ground in Lanarkshire by 1925 compared with 1921, but its supporters amounted to less than a third of the unionised workforce. However, the events of the following year were further to enhance its standing.

Notes

1. See vol. 1, Table 1.2.
2. SRO HH 31/36/1, Scottish Board of Health, Memorandum by Mr Highton, 1 October 1921.
3. SRO HH 31/36/1, District Report for Lanarkshire.
4. SRO CB 8/3, LCMA Annual Reports for 1922, 1923 and 1924.
5. SRO HH 31/36/1, Memorandum by Mr Highton.
6. *Worker*, 5 November 1921; Arnot, *History*, p. 165.
7. NMLH, CPGB Archive, un-numbered reel of microfilm from the Russian Centre for the Conservation and Study of Documents of Contemporary History, document 495/33/239a, letter from Robert Thompson, Buckhaven, 5 October 1922.
8. Long, thesis, p. 333; Arnot, *History*, p. 166.
9. *Motherwell Times*, 22 July 1921.
10. *Workers' Weekly*, 11 July 1924; *Miner*, 27 September 1924; *Worker*, 28 October 1927; NLS Dep. 258/1, AMU Delegate Meeting, 25 December 1926, 5 February 1927. The AMU was unusual in having a number of full-time 'local agents' in addition to the county officers; in 1931, there were twelve such posts (Dep. 258/5, AMU Report and Balance Sheet for the year ending 15 May 1931). The surviving balance sheets for the Crosshouse branch for 1924 and 1929 suggest that

the salaries paid to the local agent increased as a percentage of the branch income from members' contributions due to the decline in union membership: from 12 per cent in the former year, to over 20 per cent in the latter (NLS Dep. 258/5, Crosshouse AMU branch balance sheets).

11. *Communist*, 19 November 1921.
12. *Motherwell Times*, 15 July 1921.
13. Ibid., 5 August 1921.
14. Ibid., 12 August 1921.
15. Ibid., 12 August 1921.
16. Ibid., 9, 16 September 1921.
17. Ibid., 16, 23 September 1921.
18. For similar processes in the Clydeside shipbuilding industry, see G. Walker, 'The Orange Order in Scotland between the wars', *International Review of Social History*, 37, 1992, p. 192.
19. *Glasgow Herald*, 27 July 1926.
20. The FKMA had merged with the Clackmannanshire union in 1917 to form the Fife, Kinross and Clackmannanshire Mineworkers' Association (FKCMA).
21. For example, see his speech to the Fife miners' gala in 1919 (*Bellshill Speaker*, 13 June 1919). See also Macintyre, *Little Moscows*, pp. 55–6.
22. *Forward*, 10 September 1921, 30 September, 7 October 1922.
23. MPL B 022, *The Fife Miners' Union Split* (n.d. [1923]). The following account is primarily based on this detailed pamphlet which drew upon the published Board minutes; see also *Forward*, 7 October 1922, and Arnot, *History*, pp. 167, 182.
24. *Forward*, 10 September 1921.
25. *Forward*, 30 September 1922.
26. *Forward*, 30 September, 7 October 1922.
27. MacDougall, *Militant Miners*, p. 64.
28. MPL B 002, *Constitution and Rules*, rules 4, 4, 13, 44.
29. MacDougall, *Militant Miners*, p. 64.
30. NLS NF.791.d.7, NUSMW Executive, 9 October 1922; MPL B 009, MRU Auditor's report, 1924.
31. MPL B 010, MRU Branch contributions, 1923–24.
32. MacDougall, *Militant Miners*, p. 68.
33. Ibid., pp. 64–5, 76–80.
34. *Dunfermline Press*, 26 January 1924. There was a regular column of Lanarkshire notes in the *Miner*. See also the references by John Maclean to the paper in his letters to James Clunie of 23 May and 16 June 1923, reprinted in J. Clunie, *The Voice of Labour* (Dunfermline, 1958).

35. For example, *Miner*, 18 August, 1 September, 24 November 1923, 3 July 1926.
36. Ibid., 26 May 1923. See also the attack on 'Scottish independence' by Proudfoot in a letter to G. Allen Hutt: '"Henry" [i.e. Henry Dubb, the ordinary working man] can live as long as he can manage on his INDEPENDENCE, which will not last long and then we will manage to get him to move' (MacDougall, *Militant Miners*, p. 184); an extract from the letter was published in the *Workers' Weekly*, 25 July 1924.
37. *Dunfermline Press*, 1 March 1924.
38. See J. Clunie, *First Principles of Working Class Education* (Glasgow, 1920) for an example of the content of such courses.
39. Quoted in the *Miner*, 2 January 1926.
40. *Dunfermline Press*, 26 January, 2 February 1924.
41. MacDougall, *Militant Miners*, p. 64.
42. *Socialist*, 10 February 1921.
43. For the complex relationships between these parties and the formation of the CPGB, see W. Kendall, *The Revolutionary Movement in Britain, 1900–1921* (1969).
44. *Worker*, 9 April 1921.
45. For the NWCM, see R. Martin, *Communism and the British Trade Unions, 1924–1933* (Oxford, 1969), pp. 16–22, and J. Hinton, *The First Shop Stewards' Movement* (1973).
46. MacDougall, *Militant Miners*, pp. 137–8.
47. *Communist*, 15 July 1922; *Workers' Weekly*, 10 July 1925.
48. *Communist*, 27 January 1923; NMLH, CI 28, Speech by Pollitt to Political Secretariat of Executive Committee Communist International (ECCI), 10 December 1928. See also the discussions of the question at the CP Central Committee, 22 December 1923 and Political Bureau, 22 March and 6 September 1923 (NMLH, unnumbered reel, documents 495/100/58 and 104). A number of leading Fife Communists were in the leadership of the MRU: Kirker became Financial and Compensation Secretary, a full-time post, on the union's formation; Thomas Smith, Lumphinnans, was Chairman and Proudfoot, Vice-Chairman (MacDougall, *Militant Miners*, p. 62, 66, 209).
49. MacDougall, *Militant Miners*, p. 184. See MPL B 017, Hodge to Proudfoot, 29 December 1924, regretting the latter's resignation: 'You may have been influenced by the Communist Party. I know that their policy has been opposed to us all the time. They do not want us to win because it would smash their theory of boring from within'; and B 020, Hodge to Proudfoot, 16 February 1925.
50. MacDougall, *Militant Miners*, pp. 209, 222.

51. Ibid., p. 201.
52. *Workers' Weekly*, 31 October 1924; *Worker*, 1 November 1924; Macdougall, *Militant Miners*, p. 193.
53. *Workers' Weekly*, 3 April 1925; *Worker*, 4 April 1925.
54. Macdougall, *Militant Miners*, pp. 70, 118.
55. *Worker*, 17 October 1925.
56. *Workers' Weekly*, 23 July 1926. For the lingering conflicts over the MRU, see references in the letters of Proudfoot to G. Allen Hutt, 1924–6, reprinted in MacDougall, *Militant Miners*, and the recollections of John McArthur (ibid., pp. 70–71).
57. For Maclean's relationship with the CPGB, see Challinor, *British Bolshevism*, pp. 237–54 and Ripley and McHugh, *Maclean*, pp. 114–58.
58. *Socialist*, 7 April, 2 June 1921, 12 January 1922.
59. Ibid., 26 January, 9 February 1922. The SLP narrowly voted to re-adopt the de Leonite strategy of 'Socialist Industrial Unionism, as propounded by the Workers' International Industrial Union' after 'having negated same for a number of years', in 1922 (Ibid., 27 April 1922).
60. *Worker*, 27 August 1921.
61. Ibid., 14 January 1922.
62. Ibid.
63. *Socialist*, December 1923.
64. *Miner*, 15 March 1924.
65. Ibid., 10 November 1923.
66. Ibid., 2 February 1924.
67. *Worker*, 18 August 1923, 26 January 1924.
68. When Allan joined the CP is unclear. 'Comrade Allan' was reported as contributing to a discussion on left-wing unity at the SLP's conference in May 1923 (*Socialist*, May 1923). That he was Chairman of the Scottish Miners' Minority Movement in 1925 suggests that he had joined the CP by then (*Worker*, 7 March 1925). He openly declared himself a party member in February 1926 (NLS Dep. 227/42, LMU Council, 25 February 1926) and was elected to the CP Executive Committee at the party's Eighth Congress in October 1926 (J. Klugmann, *History of the Communist Party of Great Britain, vol. 2: the General Strike, 1925–26*, 1969, p. 362). For Pearson, see the *Miner*, 15 March 1924 and *Workers' Life*, 2 December 1927. For Macdougall's membership of the CP, see Knox, *Labour Leaders*, p. 174.
69. For examples, *Worker*, 16 February, 15 March 1924.
70. *Worker*, 6 June 1925.
71. Shortly after the Douglas Castle miners returned to work after a year

on strike, they were again laid idle for seven months by the national lockout (*Hamilton Advertiser*, 17 April 1926).

72. NLS Dep. 227/42, LMU Council, 13 January, 3 February 1926; Dep. 227/86, NUSMW Executive, 11 January, 16 January, 8 February, 12 April 1926. At a conference of the Lanarkshire Section MMM, the chairman's (James McKendrick) motion for a one-day county strike to prevent the Douglas Castle men being 'slowly starved into accepting the proposed wage cuts' was unanimously agreed (*Worker*, 27 February 1926).

73. NLS Dep. 227/86, NUSMW Special Conference, 11 December 1925; Arnot, *History*, pp. 168–70; Long, thesis, pp. 328–32; *Worker*, 9, 30 January 1926. For the militants' critique of earlier proposals by the NUSMW executive for reorganisation, see the *Worker*, 15 April 1922.

74. Quoted in Long, thesis, p. 330.

75. For these campaigns against non-unionism, see ibid., p. 332.

76. *Workers' Weekly*, 11 July 1924.

77. *Workers' Weekly*, 2 October 1925. See also the report from the Lanarkshire Sub-District of the CP (*Workers' Weekly*, 6 November 1925).

78. *Worker*, 19 November 1921, 22 October 1922; *Workers' Weekly*, 23 June 1923.

79. *Workers' Weekly*, 23 June 1923; *Worker*, 22 September 1923, 4 October 1924, 10 October 1925. For Aitken's and McKendrick's positions in the CP, see the *Workers' Weekly*, 16 November 1923, 26 September 1924. From the mid-1920s, the CP abandoned such educational activity in favour of internal party training. See A. Miles, 'Workers' education: the Communist Party and the Plebs League in the 1920s', *History Workshop*, 18, Autumn 1984; J. Rée, *Proletarian Philosophers: problems in socialist culture, 1900–1940* (Oxford, 1984), pp. 46–62; S. Macintyre, *A Proletarian Science: Marxism in Britain, 1917–1933* (Cambridge, 1980), pp. 72–87.

80. *Worker*, 14 November 1925. For the history of the NUWM, see R. Croucher, *We Refuse to Starve in Silence: a history of the National Unemployed Workers' Movement* (1987); for the high rate of turnover in its membership, see S. Davies, 'The membership of the National Unemployed Workers' Movement, 1923–38', *Labour History Review*, 57, 1, 1992.

81. *Workers' Weekly*, 28 March 1924.

82. NLS Dep. 227/39 and 40, LMU Council, Election Results 1924 and 1925; Dep. 227/41, LMU Council, 4 November 1925; *Miner*, 31 January 1925; *Worker*, 7 March, 14 November 1925.

83. *Worker*, 27 February 1926.

84. NLS Dep. 227/37A, LMU Council, 24 September 1921.
85. In addition to Allan standing for General Secretary and McAnulty for President, Bob Eadie contested the Vice-Presidency.

CHAPTER FIVE

1926: Solidarity under strain

Introduction

At the national level, the events of 1926 – the coal owners' insistence on wage cuts after a temporary government subsidy and the long lockout to impose them, the nine-day General Strike in sympathy with the miners before its ignominious ending by the TUC – are so well covered in the existing literature that there is no need to recount them again here.[1] In much labour and mining historiography, the seven-month mining lockout is seen as epitomising the miners' traditionally mythic virtues of industrial cohesion and communal endurance. This chapter seeks to qualify the popular stereotype of the solidaristic but essentially passive sufferings of the miners and their families through the long months of 1926 by focusing on five topics: first, the preparations made by both the state and political activists for the impending struggle; second, the maintenance of what was indeed a remarkable degree of solidarity both during the General Strike and over the summer of 1926; then the extent to which this solidarity began to crumble by the late summer and through the autumn. The conduct of the strikers, in particular the willingness of some in Lanarkshire and Fife, to continue to employ militant methods of mass picketing, direct action and sabotage is next examined. Finally, the aftermath of the dispute and its significance are assessed.

Preparations and organisation

It is generally accepted that the government effectively prepared its contingency organisation for industrial unrest in the period prior to the General Strike, commencing with the refurbishment of the Cabinet's Supply and Transport Committee (STC) in November 1924.[2] The Scottish Office Civil Emergencies files reveal similarly careful and systematic planning during 1925–6, carried out in regular consultation with the Home Office.[3] Five District Commissioners were appointed in Scotland, including Sir Arthur Rose, with responsibility for the West of Scotland, and J.W. Peck, covering most of Fife and the South East. Meetings of coal owners, sheriffs, chief constables and the military were convened to canvas their views on dealing with unrest and coordinate emergency organisation.

With vivid memories of the violent incidents which forced the suspension of pumping operations during the 1921 lockout, 'some nervousness was expressed' by the coal owners 'about Fife ... where the pits are heavily watered and there is a strong Bolshevist tendency'.[4] Sheriff Fleming of Fife, in response to a request from Captain Michael Wemyss of the Wemyss Coal Company 'for help to prevent his pits being flooded' in the event of a stoppage, informed the Scottish Office that there were 60 or 70 pits in the county but that the police force amounted to only 200 men:

> I dislike having to say that I can do nothing, and yet this is the truth without outside assistance ... I should like to know that I can count on military assistance should the occasion arise ... the Fife miners, mostly loyal, decent men, have a large admixture of disgruntled foreigners and their dupes. I want to be ready to quash these hotheads before they do much damage.[5]

In the light of such anxieties, the Secretary of State for Scotland raised the question of additional troops at the STC, and the War Office later allocated two further battalions of infantry to supplement the three battalions and a cavalry regiment already garrisoned in Scotland.[6]

These plans for military support of the civil authorities were activated immediately prior to the General Strike which commenced on 4 May 1926. During the first week of May, a battalion of the Black Watch moved south from Fort George, near Inverness, while a battalion of the South Stafford Regiment was ordered north from Plymouth. By the evening of 8 May, the disposition of military forces in Scotland was substantial. The First Battalion Royal Scots Fusiliers, two companies of the South Stafford Regiment and a squadron of mounted Hussars were based in Glasgow and a further battalion of troops was ordered to move to the city from Ireland that day. Two companies of the Staffords were also stationed in Hamilton. In Edinburgh there were two battalions of troops along with a squadron of cavalry. Two companies of the Black Watch, along with sixteen armoured cars, were based in Stirling from where they could be rapidly deployed throughout the central belt. A further two companies of the regiment were billeted at Donibristle, near Cowdenbeath in central Fife. In addition to the army, two battleships and a cruiser were anchored in the Clyde, while a battleship and a destroyer, together with marines, were stationed at Rosyth on the Fife coast of the Firth of Forth.[7]

Despite these military reserves, the use of police rather than troops was favoured by the authorities. It was felt that 'raiding parties' of strikers could be effectively dealt with if the police were more mobile and the possibility of placing 'fleets of private cars' at the disposal of chief constables was considered.[8] After the General Strike, tactics for dealing with such raids remained under review. Rose recognised the risks of deploying troops to relieve pits which came under attack: 'he thought that would lead to unnecessary bloodshed, because if a pit was being besieged by strikers, the troops advancing on it would either have to fire or to fix their bayonets and use them if necessary'. Nevertheless, if troops were already stationed at a pit, the situation would be different because 'the attackers would advance at their peril'. However, the termination of the General Strike allowed the police forces under the six 'mining sheriffs' to be augmented by 100 per cent with temporary constables, and these, together with 'loans' of police from other areas, amounted to a total 5,200 men. Even the beleaguered Chief Constable of Fife had sufficient manpower to station six to eight constables on twelve hour watches at 'a large number of important pits'. Policing nevertheless took on a paramilitary aspect with the issue of regulation service steel helmets to constables to protect them from stones and missiles.[9]

A particular concern of the authorities was the threat posed by sabotage and the use of explosives: 'The existence of these stocks in magazines scattered throughout the mining counties gives rise to considerable anxiety because if they were seized by ill-disposed persons, much mischief might be done.' Such fears were explicitly fuelled by the earlier association between Sinn Fein and militant miners.[10] The anxieties within the Scottish emergency organisation cannot have been diminished by the publication in 1924 of a lurid novel, *The Morlocks*, set in contemporary Lanarkshire mining communities. The Morlocks were a thinly disguised parody of the Minority Movement:

> a secret organisation which had been set up with very great care, and had invaded most of the great trade unions. It was composed of little bands whose aim was to take control of these organisations, whenever the miners' strike took place, with a view to bringing about a general strike of all trades. Towards this end, bridges and railways were to be destroyed, and so prevent the Government from working the roads and railways by the military forces.

Their leader was a grotesque hunchback, named Barney Blades, who introduced himself to the book's hero: 'I'm Irish though born in Blantyre ... Bein' Irish I'm always agin the government. I'm a revolutionary anarchist'. Blantyre was the scene of the book's climax, involving widespread rioting, loss of life and the destruction of pits. At one point, a gang of miners break into a pit magazine containing two tons of explosives to make home-made bombs – 'get the duff intae the syrup tins, and let us see hoo you used tae blaw up the Germans', orders their leader – before attacking Hamilton railway station to prevent troop trains leaving for the Ayrshire coalfield.[11]

Despite the book's melodramatic plot, exaggerated characterisation and political bias, it possessed genuine insight into the attitudes of revolutionaries among the miners and their perceptions of union leaders, for its author was James C. Welsh, MP, an ILP activist from Douglas Water and an LMU official since 1919.[12] The ILP's John Wheatley also warned against '*agents provocateurs* with their incitements to violence, insurrection and red armies', and condemned attempts 'by the shotgun' rather than the ballot box.[13] The *Sunday Mail* reported in 1925 that revolutionaries among the miners were stockpiling dumps of explosives and a fascist infiltrator of a Communist meeting in Lanarkshire claimed that Joseph Marcovitch of Bellshill had been commended for 'his keen interest in the explosives question'.[14] Although the Secretary for Scotland informed the Commons (in a cautious circumlocution) that inquiries had 'not resulted in confirmation being obtained of the allegations' made by the newspaper, the authorities took the threat of sabotage seriously and ordered the concentration of stores of explosives in four centres in Scotland in 1926, under a military guard totalling 175 men.[15]

The state did not plan to rely solely on police and, if necessary military, repression in the event of a stoppage. Its agents displayed careful calculation of the amount of suffering which might be tolerated in the mining communities without prompting outright revolt. One sheriff raised what Rose considered 'a point of real importance', namely that during a prolonged stoppage, the miners would 'not be inclined to see their women and children starve, and consequently will help themselves as they no longer have credit ... this would lead to very serious disturbances in many areas'. The sheriff's suggestion was 'to devise a system of Food Tickets, at any rate for women and children, the cost to be borne by the state but probably administered by Local Poor Law officials'. Such action, it was felt, would 'take the sting out of the strike'. Sir Arthur was concerned that such a course might also prolong the stoppage but nevertheless recommended its serious consideration.[16] The Scottish Office consulted on the complex question of state welfare provision and was informed by the English Board of Education that it had been constantly informed in the lockout of 1921 that the provision of free school meals to children 'was the one thing that kept the miners within bounds and that serious trouble would have followed at once if the meals had not been provided ... it seems fairly clear that there will be serious trouble if there is a strike in the mining areas and no meals are forthcoming'.[17]

The question of poor relief to the able bodied unemployed and to strikers' dependants had been a controversial issue in both Scotland and England since 1921. By the mid-1920s, confronted by the conflicting pressures of maintaining public order in the face of unrest by the unemployed and the unwillingness of ratepayers to provide adequate support, the Scottish Board of Health had evolved a policy whereby parishes were required to ensure that 'needful sustentation' was being supplied. Although parishes had considerable discretion, exceeding 'needful sustentation' could lead to a declaration by the Board that payments were illegal.[18] It is this context, and the fears of social unrest during the lockout, which helps explain the apparently contradictory policies pursued by the Scottish Board of Health during the dispute concerning poor relief, as it sought both to limit the amounts paid to strikers' dependants by Boards of Guardians sympathetic to the miners' circumstances, and also force those Boards which, under pressure from ratepayers, wished to cease relief completely, to maintain the recommended minimum scale. The Board, with Baldwin's agreement, made loans to forty parishes during the strike to enable them to continue paying relief.[19] The government's strategy, in Scotland as elsewhere, was to combine military support for the police to ensure that the authorities could 'quash hotheads' and protect mineowners' property, and at the same time prevent starvation among the miners' families which might broaden the base of support for these militants.

In contrast to the British state and its Scottish apparatus, the TUC and the trade unions made no such contingency plans for either the General Strike or a prolonged coal stoppage.[20] Only the Communist Party and its allies in the Minority Movement made any sustained attempt at a campaign to warn the miners of the impending struggle which owners and government, if not the MFGB, saw as inevitable. A Lanarkshire Miners' Minority Movement (LMMM) Conference in November 1925 recognised 'the determined intention of the Capitalists, particularly the Mineowners to attack wages, hours and conditions' and urged that 'the cardinal feature of Trade Union policy should be to prepare the Trade Unions for the coming struggle'. William Allan, LMMM Secretary, reflected on the work of the movement in the county during the previous two years: 'while a great deal of work had been done in propaganda, and in popularising the ideas of the MMM amongst the miners, they had never really settled down to organised work'. This, he concluded, was the task now facing them, although he accepted the obstacles of 'moving a very stiff and disjointed TU machine' as well as 'apathy and indifference' amongst the miners.[21] In the following months further MMM conferences were held, despite the hostility of the LMU and NUSMW leadership.[22] Reflecting on the experience of 1919, the militants were clear-sighted in their analysis of government strategy and the trade union leadership's lack of enthusiasm for confrontation. James McKendrick, the Secretary of the Blantyre CP branch, complained at one LMM conference that:

> instead of our leaders taking the offensive, they were side tracked by Report after Report; the employers came surging forward to the attack, and our leaders had got into the habit of counting it a 'victory' if they could stave off wage reductions. He instanced the Sankey Report ... and now the Samuel Report.[23]

The CP made sustained attempts at expanding recruitment and building pit organisation, with a series of tours in the Scottish coal-fields by national speakers.[24] At Blantyre, 57 new members were enrolled in the summer of 1925, while the following February Shapurji Saklatvala, Communist MP for Battersea, addressed a large demonstration in West Lothian made up of over 800 miners from villages around Stoneyburn, including one 70 strong contingent which had marched over seven miles; in the evening, a thousand heard him speak in Pringle's Picture Palace.[25] In Fife in 1925, the party's membership was reported to be 'mostly composed of miners, and their energies are concentrated on the formation of pit groups and the issue of pit papers'.[26] Ernie Wooley, the CP national organiser for factory groups, visited East Fife and instructed the Methil branch to start a pit paper.[27] John McArthur recalled: 'That was the limit of the advice we got. But we managed to acquire an old second hand typewriter, got some stencils, and found lads who could do drawing and sketching. They were asked to turn out cartoons reflecting the struggle in that pit.'[28]

A series of duplicated papers were produced by such methods in the months leading up to the lockout. The Kirkcaldy Pit Group had begun publication of the *Underworld* by July 1925 (and later in that year the *Hutch*). This was followed by the *Spark* (Methil Communist Pit Group), the *Justiceman* (Bowhill Group), and the *Torch* (Cowdenbeath Communist Pit Group). In Lanarkshire, Communists published the *Sprag* at Shotts from the autumn of 1925, the *Rebel Miner* at Rosehall, as well as a paper at Blantyreferme.[29] The Methil *Spark*, which claimed a circulation of 750 by the spring of 1926, was regarded by the CP as exemplary and conveys the tenor of such papers. Its first issue, under the heading 'Get your jackets off', urged the need for maximum unity in the face the mineowners, 'the entire capitalist press and all the resources of the state'; it carried details of miners' grievances at the Wellesley Colliery as well as an analysis of 'the worldwide nature of the coal crisis'.[30] The January 1926 issue of the *Hutch*, under the headline 'Start training for the first of May' (the date of the expiry of the national coal agreement), carried a cartoon of a boxing match in which 'United Action' knocked out the 'Coal Boss'.[31]

Solidarity and survival

At the start of the General Strike, a range of organisations were set up to coordinate action. The most all-embracing of these were local 'councils of action', containing representatives of trade councils, trade unions, Labour and Communist Parties, and other bodies such as the NUWM. According to the survey conducted by the Labour Research Department of trades councils' activities during the strike, 'the Councils of Action really united the whole of the organised Labour movement in the area'.[32] The establishment of councils of action and workers' defence forces had been central proposals of the CP in the months preceding the strike.[33] Details of those councils which are known to have been established in the Scottish coalfields are given in Table 5.1. They appear only to have been developed in Lanarkshire, where twenty-three were established under the coordination of a Joint Committee, and in Fife. In a number of them, Communists played an active, sometimes leading role, and their recently gained expertise in publishing pit papers was used to produce strike bulletins. At Methil, the duplicator and paper used to produce the *Spark* was 'put at the disposal of the Council of Action central strike committee'.[34] Workers' Defence Forces were much rarer, though Abe Moffat recalled the one at Cowdenbeath as being 'very strong ... marching along in military style through the streets, training and everything else, and we had big ex-soldiers, six feet two, taking charge of the different groups. They were very well trained and disciplined.'[35] Those at Methil and at Airdrie and Coatbridge were established after police baton charges. The corps at Methil was organised under the command of two former sergeant majors, its members wearing pit boots and helmets and armed with pokers, pickshafts and hammers. Some members of the corps at Airdrie and Coatbridge had previously been drilled by commanders with army and Sinn Fein experience and were reputedly equipped with the weighted ends of billiard cues from Rosehall Miners' Institute.[36]

However, Communist Party influence should not be exaggerated.[37] Elsewhere, such as in North Ayrshire, Stirlingshire and the Lothians, strike committees – as distinct from the more politically inclusive councils of action – under the aegis of local trades council were the norm.[38] A survey of chief constables throughout Britain commissioned shortly after the end of the General Strike by Sir

Wyndham Childs, Basil Thompson's successor as head of the Special Branch, confirms a highly uneven picture of Communist activities in the Scots coalfields during the dispute.[39] In Midlothian, Communist influence was reported as 'nil'; in East Lothian it was claimed that 'Communists as such did not show themselves but individuals holding extreme labour views were very active and usually found as picket leaders', though this assessment was contradicted by the statement that 'a communist ringleader' had been arrested during a riot in Tranent. At Kilmarnock, while there were four party members on the Trades and Labour Council, the Chief Constable was of the opinion that they exerted 'no influence'; elsewhere in Ayrshire, Communist support extended only to 'irresponsible youths'. In Stirlingshire, 'Communists were very active in organising and directing pickets', while in West Lothian their influence was 'existent but difficult to estimate'. Even in Lanarkshire, there was considerable variation. At Hamilton, 'influence negligible' was reported while at Coatbridge, despite a Communist councillor being Secretary of the council of action, it was claimed to be 'very slight'. In contrast at neighbouring Airdrie – the two towns had a joint as well as individual councils of action – there was 'no distinction between Communists and Council of Action of Trade Unions' and the activity of the former was 'particularly noticeable'. Elsewhere in Lanarkshire, the 'extremists held meetings throughout the county and formed Councils of Action which attempted to issue permits to transport workers and tradesmen'.

Fife was the main area of Communist activity. Although in Dunfermline it was reported as 'nil', at Kirkcaldy the party 'exercised considerable influence' and the local party's services were accepted by the Central Strike Committee which issued a 'permanent permit' to the party's Fife organiser to facilitate travel between Dundee and Edinburgh. At Methil, the party exercised 'great influence'; in West Fife, influence was 'pronounced', members acting as 'couriers, stewards and messengers for strikers'. It is perhaps unsafe to attribute too much accuracy of detail to these often sweeping judgements by a group of men who were not impartial observers, although surveillance of Communists was clearly widespread. Nevertheless, the broad pattern their reports reveal is congruent with that from more sympathetic sources summarised in Table 5.1.

The strike was remarkably solid throughout the industrial areas of central Scotland. In north Lanarkshire, the 'second line' of

Table 5.1 Councils of Action established in the Scottish coalfields during the general strike, 1926

Town	Communist presence	Bulletin	Workers' Defence Corps
Lanarkshire Joint Ctee of the Council of Action	Chairman + 7 out of 40 delegates		
Airdrie and Coatbridge	Chairman (AEU) + several members	Every two days	Yes
Bellshill	Chairman + 'several' of 14 members		
Shotts	'strong Communist Party presence'	Daily	Peace Corps
Cambuslang	Chairman, Secretary	Twice weekly	
Motherwell	'Active Party group'		
Blantyre	'Active Party group'		
Methil	Convenor of sub-committees	Daily	Yes, 750
Cowdenbeath			Yes, 'very strong'

Sources: J. McLean, 'The 1926 General Strike in Lanarkshire', *Our History Pamphlet*, no. 65, 1976; P. Carter, 'The West of Scotland', in J. Skelley (ed.), *The General Strike 1926* (1976); J. Klugmann, *History of the Communist Party of Great Britain, vol. 2: the general strike, 1925–26* (1969); I. MacDougall (ed.), *Militant Miners* (Edinburgh, 1981); P. Long, 'Abe Moffat, the Fife miners and the United Mineworkers of Scotland', *Scottish Labour History Society Journal*, no. 17, 1982.

Note: There were also Councils of Action formed at Wishaw, Stonehouse, Bothwell, Carluke, Salsburgh, Coalburn, Larkhall and Rutherglen plus several other places in Lanarkshire (the total for the county was 23); Stoneyburn in West Lothian; and Lochgelly in Fife.

engineering and shipbuilding workers, who were not due to strike until 12 May, came out before the end of the first week: 'the strike was so solid that an air of peace and quiet pervaded'. The response of workers called out in the Lothians and Fife 'was also generally solid'.[40] Transport was the major focus of conflict, with pickets attempting to limit the carriage of goods or passengers to the holders of TUC permits. At Methil, drivers without a permit were turned back or sent to the local trade union office where a permit could be purchased for five shillings.[41]

Beer lorries were a particular focus of attention in the attempts by strikers to control the movement of supplies, and convoys left the large Alloa breweries under military and air escort. This may have reflected a commitment to abstinence or hostility towards the Conservative affiliation of the large brewers: 'The brewers, the police and the authorities seem determined to dope the workers with beer', complained the official strike bulletin of the Dunfermline Trades and Labour Council, attempting to strike a moral tone: 'in a time like this, beer should be the last article to be transported. And yet police and the military escorts are placed at the disposal of the booze merchants.' However, the same issue reported that four barrels of beer had been removed from a lorry by pickets in Methil and that at Oakley the men were 'all in good spirits (not Younger's beer)'. The Fife authorities exploited the interests of the pickets in beer lorries by concealing policemen inside empty barrels, after the style of Ali Baba, and sending a convoy through Valleyfield whereupon a baton charge ensued.[42]

The major outbreaks of violence in Scotland during the General Strike were all related to transport. During the night of 5 May and the following day there were a series of clashes at tram depots in the east end of Glasgow. At 11.30pm, pickets attempted to force their way through police cordons at the Parkhead depot, and according to the Chief Constable 'used great violence', seriously injuring a policeman. At 3.00am, about 300 miners 'marched in military formation' from Cambuslang to reinforce a picket at the Bridgeton depot; they were only dispersed 'after a fierce struggle' following a baton charge. During the next day shops and public houses in the vicinity of the depots were looted and 'repeated baton charges were made'. Four buses were overturned and two set on fire. The following day saw renewed rioting and looting in the east end. About 200 of those arrested appeared in the Sheriff Court in the days following, including twelve young men from Cambuslang, two of whose heads were swathed in bandages.[43] In Tranent, a crowd of pickets who stopped a motor vehicle resisted police efforts to intervene and when the constables retreated to the police station, the crowd proceeded to smash its windows; eight men, including a Communist who was the alleged 'ringleader', were later imprisoned for riotous assembly.[44] In Airdrie on 11 May, a crowd of several thousand gathered at Airdrie Cross to prevent a fleet of buses travelling to Glasgow under police protection. After the Riot Act had been read, a large force of police baton charged the crowd and the resulting bitter feelings prompted the formation of the Workers' Defence Force.[45]

With the end of the General Strike, employers, government and miners dug in for a war of attrition, its outcome ultimately dependent on the ability of mining families to fend off hunger. There was some variation in the strike funds distributed by the various county unions. In Lanarkshire, the county union commenced the dispute with funds of only £4,000 and had barely recovered from the financial aftermath of the 1921 lockout. By the end of May, the *Glasgow Herald* noted signs of 'acute destitution' in the Lanarkshire mining communities and reported that 50,000 miners' dependants were receiving parochial relief in the parishes of Hamilton, Bothwell, Dalziel, Blantyre and Cambuslang.[46] In contrast in the Lothians, the MELMA had funds of almost £9,000 to support a much smaller membership. There was little in the way of destitution: 'the men in these areas are the proper type of old time miners', opined the *Herald*, 'naturally of a hardworking and thrifty disposition, and unwilling to seek relief from the parish'.[47] In Ayrshire, the union was described as being in a 'highly favoured position compared with other counties, and their larger dole from their substantial fund has made their position not quite so needful as in other quarters'.[48] One local AMU branch paid its members 30 shillings per week initially, others £1 or 15 shillings.[49] But as the dispute wore on, even the wealthier unions such as the MELMA found their funds exhausted by the end of May.[50] Unions also received via the MFGB 'Russian' money levied from workers in the Soviet Union: in the Shotts district alone, £4,000 of such funds were distributed among the three local LMU branches.[51] Money from the Soviet Union was often used to support young single men who were ineligible for parish relief, and thus reinforced political divisions based on generation.

Union funds were supplemented from a variety of sources. In Galston, Ayrshire, the local cinema mounted a weekly miners' benefit entertainment to raise money.[52] In Fife, the miners ran sports days, concerts, football matches and whist drives to raise additional funds.[53] The 'Wemyss Musical Miners', a West Wemyss male voice choir, spent several weeks in Dundee giving two or three concerts daily to raise money for the communal soup kitchens, while the 'Methil Bohemian Revellers' made a caravan tour of the borders, and the Coaltown of Wemyss band played throughout East Fife for the same purpose.[54]

Despite the calling off of the General Strike, the Mines' Inspector reported a general 'stiffening' of the strikers' morale in June, listing the reasons for this as public sympathy and the 'outwardly undivided' posture adopted by the miners' union leaders in Scotland; the speeches of A.J. Cook, General Secretary of the MFGB, were 'not without their effect on the younger men'. In addition, 'they know that feeding of schoolchildren and parish relief together are saving them seeing their wives and families go hungry'.[55] That same month, Andrew McAnulty observed that the parish councils were 'doing fairly well and are at least keeping the wolf from the door'.[56] Press reports from the coalfields confirmed miners' families were being reasonably fed. In Cowdenbeath, 3,000 children received three meals per day. In Stirlingshire, where the education authority provided two meals a day during the school holidays, the *Scotsman* concluded that 'there can be no question of the resistance of the miners being broken down through the hunger of their children'. In East Fife, the feeding system was described as the most excellent in the country: money from all sources – parochial relief, union funds and individual donations – was pooled and used to supply the communal kitchens.[57]

There was, however, considerable variation between the relief scales adopted by differing parish councils: at Newtongrange, where ten out of the eleven parish councillors were Labour representatives, 10 shillings per week were given to miners' wives, 4 shillings to the eldest child and 3 shillings to other children; at Prestonpans, 4 shillings was given to each child; yet in neighbouring Tranent, only 1 shilling was allowed for children.[58] Parish councils became a further arena for conflict between Communists and Labour Party supporters among the miners' officials whose deep-seated commitment to prudential local government conflicted with their loyalty to the miners' cause. In Ayrshire, Provost Robert Smith, an AMU agent and President of the NUSMW, sat on the Kilwinning Parish Council. When another member, a Communist and NUWM activist, urged that the council adopt the Scottish Board of Health scale, Smith argued for a reduced rate on the grounds that the strike would be a long one. Communists were similarly critical of the Labour group on Cambuslang Parish Council for their proposal to cut relief by only 10 per cent in opposition to the 15 per cent reduction imposed by the ruling 'moderates'.[59]

Some parish councils dominated by miners' representatives took a more sympathetic attitude and were the object of demonstrations of support. Lochgelly Parish Council requested the permission of the Scottish Board of Health to overdraw its bank account for poor relief but was informed that this would only be granted if the relief scales were reduced which the council refused to do. Prior to a special meeting of the council to consider the matter, a demonstration of 1,000 men and women marched from Bowhill to Lochgelly headed by a banner bearing the slogan 'We want bread'. The procession joined a demonstration of a further 2,000 in the public park which was addressed by several Communist speakers and the local ILP organiser. In response to such representations, the council agreed to issue tickets for foodstuffs as an interim measure.[60]

More significantly, ratepayers increasingly sought legal restraints on parish councils disbursing relief.[61] These ratepayers in turn became the object of the miners' ire. In Hamilton, a crowd of 2,000–3,000 paraded the town after the publication of the names of ratepayers who had sought an interdict against the parish council. Women processed 'bearing aloft effigies of some of those who had given their names as complainers in the summons ... During the afternoon the crowd visited other parts of the burgh and indulged in derisive cheering outside certain residential and business premises.' A milkman who was one of the signatories had barrels of buttermilk emptied from his cart.[62] At the end of July, the Scottish Board of Health ordered cuts in the scale of relief and some parish councils, such as Ayr and Cambusnethan, abandoned payment to miners' dependants entirely. By early August, Hamilton Parish Council was £25,000 overdrawn.[63] By the end of that month, many parish councils, dependent on Government loans, had reduced the rates of relief to strikers' dependants to half the original amount. August also saw a campaign by Scottish coal owners to stop councils paying any relief on the grounds that it was illegal.[64]

The return to work

As hardship increased by late July, the Mines' Inspector was reporting a weakening of the miners' resolve 'round the fringes of the mining areas', at Vogrie in Midlothian, at Balgonie in Fife, and at Wilsontown in Lanarkshire, while 'in the Airdrie district there are increases in the number of men employed at many of the small mines'. By that time, too, there had been some return at Thankerton Colliery, Holytown.[65] Employers were often willing to offer inducements to men willing to resume work: miners who returned to the isolated Wilsontown Colliery in August had their debts for house rent cancelled.[66] By early September, a total of 2,800 miners were working in Scotland, 1,800 of them in Lanarkshire.[67] Later that month:

> at many of the smaller mines in Lanarkshire, tempting terms are offered to induce the men to return to work so that the owners can take advantage of the present high price of coal. As much as 6 shillings bonus per seven hours shift is being given in addition to April wages.[68]

A special correspondent of the *Glasgow Herald* observed that some Lanarkshire miners were earning as much as £20 per week, but confirmed the geographical distribution of the strikebreaking on the periphery of the coalfield (where pits were usually smaller), covering a line from the Glasgow boundary, passing through Airdrie to Harthill; 'it excludes at the same time the multitude of collieries in the Hamilton and Burnbank localities [where] not a winding wheel has turned to draw up a truck of coal ... since the stoppage began'.[69] By mid-October, however, the trickle of men returning to work at Thankerton Colliery in the Holytown district had shown 'a big increase'.[70] Coalburn up till then had been regarded as 'an invulnerable stronghold of the Lanarkshire Mineworkers' Union' and 'the union's main citadel'. But the first workman's train since May ran from Lesmahagow to the Caprington and Auchlochan Colliery Company's pits on 20 October and 200 pickets were posted in the district.[71]

The Mines' Inspector stated that in Lanarkshire there was 'no difficulty' in getting men for repairing and clearing up underground workings but in Fife 'the position is different'.[72] Even in Fife, a breakaway of approximately one hundred miners commenced work in the Markinch district on the north-eastern edge of the coalfield at the end of August.[73] In early September, the Fife Coal Company sought to concentrate and protect its blacklegs by initially opening one pit in each of its five districts. At the end of the month, the Fife coal owners announced that all their pits would be open for work on Monday 4 October.[74] From the end of October, such was the price of coal that even the larger employers, who publicly insisted on the terms of an eight hour day at the rate offered in April, were reported by the Mines' Inspector to be 'desperately anxious to get miners induced to work in all their mines ... and the men are getting bonuses, extra shifts, and half shifts for small jobs usually done in the working day for nothing, remission of house rent, and so on'.[75] The effects of hunger, hardship and employers' incentives can be detected in the figures of working miners in the Scottish coalfields from the late summer. These are summarised in Table 5.2. After five months of idleness, October witnessed the critical breakthrough in the miners' solidarity with the numbers at work in Lanarkshire trebling to 14,000 in the first two weeks. A month later, the numbers of working miners in Scotland as a whole had trebled to over 26,000. By the third week in November, the NUSMW's estimate was that almost 40,000 had returned to work. Such figures must be viewed within the context of a total mining workforce of approximately 126,000 in 1925. With over thirty per cent of the miners at work, an NUSMW special conference on 27 November voted overwhelmingly, by 50–6, to resume work on the coalmasters' terms.[76]

Activists responses

The MMM activists were clear as to the necessary reaction to the increasing drift back to work in the summer: 'Big official meetings at the pits, at the homes of the blacklegs, deputations to interview the scabs, ostracism even extending to their kiddies, etc, – all these and more should be tried to keep the men from really beginning to weaken'.[77] As the incidents summarised in the appendix to this chapter indicate, working miners faced the wrath of the communities in which they lived and the traditional collective sanctions of 'rough music', besetting and parading blacklegs home, assault and damage to their houses were in daily evidence. While sometimes strikers resorted to ridicule, as when a blackleg's pet pony was

Table 5.2 Numbers working in the major Scottish coalfields, August–November, 1926

Date	Lanarkshire	West Lothian	Ayrshire	Fife and Clack.	Mid and East Lothian	Scottish Total
6 Aug	1,125	3	45	315	163	1,679
1 Sept						3,531
18 Sept						5,004
25 Sept	**3,200**	**40**	**280**	**350**	**150**	**4,080**
2 Oct	**4,700**	**40**	**330**	**700**	**200**	**6,054**
13 Oct	**14,000**	**262**	**870**	**900**	**250**	**8,353**
21 Oct					950	
2/3 Nov	14,144		2,190			
17 Nov	**14,000**	**800**	**3,500**	**3,000**	**3,500**	**26,355**
19 Nov	18,850	2,500	3,334			
22 Nov	**23,000**	**1,700**	**3,500**	**3,500**	**5,500**	**38,650**

Sources: SRO HH56/22, Bi-weekly reports furnished by Chief Constables; HH56/26, 27, 28, Situation reports and correspondence; NLS NUSMW Executive, September–November 1926; NLS Acc. 4312/12, Mid and East Lothian Miners' Association Executive, 21 October 1926.

Note: Figures in bold are derived from union records. Although figures published in the Scottish press tended to exaggerate the numbers of miners at work, there was a broad degree of congruence between union estimates and those compiled by the Scottish Office from chief constables' reports.

painted like a zebra, given a straw hat and tied to his front door, collective contempt and social stigma were more common sanctions. As one East Fife miner's wife recalled, 'the next door neebour was a blackleg at Muiredge Pit, and of course he got polis protection and ah wish ye'd seen the crowds that came home ahent [behind] him at that time, bringing him hame. I wouldnae hae the name o' it for love nor money.'[78]

Space does not permit detailed accounts of the numerous incidents summarised in the appendix, but the violence and frustration within the mining communities which the gradual return to work engendered can be exemplified by the attack on two working firemen at Hamilton Palace Colliery at the end of October. One of the crowd was reported to have shouted: 'Have no mercy on the bastard, kick him, kick him to death!'; another said: 'we will take good care he does not work tomorrow, the bastard'. After one of the victims collapsed at his home, badly bruised and bleeding, his wife ran to fetch the police, loudly booed by a crowd of 300–400 people. Seven young miners aged between 18 and 24 – two of whom lived in the same row of houses as their victims – were charged with assault on the men.[79] To avoid such communal obloquy, working miners often travelled long distances to employment at collieries in localities where they were not known: 'in such cases the men wash and change at the pits and travel by railway train or motor bus'.[80]

As more miners returned to work, conflict between strikers and working miners intensified. Because strikebreakers at Cameron Colliery in East Fife 'would not be persuaded by ordinary picketing', recalled McArthur, 'the traditional method of dealing with blacklegs soon developed. Night visits were paid, windows and front doors were smashed in.'[81] On the 13 November, the Chief Constable of Lanarkshire reported that window smashing was 'still rife' in his county.[82] Explosive detonators were often employed for this purpose, with terrifying effect on the inhabitants of the house who were liable to injury from shattered glass.[83] At Lumphinnans, the ex-servicemen's club was completely gutted by fire and the Chief Constable reported that 'there has been dissension amongst the club members for some time and those of the Communist element are believed to have been responsible for the outbreak'.[84] At the end of October, the Secretary of State for Scotland, who was concerned at such developments, directly intervened in the judicial process; he felt that the practice of fining strikers convicted of intimidation was a bad one and asked the Lord Advocate to instruct procurator fiscals to press for imprisonment in such cases.[85]

In Fife, working miners retaliated against the frequent attempts to intimidate them by window smashing. Windows of Communists in Lumphinnans were broken, as well as those in a room used by the local strike committee: 'this is believed to have been done by some party in retaliation for window breaking by extremists'.[86] In Glencraig, an explosion destroyed three boilers in the soup kitchen used by the strikers and was believed to be a reprisal 'for the recent breaking of windows of houses occupied by miners who have returned to work'. At Cowdenbeath, Provost Russell, who had taken a prominent role in miners' demonstrations, had one of his windows broken.[87]

As might be expected from the discussion of social order in the coalfields in the preceding volume, there were marked regional variations in the propensity to violence. In May, it was reported that the miners at Catrine in Ayrshire were spending their idleness in an 'exemplary manner', competing at sports for prizes donated by local shopkeepers.[88] Such outbreaks of rioting as occurred in the county during the General Strike were described by the *Ayrshire Advertiser* as 'of an isolated character' caused by hooligans.[89] The Chief Constable of Kilmarnock claimed in early November that 'there has not been a single case, here, arising out of the strike in which complaint has been made to the police of assault or intimidation or in which the police have found it necessary to institute proceedings'; three weeks later, he reported that 'miners who have returned to work are not being molested in any way'. The Chief Constable of Ayr similarly stated that 'there has been no disturbance or intimidation or anything of a like nature here in connection with the strike ...'; a month later he reported 'no change in the circumstances here – nothing doing'.[90]

A crude tabulation of all the incidents listed in the appendix to this chapter confirms this regional variation: 90 occurred in the West Central region and 59 in Fife compared with only a dozen or so each in Ayrshire and the Lothians. A similar regional contrast emerges from data on convictions for offences committed during the General Strike and the mining lockout. These are summarised in Table 5.3, with the highest number of convictions occurring in Fife, followed by West Central, with far fewer in Ayrshire and least in the Lothians. The regional percentages of the total number of convictions, when compared with mining employment for 1925, indicate that Fife, with almost half the convictions and less than a quarter of Scotland's miners, was greatly over-represented among the convicted. As with all crime statistics, the figures must be treated with caution; they may reflect differences in approach by the police, chief constables and procurator fiscals. In her study of police perceptions of labour in the 1920s, Barbara Weinberger concluded that police violence – a factor which might be expected to lead to a greater number of arrests – occurred 'most readily in areas where there was a previous history of strained police-labour relations' and that the variability in the administration of justice 'depended on how far local strikers or the unemployed were regarded as acting under Communist influence'.[91] Both these preconditions were fully met in parts of Lanarkshire and Fife. A further influence on the numbers of arrests was the tactics employed by the strikers. Fife's total was inflated by the large numbers arrested for participating in disorderly crowds; in the West Central region, injury to property was the most common conviction. But whatever the reasons for

Table 5.3 Convictions for offences related to the general strike and coal dispute tried in Sheriff Courts within the Scots coalfields, 1926

Offence	Region				Total	(Scottish Total)
	Ayrshire	West Central	Fife/ Clack.	Mid/East Lothian		
Emergency Regulation 20						
(a) injury to property	24	71	28	2	125	(187)
(b) injury to persons	1	12	11	-	24	(30)
Emergency Regulation 21						
(a) acts likely to cause sedition or disaffection	-	1	13	-	14	(16)
(b) impeding supply of food	-	9	36	-	45	(46)
(c) printing or possession of seditious documents	-	1	1	-	2	(2)
Conspiracy and Protection of Property Act 1875						
(a) using threats and violence	-	32	22	-	54	(97)
(b) forming disorderly crowd	10	17	93	5	125	(127)
Assaults						
(a) on police	-	24	3	3	30	(92)
(b) other	-	25	25	8	58	(172)
Malicious Mischief	2	5	9	-	16	(42)
Mobbing and Rioting	6	15	38	-	59	(59)
Total	43	212	279	18	552	(870)
	7.8	38.4	50.5	3.3	100.0	
% Share of employment, 1925	12.0	53.2	22.7	12.1	100.0	

Source: SRO HH56/31, Returns of convictions.

Notes:
1. The figures for convictions contained in the returns refer to crimes committed during both the general strike and the coal dispute, and includes cases not heard until as late as April 1927. There is no occupational breakdown of those convicted and some convictions refer to workers other than miners who were arrested during the general strike, particularly in Glasgow. In order to estimate those convicted in mining areas, only cases leading to conviction at Sheriff Courts within the coalfield boundaries are included in the total for each category. These courts were at Ayr, Kilmarnock, Hamilton, Lanark, Airdrie, Linlithgow, Falkirk, Dumbarton, Stirling, Dunfermline, Cupar, Alloa and Haddington. Convictions at Edinburgh and Glasgow Sheriff Courts have been excluded and these may have involved some miners; to have included these cases would have distorted the figures, but as a result the table underestimates the number of convictions of Midlothian miners. The total number of convictions under each category in all the Scottish Sheriff Courts is given in brackets.
2. There were some inconsistencies in the construction of the returns since some almost identical offences were brought before the courts under different headings; thus throwing stones at police usually led to a charge of assaulting the police but in some cases was regarded as a breach of the peace. However, the differences in the level of convictions in the different regions is apparent in the table.

such differences, the conviction figures tend to confirm the evidence in the appendix to this chapter that social disorder was concentrated in the Fife and West Central regions.

Further evidence of the variation in local responses to the lockout can be gleaned from an examination of the two most pacific of our survey localities. On the first day of the lockout, Larkhall's miners largely eschewed politics in the May Day rally, which took the form of 'a children's day with a procession through the streets and the crowning of the Queen of the May. A programme of sports followed and speaking occupied a minor part in the day's proceeding.' In contrast, at other centres in Lanarkshire 'the proceedings were devoid of picturesque trappings and concerned themselves with appeals to the workers ...'.[92]

In Newtongrange, it was reported that 'the behaviour of the community has been beyond reproach' and the miners were engaged in peaceful pursuits: 'some dig their gardens, some vent their energy on the neighbouring golf links, some walk, some cycle, and some spend their days at the seaside'.[93] Since the beginning of the dispute, 'everything has been exceedingly quiet and orderly in Newtongrange ... '.[94] By August, the inhabitants were still ready to admit 'that there are no cases of hardship in the community'.[95] Such press reports must be treated with caution, but they were reinforced by the rhetoric of class harmony during the official opening of a public park extending to seventeen acres and funded by the Miners'

Welfare Committee the following month. Mungo Mackay, the pit manager, presided over the ceremony, which was also attended by Archibald Hood, Chairman of the Lothian Coal Company and Andrew Clarke of the MELMA. The latter joined in the admiration of the new park, concluding that: 'If the standard of life throughout the country had been regulated by the standard of the social ameni-ties that had been provided in Newtongrange, they would probably not have had that measure of unhappiness that had been prevailing throughout the country during the last nineteen weeks.'[96] Before the end of October, a small number of men were reported to have com-menced work at Newbattle Colliery. By mid-November, the strike there was effectively over with the colliery fully manned: 'good feel-ing has for a long period prevailed between the management and employees at Newbattle', noted the *Dalkeith Advertiser*, 'and many of the men express satisfaction at having returned to work again'.[97]

Elsewhere, a notable feature of the lockout was attempts at sabo-tage to colliery and railway property, often involving the use of explosives. By mid-November, Masterton, Mines' Inspector for Scotland, felt that the likelihood of victimisation had induced a final desperation among 'the extreme men who will not be re-employed'.[98] The Communist, Bob Selkirk, later recalled a similar mood in central Fife:

> The brutality of the capitalists only made the miners more deter-mined and it became more difficult to prevent the adoption of ter-rorist tactics. Many a time breathtaking 'scorched earth' proposals were proposed in the basement of Lochgelly Institute and other meeting places but these inopportune tactics were always defeated. Near the end of the strike, some Glencraig miners, incensed by police terror, acting without the knowledge of the Council of Action, sent the cages rattling uncontrolled down the pit and the shaft was wrecked.[99]

Incidents of sabotage are tabulated in Table 5.4. A clear regional difference is apparent, with the majority of such incidents taking place in the West Central region. In reviewing six reported incidents involving explosives in the border area of Lanarkshire, West Lothian and Midlothian at the end of the dispute, the Chief Constable of the Lothians considered that press reports were exag-gerated. Nevertheless, the Scottish Office recorded its concern that 'in each case ... there was an attempt to injure or terrorise persons

Table 5.4 Incidents of sabotage and attempted sabotage in the Scottish mining regions during the 1926 lockout

	West Central	Fife	Ayrshire	Lothians
Use of explosives to damage colliery property	7	1	-	1
Other damage to colliery property	2	2	-	-
Attempts to damage railways by explosives	7	-	-	-
Other attempts to damage railways and trains	3	2	3	3
Total of incidents by region	19	5	3	4

Source: Calculated from Appendix to this chapter.

connected with the men who had been working during the mining dispute ... The growing use of explosives for this purpose in various districts is a disquieting feature.'[100] In response to such incidents, further police reinforcements were drafted to the coalfields. In Lanarkshire, the number of temporary constables was increased to 140 as the miners there became 'more disturbed' in October.[101] Towards the end of November, the authorities, fearful of 'outbreaks of lawlessness' in central Fife, deployed 42 additional policemen to Lochgelly and 38 to Cowdenbeath.[102]

The authorities were in little doubt as to where responsibility for such disorders lay. The Chief Constable of West Lothian reported that the Stoneyburn district, on the Lanarkshire border, remained on strike when the rest of the county's miners had resumed work and was the scene of a number of the incidents involving explosives: 'there is a strong "Red" element in Stoneyburn'.[103] Masterton was firmly of the belief that 'the troubles' in Fife 'rose largely from Communists who are connected with the Reform Union', and that there were 'dangerous people prepared to do much destruction as opportunity offers in the coal areas'; such men were 'Communists and Irishmen'.[104] Given the anti-Communist prejudice in the police, government and civil service, such assertions cannot be accepted uncritically. Yet David Proudfoot, writing from Methil in early

October, conceded that: 'A spirit of "To hell with this *peaceful* pick-eting" has now got hold of a handful of the reliable men we have and a desire for terrorism has now set in.'[105] In his memoirs, written many years later when he was a Communist county councillor, Selkirk attempted to distance the CP from sanctioning violence.[106] In his account of the attack on Glencraig Colliery, he states: 'The men arrested for this, after the strike finished, were given savage sentences. Charles Mitchell and Peter Aird, members of the Communist Party which had opposed such acts, received long terms.'[107]

It seems probable, whatever the public position of the party, that the claims of the authorities as to the participation of some Communists in sabotage and direct action, were not without foundation.[108] Given the draconian nature of the regulations issued under the Emergency Powers Act, it is not surprising that few party members are on record as advocating such tactics. But there is little evidence that the party condemned these activities, and occasional references in its press made light of them. For example, William Allan reportedly urged workers during the General Strike 'not to go without whilst food was in the shops'.[109] William Gallacher, a senior party member, noted in October that he had been unable to hold a meeting in Shotts because 'somebody had gone out one night and blown up a power station'. A few weeks previously, a Shotts member had urged the continuation 'of our guerilla warfare' on the district's scabs.[110] It was but a short step from involvement in organising Workers' Defence Corps to more offensive tactics against mines and railways, and the affinity between Communist militants and Sinn Fein activists in the early 1920s has already been noted.[111] Evidence of Communist involvement in such illegal activities is by its nature elusive, but we can note that a quarryman who was a Communist was arrested along with a miner from Blackridge, West Lothian, after breaking into an explosives store, in May 1926.[112] It is also significant that, when in his eighties, Johnny Boyle of Methil, who was a young Communist during the lockout, admitted leading an abortive night time raid in 1926 to blow up the ventilation fan at the 'scab pit' of Balgonie with a home-made bomb, on the instructions of McArthur.[113]

The authorities' belief that Communists were responsible for disorder certainly made them prime candidates for arrest, and Emergency Regulation 21, covering speeches likely to cause disaffection among the police force and civilian population, was wide enough to indict many.[114] A series of meetings in Fife to protest against police brutality provided the opportunity for the arrest of a number of Communist militants under the provisions of the regulation. For example, Alex Moffat of Lumphinnans was sentenced to two months imprisonment after he urged that young Communists should keep on 'until they tore down the Union Jack and hoisted the red flag at Westminster under a Soviet government, when there would be time of retribution on the forces of the state'.[115] Communists were required to exercise considerable circumspection to avoid incriminating statements. At a CP rally attended by 1,300 miners in Cowdenbeath, Walter Tapsell, a young London Communist, 'began a denunciation of the police but was nudged several times by the chairman and broke off'.[116]

Comprehensive details on the political affiliation of those arrested during the dispute are lacking. Wyndham Childs' circular to chief constables enquired as to the numbers of Communists arrested during the General Strike throughout the Britain. Of the 183 named Communists listed in the ensuing report as being arrested under the emergency regulations, 26 were arrested in Scotland, 23 of these within the mining counties.[117] Table 5.5 lists 43 Communists known to have been arrested in the Scottish coalfields during the General Strike and lockout, 31 of them in Fife. It should be noted, first, that not all were miners, though the majority for whom occupation is known were. Second, the listing is almost certainly incomplete, being garnered from a range of sources, and the political connections of those arrested were often only publicised in the case of leading members of the party.

From a comparison of Tables 5.3 and 5.5, it is clear that known Communists constituted a small minority of those arrested during the General Strike and lockout, though in Fife they represented over ten per cent. Moreover, a number of the arrested Fife Communists were prominent members of the party in their localities: John Bird, a Bowhill checkweigher, had been previously sentenced to three months imprisonment for incitement during the 1921 lockout; his fellow Bowhill miner, Peter Lumsden, was Chairman of the parish council; Andrew Jarvie was a leading activist in Valleyfield and a victimised checkweigher; the three Moffat brothers represented the party's cadre in Lumphinnans, along with Jim Watt of the local Young Communist League; Jimmy

Table 5.5 Communists known to have been arrested during the general strike and lockout in the Scottish coalfields, May-November 1926

Name	Charge	Conviction/Sentence
Fife		
Peter Aird, Glencraig	Attack on Glencraig Colliery	Long prison term
John Bird, checkweigher, Cardenden	Intimidating safety men	21 days
John Dick, blacksmith, Kirkcaldy	ER[1]	3 months
D. Donald, Cupar[2]	ER	£3 or 20 days
James Ednie, Cupar	ER	£3 or 20 days
R. Fowler, Lumphinnans	ER	Not known
Hugh Gardner, miner, Buckhaven	Threatening working miner	14 days
Daniel Gillies, rivet-heater, Cowdenbeath	ER	2 months
Sam Happell, NUR branch secretary, Methil	ER	£3 or 20 days
Andrew Jarvie, miner, Valleyfield	ER	Not known
Peter Lumsden, miner, Bowhill	CPPA[3]; ER	60 days
John McArthur, miner, Buckhaven	ER	Not guilty
Barney McGrory, Cupar	ER	£3 or 20 days
D. McGuiness, Cupar	ER	Not known
Robert McKersie, Cupar	ER	£3 or 20 days
Peter Munro, Cupar	ER	£3 or 20 days
Abe Moffat, miner, Lumphinnans	Leading riotous mob	Fine
Alex Moffat, miner, Lumphinnans	ER	2 months
David Moffat, miner, Lumphinnans	ER	Not known
Charles Mitchell, Glencraig	Attack on Glencraig Colliery	Long prison term
Edward Murdoch, Bowhill	Unknown	21 days
William 'Mosie' Murray, Leven	ER	30 days

Table 5.5 Communists known to have been arrested during the general strike and lockout in the Scottish coalfields, May–November 1926 (Comtinued)

Name	Charge	Conviction/Sentence
David Proudfoot, checkweigher, Methil	ER	Not proven
Robert Robertson, Cupar	ER	Not known
W. Shepherd, Lumphinnans	ER	Not known
James Stewart, miner, Lochgelly	ER, twice	£2 or 15 days; £10 or 60 days
Robert Thomson, miner, Methil	Picketing	Not known
James Watt, Lumphinnans	ER	2 months
David J. Williams, Fife	Intimidating miner	
A. Williamson, Cupar	ER	£3 or 20 days
James A. Wilson, Bowhill	Not known	21 days
Ernie Wooley, CP organiser	ER	Sentence not known
Lanarkshire		
Willam Allan, miner, Blantyre	CPPA	Not guilty
James Beecroft, miner, High Blantyre	Disorderly behaviour	Fined
John Brown, Rutherglen	ER	£3 0r 14 days
William Crichton, pit sinker, Blantyre	Assisting soldiers to desert	3 months hard labour
Frederick MacDonald, caretaker, New Stevenston	CPPA	Not guilty
Stirlingshire		
John Heeps, miner, Kilsyth	ER	3 months
Pat Lafferty, miner, Dennyloanhead	ER	Not proven
William Leishman, Dennyloanhead	ER	£10 fine
Alex Shaw, miner, Kilsyth	Demonstration against scabs	6 weeks hard labour

Table 5.5 Communists known to have been arrested during the general strike and lockout in the Scottish coalfields, May–November 1926 (Continued)

Name	Charge	Conviction/Sentence
Alfred Thomson, Bannockburn	ER	£5 fine
Ayrshire		
William Campbell, Irvine	ER	3 months
No location		
J. Shields	ER	Not known

Sources: SRO HH56/22, Police Intelligence Reports, 30 October – 7 December 1926; HH56/27, Reports and Correspondence; HH56/30, Intelligence Reports, May–November 1926; *Motherwell Times*; *Kirkcaldy Times*; I. MacDougall (ed.), *Militant Miners* (Edinburgh, 1981); B. Selkirk, *The Life of a Worker* (Dundee, 1967); A. Moffat, *My Life with the Miners* (1965), p. 45; S. Macintyre, *Little Moscows: communism and working-class militancy in inter-war Britain* (1980); P. and C. Carter, 'The miners of Kilsyth in the 1926 general strike and lockout', *Our History Pamphlet*, no. 58, 1974; 'Aspects of the General Strike', part IV, microfiche in author's possession; Sime/Gilby interview with Mosie Murray.

Notes:
1. ER = Emergency Regulations
2. CPPA = Conspiracy and Protection of Property Act.
3. It is likely that although the residence of a number of those arrested was given as Cupar in returns furnished by chief constables, this referred to the place of their trial, as the Sheriff Court for East Fife was held there.

Stewart of Lochgelly was the Chairman of the MRU, a town councillor and magistrate; McArthur and Proudfoot were the acknowledged party leaders in East Fife.[118]

Upon their release, such men were feted as heroes in their communities and their example boosted support for their party. In
Methil, at a concert held under the auspices of the Trades and
Labour Council and attended by some 200 people, six former pris-
oners were presented with medals inscribed 'International Class
War Prisoners' by Helen Crawford, a prominent Glaswegian Communist. At Bowhill, a demonstration welcomed the release of John
Bird and two other Communists after they had served sentences of
21 days.[119] Seventeen young Glencraig miners, including two
Communists, were convicted for their part in the mass attack on the
local colliery in November and sentenced to hard labour in
Barlinnie Prison. Accounts of their brutal batoning by the police as
they were arrested survive in the oral traditions of the village until
the present day – the mother of one fainted in court when she saw
her son 'beaten beyond all recognition' – and a mass demonstration
welcomed them home on their release when they were awarded
silver medals at a banquet in their honour.[120]

The authorities were well aware of the differences between such
militants and the trade union bureaucracy. In Ayrshire, James
Brown headed an AMU delegation to the County Council and
pledged that 'they would give the County Council all the assistance
in their power to maintain law and order'.[121] According to the Chief
Constable of Fife, 'the members of the old union will have nothing
to do with the Councils of Action, and they are always willing to tell
the police anything they know of the workings of the Council'.[122]
Similarly, Masterton claimed 'the troubles' in Fife 'rose largely from
Communists who are connected with the Reform Union. The old
association sits with folded hands and does nothing.' He paid credit
to William B. Small, General Secretary of the LMU, 'for his strenuous efforts to keep order amongst the men'.[123] This was echoed
by a police account of a demonstration of 4,000 to 5,000 at
Auchenraith Colliery, Blantyre, after a report that the manager had
'declared war on them on account of their threat to withdraw his
safety men ... did not please the crowd too well'; however Small
managed 'to cool them down again by some suave talking and
got them to agree to leave the matter in the hands of the strike
committee ...'.[124]

We can detect similar tensions in a press account of one of the largest demonstrations of Lanarkshire miners towards the end of the strike. According to the Chief Constable of Hamilton, the demonstration was organised by 'the extremists who have recently acquired a considerable following in this locality, mostly irresponsible youths with no inclination to work'.[125] After William Allan had received a 'rousing reception', James Beecroft, a fellow Blantyre Communist, urged the setting up of strike committees with their own leader in every street where miners lived 'and under those leaders the men on strike would see to the disappearance of black-legs'. In the midst of this combative rhetoric, two working miners were observed returning from the pit, and a large body of the crowd were only restrained by 'the presence of the police and the appeals of Mr Joseph Sullivan, MP, to keep order and remain around the platform'.[126]

The aftermath

As early as June, the Mines Inspector had presciently stated that 'the men do not realise that, no matter when or on what terms the stoppage finishes, many of them will never again be employed underground, or they would be less easy in their minds'.[127] Although Sir Adam Nimmo gave Smillie an assurance 'that he would not be a party to any victimisation', there was widespread refusal by coal owners to employ known union activists.[128] By Christmas, 10,000 miners out of the 36,000 normally employed in Lanarkshire had not restarted work; of these, some 290 were members of union branch committees, and many pit committees in the county remained completely idle; 14 checkweighmen had been refused access to the pithead and in some cases managers had ordered the demolition of the sheds used by union dues collectors.[129] Leading Communists figured prominently among the ranks of those refused work. Abe Moffat recalled that:

> my father, two younger brothers, and I were all victimised. My father was getting old by then, near retirement, and he never got back. Eventually Alex got back into another combine and David got back, but I never got back, bar when I got into a small private mine in 1938.[130]

In Buckhaven and Methil, McArthur recalled that 'victimisation for the active elements was the order of the day. Almost every one of our local active people was barred.' Like the Moffat family, the proscription on him was extended to his father and brother who were kept out of pit work for two years.[131] Mosie Murray, from Leven, who had been out of work for two years after the 1921 lockout, remained unemployed for five after 1926. Guy Bolton, who had joined the CP in Coalburn in 1924, recalled 'efter the '26 strike when they [the managers] picked a' the boys out – "Ye're no' gaun back, and you're no' gaun back"'.[132]

The dispute had seen the close involvement of employers with the state in the effort to defeat the miners. The Scottish District Coal Emergency Committee, responsible for organising the movement and distribution of coal, consisted of eleven coal owners, two representatives of coal merchants, one from the cooperative movement and two civil servants; it was chaired by J.T. Forgie, a director of William Baird and Company.[133] In October, a senior civil servant at the Scottish Office noted the 'quite good contact between the police and the mine managers' which had been brought about by the Mines' Inspector encouraging local managers to contact the police and his own request that 'the Sheriffs should instruct the Chief Constables to make contact with the Mine Managers'.[134] For their part, the LCMA expressed to the Chief Constable of Lanarkshire 'the Coal Owners' appreciation of the services which he had rendered during the strike'.[135]

Employers took the opportunity of the shift in bargaining power brought about by victimisation and the divisions created by the dispute to disorganise trade unionism during its aftermath. When the Scottish Colliery Firemen and Shotfirers' Association (SCFSA), a body not previously recognised by the employers for negotiating purposes sought recognition in October 1926, Sir Adam Nimmo was enthusiastic that such men should not be members of the NUSMW. Although he accepted that the coal owners were bound by previous agreements, he thought 'the present an opportune time for the Firemen to intimate to the Miners' Unions ... that they were no longer members of these unions and that the Miners' Unions were not entitled to speak for or act for them in future ...'. Once this step was taken, he felt that the Scottish owners 'ought not to put any obstacle in the way of negotiating with them and of ultimately giving them industrial recognition'.[136] Relations between the

NUSMW and SCFSA were strained throughout the inter-war period and the latter body remained a thorn in the flesh of the larger union until an accommodation was reached in 1946.[137]

More serious, however, were employers' attempts at disruption of workplace trade unionism. David Meek recalled that at Hamilton Palace Colliery there were two checkweighers or 'justicemen', at no. 1 and no. 2 pits, who were Secretary and President of the union branch:

> ... so the undermanagers went round all the men, the newcomers [i.e. former strikebreakers] and asked them to sign a petition that they wanted to do away with the present justicemen and put in ... for nomination for two new justicemen. Well, in the ensuing vote, the two justicemen were voted off. Well, we nominated them back again, the people who had stayed out right to the very end, we nominated the two men back on again and when a vote was taken place, of course, we knew there was no chance of getting them back again, and we brought on our own justicemen, and of course that started the deterioration of the union as well, till finally there were only a matter of about, oh, less than a hundred of us that got started after October '26 was left in the union, till finally it just drifted away and there was no union whatsoever.[138]

Such divisions accelerated a tendency towards political sectarianism by members of the Communist Party which had been apparent even before the lockout. As early as June 1925, the tone of a complaint that three left-wing members of Gateside LMU branch committee had been victimised and had not received sufficient support from the full-time union agent was symptomatic of this mood: 'our own union officials helping the boss to down working class fighters'.[139] It was further reflected in the statement issued by the party's Executive Committee after the calling off of the General Strike by the TUC which condemned the failure of the right-wing leadership: 'they have been the agents of capitalism in the labour movement'.[140] When Duncan Graham, an LMU official and MP for Hamilton, addressed a meeting in Motherwell in May, he was constantly heckled by the 'younger element ... clearly spoiling for a fight'. The gap in generational attitudes was readily apparent. When Graham's defence of the TUC and his hint that the MFGB might advocate a return to work brought 'cries of "shame" from the younger element', he retorted angrily that it would be 'a greater shame if the miners had to daun'er back in twos and threes'. Recalling his forty years in the miners' movement – 'I have done as much in this movement and more than you are ever likely to do' – he insisted that 'the leaders are more competent to deal with the situation than young irresponsibles'. One of the latter argued for the withdrawal of the safety men and to 'allow the pits to go to hell'.[141]

By August, Allan was openly contemptuous of his elderly fellow officials. Writing in the *Worker* under the headline 'The Cowardly Leaders of Lanarkshire', he complained of the 'innumerable instances of capitulation and spineless policy' of the county leaders since 1921 and 'cases of starving miners being comforted by shallow-pated prigs who blithely inform them that it is all their own fault since they did not send the Labour Party back into power'.[142] At the NUSMW Executive that same month, Allan insisted on his right to submit his views to the membership irrespective of the position of the union's governing body. Challenged by Smillie as to whether he believed the Executive and himself were sincere, Allan asserted that 'he did and does doubt the sincerity of Mr Smillie on behalf of the miners'. When asked to withdraw the remark, Allan refused and the meeting adjourned.[143] At a 'packed meeting' in the Cooperative Hall, Hamilton, two weeks later, Allan defended himself against moves to expel him from the Executive. According to the local press, 'it was quite evident that he had the wholehearted support of the meeting'.[144]

Yet despite such divisions and the significant numbers returning to work before the end of the lockout, attempts to establish 'non-political' unions in Scotland in its aftermath were much less successful that those in Nottinghamshire, and, to a lesser extent, in South Wales.[145] A Stirling and Clackmannan Miners' Industrial Union (SCMIU) was formed in 1927 but secured only 94 members in its five branches and was dissolved in 1929. A similar body, the Fife and Kinross Miners' Industrial Trade Union (FKMIU) was set up by a group of former Adamson supporters in Lochgelly but it had only 76 members by 1930.[146] The limited membership of such bodies may well have been atypical of the mass of the miners. In the Kilsyth district, the SCMIU Secretary was John Heeps, a former Communist who had been imprisoned for sedition in 1926; in the village of Longcroft, his sole member was 'the local Orangeman'.[147] Bert True, an official in the FKMIU was also a former militant; a Welshman resident in West Wemyss, he was unusual in that he 'was always immaculately dressed ... always had a soft hat, tie and coloured hand gloves'.[148] Some 'non-pols' were merely disillusioned by the defeat of politicised trade union activity while their officials may have been seduced by the bureaucratic rewards of £6 per week and a Triumph motorcycle.[149]

The 'non-political' movement nevertheless touched a sympathetic chord in the consciousness of some older miners within the tradition of the independent collier. A Larkhall miner, writing in June 1926, argued that the dispute could be resolved by offering an eight hour day with no reduction in wage rates. He went on to combine nostalgia for an earlier period of union organisation with an anti-bureaucratic critique of miners' agents who became MPs:

> these people are protected by their two or three jobs and paid for by the man who lowered his independence by receiving parish relief ... win back our independence, brush these people aside, and look after our own business from a sensible point of view and not by a political movement made up of people out for good jobs and money.

The solution, he argued, lay in a district union, 'which could be worked by a secretary and treasurer and a Board of workmen from the various pits in the district ... then the miner would get his independence back by having money in the bank for the wife and family of the miners when there was a dispute on'.[150]

The primary reason for the failure of such non-political initiatives, in contrast to Nottinghamshire and South Wales, lay in the unwillingness of Scottish coal owners to sponsor them. This in turn reflected the organisational weakness and conciliatory policies adopted by the leadership of the NUSMW and the county unions which, from the employers' point of view, rendered non-political unionism redundant in Scotland. It is to developments within these unions that we return in the following chapter. Before doing so, however, it is appropriate finally to address a broader historiographical debate on the significance of the General Strike from the specific perspective of the Scottish coalfields.

There is some controversy in the existing literature as to whether the General Strike represented a 'watershed' in British industrial relations. Whereas writers from varying points within the Marxist tradition, such as Martin Jacques and John Foster, have pointed up the dislocation which 1926 represented – in terms of a greater defensiveness and class collaboration – within the trajectory of British trade unionism, others such as Hugh Clegg and Gordon Phillips have emphasised the continuities in pre-existing tendencies towards industrial accommodation by the trade union bureaucracy.[151] As in all such debates, it is possible to detect both continuities and ruptures. From the viewpoint of the Scottish coalfields, the acceleration of certain pre-existing trends after 1926, notably the divisions between left and right and the fissiparous tendencies within the miners' unions, can be detected. But 1926 can also be considered as marking the climax of the syndicalist insurgency which had developed since 1912.

The lockout also represented a turning point or 'hinge' in the 'repertoire' of popular protest elaborated since the early nineteenth century.[152] Thereafter, collective violence and sabotage, rough music and public ritual displayed a much more limited salience during labour disputes. In part this merely reflected the fact that the communal mobilisations associated with national mining disputes did not re-appear for almost fifty years. But as was noted in the preceding volume, industrial conflict dramatically increased in the Scottish coalfields after 1926 as miners resisted employers' attempts to take advantage of the defeat to drive forward changes in the labour process and intensify the rate of exploitation. As will become evident in the following chapters, these struggles were often conducted under the leadership of the Communist Party. In the absence of empirical evidence, we can only note the divisions over direct action evidenced above in the views of Proudfoot and Selkirk, and speculate that the success of police repression encouraged a focus on militant trade unionism within the workplace rather than a reliance on sabotage, 'terrorism' and mass insurgency. Despite the increasingly revolutionary rhetoric espoused by the Communist Party by the end of the 1920s, it is clear that the tactics of most of its mining cadre were directed towards industrial militancy rather than insurrection. 1926 can thus be seen as a significant point in the 'modernisation' of social conflict in the Scottish coalfields.

Appendix

Chronology of incidents involving mass picketing, assaults on working miners, attacks on property and sabotage in the Scots coalfields, May–December 1926

Date	Incident
1 May	**Lanarkshire**: windows smashed and police assaulted during fracas in Hamilton; one miner arrested.
4 May	**Lanarkshire**: stoning of buses at Airdrie. **Glasgow**: bus overturned by strikers at Parkhead.
5 May	**Renfrewshire**: 3 arrests for stone throwing. **Ayrshire**: a crowd of 300 broke the windows of buses and blocked the road between Galston and Hurlford. **Dunbartonshire**: miners attacked commercial vehicles near Condorrat. **Lanarkshire**: buses stopped running after their windows were broken by stone throwing. **East Lothian**: train stoned near Musselburgh.
6 May	**Glasgow**: riots continued in the east end throughout the day after a picket of miners (estimates range from 300–500) marched from the Cambuslang and Newton districts in the early morning to assist pickets at tramway depots; they were dispersed by police 'after a fierce struggle'; later in the day the pickets were again dispersed by repeated baton charges and the retreating crowds looted shops; 66 arrests were made. **Ayrshire**: 5 men, including two miners, were arrested in Irvine after crowds attacked buses carrying shipyard workers.
7 May	**Glasgow**: further rioting and looting in the east end and around 60 arrests were made during repeated baton charges. **Lanarkshire**: attack made on police by a crowd of 500–600 after the police foiled a raid on a public house in Cadzow, Hamilton. **Lothians**: in Tranent, a crowd which had stopped motor vehicles attacked the police station and smashed shop windows; another crowd stoned a train near Wallyford.

Fife: a crowd of 1,000 blocked the level crossing at Leven and damaged the points; a car was damaged by a crowd at Gallatown.

Early May

Fife: a 'large and disorderly mob' armed with crowbars and missiles stoned beer lorries at Valleyfield.

Lothians: 13 miners were arrested on charges relating to the stopping of vehicles and demanding TUC permits.

10 May

Ayrshire: two lorries were held up by pickets at Cumnock; a quarrymaster was stoned near Cumnock; the Dumfries-Glasgow train was stoned by a crowd of 1,000 at Auchinleck and timber thrown onto the engine from a bridge.

Lanarkshire: police baton charged to disperse a picket near Douglas.

Fife: a crowd halted lorries in Kirkcaldy and removed two bags of coal; a picket at Muiredge Colliery, Buckhaven, was dispersed by a baton charge; three policemen were injured and five miners arrested.

Lothians: 12 miners were arrested after a crowd attacked a signal box at Newcraighall.

11 May

Lanarkshire: the Riot Act was read in Airdrie and a crowd of several thousands dispersed by baton charges.

Ayrshire: a crowd of 200 blocked the railway line and jammed the points near Auchinleck; 19 miners, 'all young men', were arrested.

West Lothian: a checkweigher and two miners were arrested after preventing delivery of fuel to a shale mine.

Fife: a crowd of several hundred attacked a beer lorry at Buckhaven.

12 May

Ayrshire: a length of railway line was removed near Auchinleck.

Lanarkshire: explosives were used to damage a railway line at Omoa; the repair gang were stoned by a crowd.

Fife: a crowd at Thornton, led by a melodeon player and carrying a banner inscribed 'Scab's escort', followed a railway clerk from work.

14 May

Ayrshire: 11 miners were arrested and later found guilty of stopping traffic on the Ayr-Patna road by smashing bus windows.

31 May	**Lanarkshire**: a railway line near Whiterigg Colliery, was blown up and the cylinder of a steam engine at No. 3 Whiterigg Mine was also destroyed by explosives. **West Lothian**: two men from Blackridge, one of whom was a Communist, were arrested for stealing explosives from a Harthill quarry with the intention of blowing up a railway bridge.
12 June	**Fife**: 3,000 men and women from Bowhill and Lochgelly demonstrated outside a Lochgelly Parish Council meeting demanding relief.
18 June	**Fife**: a mass picket at Jenny Gray Colliery, Lochgelly was dispersed by a police baton charge and 17 were arrested; 13 men were later sent to prison. Two railway coal wagons were derailed and others discharged by a crowd at Mary Pit, Lochore.
20 June	**Fife**: 3,000 'miners and their womenfolk' from East Fife marched in procession from Methil to Thornton Poor House demanding admission for 1,000 single miners refused parish relief; 6,000 miners and women pithead workers marched to Dunfermline Poor House in a similar protest.
29 June	**Lanarkshire**: a large picket met repairers who had worked on airways at a Bellshill pit.
30 June	**Lanarkshire**: a miner working at Parkhead Colliery was subjected to rough handling in Bellshill and four arrests were made.
1 July	**Lanarkshire**: a crowd of two dozen raided a coal train near Rutherglen.
2 July	**Lanarkshire**: the railway siding at Longrigg Colliery was damaged by two charges of explosive; at the same time, the doors of 74 railway wagons containing anthracite were maliciously opened and allowed to run onto the track.
4 July	**Lanarkshire**: the cylinder of a haulage engine at Greenside Colliery, Newhouse, was 'completely wrecked' after being blown up by explosives.
7 July	**Lanarkshire**: anonymous letters were sent to miners working

at Blackridge Colliery threatening that their houses would be burned down; the men immediately stopped work.

8 July   **Lanarkshire**: a crowd of 2,000–3,000 paraded through Hamilton carrying 'grotesque effigies' of ratepayers who had taken legal action against the parish council to stop poor relief to miners and picketed their homes and offices.

20 July   **Lanarkshire**: 20 working miners at a small colliery near Baillieston refused to go to work until police protection was given to the mine after a rumour that it was to be blown up.

21 July   **Lanarkshire**: a crowd of men and women picketed 30 miners who had returned to work at Thankerton Colliery, Holytown; 'derisive characterisations of the men were profusely tendered'; only one man worked the following day.

23 July   **Ayrshire**: a large body of miners' wives marched to the Ayr Poor House demanding admittance after being refused parish relief.

2 August   **Lothians**: a hundred men, women and children jeered and stoned miners going to work at Vogrie Colliery.

7 August   **Fife**: picketing took place at Balgonie Colliery where approximately 100 men were working; it 'took the form of jeering, especially by the women'.

9 August   **Lanarkshire**: a miner returning from work in Coatbridge was molested by a large crowd which broke the windows of his house; 10 arrests were made.

10 Aug.   **Lanarkshire**: mass stealing of coal from Bardykes Colliery, Blantyre.
              Dunbartonshire: miners invaded the farm owned by the Chairman of Cumbernauld Parish Council and damaged walls and fences after the council decided to stop payment of relief to miners' dependants; the council later voted to continue relief on a reduced scale.

12 August   **Fife**: about 1,500 miners assembled in Coaltown of Balgonie where 160 men were working in the Balgonie Coal Company's pits; they had with them 'music of the ragtime order and were armed with cudgels'; nine 'young miners'

were later found guilty of 'shouting and bawling and flourishing their sticks'.

17 August   **Lanarkshire**: two working miners at Kingshill Colliery were molested in Wishaw by a crowd of men and women; two arrests were made.

19 August   **Fife**: two working miners at Lochside Mine were followed home by a crowd hissing and booing, two arrests made; two 'ringleaders' of a picket in Dunfermline were also arrested.

27 August   **Lanarkshire**: a large number of strikers badly damaged a bus containing working miners at Woodhall Colliery and injured a policeman.

28 August   **Ayrshire**: 10 men and 39 women were arrested for being part of a 'disorderly crowd' at Auchinleck, 'shouting, bawling, beating tin cans and trays, surrounding [working miners] and following them and besetting the house of one of them'.

31 August   **Lothians**: police baton charged a demonstration of miners and their families demanding poor relief at West Calder Parish Council Chambers.

1 Sept.   **Lanarkshire**: the driver of a goods train was injured by stone throwing near Glenboig.

3 Sept.   **Lanarkshire**: a miner was arrested for throwing a hutch and props down the shaft of Lochrigg Colliery, Airdrie.

7 Sept.   **Lanarkshire**: the windows of a miners' house at New Logan's Rows, Motherwell, were smashed and the garden destroyed after he started work at Woodhall Colliery;

11 Sept.   **Lanarkshire**: 26 men started work at Dewshill Colliery, Salsburgh, under police protection from a large picket.
Fife: a 'disorderly crowd' beset a fireman working at Glencraig Colliery and six miners' wives were arrested.

17 Sept.   **Fife**: pickets were out in force at Cowdenbeath, Lochgelly, Glencraig, Lochore, Methil and Buckhaven.

19 Sept.   **Fife**: police baton charged a crowd of 300–400 strikers who attempted to force entry to Glencraig Colliery.

20 Sept	**Fife**: some miners returning from work were followed and booed by several women in Lochore; police baton charged a crowd of 300 pickets at Glencraig Colliery which attempted to storm the pit; police baton charged another crowd which stoned them in nearby Lochore in the evening.
23 Sept.	**Lanarkshire**: a railway line at Shotts Iron Works was damaged by gelignite placed under a sleeper; a bucket of tar was thrown over the windows of the house of a working miner in Baillieston. **Fife**: every window in the house of a working miner near Dunfermline was blown out by detonators which caused considerable damage; the windows of working miners were smashed at Valleyfield.
25 Sept.	**Lothians**: two miners were arrested for threatening a safety man at Ormiston.
27 Sept.	**Lanarkshire**: the water pipe on the electrical plant supplying Shotts Iron Works and Northfield Colliery was blown up by three explosive charges.
3 Oct.	**Fife**: a local Communist was charged under the Conspiracy and Protection of Property Act and later sentenced to 40 days; a crowd at Bowhill prevented a miner from going to work and three local Communists were later sentenced to 21 days imprisonment for their part in the incident.
4 Oct.	**Fife**: the windows of a house at Crosshill were broken by a detonator.
5 Oct.	**Lanarkshire**: a crowd assaulted five working miners in Larkhall.
6 Oct.	**Fife**: a crowd of 1,000 men and women picketed the first working miners at the Wellesley Colliery, Denbeath; a crowd of 300 followed 3 working miners at Coaltown of Wemyss. **Clackmannanshire**: pickets from Fife 'raided' the garden of a working miner and broke window panes.
7 Oct.	**Fife**: 1,500 people picketed Wellesley Colliery.
9/10 Oct.	**Lanarkshire**: 'huge crowds' demonstrated at the house of a working miner in Motherwell.

Lothians: dynamite was used to blow a large hole in the roof of a garage belonging to the Edinburgh Collieries Company and damaged vehicles.

11 Oct.   **Lanarkshire**: a crowd of 200 strikers attacked a number of working miners in Holytown Main Street as they returned from work; a police baton charge led to a dozen arrests; the windows of five working miners in Holytown were broken during the night.
West Lothian: the windows of working miners living near Bo'ness were broken.

15 Oct.   **Lanarkshire**: the windows of a miner's house at Cleland were blown in by explosives.

16 Oct.   **West Lothian**: two Tarbrax miners were charged with intimidating workmen at Baads Mains Colliery, West Calder.

18 Oct.   **Lanarkshire**: a crowd marched to Blairmuckhill Colliery, Harthill, and put two working miners into a 'state of fear and alarm'.
Fife: a Communist miner from Buckhaven was arrested for threatening a working miner under police escort and later sentenced to 14 days imprisonment.

19 Oct.   **Lanarkshire**: two working miners at Hamilton Palace Colliery were attacked and seven young miners were arrested.

20 Oct.   **Lanarkshire**: a crowd of 700 at Blantyre attacked three men employed as safety men at Auchenraith Colliery; the crowd was dispersed by a police baton charge and seven arrests were made; a crowd of 400–500 at Bothwellhaugh stoned buses used for carrying blacklegs and assaulted two firemen working at Hamilton Palace Colliery on their return from work before the police baton charged; five other safety men from Hamilton Palace were threatened as they returned to Bellshill.

21 Oct.   **West Lothian**: daily demonstrations were mounted against firemen working at Castleloan and Cumlouden Collieries; a fireman's windows were broken at Castleloan.
Lothians: report of windows being broken in the house of a blackleg at Poltonhall.

22 Oct.   **Lanarkshire**: 2.5 pounds of gelignite were stolen from Craighead Quarry.

25 Oct.   **Lanarkshire**: three miners were arrested for breaking the windows of houses occupied by working miners at Batonrigg Colliery, Shotts.

27 Oct.   **Lanarkshire**: eight men were arrested after miners from Viewpark Colliery were assaulted in Uddingston as they returned from work.
Dunbartonshire: three miners were arrested after a crowd followed a colliery contractor through the streets of Kilsyth.
West Lothian: three Bathgate miners were arrested for intimidating miners working at Eaton Pit.
Dumfriesshire: the windows of a working miner at Kirkconnel were broken.

29 Oct.   **Lanarkshire**: a crowd threatened four apprentice mining engineers near Blantyreferme Colliery.

30 Oct.   **Lanarkshire**: eight cases of window breaking, including one case at Fauldhouse where a detonator was used; a Hamilton miner imprisoned for assaulting a working miner, and a youth sentenced to 30 days for throwing a stone at the manager of Greenfield Colliery.
Dunbartonshire: several cases of window breaking occurred at houses of working miners near Kirkintilloch.
Fife: two working miners were assaulted by a number of men in Glencraig; explosives were later used to blow out the windows of one of the assaulted men.

1 Nov.   **Fife**: during the night a number of windows at the houses of working miners were broken by stones in Lochgelly and Bowhill; daily demonstrations were organised against miners going to work under police escort at Bowhill and Dundonald Collieries.

2 Nov.   **Lanarkshire**: the pithead winding gear at Kirkwood No. 1 pit was destroyed by fire after men from other districts went to work there; the windows of working miners at Hamilton Palace Colliery were broken during the night.
Fife: a Cardenden miner was arrested under the Conspiracy and Protection of Property Act and later sentenced to 21 days imprisonment.

3 Nov.   **Lothians**: nine Bonnyrigg miners appeared in court charged with breaking the windows of a house occupied by a family of working miners.

Stirlingshire: a lump of cement was thrown through the window of a safety man.

4 Nov.   **West Lothian**: a man was arrested for assaulting police escorting working miners.

Fife: a crowd of 200 intimidated blacklegs at the Aitken Pit, Kelty, and 19 men were arrested; 'disorderly and hostile' crowds demonstrated against working miners returning from Bowhill Colliery.

5 Nov.   **Lanarkshire**: a large crowd raiding coal waggons at Southrigg Colliery, Harthill, were dispersed by baton charges; an unsuccessful attempt was made to blow up a bridge over the railway leading to Dewshill Colliery, Shotts.

Stirlingshire: five men were arrested for intimidation after a mass picket at Plean Colliery was dispersed by a baton charge.

6 Nov.   **Stirlingshire**: five arrests were made after a picket at Plean Colliery was dispersed by a baton charge.

Fife: the stable and three horses of a Buckhaven carter (who had previously reported eight miners to the police for throwing sand and rubbish in his coal) were destroyed by fire; incendiarism was suspected.

9 Nov.   **Lanarkshire**: five married women reported to Procurator Fiscal for 'booing, shouting and throwing mud' at working miners returning from Tannochside Colliery; eight married women from Stane similarly reported for 'behaving in a disorderly manner and jeering and using taunting expressions' at the house of three working miners.

Ayrshire: 15 men and 9 women were reported to the Procurator Fiscal for intimidation and besetting the homes of six working miners at Hurlford; a railway sleeper was dropped from a bridge onto a bus driving miners to work in the Cumnock district.

Stirlingshire: the windows of three houses occupied by working miners were broken.

10 Nov.   **Fife**: the window of a workman's house at Crosshill was blown in by explosives.

11 Nov.	**Fife**: the window of a workman's house at Glencraig was damaged by a detonator.
	Lothians: a bus carrying working miners was stoned in Tranent High Street.
12 Nov.	**Lanarkshire**: a quantity of explosives were stolen from a colliery.
	Stirlingshire: the window of a working miner's house was broken.
	Fife: the window of a workman was broken at Lochgelly.
13 Nov.	**Lanarkshire**: the haulage wheel at Hartrigg Colliery was destroyed by explosives; explosives were also used to damage a colliery railway line near Holytown.
	Fife: windows were broken by a detonator in Lochore and by stones in Lumphinnans.
15 Nov.	**Fife**: three cases of window breaking in Lochgelly and Bowhill.
16 Nov.	**Lanarkshire**: a working miner was assaulted as he returned from Broomside Colliery, Motherwell.
	Lothians: a crowd of strikers threatened a working miner at Prestonpans.
17 Nov.	**Lanarkshire**: a charge of gelignite exploded on a boiler at Kirkwood Colliery; eight people were arrested after a crowd from Blackwood assaulted two working miners.
	Fife: an explosion occurred in a soup kitchen used by strikers, believed to be an act of retaliation by working miners.
19 Nov.	**Lanarkshire**: 60–70 miners, 'mostly youths', marched from Stonehouse to Larkhall where they attacked a working miner before being dispersed by a baton charge; five arrests were made.
20 Nov.	**Fife**: a large procession 'composed for the main part of youths and women' and headed by a pipe band picketed Nellie Pit, Lochgelly; 18 miners were arrested after five miners working at the Mary Pit were attacked by members of a crowd of 150 pickets.

21 Nov.   **Fife**: an explosion occurred at the Jenny Gray Pit, Lochgelly, after a bomb was thrown into the electricity distribution plant.

22 Nov.   **Lanarkshire**: several windows of working miners were broken in the Hamilton district during the night.
Fife: a crowd of 300–400 stormed the pithead at Glencraig Colliery, smashed windows, wrecked the boiler and cage, and attacked the police and working miners; the windows of a house in which a policeman took refuge were smashed by the crowd; 48 people were later charged with mobbing and rioting; several windows of working miners were broken at Bowhill, Cowdenbeath and Valleyfield.

23 Nov.   **Lanarkshire**: an explosion damaged the boiler at Shotts Iron Works in an attempt to cut off the water supply to eight adjoining pits; a Tannochside miner was charged with intimidating a fireman working at Tannochside Colliery.
Fife: a crowd of 60 strikers stoned three working miners and broke windows and cut the phone lines at Kinglassie Colliery; at Valleyfield, the windows of both working miners and 'extremist strikers' were broken.

24 Nov.   **Fife**: two windows were broken in workmen's houses in East Wemyss.

25 Nov.   **Stirlingshire**: the windows of two workmen's houses were broken by stones at Cowie.

26 Nov.   **Fife**: Lumphinnans Ex-servicemen's Club was destroyed by a fire allegedly started by 'the Communist element'.

27 Nov.   **Fife**: at Lumphinnans, the windows of two houses occupied by 'extremists' and of the committee rooms used by the 'extremists' were broken, allegedly 'in retaliation for window breaking by extremists'.

28 Nov.   **Fife**: an explosion in a partly-built house was thought to have been caused by strikers.

30 Nov.   **Fife**: an attempt was made to blow up power lines from the electricity generating station at Aitken Pit, Kelty.

End of Nov.
West Lothian: power cable at Foulshiels Colliery, Stoneyburn, blown up; explosives were used to damage a window and stonework of a safety man at Breich; a detonator smashed the windows of a house near West Calder.

4 Dec.
West Lothian: the window of a house at Stoneyburn occupied by a family who were prosecution witnesses against strikers was blown in by explosives; the doorstep of the father of one of the strikers was later damaged by a charge of gelignite in retaliation.

9 Dec.
West Lothian: a pit contractor who had been 'subject to the attentions of the strikers' was allegedly shot at from a passing car by men armed with a revolver.

Sources: SRO HH 56/22, 26, 27, 28, 30, 35, Reports and correspondence concerning the coal dispute, 1926; the following newspapers were searched from May_December, 1926: *Emergency Press, Kirkcaldy Times, Leven Advertiser and Wemyss Gazette, Hamilton Advertiser, Motherwell Times, Dalkeith Advertiser, Glasgow Herald, Scotsman, Kilmarnock Standard, Weekly Supplement and Advertiser for Galston, Newmilns, Darvel and Hurlford, Ayrshire Advertiser*; J. McLean, 'The 1926 General Strike in Lanarkshire', *Our History Pamphlet*, no. 65, Spring 1976.

Notes

1. For the general strike, see P. Renshaw, *The General Strike* (1975); M. Morris, *The General Strike* (Harmondsworth, 1976); G.A. Phillips, *The General Strike: the politics of industrial conflict* (1976). The most recent study is K. Laybourn, *The General Strike of 1926* (Manchester, 1993) which contains a comprehensive review of the literature. The miners' lockout is covered in detail in R.P. Arnot, *The Miners: years of struggle* (1953), pp. 457–523, while the economic context is analysed by B. Supple, *The History of the British Coal Industry, vol. 4, 1913–1946: the political economy of decline* (Oxford, 1987), pp. 214–70. Relevant local studies include Arnot, *History*, pp. 161–82; S. Bhaumik, 'Glasgow', in Morris, *General Strike*, pp. 394–410; I. MacDougall, 'Edinburgh' in J. Skelley (ed.), *The General Strike 1926* (1976), 'Some aspects of the 1926 general strike in Scotland', in I. MacDougall (ed.), *Essays in Scottish Labour History: a tribute to W.H. Marwick* (Edinburgh, n.d., [1978]), and 'The '26', in B. Kay (ed.) *Odyssey: the second collection* (Edinburgh, 1982), pp. 101–11; P. and C. Carter, 'The miners of Kilsyth in the 1926 general strike and lockout', *Our History Pamphlet*, 58, Spring 1974; P. Carter, 'The West of Scotland', in Skelley, *General Strike*; J. Maclean, 'The 1926 general strike in Lanarkshire', *Our History Pamphlet*, 65, Spring 1976; Duncan, *Shotts Miners*, pp. 11–20.
2. Laybourn, *General Strike*, pp. 32–4; Jeffery and Hennessy, *States of Emergency*, pp. 82–107; Weinberger, *Keeping the Peace?*, pp. 192–8.
3. Long, thesis, pp. 371–81.
4. SRO HH 1/608, Memorandum 'on the question whether protection is likely to be needed', 30 July 1925.
5. SRO HH 56/14, Sheriff Fleming to Sir John Gilmour, 13 July 1925. The term 'foreigners' here can only refer to miners from outside Fife, such as Lanarkshire or Ireland, rather than foreign nationals.
6. SRO HH 56/14, Scottish Office to Sir A. Rose; J.W. Peck to Sir A. Rose, 22 March 1926; Notes of Conference at Scottish Office, 16 March 1926.
7. HH 56/25, 'Military position as at evening of 5 May 1926' and 'Military position as at evening of 8 May 1926'. In the light of suggestions that soldiers had fraternised with Fife miners during the 1921 lockout (see above, ch. 3), it is significant that fears of such sympathies re-emerging were apparent in the Scottish Office in 1926. At the end of May, the companies from the Black Watch regiment in the coalfields were returned to Fort George, a civil servant observing: 'the men in the Black Watch have many connections in Fife and it is

thought preferable to replace them with non-local troops' (HH 56/26, P.J. Rose to W. Hogg, 31 May 1926).

8.   SRO HH 56/36, 'Guarding of pits: use of military guards'; HH 56/14, Sir A. Rose to P.J. Rose, 30 October 1925.

9.   SRO HH 56/35, J.W. Peck to P.J. Rose, 7 July 1926; HH 56/26, P.J. Rose to W. Hogg, 21 June 1926; *Scotsman*, 22 September 1926.

10. SRO HH 56/21, P.J. Rose to Vice-Admiral Cowan, 24 March 1926; Long, thesis, p. 377.

11. J.C. Welsh, *The Morlocks* (1924), pp. 172, 198–210. The book's title was taken from H.G. Wells, *The Time Machine*: 'Above ground you must have the Haves, pursuing pleasure, comfort and beauty, and below ground the Have-Nots. The Morlocks was the name by which these creatures were called.' See T. Rodgers, 'Politics, popular litera-ture and the Scottish miners: the poetry and fiction of James C. Welsh', *Scottish Labour History Society Journal*, 27, 1992.

12. For an example of caricature, the villain, Barney Blades, is described as 'small in stature, hunchbacked and misshapen, with inordinately long arms, and one of the ugliest faces that ever sat upon human shoulders ... the ears were large, and his mouth resembled a long slit across his face ...' (Welsh, *Morlocks*, p. 199).

13. *Forward*, 22 August 1925.

14. Long, thesis, pp. 376–7.

15. Parliamentary Debates, 187 HC Deb. 5s, 28 July 1925, col. 229; SRO HH 56/14, Sir A. Rose to P.J. Rose, 30 October 1925; HH56/21, P.J. Rose to Vice-Admiral Cowan, 24 March 1926. The Explosives Substances (Scotland No. 2) Order made by the Secretary of State for Scotland under the Emergency Regulations empowered Chief Constables to control the storage of explosives (*Glasgow Herald*, 6 May 1926). A request from the military authorities to remove the guards in June was refused by the Solicitor General on the grounds that: 'It is very important to .protect the explosives and detonators which have been concentrated at these points because of the possi-bilities of mischief being done in the mining districts' (HH 56/26, P.J. Rose to W. Hogg, 11 June 1926).

16. SRO HH 56/14, Sir A. Rose to P.J. Rose, 30 October 1925.

17. SRO HH 56/15, Scottish Office to J. Jeffrey, Scottish Board of Health, 3 December 1925; Ewan MacPherson, Scottish Board of Health to Capt. W.E. Elliot, Scottish Office, 28 July 1925; Board of Education to P.J. Rose, 29 July 1925.

18. I. Levitt, *Poverty and Welfare in Scotland, 1890–1948* (Edinburgh, 1988), pp. 104–32.

19. Ibid., p. 129.

20. Morris, *General Strike*, pp. 165–83; Laybourn, *General Strike*, pp. 34–6; J. Foster, 'British imperialism and the labour aristocracy',

in Skelley, *General Strike*, pp. 44–5; Long, thesis, pp. 364–71, 384; MacDougall, '1926 general strike', p. 170.

21. *Worker*, 21 November 1925.
22. *Worker*, 27 February, 10, 24 April 1926. For the antagonism of the union leadership, see NLS Dep. 227/86, NUSMW Executive, 16 March, 19 April 1926.
23. *Worker*, 24 April 1926.
24. *Workers' Weekly*, 24, 31 July, 6 November 1925, 19 February 1926.
25. *Workers' Weekly*, 24 July 1925, 19 February 1926.
26. *Workers' Weekly*, 10 July 1925.
27. *Workers' Weekly*, 1 May 1925; MacDougall, *Militant Miners*, p. 140.
28. MacDougall, *Militant Miners*, p. 140.
29. For the *Underworld* and the Blantyreferme paper (title unknown), see MacDougall, *Militant Miners*, pp. 225, 238; copies of the *Spark*, *Hutch* and *Torch* are in the Proudfoot Papers, MPL; for the *Sprag*, see Duncan, *Shotts Miners*, p. 12; for the *Rebel Miner*, see *Workers' Weekly*, 19 January 1926.
30. *Workers' Weekly*, 26 March 1926; first issue of *Spark* (un-numbered, no date), MPL.
31. MPL, *Hutch*, 4, January 1926.
32. E. Burns, *The General Strike 1926: trades councils in action* (1926), p. 14.
33. Klugmann, *History, vol. 2*, pp. 148–53.
34. MacDougall, *Militant Miners*, p. 89.
35. Long, 'Abe Moffat', p. 9.
36. MacDougall, *Militant Miners*, pp. 90–2; McLean, 'General strike in Lanarkshire', pp. 13, 22.
37. Cf Klugmann: 'No one should attempt to paint the tremendous apparatus of strike committees and Councils of Action that grew up throughout Britain as the monopoly of Communists' (*History, vol. 2*, pp. 147–8). Laybourn argues that 'Government victimisation of the Communists greatly exaggerated their true importance' (*General Strike*, p. 73), but it is evident from the following account that Communists did play a much more significant role in Lanarkshire and Fife than in many other parts of Britain.
38. Carter, 'West of Scotland', pp. 119–24; MacDougall, 'Edinburgh', p. 149.
39. Sections of the resulting report, 'Aspects of the General Strike', were reprinted in B. Weinberger, 'Communism and the general strike', *Bulletin of the Society for the Study of Labour History*, 48, 1984, pp. 31–57. Sections 2 and 4 of the report, summarising responses of Chief Constables, were not reprinted but have been made available to me on microfiche by the Society for the Study of Labour History.

40. Carter, 'West of Scotland', p. 115; MacDougall, 'Edinburgh', pp. 146–7.
41. 'Aspects of the General Strike', section 2, Fife and Kinross.
42. SRO HH 56/33, *Dunfermline Trades and Labour Council Official Strike Bulletin*, no. 9, 11 May 1926, no. 10, 12 May 1926.
43. 'Aspects of the General Strike', Section 2, Glasgow; *Emergency Press*, 7, 8, 11, 12 May 1926.
44. *Scotsman*, 8 May 1926; 'Aspects of the General Strike', Section 2, East Lothian.
45. McLean, 'Lanarkshire', p. 13.
46. *Scotsman*, 1 June 1926; *Glasgow Herald*, 25 May 1926.
47. *Dalkeith Advertiser*, 20 May 1926; *Glasgow Herald*, 28 May 1926.
48. *Weekly Supplement and Advertiser, for Galston, Newmilns, Darvel and Hurlford*, 28 May 1926.
49. *Ayrshire Advertiser*, 3 June 1926.
50. *Scotsman*, 31 May 1926.
51. *Hamilton Advertiser*, 25 December 1926.
52. *Weekly Supplement and Advertiser, for Galston, Newmilns, Darvel and Hurlford*, 28 May 1926.
53. *Scotsman*, 1 June 1926.
54. *Kirkcaldy Times*, 25 August 1926.
55. SRO HH 56/26, Situation report of J. Masterton to Chief Inspector of Mines, 15 June 1926.
56. *Workers' Weekly*, 25 June 1926.
57. *Scotsman*, 10 July 1926.
58. *Scotsman*, 31 May, 9 July 1926.
59. *Workers' Weekly*, 18, 25 June 1926.
60. SRO HH 56/26, Fifeshire Constabulary. Police Report. Miners' Strike, 12 June.
61. *Scotsman*, 9 July 1926.
62. *Glasgow Herald*, 9 July, 14 August 1926.
63. *Scotsman*, 24, 31 July, 7 August 1926.
64. *Motherwell Times*, 3 September 1926. See also *Scotsman*, 1 June, 24 29, 31 July, 6, 13, 14, 19, 31 August, 4 September 1926. Kilsyth Council maintained its original level of relief payments until October but its request of a loan of £4,000 from the Board of Health was refused until the rates were cut by between 10 and 20 per cent (Carter and Carter, 'Miners of Kilsyth', p. 19).
65. SRO HH 56/26, J.W. Peck to P.J. Rose, 28 July 1926, G.M.A. Macleod to P.J. Rose, 7 August 1926; *Glasgow Herald*, 27 July 1926. For Thankerton, see ch. 4 in this volume. Balgonie, some five miles inland from Buckhaven was not covered by the relatively efficient feeding arrangements in Wemyss Parish; moreover, the village was surrounded by drift mines into the colliery workings so that strike-

breakers did not have to appear at the pithead (MacDougall, *Militant Miners*, p. 109).

66. SRO HH 56/27, Situation Report from J. Masterton to Chief Inspector of Mines, 20 August 1926.

67. SRO HH 56/27, Weekly Report. Coal Emergency Organisation. Scottish Division.

68. SRO HH 56/27, J.W. Peck to W. Hogg, 15 September 1926.

69. Reprinted in the *Motherwell Times*, 3 September 1926; see also the similar report reprinted ibid., 24 September 1926.

70. *Motherwell Times*, 15 October 1926.

71. *Glasgow Herald*, 21, 22 October 1926.

72. SRO HH 56/27, C. Campbell to W. Hogg, 18 September 1926.

73. SRO HH 56/27, C. Campbell to R.N. Duke, 26 August 1926.

74. *Kirkcaldy Times*, 8 September, 6 October 1926.

75. SRO HH 56/28, J. Masterton to J.W. Peck, 28 October 1926.

76. NLS Dep. 227/87, NUSMW Special Conference, 27 November 1926.

77. *Worker*, 21 August 1926.

78. MacDougall, 'The '26', p. 107.

79. SRO HH 56/28, Police report, with J.W. Peck to P.J. Rose, 22 October 1926.

80. SRO HH 56/27, Situation Report, J. Masterton to Chief Inspector of Mines, 1 October 1926.

81. MacDougall, *Militant Miners*, p. 109.

82. SRO HH 56/22, Report from Chief Constable of Lanarkshire, 13 November 1926.

83. For example, a detonator placed on the window sill of the house of working miner near Dunfermline caused 'a terrific explosion' which shattered four windows and the sleeping family were cut by glass (*Scotsman* , 22 September 1926).

84. SRO HH 55/22, Report from Chief Constable, Fife and Kinross, 26 November 1926. .

85. SRO HH 56/28, P.J.R[ose] to J.W. Peck.

86. SRO HH 55/22, Report from Chief Constable of Fife and Kinross, 30 November 1926.

87. SRO HH 56/22, Chief Constable of Fife and Kinross to Under-Secretary for Scotland, 18 and 24 November 1926.

88. *Kilmarnock Standard*, 29 May 1926.

89. *Ayrshire Advertiser*, 20 May 1926.

90. SRO HH 56/22, Chief Constable of Kilmarnock to Under-Secretary for Scotland, 2 and 23 November 1926; Chief Constable of Ayr to Under-Secretary for Scotland, 2 November, 7 December 1926.

91. B. Weinberger, 'Police perceptions of labour in the inter-war period: the case of the unemployed and of miners on strike', in F. Snyder and

D. Hay (eds), *Labour, Law and Crime: an historical perspective* (London and New York, 1987), p. 174.

92. *Glasgow Herald*, 3 May 1926.

93. *Scotsman*, 31 May 1926; *Dalkeith Advertiser*, 20 May 1926.

94. *Dalkeith Advertiser*, 20 May 1926.

95. Ibid., 19 August 1926.

96. Ibid., 16 September 1926.

97. Ibid., 18 November 1926.

98. SRO HH 56/28, quoted in J.W. Peck to P.J. Rose, 20 November 1926.

99. Selkirk, *Life*, p. 19.

100. SRO HH 56/22, copy of unsigned letter to the Chief Constable of the Lothians and Peebles.

101. SRO HH 56/28, Chief Constable of Lanarkshire to J.W. Peck, 21 October 1926.

102. SRO HH56/22, Chief Constable of Fife and Kinross to Under-Secretary for Scotland, 23 November 1926.

103. SRO HH 56/22, Report from Chief Constable of West Lothian, 19 November 1926.

104. SRO HH 56/27, Situation Report from J. Masterton to Chief Inspector of Mines, 24 September 1926; HH 56/28, quoted in J.W. Peck to P.J. Rose, 20 November 1926.

105. MacDougall, *Militant Miners*, p. 299.

106. Selkirk was temporarily expelled from the party for ultra-leftism in the 1930s (*Daily Worker*, 26 June 1930). His much later, retrospective public condemnation of acts of sabotage may have been influenced by this.

107. Selkirk, *Life of a Worker*, p. 19.

108. Martin observes that 'the Communists maintained a strictly "constitutional" attitude throughout' and the CP's own later analysis noted that its slogans 'were inevitably defensive in character' (R. Martin, *Communism and the British Trade Unions*, Oxford, 1969, p. 72)

109. Quoted in McLean, 'General strike in Lanarkshire', p. 11.

110. *Workers' Weekly*, 8, 22 October 1926.

111. See above, ch. 3.

112. SRO HH 56/35, Memo. for Solicitor General, with P.J. Rose to W. Hogg, 3 June 1926.

113. Interview with Johnny Boyle, Methil, 6 August 1986. Boyle decided to abort the mission and bury the bomb after a local miner who was guiding them took fright. It is significant that another veteran Fife Communist, Hugh Sloan, who was also present at the interview spontaneously interjected after this anecdote, by way of explanation for the incident, that 'in thae days ... there was tremendous support for the IRA and the Irish question ...'.

114. See Weinberger, *Keeping the Peace?*, p. 197.
115. MacDougall, *Militant Miners*, p. 111; *Scotsman*, 16 July 1926.
116. SRO HH 56/26, Fifeshire Constabulary. Police Report. Miners' Strike, 11 June.
117. On the basis of cross checks with other sources, Weinberger argues that the figures in the Childs' report 'are pretty accurate, and offer as close an approximation on the regional distribution of arrests as we are likely to get'. On this assumption, she criticises Arnot's figure of over 200 arrests of pickets because the Chief Constable of Glasgow listed only 13 strikers and 9 Communists as being arrested ('Communism and the general strike', p. 32). However, according to the *Emergency Press* of 8 May, 80 men appeared in court the previous day charged with offences arising from the disorders; the paper's edition of 11 May recorded that 100 more people appeared in court the day before on similar charges; the next day, further trials were reported, including that of 14 young men who were part of a crowd shouting anti-government slogans (*Emergency Press*, 8, 11, 12 May 1926). Arnot's estimate is therefore accurate. Weinberger also uses the chief constables' reports to Childs to challenge the Communist Party's estimate in June that 1,250 of its members had been arrested. This may well be an inflated estimated but it is not clear from Childs' report how chief constables ascertained the numbers of Communists arrested. While Special Branch officers would doubtless be familiar with leading Communists in the localities, rank and file party members among those arrested may have gone undetected and were unlikely to have drawn attention to their political affiliation. A further complication is that Part IV of the Childs' report lists by name 'Communists prosecuted under the Emergency Regulations'. It is not clear that Communists arrested for other offences are included.
118. MacDougall, *Militant Miners*, pp. 19, 76, 111, 292; Macintyre, *Little Moscows*, pp. 58, 62.
119. SRO HH 56/26, P.J. Rose to J.W. Peck, 23 July 1926; HH 56/22, Chief Constable Fife and Kinross to Under Secretary for Scotland, 18 Nov 1926.
120. Gallacher Memorial Library, Glasgow Caledonian University, Anni Cairns to John Foster, 22 November 1984.
121. *Kilmarnock Standard*, 15 May 1926.
122. SRO HH 56/26, Fifeshire Constabulary. Police Report, Miners' Strike, 11 June. The report goes on to give details, supplied by a member of the 'old union', of an unsuccessful approach by the MRU to jointly coordinate collections and communal feeding arrangements.
123. SRO HH 56/27, Situation Report from J. Masterton to Chief Inspector of Mines, 24 Sept 1926.

124. SRO HH 56/28, Chief Constable of Lanarkshire to J.W. Peck, 21 October 1926.
125. SRO HH 56/22, Report of Chief Constable of Hamilton, 16 November 1926.
126. *Glasgow Herald*, 19 November 1926.
127. SRO HH 56/26, Situation Report of J. Masterton to Chief Inspector of Mines, 15 June 1926.
128. NLS, NUSMW Special Conference, 27 November 1927.
129. *Worker*, 24 December 1926.
130. Morris, *General Strike*, p. 103.
131. MacDougall, *Militant Miners*, pp. 113–15.
132. I. MacDougall, *Voices from the Hunger Marches, vol. II: personal recollections by Scottish hunger marchers of the 1920s and 1930s* (Edinburgh, 1991), pp. 331, 397.
133. Long, thesis, p. 384.
134. SRO HH 56/27, J.W. Peck to P.J. Rose, 14 October 1926.
135. UGBRC UGD 159/1/16, LMCA Executive Committee, 13 December 1926.
136. Ibid., LMCA Executive Committee, 25 October 1926.
137. Long, thesis, pp. 348ff; Arnot, *History*, pp. 234–5, 277.
138. Interview with David Meek, 25 July 1984.
139. *Workers' Weekly*, 26 June 1925.
140. Ibid., 4 June 1926.
141. *Motherwell Times*, 21 May 1926. The authenticity (and self-serving character) of some events portrayed in *The Morlocks* is suggested by a scene which anticipated this incident, and reflected Welsh's intimate knowledge of the vernacular views of his critics. When a union official addressed a meeting in a Blantyre cinema of striking miners demanding 'a fight to the finish', he met a barrage of hostility: 'They're oot tae preserve their jobs first: no tae look after your interests. Whenever they see the funds gettin' low they ca' off the fight, so that you'll go back to work, an' pay intae the union, tae let them gang jauntin' tae London tae haud conferences', stated the militant Barney Blades. '"Ay, there's too muckle jauntin' tae London, an' haudin' conferences", said another young man, "If you meet a miners' agent at a', he's either gaun tae a conference, or comin' hame frae yin, but it's a different thing if we need them. They hinna time then ... but naebody ever heard o' a leader wha couldna gang tae a conference ..." ... During the period of waiting, the young men amused themselves by firing off rough jests ... "Send out the champion wheedler", some of them called, as the time drew near for the meeting to begin. "Bring out auld Joe Ginger-snaps", cried another, then a storm of cat-calls burst forth, and amid the howls and the noise ... the speaker, without allowing the chairman to introduce

him, began a most courageous attack upon the young men for their unruly conduct, and a babel of noise broke forth afresh: the speaker shouting from the platform, and the young men hurling back every form of insult that they could think of ... Losing his temper somewhat, he began to be personal in his reply, and knowing the individual who had put the question, he was not too polite in the things he said; and this brought such a storm of protest and abuse from the young men that the meeting broke up, and the speaker withdrew by a back door, and got away, leaving the angry mob to get out on to the street, breathing all manner of threats and vengeance against him' (Welsh, *Morlocks*, pp. 189–93).

142. *Worker*, 21 August 1926; for similar criticisms, see the report of the Lanarkshire MM conference in the same issue.

143. NLS Dep. 227/86, NUSMW Executive, 28 August 1926.

144. *Hamilton Advertiser*, 11 September 1926.

145. See A.R. and C.P. Griffin, 'The non-political trade union movement', in A. Briggs and J. Saville (eds), *Essays in Labour History, 1918–39* (1977). For Nottinghamshire, see A.R. Griffin, *The Miners of Nottinghamshire, 1914–44* (1962), D. Gilbert, *Class, Community and Collective Action: social change in two British coalfields, 1850–1926* (Oxford, 1992), pp. 188–205, and 'The landscape of Spencerism', in Campbell, Fishman and Howell, *Miners, Unions and Politics*. For South Wales, see H. Francis and D. Smith, *The Fed: a history of the South Wales miners in the twentieth century* (1980), pp. 113–38.

146. Griffin and Griffin, 'Non-political trade union movement', p. 156; SRO FS 10/19, Stirling and Clackmannan Miners' Industrial Union; MacDougall, *Militant Miners*, p. 115.

147. Carter and Carter, 'Miners of Kilsyth', p. 20.

148. MacDougall, *Militant Miners*, pp. 81, 115.

149. Ibid., p. 115; Carter and Carter, 'Miners of Kilsyth', p. 20.

150. *Hamilton Advertiser*, 19 June 1926.

151. J. Foster, 'British imperialism and the labour aristocracy', and M. Jacques, 'Consequences of the General Strike', in Skelley, *General Strike*; Phillips, *General Strike*; H.A. Clegg, *A History of British Trade Unions since 1889: vol. 2, 1911–39* (Oxford, 1985). Foster concludes that: 'It would seem that in the twenties we are faced with an altogether new *type* of control: that the previous manipulation of labour organisation had so expanded as to take on an altogether new character' (p. 51); Jacques points to the TUC General Council's 'reduced emphasis on the efficacy of militancy and strikes in general' and its new-found acceptance that 'wage-labour and employers had common interests' (pp. 385, 388). For Phillips, the General Strike instead reveals the unchanging character of the British labour move-

ment (p. 294). The debate is reviewed in Laybourn, *General Strike*, pp. 108–16.

152. The concept of 'repertoires' of collective action was developed by Charles Tilly. For examples of its application by Tilly and others, see M. Traugott (ed.), *Repertoires and Cycles of Collective Action* (Durham, NC and London, 1995).

CHAPTER SIX

Schism and sectarianism, 1927–29

In 1926 we had shouted and protested, we had had our meetings and our marches. In 1927 we had time to notice how shabby and disheartened everyone looked. Essential food and clothing got on credit during the lock-out had now to be paid for. So had arrears in rent; bit by bit, week by week, in instalments that left everyone bare to the bone ... looking back even in our worst times, we seemed to have been living in a golden Eldorado compared with what was now happening. The year 1927 was like living in a beleaguered city.

Jennie Lee's recollection of 1927, with her father blacklisted from the Fife pits, was probably atypical. As a schoolteacher, she was able to support her family: 'most of our neighbours ... were worse off'.[1] In Lanarkshire, the scale of colliery closures – fifty-three mines were abandoned and a further seventeen temporarily closed or discontinued in 1927 – created 'unprecedented unemployment and distress in the mining population'. Evictions from company-owned houses were widespread.[2] A survey of the Inspectors of Poor in mining parishes in 1927 revealed an often depressing, if uneven, picture of unemployment and poverty. Of sixteen parishes in Lanarkshire, three reported their situation as 'fairly good', three as 'fair', the remainder were 'distinctly gloomy'. Blantyre parish had the highest rate of pauperism with 1,170 per 10,000 of the population receiving poor relief, followed by Dalserf with 884. In Fife, the important mining parishes 'have heavy unemployed lists with very little prospect of re-employment in the near future'. In contrast, in the Lothians, seven out of eleven parishes regarded the situation as 'fairly promising' while three out of six consulted in Ayrshire were reported as 'fairly good'.[3]

By the end of the following year, the effects of increased mechanisation, speed-up and rationalisation following the lockout were also being reported:

As a result of these permanent changes in method there has been going on apparently a sifting process by which the unemployed now largely consist in several areas of those who are unfit for the present methods of production ... It seems fairly certain that there is a large mass of labour in the coalfields that is permanently surplus ...

Lanarkshire was the worst placed county, with unemployment 'blackspots' at Larkhall, Ferniegair, Burnbank, Blantyre, Bellshill, Wishaw and Shotts.[4]

One encouraging element was the unification of the two Fife unions. Prolonged negotiations had been brokered by the NUSMW and agreement reached in December 1926, when Smillie 'hoped that the amalgamation would be the means of creating a new spirit throughout the coalfields of Fife, Kinross and Clackmannan'. The merger was approved by a large majority of the FKCMA and Adamson similarly expressed the wish that its consummation 'would be fruitful of good results in the mining interest'.[5] Far from these aspirations being realised, the Scottish miners' unions were to suffer political divisions of greater intensity than any elsewhere in the British coalfields.

The clash between the ideology of the militant miner and a bureaucratic reformism still inflected with the values of the independent collier was symbolised at an NUSMW Executive meeting in 1928. Duncan Graham, MP, proposed a meeting with the coal owners to consider 'the means by which trade can be organised to keep the pits that are economic in operation'. If the owners refused, a 'Special Sub-Committee should be appointed to consider the best means by which a restrictive policy can be carried out', and the MFGB asked to adopt this remedy throughout the British coalfields. If such an unrealistic policy had failed before 1926 – as it had also failed to attract MFGB support – it could scarcely begin to address the problems facing the industry in the subsequent years.[6]

William Allan, supported by his comrade Andrew McAnulty, moved an amendment mapping out a very different strategy which encapsulated their conflicts with their right-wing opponents:

That the crisis shown by increased unemployment, renewed attacks on wages and conditions, can only be effectively tackled by the immediate holding of the long overdue Annual Conference of the Scottish Mine Workers, the operating of the rule relating to election and re-election of Officials and Executive, the framing of a policy that will make for 100 per cent membership, the breaking down of the county barriers between the unions, actively leading the men in their fight against new impositions and attacks, and to so organise the large army of unemployed miners as to prevent them being used against those still working, and to secure for them better treatment and a higher scale of relief from the Parishes and from the Labour Exchanges.

While this policy faced enormous practical difficulties, it at least recognised the crisis confronting the industry and the unions. However, Graham's motion was carried by 15 votes to 2.[7]

If Allan's amendment pointed to the critical tactic which the NUSMW leaders were to use to retain power – the refusal to convene the Annual Conference – this vote obscures his support among left-wing union activists in the coalfields whose constituency had increased during the lockout. The conflict between left and right led to a major split less than a year later with the formation of the Communist-inspired United Mineworkers of Scotland (UMS) in April 1929. Its establishment was the outcome of a complex interplay of influences, the roots of which lay within both the miners' unions as well as the evolving policies of the international Communist movement and its British party. The aim of this chapter is to disentangle and analyse these forces through twin narratives set in the unions and the CP.[8] But as the chapter also demonstrates, the tragedy of the situation was that the battle between left and right was conducted within organisations with a dramatically diminished membership, the consequence not only of pit closures and unemployment, but also of these political conflicts.

Developments in the unions

In order to understand the byzantine politics of the Scots mining unions during this period, a résumé of their government is necessary. The NUSMW was a federation of six largely autonomous county unions covering Lanarkshire, Fife, Ayrshire, Stirlingshire, West Lothian, and Mid and East Lothian.[9] The governing body of the NUSMW was the Annual Conference which formally appointed the Executive and the four officials (President, Vice-president, Treasurer and Secretary) for the ensuing year. The officials were elected at the Annual Conference from nominations made by the county unions; if the same nomination was supported by counties comprising the majority of the affiliated membership, it would automatically be carried at the conference. Appointment of Executive members was made by the county unions according to a quota determined by their affiliated membership: Lanarkshire had nine, Fife, five, and so on. The procedures for officials' nominations and Executive appointments were left to individual unions. Only Lanarkshire and Fife decided their nominees and Executive members by branch or individual ballot; Ayrshire and Stirlingshire decided at their executives which were dominated by agents and local officials; in the Lothians' unions, the agents were appointed as county representatives on the Executive. The new Executive took up office at the Annual Conference when the sitting Executive retired. No conference was held in 1926 due to the lockout, and it was eventually agreed by the existing Executive in July 1927 to hold the conference in September; this was subsequently postponed until December.

The first indications of the growth of left-wing support after the lockout came in Lanarkshire. In the LMU elections in June 1927, Allan and McAnulty defeated Small and Smillie for the posts of General Secretary and President, while four other MM candidates were among the twelve elected members of the LMU Executive, as were four out the six members of the Finance Committee.[10] Yet the numbers voting also indicated the predicament of trade unionism in the county – only 13,000 out of a workforce of 40,000.

In Fife, the situation was complicated by the recent merger of the MRU with the FKCMA. Fife's representatives on the NUSMW Executive had been appointed to these positions in 1925 by the 'Old Union' which no longer existed. In the light of the proposed NUSMW conference in September, the new Fife Executive Board called in June for branches to nominate five candidates for the Scottish executive. That same meeting also requested nominations from branches for two agents. The terms of the amalgamation had prescribed that Philip Hodge, former General Secretary of the MRU, be made an agent of the FKCMA, but that 'all other vacancies for agents to be filled by ballot vote of the joint membership after amalgamation'.[11] There were two such positions to be filled, held temporarily by Adamson supporters. Thus there were seven vacancies in the Fife union in the summer of 1927.

The CP had a 'fraction' of fourteen out of the fifty-four members of the Fife Executive Board following the post-merger elections of branch delegates in February. That party influence extended beyond this core was indicated by the twenty-one votes received by the Communist Jimmy Stewart when he contested the Board Chairmanship, compared with thirty-three for the 'old union' candidate.[12] The forthcoming elections presented the Communists in the Fife union with a major opportunity to expand their support. A series of CP meetings agreed a slate of five candidates for the NUSMW and Proudfoot and McArthur as the party's nominees for agents.[13]

The elections were to suggest that for some party members personal ambitions were not always amenable to party discipline. It was reported that Jimmy Stewart and John Bird intended 'running against all-comers' for the agents' posts. Bird had a reputation as being a maverick or 'stunt merchant' and he and Stewart disobeyed the party decision. Proudfoot lamented 'supposed leading Party members running against each other' since it would give 'some semblance of truth to Adamson's oft repeated statement "A gang of job hunters"'.[14] Although the party instructed that only the approved slate was to be supported, branches where party influence was strong in central Fife, the local base of Bird and Stewart, did not always pay heed. Proudfoot noted that 'Cowdenbeath, Lochgelly, Glencraig, Lochore and Kirkford have not toed the line', and pondered 'whether it is due to McArthur and I being in the East'.[15]

There emerged what Proudfoot accurately described as 'the MESS': for the two agents' posts, there would be two clear right-wing candidates, two official CP candidates, and seven left-wing candidates, including four other CP members. At a subsequent Fife CP aggregate meeting, members who were not the official party candidates were instructed to immediately withdraw their names. In an attempt to prevent any further breaches of discipline after their election to union office, all official candidates were asked to provide the Fife party organiser with an undated letter of resignation from their future union post.[16]

The unfortunate legacy of this wrangle was that names of CP members who were not party nominees remained on the ballot papers. The five Communists for the two agents' posts secured a total of 51.7 per cent of the votes, but the 'unofficial' candidates served only to dilute the party's electoral impact and prevented Proudfoot and McArthur from achieving a commanding lead in the first ballot.[17] In the following months there were a further two ballots involving a diminishing number of candidates and much manoeuvring by both left and right factions until the final results were declared in December. McArthur and Proudfoot secured 6,586 and 6,467 votes respectively for the agents' posts against 5,223 and 5,144 for their right-wing opponents. Hodge, McArthur, Proudfoot, Stewart and Bird won Fife's support for the NUSMW Executive, defeating Adamson and four of his supporters.[18]

Important as the left's success in these elections was, the outcome of a separate branch vote for Fife's nominations for NUSMW officers declared on the same day assumed even greater significance. The Scottish Miners' MM had put forward a regionally balanced team for these posts: Bird for President, Allan for Secretary, Alex Thomson of Stirlingshire for Vice-President and Dan Sim of Ayrshire for Treasurer. A majority in Fife voted to support these candidates. This result assumed enormous implications as it followed the announcement of the LMU nominations for the Scottish official posts a few days before. On a proportional, 'financial' vote, the LMU branches supported the MM nominees for President, Vice-President and Secretary, as well as electing five MM candidates among the nine Lanarkshire representatives to the NUSMW Executive.[19] These results in Fife and Lanarkshire were devastating for the established NUSMW leadership, for the combined membership of the Fife and Lanarkshire unions commanded a majority of votes at the Annual Conference. Faced with the prospect of Communists as President, Vice-President and Secretary of the national union, together with a large minority of ten MM supporters on the new Executive, the leadership desperately sought to stave off defeat. At a meeting of the NUSMW Executive in late December, it was decided to accept the recommendation of the Committee on Organisation and Finance (COF), four of whose eight members were among those defeated as officials or Executive members, to again postpone the Annual Conference because of the serious financial situation which the union faced and the heavy arrears of some of the county unions.[20]

In 1928, effective trade unionism in the Scots coalfields was paralysed as the dispute between left and right plunged the NUSMW into chaos.[21] A majority of branches in both Fife and Lanarkshire voted that the Conference be convened at an early date and mandated their NUSMW representatives to oppose further postponement. The leadership's response was to delay any meeting of the Executive for several months. When it finally met in April, the Fife and a majority of the Lanarkshire representatives defied their mandates, supporting further postponement on the grounds of arrears by a number of the county unions, although such arrears had not precluded previous Annual Conferences.[22]

The meeting also empowered the COF to circulate a statement to members explaining the delay. The document issued was signed by twenty-two members of the union's right-wing faction and argued that a national conference 'must be thoroughly representative of an actual real membership in each of the Districts, having their numbers definitely ascertained and paid for'. The 'paramount reason' for this situation was 'the subversive actions of the Communist and Minority Movements' in Fife and Lanarkshire. The statement went on to attack the CP and Comintern as an 'alien and Hybrid Junta' which was 'endeavouring to capture the Executive Authority' of the union. It concluded with a rallying call to support 'the leaders you have chosen and tested, and found not wanting ...', a phrase whose irony was seized on by Communist propagandists.[23]

In May, a deputation from the COF presented their version of events before the MFGB Executive, a body which itself reflected the increasingly strident anti-communism within the wider labour movement.[24] The MFGB recorded its 'strong condemnation' of Communist tactics and pledged all possible help to 'the bona-fide Scottish Miners' Federation and all other districts which are carrying out the principles of the Miners' Federation, the Trades Union Congress, and the British Labour Party'. This resolution was later endorsed by the MFGB conference in July, where Allan was physically ejected from the hall by the MFGB President, Herbert Smith, amid angry scenes. The conference also appointed a Commission of Inquiry into the Scottish situation.[25]

Both factions in Scotland exchanged a flurry of legal actions. In June, the annual elections in Lanarkshire showed further gains for the left. However, two right-wingers, who had urged their supporters not to participate in the ballot after McAnulty had ruled out of order a motion on the Executive declaring MM supporters ineligible to stand, used this to secure an interdict maintaining the Executive in office until a full hearing.[26] In Fife, Hodge sought an interdict against the NUSMW Executive if no conference was convened by August. The Executive agreed to a conference in August but ruled that no county union would be entitled to representation if three months in arrears of dues to the national union. This would have excluded the Fife, Lanarkshire and Stirlingshire unions and accordingly, at a meeting of the NUSMW Executive, nominations of the old officials from the MELMA and the Ayrshire union were accepted, while those from Fife and Lanarkshire were declared out of order. In response, the FKCMA secured a further interdict restraining the NUSMW from convening this rump conference representing a minority of the organised miners.[27]

Within the LMU, the division was fairly evenly balanced and the antagonism between the factions correspondingly sharp. While the Communists Allan and McAnulty were Secretary and President, the right-wing dominated the Executive. An attempt on the LMU Executive to censure Small, Graham, Welsh and others for opposing the clearly expressed will of the LMU Council (which had voted 31 to 24 against postponing the Annual Conference) was lost by 10 votes to 6.[28] Yet their actions were repudiated by a subsequent meeting of the LMU Council in May by a financial vote of £438 5s 10d against £385 18s 7d.[29] Nevertheless, the refusal of McAnulty to allow the motion declaring MM members ineligible for election spurred the right wing to disrupt Executive meetings. Although the right had voted to remove McAnulty from the chair, he steadfastly refused to vacate it, insisting he was elected by the membership not the Executive.[30] Allan complained that at subsequent Executive meetings, 'every attempt to read the minutes or correspondence had been deliberately blocked by Mr Small and his friends, talking, stamping and bawling in order to drown the voice of the secretary. On these five occasions from 5.30 to 8 o'clock bedlam had existed ...' However, a motion at the Council to suspend these Executive members failed by 47 votes to 21.[31]

This failure marked a turning tide against the left in Lanarkshire. This ebbing away of support over the summer of 1928 had a number of causes. In part, it reflected the despair of union activists at the chaos into which the LMU had descended; an enduring loyalty to old leaders who had the support of the MFGB; the impact of sustained anti-communist propaganda in the popular press and broader labour movement; hostility to the increasing stridency of Communist rhetoric and, on one occasion when James McKendrick assaulted Small, physical violence; and a desire to restore a semblance of unity.[32] According to Proudfoot, a well-informed observer, the position in the LMU was 'very bad. Contributions dropped from over £1000 in March to £175 for July. 40 out of 80 branches retaining contributions collected. Members, mainly our supporters, leaving the union wholesale.'[33]

At the September LMU Council, a delegate asked Allan if he 'was prepared to cease ridiculing our people at street corner meetings and refrain from taking instructions or dictation from an outside organisation?' He also appealed to Graham and Welsh 'to try to come to some agreement. "Bury the hatchet", he said: the workers were suffering and that only by united effort would they be able to achieve anything good on behalf of the men.' The delegate from the militant Priory branch complained that 'everybody was out to play their own game, and the game has ended in chaos'. The Thankerton representative urged both sides to withdraw from legal action and arrange for new elections: 'He had lost 50 per cent of his members. The men were insisting on this question being settled before joining or coming back to the union.'[34]

Such pleas had little effect. The success of their interdict sustaining the sitting LMU Executive in office encouraged the right wing further to harry the left-wing officers. The elderly McAnulty resigned as President in August, complaining of the 'insulting and disruptive tactics' of Graham and others on the Executive.[35] The previous month, Allan had been ejected from the NUSMW Executive meeting by police after allegedly insulting Smillie and remained excluded until apologising in November.[36]

After Allan, McKendrick and other Lanarkshire MMM supporters sponsored a Scottish 'Save the Union' conference at Falkirk in October, the right-wing majority on the LMU Executive accused them of planning to set up a rival organisation and initiated steps to suspend them. The suspension procedure involved a lengthy series of meetings which further intensified the factional conflict: one meeting of the Council was adjourned in disorder after 'an altercation between two members of the Executive was responsible for creating a scene which brought the business to a standstill'.[37]

The situation in Fife was the opposite of Lanarkshire: there the left had built up a slim majority against an embattled right-wing Secretary.[38] The growth in support for the left in the larger branches was indicated by the election of Stewart as Executive Chairman on a financial vote in 1928.[39] Adamson's breach of his mandate to support a Scottish conference, as well as his voting for the exclusion of his own union from the proposed rump conference, led the FKCMA Board to suspend him as Secretary. During a membership ballot seeking approval of this action in September, Adamson resigned and immediately set about the formation of a new union, confusingly titled the Fife, Clackmannan and Kinross Miners' Union (FCKMU). His old rival Hodge was appointed Interim General Secretary of the FKCMA.[40] Notwithstanding his resignation as Fife Secretary and this hostile initiative against an NUSMW affiliate, Adamson remained a member of the NUSMW Executive despite protests from the FKCMA.

While Lanarkshire and Fife were the principal arenas of factional conflict, there were echoes of the battle in the other county unions. It was indicative of the radicalising effect of the lockout that Ayrshire, which had previously lacked any significant militant reform tendency, now exhibited a greater degree of democratic radicalism in some of its branches. In April 1927, seven branches supported a proposal that one agent be subject to re-election by ballot each year, a move defeated by the remaining ten branches. At the AMU Annual Meeting in August, the proposal of the Galston branch that the union's representatives on the NUSMW Executive be elected by ballot for a maximum of three years was defeated, as were seven further motions on union democracy submitted by the Hurlford branch. In the votes for the NUSMW officers, Allan received the support of five AMU branches for Secretary against fifteen for the incumbent Robert Smith, the AMU chairman; Bird received four votes against Smillie's fourteen for President. Dan Sim, the MM candidate for Treasurer was an AMU organiser and received eight votes against twelve for the right-wing, Lanarkshire candidate.[41]

After the publication of the anti-communist manifesto by the NUSMW leadership in April 1928, six AMU branches supported its rejection against thirteen endorsing it. In August, a left-wing resolution from the Auchinleck branch supporting A.J. Cook's 'solitary fight' on the TUC General Council against the 'Industrial Peace propagandists' led to a 'spirited discussion' at the AMU Annual Meeting but was defeated 13–8. A resolution from the same branch condemning the actions of the Scottish Executive and calling on the Ayrshire representatives on it to resign was lost 13–6. Nevertheless, a further motion from Galston demanding the annual election of NUSMW officers and Executive by ballot was lost by only one vote. A subsequent financial vote carried this motion by £7,729 to £6,110, and, according to one press report, James Brown offered his resignation. However, the Chairman, Robert Smith (who was also the defeated Secretary of the NUSMW) later ruled that the resolution involved a constitutional change which required a two-thirds majority. A financial vote on the Chairman's ruling was refused. This represented the high-tide of the left's challenge in the AMU.[42]

On the executive of the West Lothian union, left-wing support was mainly confined to three out of the union's ten branches: Loganlea and Foulshiels in the Stoneyburn district and Kinneil near Bo'ness. In August 1928, there was a vote of 6–3 in favour of right-wing candidates for NUSMW officers; in September, a motion from Loganlea pledging support for an NUWM march to Edinburgh was defeated by a identical margin, as was a motion in November demanding that Adamson be suspended from the NUSMW Executive.[43] In the MELMA, there was broad backing for the right-wing leadership. MM support on the Delegate Board was largely confined to the Prestongrange and Prestonlinks branches at Prestonpans, typified by the 18–2 defeat of their motion protesting against the postponement of the NUSMW conference.[44]

By the closing months of 1928, the left was in the ascendant in Fife, in retreat in Lanarkshire and had only the support of approximately a third of the delegates in the Ayrshire and West Lothian unions. After months of prevarication and manoeuvring, the right-wing leadership of the NUSMW then proceeded with alacrity and ruthless determination to outflank and isolate the militants. The MFGB Commission of Inquiry took evidence from the NUSMW Executive on 23 November but refused to meet FKCMA representatives.[45] On 10 December, Adamson applied to the NUSMW Executive for affiliation of his FCKMU. While approval was given in principle, decision was deferred pending the MFGB report.[46] This may have been a subterfuge to delay until the existing troublesome Fife affiliate had been dealt with. In February 1929, a special meeting of the NUSMW Executive was convened at two days notice by the COF and agreed to summon a Special Conference a week later with the sole item of business an alteration of the union's constitution to exclude any district union in arrears by four quarterly contributions: this would have the effect of disenfranchising both the FKCMA and the Stirlingshire union and soon the LMU also.[47]

On 18 February, prior to the Special Conference later that day, the Executive met to receive the report of the MFGB Commission which concluded that the 'interference by the Communist Party complained of by the deputation has been proved'. The Executive regarded this decision as 'very satisfactory' and had little difficulty in persuading the conference to approve the change of rule. A motion moved by Hodge and seconded by McKendrick urging delay until the matter could be discussed in the districts, was defeated by 45 votes to 25.[48]

The scene was thus set for the final moves. For Allan, the conference was 'the last straw' and, on behalf of the Save the Union Council, he issued a manifesto in early March calling for the formation of a new Scottish Mineworkers' Union and accusing the 'old gang bureaucrats' as being 'the allies of the masters and the enemies of the miners'.[49] On 8 March, the MM's *Worker* proclaimed: 'the onus for splitting the unions rests entirely on the shoulders of the fakers ... A new Miners' Union in Scotland is no longer a bogey.'[50] At the NUSMW Executive on 11 March, it was decided to convene the Annual Conference on 28 March. It was reported that Allan had been suspended by the LMU Executive, and the meeting voted also to suspend him from the NUSMW for his activities in connection with the Save Union Council.[51]

At the Annual Conference, the Chairman, James Doonan of West Lothian, attacked the Save the Union Council in his opening address, disingenuously complaining that 'if they thought that any of their officials had reached the stage in which their capacity of service to the men had ceased then they could be told to resign'. The conference then proceeded to approve the affiliation of the FCKMU and the readmittance of the Stirlingshire union which had paid sufficient dues. Even had the FKCMA been able to pay off its arrears in future, it is probable that it would have been refused membership of the national union since there was now a recognised Fife affiliate. The Executive's recommendation that it should continue in office until the next conference in August 1929 was also approved.[52] A little over two weeks later, a meeting organised by the Save the Union Council, to which we return below, took the decision to establish the United Mineworkers of Scotland (UMS).

The parameters of Minority Movement support

The foregoing account has been conducted within the interlocking structures of the NUSMW and county unions. The views of rank and file union members are impossible to ascertain from the records of these bodies or the partisan accounts of the leading protagonists in the national and Communist press. Yet the ballots conducted in the main unions during this period allow at least some evaluation of support for left and right factions among the membership.

In Lanarkshire, union branches were usually based on single collieries. Since the LMU published ballot results by branches, these allow a comparative assessment of political support at individual mines. In 1927, the combined votes for the MM candidates for the posts of LMU President, Vice-President and Secretary amounted to 40 per cent of the total. But the distribution of these votes was uneven, being greatest in the concentration of pits in the central Clyde valley districts of Blantyre, Hamilton, Motherwell, Bellshill and Uddingston, and on the borders of the county at Shotts in the east, Douglas and Coalburn in the south, and at the large Auchengeich and Bedlay collieries near Glenboig in the north. It was weakest in two bands skirting the central Clyde valley, the first stretching through Baillieston to Airdrie and Caldercruix, the second lying across the Wishaw, Carluke and Larkhall districts.[53] Left-wing support, although enlarged, therefore displayed a broadly similar geographical pattern to the 1925 LMU elections previously discussed in chapter four.

To locate more clearly branches with a consistent record of strong or weak MM support, those where the vote was five per cent or more above and below the mean MM vote in both 1925 and 1927 were identified. Fourteen branches were found in the first category, indicating strong MM support, and these are listed in Table 6.1; the twenty-one branches where support for the MM was consistently weak are described in Table 6.2. These two tables bring together several strands of the analysis of the varied nature of work and community in Lanarkshire developed previously. MM support tended to be stronger in larger collieries. The average underground workforce in 1927 for those listed in Table 6.1 for which information is available was 516; the mean workforce of the weak MM collieries was 228. Although data on strikes at individual collieries are incomplete, 23 strikes have been identified at mines listed in Table 6.1

Table 6.1 LMU branches displaying strong MM support, 1925–7.

Branch	Locality	Minority Movement support				Underground workforce 1927	Owner
		1925		1927			
		% vote	Number voting	% vote	Number voting		
Auchinraith	Blantyre	40.6	249	57.7	299	382	Merry & Cunninghame
Priory	Blantyre	48.6	392	51.4	328	634	Wm Baird
Earnock	Burnbank	43.4	252	62.7	106	712	John Watson
Whistleberry	Burnbank	41.3	110	47.6	66	184	Arch. Russell
Bothwell Castle	Bothwell	36.6	161	61.3	245	470	Wm Baird
Hamilton Palace	Bothwell	53.9	373	43.2	41	694	Bent Colliery Co.
Blantyreferme	Uddingston	48.0	177	52.6	179	668	A. G. Moore
Rosehall	Bellshill	51.5	32	70.6	33	776	Robt Addie
Woodhall	Bellshill	39.0	154	48.6	110	734	Barr & Higgins
Jerviston	Motherwell	42.5	29	70.6	11	74	Stewarts & Lloyd
Douglas	Douglas West	36.8	58	46.0	79	256	Wilsons' & Clyde
Auchengeich	Glenboig	31.8	352	51.8	472	541	Jas Nimmo
Bedlay	Glenboig	42.6	42	74.7	81	582	Wm Baird
Loganlea	[West Lothian]	36.7	48	61.5	14		

Sources: NLS Dep. 227/41 and 43, LMU Council, 1 July, 1925, 6 and 13 July, 1927; List of Mines, 1927.

Note

The degree of MM support has been calculated from the branch voting records for MM candidates for the posts of president, vice-president and general secretary in 1925 and 1927. The 'percentage vote' columns give the combined vote for these candidates expressed as a percentage of the total votes cast for all candidates in each year. The 'numbers voting' columns list the total number voting for the post of general secretary in each year. Although there was some slight variation in the total votes cast for each post, this provides a reasonably accurate indicator of the numbers participating in each branch in the relevant year.

The mean percentage vote for MM candidates for the three posts was 28.3 per cent in 1925 and 40.4 per cent in 1927. The branches listed here are those where the MM vote was five per cent or more above the mean in both years.

Table 6.2 LMU branches displaying weak MM support, 1925–7.

Branch	Locality	Minority Movement support				Underground workforce 1927	Owner
		1925		1927			
		% vote	Number voting	% vote	Number voting		
Allanton	Larkhall	23.2	79	28.8	41	272	Wm Barr
Ferniegair	Larkhall	11.7	131	14.2	105	314	Arch. Russell
Netherburn	Larkhall	17.4	50	23.3	53	155	Jas Gemmell
Larkhall	Larkhall	23.3	393	16.1	203	c1500	Residential branch
Garriongill	Wishaw	23.6	146	10.1	143	197	Coltness Iron Co.
Glenclelland	Wishaw	23.4	44	31.4	70	140	Jas Gemmell
Law	Wishaw	21.3	263	28.0	166	103	Wilsons & Clyde
Wishaw	Wishaw	13.1	61	5.3	38	57	Glasgow Iron & Steel Co.
Caldercruix	Airdrie	18.2	58	21.5	62	n/a	[Residential branch?]
Kippsbyre	Airdrie	19.3	130	17.4	123	312	John Watson
Monkland	Airdrie	20.3	59	30.1	115	n/a	[Residential branch?]
Calderbank	Baillieston	20.9	46	31.0	17	117	Summerlee Iron Co.
Ellismuir	Baillieston	14.8	92	12.4	38	145	United Collieries
Clyde	Tollcross	9.2	61	18.1	51	115	Jas Dunlop
Clydeside	Uddingston	2.7	61	14.6	31	257	United Collieries
Hattonrigg	Bellshill	15.9	21	27.1	16	560	Summerlee Iron Co.
Climpy	Wilsontown	20.4	104	17.0	75	193	Coltness Iron Co.
Auldtonhill	Lesmahagow	22.5	127	9.5	37	n/a	[Residential branch?]
Batonrigg	Shotts	12.6	147	14.4	162	323	Shotts Iron Co.
Blackhill	Shotts	7.9	51	6.1	125	389	Summerlee Iron Co.
Morton's Mine	-	21.2	179	29.7	39	n/a	n/a

Sources: As for Table 6.1.

Note: See Table 6.1. The mean percentage vote for MM candidates for the three posts was 28.3 per cent in 1925 and 40.4 per cent in 1927. The branches listed here are those where the MM vote was five per cent or more below the mean in both years.

during the period 1921–7 compared with only 8 at those in Table 6.2.[54] Despite the incompleteness of the data, particularly in relation to residential branches, it is likely that the MM supporting branches were at more militant mines. Militancy, however, was not universal in the Lanarkshire coalfield.[55]

There were few other obvious differences between the collieries in both lists. Almost all were mechanised to some degree by 1927 and several employers appear on both lists. Employer policy may nevertheless have exerted some influence. The paternalism of William Barr and other Larkhall employers has been previously discussed and the relatively small scale of productive units in the district could foster collaborative aspects of the independent collier.[56] This points to the importance of locality, and both groups conform to the broad geographical divisions suggested above. In Table 6.1, two collieries are listed in Blantyre – a third Blantyre branch, Dixon's, narrowly missed inclusion – and two at adjacent Burnbank, districts with well-established traditions of militancy and radicalism by 1927. In Table 6.2, the majority of mines fell within the two bands lying outside the central Clyde valley.

Religious divisions could often take on a spatial dimension. The Larkhall and Airdrie districts, featured prominently in Table 6.2, were predominantly Protestant. In the Shotts district, the adjacent villages of Stane and Dykehead were regarded as tending to be Catholic and Protestant respectively. Such divisions are relevant to the previous discussion of the SNTUA and the hostility of Orangemen towards communism.[57] That both Allan and McAnulty came from Catholic backgrounds is a further factor to be considered. These divisions may explain the weak MM support at Batonrigg colliery, a mile or so from Dykehead and two miles from the Protestant village of Harthill, in contrast with the 87 per cent vote for MM candidates in 1927 in the LMU Kepplehill and Stane branch. The Thankerton branch, a former SNTUA stronghold, showed strong support for MM candidates in 1927 – 60 per cent – but this was limited to the 18 union members who voted at a mine with an underground workforce of 477, suggesting that the Orangemen had either not returned or had again left the LMU. Similarly, at Hamilton Palace, where there was friction between scabs and unionists after the lockout, only 41 union members voted out of 694 underground workers.[58] The low membership which such levels of electoral participation suggest was not confined to the MM supporting branches, but points to how the factional conflict in the LMU was increasingly conducted within a hollow shell.

In Fife, branches were based on residence. The figures for the second ballot in 1927 – the only one for which votes in individual branches is available – were scrutinised and the following villages were identified as 'Communist supporting': Bowhill, Denbeath, Dunnikier, Glencraig, Hill of Beath, Leslie, Lochgelly, Lumphinnans, Methil, Milton of Balgonie, Raith. These were typically large branches, generally situated in the densely populated mining villages of central or East Fife where the pits were largest and there had been the greatest in-migration from elsewhere in Scotland. 'Right-wing strongholds' were found in Alloa, Blairhall (Lower), Dunfermline, Halbeath, Kincardine, Lassodie, Lethans, Markinch, Oakley, Rosebank, Saline Valley, Sauchie, Tillicoultry, Townhill and Wellwood.[59] These were geographically concentrated in West Fife, around Dunfermline and in the smaller villages extending westwards into Clackmannanshire, with its strongly established tradition of industrial tranquillity, where pits were generally smaller.[60]

A memorandum to the Political Bureau (PB) of the CP in 1928 claimed that the party and MM had the support of about one third of the Ayrshire miners.[61] Approximately a third of the AMU delegates were prepared to support MM policies in 1928 but the views of their membership cannot be inferred from this, a point argued forcibly by AMU Secretary, James Brown:

> Galston, Hurlford, Drongan and Springside [branches] can be looked upon as Communist, in respect that the Delegates representing them at the [AMU Annual] Conference were avowed Communists, but in none of these, with the possible exception of Hurlford, would they have anything like a majority if a ballot vote were taken.[62]

Nevertheless, an election for the post of AMU County Agent in 1928 provides some support for the CP's assessment. The contest was between Brown and George Gilmour, a left-wing candidate who, though not a Communist, was a sponsor of the Save the Union Council and had CP support.[63] Gilmour secured 32.5 per cent of the vote, receiving majorities, but very large ones, in only five out the AMU's twenty-two branches: Galston, Hurlford, Drongan, Springside and Crosshouse, suggesting a greater degree of support for their Communist delegates than Brown allowed.[64] Although AMU branches were based on residence rather than collieries, none of the mines listed in the vicinity of these villages belonged to the giant firm of William Baird which dominated mining in the county.[65] Moreover, four out of the five villages were within a five mile radius of the town of Kilmarnock, where the only CP Local in Ayrshire was situated. The corollary of these characteristics was that the power of the employers' blacklist and dependency on company housing in Ayrshire's typically scattered rural settlements restricted the potential for mobilisation behind Communist policies.[66] It is the nature of these policies and their influence upon the miners' unions that must now be considered.

Communist policy

A central controversy in the burgeoning historiography of British communism is the relationship between the CPGB and the Comintern. Andrew Thorpe identifies one broad strand in the literature as portraying the British party as a subservient creature of Moscow, although this characterisation could take both a right and left-wing form, stemming either from Cold War stereotypes or from principled anti-Stalinism.[67] In rejecting such approaches, a second band of literature emphasised the autonomy which the party enjoyed. This analysis traditionally figured in party histories anxious to avoid confirming a central tenet of political opponents. Walter Kendall, for example, notes that 'official Communist hagiography treats the Party as essentially a British institution'.[68] An alternative, non-party, source of this general approach lay in historians' concern to explore Communist culture in particular localities, to reconstruct a history of the party 'from below'.[69]

More recently, Nina Fishman's important revisionist text, *The British Communist Party and the Trade Unions, 1933–45*, displays some affinities to this second strand of historiography. While Fishman provides a finely nuanced account of the trade union cultures in which the party operated, the influence of the Comintern is less directly addressed and it appears as a fluid and shadowy entity.[70] She suggests that historians have failed to recognise 'the Comintern's flexible interpretation of its own line', a flexibility she finds evident even in the earlier history of the CPGB by Macfarlane.

The British party is allowed considerable autonomy within the convoluted rhetoric of Comintern policy. Its 'revolutionary pragmatists' – notably Harry Pollitt and J.R. Campbell – were able to draw on very British working class traditions: 'Their model of democratic centralism was highly derivative of working class non-conformism. It relied on individual consciences to interpret the real world according to their own lights ...'.[71]

There are some problems with such an interpretation. The capacity of Moscow apparatchiks to hedge their bets on the outcome of factional struggles certainly led to ambiguities in Comintern formulations, but it would wrong to construe this as intentional flexibility of policy or the deliberate fostering of national autonomy.[72] The interventions of the Comintern were ultimately always decisive. Eric Hobsbawm was highly critical of Klugmann's authorised history of the British party precisely for neglecting this aspect.[73] Macfarlane, during a lengthy correspondence with Palme Dutt in the pages of *The Times Literary Supplement* following the publication of the former's book, was insistent that, despite some instances of protest to the Comintern by the CPGB: 'Such examples must not blind us, however, to the fact that in the last analysis the Comintern determined the broad lines of policy which all member Parties had to follow.' When Dutt disingenuously invoked 'the absolute democratic sovereignty of the Congress of our Party in the election of its leadership', Macfarlane rightly accused him of talking 'nonsense', citing Condition 16 of Comintern membership which explicitly denied such national sovereignty.[74]

Such debates have led to a rejection of conceptions of the relationship between Comintern and CPGB as either entirely determined or largely autonomous. 'Post-revisionist' writing, in Thorpe's characterisation, now recognises that the relationship between the party and Moscow was important. Thorpe himself has identified a number of 'mechanisms of control' available to the Comintern in dealing with its member parties. These included significant financial assistance; supervision of party activities by Comintern representatives; monitoring of party minutes and publications; interception of mail from foreign Communists in Moscow; provision of foreign Communist personnel to assist in party campaigns; supply of slogans and articles from Moscow; the sponsorship of factions in national parties; secret training of national cadres at the 'conspirative' International Lenin School (ILS) in Moscow; as well as intimidation and terror. However, despite this impressive battery of control techniques, Thorpe concludes that Comintern subordination of the British party was inevitably incomplete, the implementation of Comintern policy always rendered problematic through its long chain of command: 'democratic centralism became weaker the further it had to stretch'.[75]

In another recent 'post-revisionist' study, McDermott and Agnew also distinguish between Comintern decisions and their actual implementation at national and local levels, speculating that national parties which operated within parliamentary democracies may have been 'more susceptible to the countervailing pressures of national political life'. Nevertheless, with a lesser inclination towards autonomy, they caution against any,

> propensity to underestimate the mechanisms of control employed by the Comintern at the international level and by the party leaderships at the national level. Stalinist discipline demanded that members loyally fulfil the party line, deviations were rarely tolerated for long, and space for debate and discussion was severely restricted. While scope for regional local and individual initiative did exist and should be recognised, it must be treated with a fair degree of circumspection.[76]

Similarly, in an extensive review of recent international research on the Comintern, Studer and Unfried argue that western Communists were 'neither will-less puppets on Moscow's strings nor did they live in self-sufficient national or regional cultures'. But they conclude that 'the leeway allowed any one Communist Party was constricted further in the 1930s, on several levels and at an accelerating pace'.[77] So even within this 'post-revisionist' literature the degree of independence either allowed to, or grasped by, national Communist parties and their local cadres remains a matter of considerable debate which can only be resolved by empirical investigation.[78]

The mining industry was an important area of Communist activity in Britain and the unique situation in the Scottish coalfields in particular commanded frequent discussion in the PB and Central Committee (CC) of the CPGB, as well as detailed coverage in the party press. The significance of developments in the Scottish coalfields was far from unnoticed in Moscow. In February 1929, for example, in a 'closed letter' to the Central Committee of the CPGB, the Presidium of the Comintern emphasised that work in trade unions, 'particularly in Fife and Lanarkshire', should be regarded 'as a most important task of the party as whole'.[79] Before considering the context and implementation of this directive, it is necessary to outline the important shifts in Comintern policy which were under way by 1927.

That year marked the beginning of the formulation of the theory of the 'third period', so-called because it postulated that, after the initial phase of revolutionary upsurge beginning in 1917, and the subsequent temporary stabilisation of international capitalism from 1923, there would be a new wave of imperialist wars and also sharpening class struggles which social democratic parties – increasingly characterised as 'social fascist' – would endeavour to suppress. The use of the term 'third period', and the conventional notations of the 'new line' of 'class against class', to summarise the Comintern policies derived from this fundamentally misconceived analysis have often obscured the tempo and trajectory of their evolution.[80] With the defeat of Trotsky, who was expelled from the Communist Party of the Soviet Union (CPSU) in November 1927, Stalin manoeuvred to shift leftwards in order to defeat his 'rightist' rival Bukharin. As early as October and November 1927, Pollitt, then Secretary of the MM, was in discussions in Moscow with leading figures, including Stalin, on the new policy involving a breach with the Labour Party. After receiving a verbal 'hammering' for his initial resistance, he adopted the new perspective and on his return to Britain persuaded a minority in the CPGB CC.[81] At the Fifteenth Congress of the CPSU in December, Stalin proclaimed 'a new revolutionary upsurge' and the Ninth Plenum of the Executive Committee of the Comintern (ECCI) in February 1928 saw the first political implications of the new approach: the British and French CPs were forced to abandon their previous commitment to the united front with social democratic parties.[82]

By the Sixth World Congress of the Comintern in the summer of 1928, the new line was clearly enunciated of a 'turn to the left'.[83] Harry Wicks recalls the foreign students at the ILS being briefed on the new danger of the 'right deviation' in addition to the previous Trotskyist sin of 'left deviationism' and instructed to meet the delegates from their home parties to report on the situation within the CPSU: 'often the vast hall was pretty empty, the real congress was taking place wherever Stalin's supporters could lobby the delegates'.[84] By the autumn of 1928, Stalin's victory over Bukharin was evident.

The battle for control of the CPSU and the Comintern meant that for much of 1928 the implications of the 'new line' for trade union policy were confused.[85] During the discussions of the British Commission of the Ninth Plenum of the ECCI in February, Page Arnot detected 'a very leftward swing among the masses' and argued that 'the startling Communist victories' in the Scottish miners' unions were evidence 'of a solid working class revival'. But little was said of any shift in party industrial policy.[86] The Plenum's general resolution on the trade union question was couched in abstract generalisations.[87]

The Fourth Congress of the Red International of Labour Unions (RILU), held in April, did not clarify the situation. Losovsky, RILU Secretary General, had supported the formation of 'red' unions as early as 1927 and calls for this policy were in evidence at the congress.[88] However, although the theses adopted noted a 'leftward drift of the masses' and the 'united front of reformists and employers for the purpose of purging the factories of revolutionary workers', they argued that the 'chief task' of RILU supporters in Britain and Germany remained winning workers organised in reformist unions. They predicted that as 'the alliance between the trade union bureaucracy and the employers' became closer, the former would launch 'ever more furious attacks' on militants and that 'the struggle against expulsions must be conducted with maximum determination'. The programme of action specifically outlined for the MM insisted on the slogan 'No splitting the unions', and the need to show the workers 'that the reformist leadership alone is guilty of splits and disruption. (A striking example is the action of the Scotch Miners' officials, adherents of the Minority Movement). The Minority Movement shall mobilise the broadest masses against the Reformist Splitters.'[89] It was this perspective which consistently informed reports on the Scottish miners' unions in the *Worker* during 1928.[90]

Such a policy did not necessarily imply the formation of new, revolutionary unions, but this was the direction in which Comintern thinking was moving. The PB complained that some British delegates to the Sixth Congress had returned from Moscow with 'a new union complex'.[91] With the defeat of Bukharin in the autumn of 1928, the ambiguities of the Fourth RILU conference were increasingly re-defined by Losovsky as initiating a trend towards 'independent leadership': 'The masses must be organised and led, if necessary without the trade union apparatus and if necessary against it; no fetish must be made of the trade unions; the reformist organisations must not be transformed into objects of worship.' By December, he accused those who feared splits as displaying 'a conciliatory attitude towards the bureaucracy'.[92]

At the end of November an authoritative article appeared in the *Worker* under the name of 'A. Bergson' which was critical of the MM generally and of its tactics in Lanarkshire in particular:

> Today the Minority Movement is operating under circumstances which demand rapid changes in tactics and flexibility in organisational principles. The failure to recognise this has resulted in many mistakes being committed. Comrades are showing a tendency to worship effete slogans and to employ mechanically the same tactics in changing situations.

One such slogan was 'save the unions', which had been wrongly interpreted as 'meaning the complete subordination of all their activities to working in and through official channels'. This tendency to 'legalistic tactics' had been demonstrated 'quite clearly in Lanarkshire ...'. Although it did not explicitly call for the formation of a new miners' union, the article asserted the need for Communists to come 'to the forefront of the struggle as an independent force' and lead unofficial strikes.[93]

Although a majority of the leadership of the CPGB resisted these interpretations, they were under increasing pressure to form a new 'red' union in the Scots coalfields. In 1930, Pollitt stated that 'in resolution after resolution we have been condemned for not forming the UMS before we had formed it, [that] we were missing the tide'.[94] The previous year, Campbell claimed that by the end of August 1928, 'it had become perfectly clear that we had gone as far as we could within the reformist apparatus' and that a decision had been taken in the PB 'that preparations should be made to form a new union in Scotland. For that purpose we called a conference in Falkirk last October.' Nevertheless, he rejected 'the criticism subsequently expressed by the Profintern [i.e. RILU] that we ought to have formed a new union at this conference. A new union, comrades, is a serious business. It has got to be well prepared.' After preparing 'the mass of our members ... the favourable opportunity we selected' was when the MFGB Commission reported: 'That was the point to break, and when that point came, the membership in Scotland were ready.'[95]

There is considerable rationalisation in Campbell's retrospective account before a critical Comintern audience. Contemporary documentation suggests that the perspective of forming the UMS involved more long term preparation than his testimony allowed. In December 1928, Pollitt stated to the Political Secretariat (PS) of the ECCI that 'the most serious danger, however, that we are facing in the party is an attempt to interpret the resolution of the Ninth Plenum as meaning that we are, whenever possible and on every occasion that presents itself, to establish new trade unions ...'. However, the majority position, was:

> to hold on to the positions that we have already in the unions at present ... to intensify the campaign against the splitters and to fight against the new-union danger, to become more flexible in our trade union work and not make a fetish of constitutionalism; because the first two tendencies merely lead to the same thing: the isolation of the party and the development of sectarianism within the party.

With regard to the mining situation he recalled the earlier split by the MRU and depicted the present disunity as 'a harvest to the coal capitalists in Fife'. Pollitt was realistic (and prescient) about the concerns of rank and file miners:

> both in Lanarkshire and Fifeshire, there is a feeling amongst those who have left the union that they are not prepared to join a union again until they can see that the union is going to be strong enough to defend the everyday conditions of the miners; and they are afraid in many cases of joining a Red Union because they believe that such a union will not be recognised by the capitalists or by the TUC and that therefore the possibility of defending or bettering their economic conditions will be considerably lessened.

It was only in Fife, he stated, that there was a sufficiently experienced cadre to manage the affairs of the union. In Lanarkshire, the party lacked control: 'the situation is about as bad as it can be ... The economic effects of the situation in Lanarkshire baffle description':

> The line of the Party now with regard to the Scottish situation is to develop a campaign on the basis of political and economic demands that will raise the whole fight out of a struggle for official positions into a definite struggle for better conditions for the miners, and out of the struggle making the necessary organisational changes.

Therefore we believe this struggle is best launched under the auspices of 'Save the Union from the splitters and strike-breakers'. We oppose any suggestion that there should be a date fixed to form a new union in Scotland. Such a step would be *suicidal, ridiculous and premature*. We have practically no influence at all in considerable sections of the Scottish coalfield, and the line of the Central Committee is therefore to develop this Save the Union campaign in order that, as a result of the campaign, we can mobilise all sympathetic elements, get them to organise them into committees, then upon the basis of the response to this campaign, making the decision, *if necessary*, of forming one union for the Scottish miners.(my emphasis)[96]

We can note the long term and conditional nature of Pollitt's commitment to a new union. But as his statement indicates, he was not only under pressure from the Comintern to form new unions but also from sections of his own cadre in the Scots coalfields. As early as July 1928, Proudfoot queried whether a call in the party's *Workers' Life* for an alliance of Fife and Lanark was intended as the basis for a breakaway Scottish union: 'I know that some of the Lanarkshire chaps are in favour of that policy ... I am afraid that policy will not find much support in Fife.'[97] It was symptomatic of such views that a report in the *Worker* of 30 November, under the headline: 'No breakaway unions – dangerous move by Lanark branch', described how the Blantyre LMU branch had decided to withdraw from the union in protest at the actions of the LMU Executive:

Left-wing sentiments may have been the cause of this breakaway but these comrades must understand that no progressive worker can back such a policy. In essence this is a reactionary move which can only have the effect of assisting both the right-wing and the local manager ... the Lanarkshire comrades are dissociating themselves from this split.[98]

Despite this final disclaimer, when Proudfoot visited Blantyre a few weeks later, he found that: 'The prevalent feeling in Lanarkshire is that there is no Union to save, that we should immediately set about the formation of a new Union.' In contrast, Proudfoot took a strategic view of the party's interests:

The line I took at Blantyre and still believe to be right: – Organise the Lanarkshire mineworkers around struggle at the Pits (unionists and nons) continually appeal to them to come into the union to fight the

R.W. who refuse to struggle at the pit and who also refuse to accept rank and file decisions on struggle, thereby ORGANISING opposition to the R.W. and support to ourselves which would ultimately drive the R.W. into FORMATION of new unions as has been demonstrated by Adamson.[99]

A few days later, he expanded his views further in a realistic appraisal of the rank and file miners' attitudes:

I hope my statement re the Party line on the Lanarkshire situation did not convey the impression that I was opposed to the formation of New Unions *when the time is ripe*. Some of our chaps who are 'rushing into print' with some of these suggestions at present should be handed something to play with. It is a very easy thing to declare and prove that the Workers are getting fed up with the R.W. leadership, but they are *not so fed up* that they have come solidly over to us or we should have them along with us inside the Unions fighting the R.W. Some of our 'Red' Union advocates will possibly put up the argument to that, by stating that the wholesale leaving the Unions (as in Lanarkshire) is the manifestation of the 'fed up' feeling and if a New or 'red' Union was formed we should have these 'fed ups' joining up with us. Looks very nice but what should not be forgotten is the fact that the Unions (Miners' Unions) membership was not built up by the miners joining voluntary but continuous pressure, card inspections, threats of, and strikes at pits which compelled many to retain membership. (emphasis in original)[100]

The CPGB's Tenth Congress in January 1929 devoted considerable attention to the Scottish coalfields.[101] One third of the lengthy Resolution on the Mining Situation was concerned with Scotland. It admitted that 'the main defect in our Party work was to allow the inter-Union struggle to appear as a struggle between the Communists and the Right Wing Leadership over positions for monetary gain and personal advantage, instead of keeping the demands of the workers to the forefront'. In reviewing the future strategy of the party, attention was paid to the 'special tasks' arising from the Scottish situation. These included a campaign outside Scotland to expose the attitude of the MFGB Executive and in the other Scottish coalfields to establish 'Save the Union' Councils 'with a view to mobilising all possible support in the event of the bureaucrats forcing split'. It is clear that the party by this stage was engaged 'in preparation for the inevitable split of the union by the bureaucrats'. Nevertheless, its perspective remained one of preparation within the existing unions: 'The whole line of the "Save the Union" Committees in Scotland should be to gather support for Fife by fighting inside the Scottish Mineworkers' Union, and to prepare for the formation of one miners' union for Scotland.'[102]

Such ambiguous rhetoric could encompass both the long established reform movement demand for the amalgamation of the existing Scottish county unions into a more centralised organisation as well as a breakaway red union. The Report of the Central Committee to the Congress emphasised the former interpretation although kept the latter option open:

'Save the Union' committees have been set up under Left-Wing or Minority Movement auspices for the purpose of building up the existing unions and to counter the attempts of the bureaucracy to smash the unions ... These committees, in addition to forming a buttress against the attempts of the bureaucrats to split the union, will also provide a basic framework for a new union in the event of a split being forced by the bureaucrats.[103]

The Congress discussion of this resolution – which was adopted unanimously – displayed similar ambivalence. It was opened by Arthur Horner of South Wales, a staunch opponent of 'new unionism', who accepted that 'splits are acceptable in certain circumstances' and that the Save the Union Committees provided 'the necessary basis for alternative Unions when such unions are forced upon us'. Although the failure to establish such a new union in Scotland was 'alleged to be one of the Party's mistakes',

Yet in Scotland, and especially in Lanarkshire, we have been handicapped by not having the necessary personnel and resources for such a task. To have set up a new union in Lanarkshire would have meant the liquidation of the Party. Our first objective in Lanarkshire must be the building up of a solid Party cadre, which does not at present exist in that region. None the less we retain as our objective the establishment of an independent Scottish Miners' Union; and the time for its establishment will come with the exclusion of the revolutionary Fife Union from the Miners' Federation.

Such goals were to prove contradictory: cadre development could not be carried out in a matter of weeks. This was implicit in the contribution of Abe Moffat who warned it would be 'dangerous' to establish a new union until the Save the Union Committees 'had gained much more strength' by 'going out to the unorganised miners in the pits'. Allan accepted that too much emphasis in Lanarkshire had been placed on 'a palace revolution' inside the union office, but did not agree that all avenues inside the MFGB yet had been closed: to form a new union would be 'a very big mistake'. Horner summed up: 'to advocate the immediate formation of a new Scottish Miners' Union, without mass support, would simply mean isolation'.[104]

On 11 February, three weeks after the CPGB Congress ended, the NUSMW Executive suddenly called the conference for 18 February which paved the way for the expulsion of the Fife union. This move effectively precluded the long term campaign planned by the party. The *Workers' Life* discussion on the MFGB report received on the day of the conference not only urged the formation of Save the Union committees but raised the slogan 'Prepare for the formation of one Scottish Mineworkers' Union'.[105] At the end of February, the CC received a long and highly critical 'closed letter' from the Presidium of the ECCI in response to reports it had received of the party Congress, which 'disclosed serious deficiencies in the leadership'. It condemned the leadership's failure to address 'mistakes and shortcomings in the sphere of trade union activity'. It demanded that an end be put:

> to vacillation and wavering in the sphere of trade union work ... The most vigilant attention must be paid to those branches of the unions in which the Communists have already secured the leadership ... particularly in Fife and Lanarkshire, where it is necessary to correct the mistakes pointed out by the Party Congress ...[106]

While the letter did not explicitly call for the formation of a new union, it did not have to spell out this demand to a leadership well aware of what the Comintern's views now were.

In early March, Allan issued the call for a new union. At a meeting of the PB on 6 March, after William Gallacher reported on the NUSMW decision to disaffiliate Fife and Allan's statement, it was unanimously agreed that the 'time was ripe for launching United Mineworkers of Scotland'. A move which two month's before had been deemed 'suicidal, ridiculous and premature' had been forced on the party by the able manoeuvring of the NUSMW right-wing. Gallacher warned of the need 'to avoid the danger of impatient cds who will try to make it an appendage to the P[arty]. Our aim is not a small C[ommunist] Union, but a rev[olutionary] Union of Scottish Mineworkers'. At the PB of 20 March, it was agreed to call a conference for the setting up of the new union on 14 April with two agenda items: the economic struggle in the industry and the provisional rules of the new union.[107] Three days later, these decisions were formally ratified by the CC. It heard that following Allan's suspension, a conference of Lanarkshire Save the Union Committees had been attended by 42 delegates and a 16 strong campaign committee, 11 of whom were CP members, established.[108] In Moscow, the secretariat of the RILU discussed Allan's suspension, declared that the tactics of the union bureaucracy had entered a 'new stage', and fully endorsed the call for a new union.[109] In Fife, the decision was loyally supported by those party members who had previously urged caution. The non-CP left on the FKCMA Executive, led by Hodge, were opposed to 'any new or rash adventure' and anxious to pursue matters further with the MFGB. The Board agreed by 13–10 to attend the forthcoming conference to establish the new union only with a 'watching brief'.[110]

The founding conference of the UMS was attended by 132 delegates whose county affiliations reflected the areas of Communist influence: 64 from Lanarkshire, 47, Fife, 8, Ayrshire, 6, West Lothian, 4, Stirlingshire, and 3 from Mid and East Lothian.[111] It appointed a provisional committee with Allan as General Secretary and adopted resolutions committing the new union to 'a definite class policy designed to organise the miners for a real struggle to combat the attacks of the employers', as well as a constitution guaranteeing 'the fullest possible democratic rights' and the regular election by ballot of its officials.[112]

In June, the FKCMA Executive agreed to hold a ballot of the members on whether to join the UMS. The ensuing campaign led to a rupture within the union as Communist officials such as Proudfoot, McArthur and Stewart strongly urged support for the UMS against the wishes of Hodge and his supporters. Amid claims that Hodge was manipulating the ballot, the Fife Communists convened a conference of militants in Lochgelly and agreed to set up branches of the UMS in the coalfield and abandon the FKCMA.[113] The FKCMA Board denounced their former Communist allies as 'disruptionists and Union smashers' and declared the ballot null and void.[114] The UMS had been launched with a desperate optimism, Allan declaring that 'the only line of salvation' lay in 'getting away from the self wrecked and discredited rump and establishing One Union for the whole of the coalfield'.[115] Two months after its foundation, there were three unions in the Fife coalfield alone, although Hodge's FKCMA was soon to disintegrate.[116]

Conclusion

The crisis in the Scottish unions during 1927–9 represented the climax of the struggle between the cohort of young militants which had emerged during and after the First World War and the generation of miners' leaders who had founded these unions. When Allan secured the LMU secretaryship from Small and Bird defeated Smillie for the NUSMW presidency in 1927, Allan was only 27 and Bird 31, while Small and Smillie were 54 and 70 respectively. Proudfoot and McArthur were 35 and 28 when they won the posts of agents that same year. They defeated James Cook, the former General Secretary of the Clackmannan Miners' Association and an FKCMA agent who was 49, and Sandy Smith, a temporary agent in his sixties.[117] Of the twenty-two agents, MPs and NUSMW Executive members who signed the anti-Communist manifesto in 1928, biographical details are available for seven; their average age was 59.[118]

Generation was explicitly referred to in these conflicts. At an LMU Council meeting in 1928, the 61 year old Duncan Graham, MP, a member of the LMU Executive since its foundation in 1894, and a former General Secretary, accused Allan and his comrades of attempting to set up a rival organisation. He defiantly reviewed the progress of the union: 'They had come through very many difficulties and had all kinds of opposition manifested both from inside and outside, to the various policies that had been ... carried into effect during more than thirty years.' Past progress counted for little with the young militants concerned with the contemporary crisis in the coalfield. McKendrick retorted that 'it was not his fault that he was born thirty years after Mr Graham. Was Mr Graham entitled to any more credit for being born before him?'[119] The politics of the young militants had been forged in the reform committees, the MM and the MRU, and had been further tempered by the experiences of 1926: all the leading Communists in Fife as well as Allan in Lanarkshire had been arrested during the General Strike and lockout.[120] They were now to attempt to put these politics into trade union practice in their new 'red' union, which significantly had as one of its founding principles the need to organise 'young miners' and secure 'special conditions for them from the owners'.[121]

The events described in this chapter also illustrate the complexity of the debates concerning CP autonomy from the Comintern. It is clear that the UMS had indigenous roots in the conflicts within the Scottish miners' unions. Even without pressure from the Comintern, it is probable that some new union would have been formed by militants in Fife and Lanarkshire. The experience of the MRU pointed to the difficulties which the party leadership had in enforcing its policies against the wishes of its militants on the ground, just as the FKCMA elections in 1927 highlighted elementary problems of party discipline. Moreover, despite the caution of the CPGB leadership, there was clearly enthusiasm for a split among sections of the party in Lanarkshire – though not by leading cadres such as Allan and McKendrick – and in central Fife.

The growing sectarianism within the CPGB following the apparent 'betrayal' of the General Strike by the TUC has already been noted.[122] This current developed further momentum as the 'old gang' of NUSMW officials manoeuvred to retain their positions. Eddie Laughlin, a 28 year old Blantyre miner, symbolised its ultra-left inclination when he asserted before the Tenth CPGB Congress that: 'We have to fight the right-wing with our fists, our heads and our boots'.[123] In Fife, the CP's pit papers in Cowdenbeath were criticised by Proudfoot and McArthur for their sectarianism. Proudfoot's irritation was manifest at an article in the *Stripper* which criticised CP allies 'because they do not support the whole Party line re. the General election and TO DRAW THEM CLOSER TO THE PARTY AND ACCEPT THE PARTY'S GEN. ELECTION LINE ... THEY MUST BE DENOUNCED AS "HYPOCRITES" ETC. They further state that THIS IS THE PARTY LINE. Holy Christ'.[124]

In 1929, Selkirk, the Fife CP Organiser and a former anarchist who readily accepted the apocalyptic predictions of the 'new line', wrote a letter to the *Workers' Life* complaining that party propaganda 'does not prepare the workers for British civil war conditions. Guns will be used in the civil war', and quoting Lenin after the 1905 Revolution: 'Our workers' battalions must be trained for the mass production of bombs ...'.[125] Such views drew not only on the Comintern's new analysis but also evoked the militaristic insurgency in the Scots coalfields of the post-war years. Proudfoot was unimpressed but observed that Selkirk 'was not alone in this as some of his associates are imbued with this particular bug'. They had published a pit paper for the Mary colliery at Lochore, 'called the "Red Guard" with crossed rifles and bayonets as the design on the title. Some bloody design for a pit paper.'[126] Proudfoot was similarly critical of his East Fife comrades who insisted 'our job was to intensify the fight' and who wanted to put forward a 17 year old YCL member to replace him as Denbeath FKCMA branch delegate upon his election as union agent: 'he had little or no experience at the "face", had never seen a Pan Run, had no brushing experience, knew nothing of the seams or rates in the Wellesley and was employed at Muiredge. You can imagine what this would have meant at the biggest pit in Fife with over 1,000 men.'[127]

The leftward shift in Comintern policy was thus highly congenial to some sections of the CP's membership. Margaret McCarthy, a young Communist who worked in the Glasgow CP office in 1930 recalled that:

> The young Communists adopted, too, the new line of the Party without doubt or hesitation. It accorded completely with our mood of frustration and despair, with our lack of confidence in the recognised Labour leadership, our desire for something sharp, short and spectacular to end the hopeless stalemate of our existence.[128]

Faced with the industrial dereliction of Lanarkshire and the activities of the NUSMW leadership, such views are perhaps understandable. They point to the ways in which local conditions could generate support for the 'new line' rather than seeing it as an entirely artificial imposition by the Comintern. But if such evidence adds credence to the indigenous elements in the evolution of CPGB policy in 1927–9, in the following years both the Comintern and the CP leadership were to take a strong interest in the development of Britain's most important red union.

Notes

1.   Lee, *Great Journey*, pp. 79, 87.
2.   NLS NUSMW Executive, 9 April 1927, 5 April 1928; *List of Mines*, 1927.

3.   SRO DD 10/258, Memorandum as to unemployment and pauperism in mining parishes in Scotland.

4.   SRO DD 10/205, Inspectoral report on distress in the Scottish coal-fields, 19 December 1928. For the effects of mechanisation, see vol. 1, ch. 3.

5.   NLS NUSMW, Fife Dispute Committee meeting, 13 December 1926, Executive, 27 January 1927; MPL A006, FKCMA Executive Board, 4 April 1927.

6.   See ch. 2 in this volume.

7.   NLS NUSMW Special Executive, 8 June 1928.

8.   The most detailed account of these conflicts is in Long, thesis, pp. 403–29, but the focus is very much on the miners' unions. Arnot, *History*, pp. 182–95, concentrates exclusively on internal develop-ments in the unions and makes no mention of the role of Communist policy, despite the fact that as a member of the CPGB Central Committee he was a central actor in the events he describes. Martin, *Communism*, pp. 90–2, deals briefly with the factional conflict in the Scottish coalfields in the context of Communist policy, while Macfarlane, *British Communist Party*, pp. 265–74, treats them at greater length in an account largely based on published party sources. Martin Sime, 'The United Mineworkers of Scotland: an appraisal of its origins', (unpublished paper, c. 1978), bases his analysis, which is heavily weighted towards Fife, largely on sources in the Proudfoot Papers. The account in this chapter is based on a wider range of union, CPGB and Comintern sources than were avail-able to previous researchers.

9.   A seventh constituent, the tiny Kirkintilloch and Twechar Miners' Union voted to dissolve itself and merge its membership with the LMU in October 1927 (NUSMW Executive, 17 October 1927).

10.   NLS Dep. 227/43, LMU Council, 6 and 13 July 1927; *Workers' Life*, 15 July 1927; W. Gallacher, 'The position in the Scottish coalfield', *Labour Monthly*, 10, 1928, p. 678; *Forward*, 16 July 1928.

11.   D. Proudfoot and J. McArthur, *Barriers of the Bureaucrats: Fife breaks through* (n.d., 1929), p. 6.

12.   MPL A006, FKCMA Executive Board, 4 April 1927.

13.   PL, 9, 16 June 1927.

14.   MacDougall, *Militant Miners*, p. 37; PL, 23 June 1927.

15.   PL, 27 June 1927.

16.   MPL G008, Fife Sub-District Party Committee circular, 12 July 1927.

17.   Proudfoot and McArthur, *Barriers*, p. 7.

18.   Ibid., p. 9.

19.   Ibid., pp. 10–11; NLS Dep. 227/43, LMU Council, 7 December 1927. It was indicative of the growing willingness of the Scottish MMM to

cross traditional regional boundaries that the Lanarkshire Section issued a leaflet to miners in Fife during the campaign, reporting on the LMU vote supporting the MM candidates and urging a similar outcome in Fife (MPL G040, Scottish Miners' Minority Movement).

20.   Proudfoot and McArthur, *Barriers*, p. 15; NLS Dep. 227/87, NUSMW Executive, 26 December 1927; G.A. Hutt, '"Democracy" in the Scottish miners' union', *Labour Monthly*, 10, 1928, p. 353. Hutt claims that the number of defeated officials was seven out of nine. The figure of four out of eight is taken from Proudfoot and McArthur.

21.   Proudfoot and McArthur, *Barriers*, provides an accurate, if politically partisan, account. The most detailed study is contained in Long, thesis, ch. 12. See also Arnot, *History*, pp. 182–95; Martin, *Communism*, pp. 91–2; Macfarlane, *British Communist Party*, pp. 265–9.

22.   Arnot, *History*, p. 187.

23.   The leaflet is reproduced in the minutes of NUSMW Executive, 23–7 April 1928. For Communist commentaries upon it, see Hutt, 'Democracy', pp. 355–6, and Proudfoot and McArthur, *Barriers*, pp. 20–1.

24.   Martin, *Communism*, pp. 95–101. Walter Citrine, TUC General Secretary, used the example of the LMU in articles condemning Communist tactics in the unions (W.M. Citrine, 'Democracy or disruption', *Labour Magazine*, 4, 11, 1928). The 'attempts to disrupt' the Scottish mining unions were also condemned in the report of the TUC's 'Inquiry into Disruption', *Report of 61st Annual Trades Union Congress* (1929), p. 180.

25.   Arnot, *History*, p. 189; Proudfoot and McArthur, *Barriers*, p. 23; NLS Dep. 227/88, NUSMW Executive, 18 February 1929, Appendix; *Glasgow Herald*, 19 July 1928. Although Allan, McKendrick and two others were elected as Lanarkshire delegates, the NUSMW Executive refused to endorse their conference credentials (*Workers' Life*, 19 July 1928).

26.   Gallacher, 'Scottish coalfield', p. 679; NLS Dep. 227/44, LMU Council, 25 June, 8 August 1928; *Glasgow Herald*, 10 August 1928.

27.   Proudfoot and McArthur, *Barriers*, pp. 24–5; NLS Dep. 227/70, LMU Executive, 28, 31 August 1928; *Glasgow Herald*, 29 August 1928.

28.   NLS Dep. 227/70, LMU Executive, 17 February, 15 April 1928.

29.   NLS Dep. 227/44, LMU Council, 2 May 1928.

30.   Macfarlane, *British Communist Party*, p. 267.

31.   NLS Dep. 227/44, LMU Council, 20, 25 June, 8 August 1928.

32.   McKendrick later apologised to Small for his 'unmanly action' (NLS Dep 227/43, LMU Council, 1 June 1927).

33. PL, 20 August 1928.
34. NLS Dep. 227/44, LMU Council, 5 September 1928.
35. Cited in Long, thesis, p. 419.
36. NLS Dep. 227/87, NUSMW Executive, 23 July 1928; Dep. 227/88, NUSMW Executive, 2 November 1928. After the NUSMW Executive had refused to accept the LMU's nomination of James McKendrick as a Scottish delegate to the MFGB Conference, Allan nominated him again. When Smillie asked if Allan wanted to make fools of the Executive, the latter allegedly replied, 'Do you not think you have made b——y fools of the miners long enough?' (Executive, 23 July 1928). Allan later strenuously denied using the word 'bloody' (Dep. 227/70, LMU Executive, 11 September 1928). A few weeks after his return to the Executive, Allan was again threatened with suspension for an article he had written in the *Miners' Voice*, which allegedly insulted and attacked members of the Executive (NUSMW Executive, 22 November 1928).
37. NLS Dep. 227/70, LMU Executive, 25 September, 12, 16 October, 7 December 1928; Dep. 227/44, LMU Council, 1, 24 October 1928; Dep. 227/45, LMU Council, 6 February 1929.
38. Proudfoot compared Lanarkshire where 'they have got a first rate *team* of R.W^{ers}, Smillie, Graham, Welsh, Small & C^{cy} to oppose while we in Fife have only one prominent but exceedingly crafty R.W^{er}, Wullie, with a team of third raters who are imbued with no other aim than opposing the "Reds" ...'. (PL, 28 July 1928).
39. MPL A025, FKCMA Executive Board, 5 May 1928. The right-wing candidate, Toner, received the support of 28 delegates to Stewart's 24, but the financial vote was £424 to £334 in favour of Stewart. The left's growing support was demonstrated by the same meeting approving a motion from Toner's own East Wemyss branch demanding the resignation of the Fife NUSMW representatives by 27–17, and a demand to prevent agents also being MPs by 27–20.
40. MPL A027, FKCMA Executive, 28 July 1928; A028, FKCMA Executive, 20 September 1928; Proudfoot and McArthur, *Barriers*, p. 28.
41. NLS Dep. 258/1, AMU Delegate Meeting, 14 April 1927, Annual Meeting 13 August 1927, Delegate Meeting, 29 October 1927.
42. NLS Dep. 258/1, AMU Special Delegate Meeting, 19 May 1928, Annual Meeting, 23 August 1928; *Forward*, 11, 25 August 1928; *Workers' Life, 10 August 1928*.
43. NLS Acc. 4312/3, West Lothian Mineworkers' Union, Special Executive, 18 August 1928, Executive, 14 September, 21 November 1928.
44. NLS Acc. 4312/12, MELMA Board, 31 December 1927; see also MELMA Board, 28 May 1927, 29 September, 27 October 1928.

45. NLS Dep. 227/88, NUSMW Executive, 22 November 1928; Proudfoot and McArthur, *Barriers*, p. 29.
46. NLS Dep. 227/88, NUSMW Executive, 10 December 1928.
47. NLS NUSMW COF, 9 February 1929; NUSMW Executive, 11 February 1929; *Inprecorr*, 15 March 1929.
48. NLS NUSMW Special Conference, 18 February 1929.
49. *Workers' Life*, 8 March 1929.
50. *Worker*, 8 March, 19 April 1929; Arnot, *History*, p. 194.
51. NLS NUSMW Executive, 11 March 1929.
52. NLS NUSMW Annual Conference, 28 March 1929.
53. NLS Dep. 227/43, LMU Council, 6, 13 July 1927.
54. PRO LAB 34/39–46, Trades Disputes Books; *List of Mines*, 1921–7.
55. See vol. 1, ch. 3, for discussion of strike incidence.
56. See vol. 1, ch. 6, for paternalism in the Larkhall district.
57. See vol. 1, ch. 7, for religious divisions, and ch. 4 of this volume for the SNTUA.·
58. See above, ch. 5, of this volume.
59. From the branch voting returns in the second ballot, lists were compiled according to the following criteria: branches were defined as displaying strong CP support if (a) their vote was more than 50 per cent for the CP candidates for agents (the mean vote was 41.9 per cent) and (b) their vote was less than 30 per cent for the right-wing candidates for agents (mean 38 per cent). Votes for the NUSMW panel were not used in this calculation because the results were complicated by the CP supporting the non-Communist Hodge in this ballot. Right-wing strongholds were identified by (a) where the votes for the right-wing candidates were 60 per cent or more (b) where the support for the left slates for agents and Executive was less than 25 and 35 per cent respectively (MPL A118, 'Ballot Returns re appointment of 2 Agents' and 'Ballot Returns re appointment of 5 for National Executive').
60. See vol. 1, ch. 1, for the industry in Fife, and vol. 1, ch. 4, for the characteristics of the mining population. These findings confirm Proudfoot's observation that the 'Old Gang ... rule the roost in Clackmannanshire' (PL, 16 June 1927).
61. NMLH, CP/IND/KLUG/05/01, Notes made the late James Klugmann in Moscow, 'The mining situation in GB', signed 'JRC' [J.R. Campbell] for Political Secretariat'. Hereafter material from Klugmann's notes will be indicated by 'JK'. They are described in N. Branson, *History of the Communist Party of Great Britain, 1927–41* (1985), pp. vii-viii.
62. *Forward*, 11 August 1928.
63. NLS Dep. 258/1, AMU Delegate Meeting, 29 September 1928.

Gilmour also seconded the motion rejecting the anti-Communist manifesto at the AMU (ibid., 19 May 1928).

64. NLS Dep. 258/1, AMU Delegate Meeting, 30 August 1928. Gilmour also gained a substantial minority vote in the Auchinleck branch which had sponsored left-wing resolutions. Brown received overwhelming support in his own village of Annbank (696 votes out of 746) and neighbouring Mossblown (183 out of 271).

65. See vol. 1, ch. 1.

66. See vol. 1, ch. 6, for company housing and other forms of social control in Ayrshire.

67. A. Thorpe, 'Comintern "control" of the Communist Party of Great Britain, 1920–1943', *English Historical Review*, 113, 1998, pp. 637–8. See also P. Anderson, 'Communist Party history', in R. Samuel (ed.), *People's History and Socialist Theory* (1981), pp. 145–55, and P. Latham, 'Methodological approaches to Communist Party history', *Our History Journal*, October 1978, for earlier attempts at categorising the literature.

68. W. Kendall, 'The Communist Party of Great Britain', *Survey*, 20, 1, 1974, p. 119.

69. Macintyre, *Little Moscows*, is one example. See also Geoff Eley's recent strictures (from which he excludes Macintyre) against 'the common mistake' whereby 'the history of indigenous radicalisms and local communities' amounts to 'the history of communism with the communism left out' (G. Eley, 'From cultures of militancy to the politics of culture: writing the history of British communism', *Science and Society*, 61, 1,1997, p. 126).

70. N. Fishman, *The British Communist Party and the Trade Unions, 1933–45* (Aldershot, 1995). There are far fewer index entries to the Comintern than to the Transport and General Workers' Union, for example.

71. Fishman, *British Communist Party*, pp. 36, 333.

72. Cf Pelling's observation on the capacity of RILU functionaries to draft 'hedging' resolutions (H. Pelling, *The British Communist Party: a historical profile*, 1958, p. 57) and the characterisation of Losovsky as a 'trimmer' by one of his fellow Comintern cadres in 1929: 'If [Losovsky] wants to find a vague formulation which offers a way out in any direction, he would do best to look for it in his own collected works' (quoted in Martin, *Communism*, p. 15). Such hedging became increasingly important as the full weight of Stalinist terror fell with disproportionate brutality on the Comintern and its subsidiary organisations: see K. McDermott, 'Stalinist terror in the Comintern: new perspectives', *Journal of Contemporary History*, 30, 1995.

73. E.J. Hobsbawm, 'Problems of communist history' in his *Revolutionaries* (1973), p. 9.

74. *TLS*, 21 April, 5, 12, 19, 26 May, 2, 9, 16 June 1966. The tenor of the recent biography of Pollitt supports earlier accounts that Pollitt was installed as British leader with Comintern sponsorship (K. Morgan, *Harry Pollitt*, Manchester, 1993, p. 65).

75. Thorpe, 'Comintern control', pp. 638, 662. See also A. Thorpe, 'The Communist International and the British Communist Party', in T. Rees and A. Thorpe (eds), *International Communism and the Communist International, 1919–43* (Manchester, 1998), where he argues that Comintern influence over the British party has been exaggerated.

76. K. McDermott and J. Agnew, *The Comintern: a history of international communism from Lenin to Stalin* (1996), pp. 118, 215. See K. McDermott, 'The history of the Comintern in the light of new documents', in Rees and Thorpe, *International Communism*, p. 37.

77. B. Studer and B. Unfried, 'At the beginning of history: visions of the Comintern after the opening of the archives', *International Review of Social History*, 42, 1997, pp. 432, 439.

78. For one analysis of 'the field of tensions' encompassed within 'the parameters of Comintern politics', see K. Morgan, 'Harry Pollitt, the British Communist Party and international communism', in T. Saarela and K. Rentola (eds), *Communism: national and international* (Helsinki, 1998).

79. Macfarlane, *British Communist Party*, p. 318.

80. There are sometimes differences between different writers as to the precise chronology of the 'third period': for example, Hallas defines is as the years 1928–34 (D. Hallas, *The Comintern*, 1985, pp. 123ff.), McDermott and Agnew prefer 1928–33, although they note the increasing sectarianism from 1926 as well as the initial use of the idea (ironically by Bukharin) at the end of that year (McDermott and Agnew, *Comintern*, pp. 68, 81ff.). Squires points to the difficulties of periodisation, suggesting a broad interpretation might extend from the end of 1927 until 1935, but adopting the 'narrower limits' of 1930 until March 1933 (M. Squires, 'The CPGB and "class against class"', *Socialist History*, 3, 1993, pp. 6–7). The most detailed discussion of the question is by Worley, who adopts the period 1927–32 whilst locating the origins in 1926 (M. Worley, 'Class Against Class: the Communist Party of Great Britain in the Third Period, 1927–1932', unpublished PhD thesis, University of Nottingham, 1998).

81. Morgan, *Pollitt*, p. 64.

82. Quoted in B. Fowkes, *Communism in Germany under the Weimar Republic* (1984), p. 145; Martin, *Communism*, p. 106.

83. McDermott and Agnew, *Comintern*, p. 82.

84. H. Wicks, *Keeping My Head: the memoirs of a British Bolshevik* (1992), p. 102.

85. Martin, *Communism*, p. 107.
86. *Communist Policy in Great Britain: the report of the British Commission of the Ninth Plenum of the Comintern* (1928), pp. 108, 126; see also the comments by Losovsky, p. 89; *Inprecorr*, 1 March 1928; Branson, *History*, p. 39.
87. J. Degras (ed.), *The Communist International, 1919–43: Documents, vol. 2, 1923–29* (1971), pp. 432–6.
88. Worley, thesis, pp. 67–8.
89. *Report of the Fourth Congress of the RILU* (1928), pp. 13, 19, 21, 103.
90. *Worker*, 6 January, 18 May, 13 July, 19 October 1928.
91. Branson, *History*, p. 40.
92. Quoted in Martin, *Communism*, p. 109.
93. *Worker*, 30 November 1928. The identity of the author is unknown.
94. NMLH CI 32, Anglo-American Secretariat, 11 August 1930.
95. *Inprecorr*, 9 October 1929.
96. NMLH CI 28, PS ECCI, 10 December 1928.
97. PL, 15 July 1928; *Workers' Life*, 13 July 1928.
98. *Worker*, 30 November 1928.
99. PL, 25 December 1928.
100. PL, 28 December 1928.
101. NMLH CP/CENT/CONG/02/06, *The New Line: documents of the 10th Congress of the Communist Party of Great Britain*. See Political Report of the Central Committee (pp. 19–20), Organising Report of the Central Committee (pp. 39–40).
102. NMLH CP/CENT/CONG/02/07, Resolution on the Mining Situation.
103. CP/CENT/CONG/02/06, *The New Line*, pp. 39–40.
104. *Inprecorr*, 1 February 1929. For Allan's comments, which were not fully reported in *Inprecorr*, see NMLH CP/IND/KLUG/04/03, JK 'Verbatim report of 10th Congress'.
105. *Workers' Life*, 22 February 1929.
106. The letter, dated 27 February 1928, is reprinted in Macfarlane, *British Communist Party*, pp. 308–19.
107. NMLH, JK, PB, 6, 20 March 1929; CP/CENT/PC/01/15, Report of voting in Executive Committee and Political Bureau from the 10th to 11th Congress. Pollitt was absent from these PB meetings, acting as Comintern emissary to the CPUSA (Morgan, *Pollitt*, p. 61).
108. NMLH CP/IND/KLUG/05/01, JK, PB 6, 20 March 1929, CC, 23–25 March 1929.
109. *Workers' Life*, 29 March 1929.
110. PL, 9, 25 March 1929; MPL A041, FKCMA Executive Board, 9, 23 March 1929.
111. *Worker*, 19 April 1929.
112. Ibid.

113. *Workers' Life*, 21 June 1929; MacDougall, *Militant Miners*, pp. 126–7.
114. MPL A046, FKCMA Executive Board, 29 June 1929. Bird, who had increasingly distanced himself from the CP, did not leave the union and became the new Chairman of the FKCMA.
115. Allan, 'Position of the Scottish miners', p. 284.
116. Arnot, *History*, p. 195; MacDougall, *Militant Miners*, p. 127; *Daily Worker*, 25 February 1930.
117. MacDougall, *Militant Miners*, pp, 119–20, 172, 177.
118. Calculated from Knox, *Labour Leaders*.
119. NLS Dep. 227/44, LMU Council, 1 October 1928; Knox, *Labour Leaders*, p. 127.
120. See ch. 5 of this volume.
121. *Worker*, 19 April 1929.
122. See ch. 5 of this volume.
123. NMLH CP/IND/KLUG/04/03, JK, 'Verbatim Report of 10th Congress of the CPGB'; CP/IND/MISC/21/05, 'Peter Kerrigan's notes for orations at the funerals of deceased comrades: Eddie Laughlin, died 28 December 1960'.
124. PL, 17 September 1928. See also PL, 7 January 1929, complaining about the 'volume of abuse' published in the *Stripper*.
125. *Workers' Life*, 23 August 1929.
126. PL, 5 September 1929.
127. PL, 28 July 1928.
128. M. McCarthy, *Generation in Revolt* (1953), p. 138.

CHAPTER SEVEN

Dual unionism and its aftermath, 1929–39

Introduction

The UMS was the more important of the two 'red' unions formed by the CPGB in 1929 (the other was the small United Clothing Workers' Union), yet it has received remarkably little detailed examination.[1] The first aim of this chapter is therefore to provide an account of its development, activities and membership. The second is to explore further the debates outlined in the previous chapter concerning the implementation of CP and Comintern policy. Although the UMS had strong indigenous roots within the fissiparous tendencies of Scottish mining trade unionism, its evolution and strategy can only be understood through its relationship with the CPGB and the International. Both these bodies closely monitored the new union's progress and exerted a powerful control over its activities before the decision was taken to liquidate it in 1935. The ultimate failure of the UMS to build a more militant and democratic alternative to the existing county unions, as the MRU had done in Fife in the 1920s, lay not only in the more unpropitious economic conditions in the early 1930s but was also due to the policies imposed upon it by the CPGB. The final section addresses developments in the NUSMW and county unions.

The United Mineworkers of Scotland

The formation of the UMS, unfettered by the previously alleged constraints of an established, right-wing union bureaucracy, provided the opportunity for Communist miners to develop a new kind of revolutionary union. According to J.R. Campbell, after the split it was 'up to the militants to organise their section of the union in such a way that it can organise the unorganised workers and become the representative union in the area', while McArthur recalled that in the UMS 'we tried to carry out a lot of the theories that we had been propagating'.[2] Pollitt urged that in the new situation of economic crisis and increasing class struggle, trades unionism had 'now to be adapted to modern conditions', reorganised 'as a fighting force against capitalism and not an appendage of capitalism'.[3]

The UMS constitution reflected such aspirations. While its first objective was a conventional defence of wages, this was combined with simultaneously 'mobilising and organising the Scottish mineworkers to play their part in the general struggle of the working class for the overthrow of the capitalist system and the establishment of a Revolutionary Workers' Government'. It was a condition of entry that the member delegated to his branch committee 'full power to issue notices relating to work or cessation of work on his behalf'. Branches were intended to be formed 'at every colliery in Scotland', although two or more collieries might be grouped together. The Scottish coalfields were elaborately divided into sixteen areas, each with an Area Committee composed of branch delegates. A National Executive, which met monthly, was elected annually by ballot, as were full-time agents, the national officials every two years. Day to day running of the organisation was the responsibility of a Sub-Executive Committee consisting of the President, General Secretary and three Executive members, while the 'supreme authority' of the union was vested in the Annual Conference.[4]

These ambitions to establish a pit-based, activist democracy reaching into the ranks of the unorganised were at best only imperfectly realised, as was apparent in the early attempts to build 'committees of action' to include non-unionised miners at the pits. In November 1929, Proudfoot reported a 'lack of clarity' among Communists in the UMS on this CP-inspired campaign, some arguing that the committees were an end in themselves, others that the campaign should be used to recruit to the union. A meeting of 'leading Party members' in the UMS endorsed a statement on the issue from Proudfoot, Alex Moffat and McArthur. It recognised the 'disgust' of the mineworkers at the 'sabotage' by the county union officials that had manifested itself 'along two distinct lines': the formation of the UMS by 'the more advanced militant mineworkers' and 'the mass of the Scottish Mineworkers divorcing themselves from the trade union movement'. It argued not only for an intensive campaign for 'all-inclusive pit committees' but that 'a strong emphasis be made for recruiting members to the UMS ...', otherwise the policy might be misinterpreted as 'bolstering up non-unionism' and the committees considered as 'an alternative machinery to the UMS'. The UMS, they felt the need to emphasise to the meeting, was 'not merely a propagandist body but is a Trade Union ...'. A subsequent UMS leaflet advocated the formation of committees of action, 'comprising organised and unorganised' around a set of demands including a seven hour day and guaranteed wages, but simultaneously urged 'Join the UMS'.[5]

A UMS meeting at Wellsgreen Colliery, near Buckhaven, succeeded in appointing an eleven-strong committee, only half of whom were UMS members. At the Victoria Pit, West Wemyss, the committee was not so 'all embracive', all but one of its nine members being UMS activists. However, the changes in the labour process and workforce recruitment in the 1920s rendered the operation of such committees problematic: their members might work on three or even four different shifts and could be drawn from a number of villages six or eight miles apart.[6] Proudfoot, who had conducted as many as five pithead meetings a day during the campaign, admitted that 'much energy has been expended but few Committees have been formed ... In Lanarkshire our chaps at many pits have been unable to get the men to stand and listen to them.'[7]

A further factor in the failure of the campaign was the refusal of non-party members of the UMS to see the relevance of the committees, especially given the lack of clarity on the relation between them and the formal union structures. Proudfoot lamented the lack of support from UMS branch officials in Fife: 'they do not voice opposition to the formation of the Cttees but sit tight and do nothing'. They had 'got into the orthodox T. U. rut, out of which the majority refuse to be moved'.[8]

In July 1930, Allan reported that of the union's branches, seven covered six, seven or eight pits, and only eight had single pit committees; 'all the rest are geographical branches with poor representation from the pits. We have failed to get our roots into the pits.'[9] By that year, Proudfoot was firmly of the view that the branch committees would remain 'as passive as ever' – though he recognised that this would be condemned as evidence of his 'Right Wing' tendencies by the '100% new liners'. Nevertheless, Proudfoot provided an acute insight into the motivations of the great majority of UMS members in Fife who were not members of the CP. Many, he argued, were in the union because they were anti-Adamson and the focus of the earlier agitation in the county unions upon union reform, 'stressed to the exclusion of any positive policy we had for operating at the pits, has surrounded us with Committee members who are convinced the fight has been won because we have all those "reforms" incorporated in our Rules and Constitution ...'. His 'candid opinion' – which he insisted was not the 'vapourings of someone who hasn't made intensive attempts to operate the new line, but is the sum total of my experiences during the past three months of intensive activity at the pits' – was that these local officials were 'now realising the class nature of the UMS and have no desire to be actively identified with it'.[10]

Proudfoot claimed a similar inertia permeated the UMS Executive which was 'the most awful dud EC that I have ever run across':

> This arises from the syndicalist approach and decisions of the West of Scotland representatives on the Rules Ctee, when we were drafting the Rules. Because they had advocated 'rank and filers' only on the EC of the Reformist Unions, they contended that we were in honour bound to carry this out in the UMS although at the same time admitting that we were crippling the EC by keeping out the most experienced militants ... This passivity is carried by the EC members into the Area Committees and thence by area delegates into the branches.[11]

Proudfoot's views were echoed by a member of the CP's CC: 'The mass at present time are passive and most of the work is carried out by the pit organisers – only 14 or 15 – actually do this work and the whole bulk of the members do nothing.'[12]

To counter such tendencies, the union and party leadership sought to develop a new union culture which was distinct from the bureaucratic practice of the county unions:

> In the old corrupt unions the local officials took no effective part other than to draw local official salaries, which, so long as they were regularly paid, kept the local officials 'loyal' to the Mondist bureaucrats. Such a condition of affairs would be fatal for a class union like

the UMS. Petty graft, which was and is a feature of the old unions, will not be tolerated in the UMS.[13]

Initially the UMS had adopted a similar system of fees and salaries for local work, with branch secretaries and dues collectors remunerated on a scale proportional to their membership: for example, a branch secretary with 165 members received a monthly salary of 10s 1d in July 1929.[14] The following year, however, the Executive campaigned 'to put the Union on a proper class basis so far as officials' fees was concerned'.[15] In August 1930, the Dysart representative on the UMS East Fife Area Committee announced that his branch committee had agreed to perform their duties on a 'voluntary basis' and urged other branches to follow suit in order to demonstrate the difference between the UMS and the 'reformist unions'.[16]

The issue was not immediately resolved. The following month Pollitt admitted that the union had 'not made the progress it should have made' because the mass of miners were not yet convinced that it represented a fundamentally different type of organisation. Because the factional conflict preceding its formation had been viewed 'as struggles for jobs and positions', it was the duty of every CP member in the union to give his services voluntarily: 'There should be no further taking of fees ... it would strike a deadly blow at the financial corruption that has been the curse of trade unionism for years.'[17] A *Daily Worker* editorial returned to the theme of the need to extend the voluntary principle in the UMS to highlight the contrast with 'the corruption practised by the reformist trade union officialdom. Large salaries and sheer robbery disguised under the name of "expenses" play their part in turning the trade union official into a boss hireling and removing him from any sympathy with the class from which he sprung.'[18] Nevertheless, when Proudfoot took over as UMS General Secretary in January 1931, he complained of 'a sullen revolt amongst the majority of the Branch officials' due in part 'to non-payment of salaries'.[19] A UMS commission that same month strongly objected to the practice of some branches deducting 'salaries due to them from the contributions drawn, before sending to Head Office', and sought to extend further the voluntary principle.[20]

Such campaigns had some effect in the long term. In September 1930, 26 per cent of the union's income from dues was paid out in branch salaries and expenses, a figure which had dropped to 14 per cent in February 1931 and to less than 4 per cent three years later. However, in the context of a declining membership – of which more below – this reduction may reflect the sloughing off of a stratum of lay officials imbued in the traditional practices of the Scottish mining unions as much as a transformation of the attitudes of UMS activists.[21]

One way in which the UMS sought to transcend union routinism and build a base in the pits was through the establishment or revival of pit papers. The Executive reported to the Annual Conference in 1930 that the re-issued *Sprag* had played a significant role during a strike at Shotts, and noted the publication of similar papers elsewhere. In that year, sixteen pit papers have been identified as circulating in the Scottish coalfields. They typically comprised four duplicated pages sold for a penny, their circulation ranging from 250 to 650 per issue.[22] The fugitive, ephemeral nature of such publications has left only a fragmented archival presence. This, together with their crude, sometimes almost illegible, reproduction, has led them to be largely ignored by historians.[23] Nevertheless, they represented a significant attempt by UMS activists to reach out politically to the mass of miners. A list of those produced during 1929–34 is contained in Table 7.1.

The titles of the papers often sought to link the imagery of some aspect of pit life with their agitational purpose. For example, a 'sprag' was a pin which locked the wheels of a coal hutch.[24] Some picked up the theme of illumination – the *Headlamp* and *Reflector* – while others referred to the miner's tools – *Hammer*, *Mash* – echoing the symbols of the October Revolution. Some displayed a mischievous ingenuity in their appropriation of local incidents. Rab Smith recalled how the *Panbolt* – a long bolt used for connecting conveyor sections – got its name: '... a fella Mulligan ... he hit the manager in the heid. Split his heid 'n' he got six months in gaol. Split his heid wi' a panbolt. So tha's hoo th' paper got its name, Th' Panbolt.'[25]

The papers sought to combine items on national campaigns and local issues together with items of pit gossip, readers' letters, jokes and cartoons. Achieving a popular and readable style, as well as balancing the contents between political didacticism, union affairs, pit grievances and news of local interest was a considerable challenge to the amateur journalists of the mining villages and inevitably one not always met. Papers often had to rely on snippets of pit gossip

Table 7.1 Pit papers published in the Scottish coalfields, 1929–34

Paper	Publishing group or locality	Year(s) of known publication
Fife:		
Bogie	Brighills Pit Group CPGB	1932
Buzzer	Organ of the Militant Miners of Glencraig	1930
Fan	Organ of the Militant Section, Muiredge Workers	1931
Flame	Michael Militant Miners	1933
Pan Bolt	Organ of Peeweep Communist Pit Cell	1930
Red Checkweigher	Peeweep, Lumphinnans Nos. 11 & 12 Pits 'Reissued'	1929 1930
Red Guard	Mary Pit, Lochore	1929
Reflector	Hill of Beath	1930
Spark	Organ of the Methil Communist Pit Group	1930–1
Torch	Organ of the Militant Section: Frances Workers	1930–1
Lanarkshire:		
Clipper	Organ of the Viewpark Militant Miners	1930
Fan	Organ of the Militant Miners South Lanark	1930
Fan	Broomfield Edition	1930
Headlamp	Organ of Militant Group of Priory Miners	1933
Spark	Organ of the Bardykes Militant Group (UMS)	1933
Sprag	Organ of the Militant Miners of Shotts	1930

Table 7.1 Pit papers published in the Scottish coalfields, 1929–34 (Continued)

Paper	Publishing group or locality	Year(s) of known publication
Stripper	Rosehall	1930
Title unknown	Palace Colliery	1934
Title unknown	Viewpark Colliery	1934
West Lothian:		
Mash	Dardanelles Pit	1930
Shovel	Fauldhouse	1930
Ayrshire:		
Kenneth's Hawk	Kenneth's Colliery, Dreghorn	1930
Jigger	Barony, Auchinleck	1930
East Lothian:		
Links	Organ of the	1930
Reflector	Preston Links Communist Cell	

Sources: E. and R. Frow, *Pit and Factory Papers Issued by the Communist Party of Great Britain, 1927–1934* (Salford, 1996); R. Harrison, G. Woolven, R. Duncan, *The Warwick Guide to British Labour Periodicals* (Hassocks, 1977); Methil Public Library, Proudfoot Papers; Modern Records Centre, University of Warwick, Mss 88, Miners' Minority Movement collection; information from Bill Moore, Sheffield; *Daily Worker*.

under headings such as: 'We want to know ... if the inspector during his last visit inspected the travelling roads in some of the sections ... if he did then he accomplished the impossible', or: 'Things we want to know: Who is the wee gaffer that said "kick the pope" when he was sitting drunk at the fire on Seterday nicht.'[26]

Communist activists faced considerable technical and organisational difficulties in the regular production of a local pit paper. Skills in typing, lay out and duplication were lacking, and the resulting publications frequently amateurish. Bob Selkirk recalled: 'Many a night shift was worked to produce the Pit Papers for sale on pay-day. Clumsy brushers, consulting the dictionary and the

Party Organ, typing with one finger, became "expert" journalists with no fear of the law of libel.' Rab Smith remembered 'the sacrifice' of the party comrades involved in producing the papers: 'the hoors that were spent ... Through the night ... and the machine jammed ... Ah've seen it four o' clock in the mornin' before we finally got the paper published'.[27] Given the restricted activist base of the UMS, such demands could not be sustained for long and it is significant that many pit papers did not survive after 1930, despite the continuing exhortations of the CP and Comintern.[28]

Another brave attempt at changing the culture of trade unionism by breaking down gender divisions was the involvement of women in the UMS. The UMS founding conference had adopted the principle that the union should 'assist in creating guilds for miners' women folk'. Such guilds already existed in the National Union of Railwaymen, but the 1926 lockout had highlighted the role of miners' wives in supporting strikers.[29] At a meeting of the UMS 'Sub-Organising Committee' [sic] in September 1929, four 'women comrades' were invited to discuss methods for the formation of UMS women's guilds. It was agreed that every member of a guild would be allowed to attend the branch to which it was linked but that two delegates would be formally appointed, while two branch delegates would be appointed to the guild. The guilds would also elect one delegate to a guild Area Committee which in turn would send two delegates to the cognate UMS Area Committee.[30]

An early meeting of the national UMS Women's Guild Committee, chaired by the union President, indicated the functions of what were clearly seen as auxiliary units of the union rather than autonomous organisations of women in the mining villages. The reciprocal representation was intended to prevent the possibility 'of the Guilds pursuing one policy and the Union another'. A list of topics on which visiting speakers could be provided had been drawn up by the union 'and would be submitted to the Guilds at an early date'. The activities which guilds were encouraged to engage in were demonstrations to collieries, parish councils, labour exchanges, education authorities and county councils, and selling the UMS journal, the *Mineworker,* as well as the CP's *Daily Worker.*[31]

Proudfoot's concern that, because the guilds were composed 'of raw, inexperienced women', they would require careful attention to prevent them becoming 'mere echoes of the Co-op Guilds, slander clubs and tea parties', was probably typical of even the more progressive UMS activists.[32] At a conference attended by twenty-four delegates from eight guilds, the proceedings were dominated by reports from male UMS officials.[33] In 1932, Alex Moffat complained of the guilds 'carrying out activity to the detriment of UMS activity' and insisted that 'all outside activity must become secondary to the tasks confronting the Guilds'. He clearly spelt out these 'main tasks' in a way which emphasised the guilds' subordinate role: 'to bring the Miner's wives into the Guilds so that they can be convinced through the policy of the UMS [of] the need for their husbands and sons joining up in the ranks of the UMS'.[34]

Establishing the guilds within the strictly gendered world of mining trade unionism was an uphill struggle, dictated by party policy rather than spontaneously demanded by rank and file activists.[35] Proudfoot reported that the formation of women's guilds was 'part of the organisation that almost every Cttee without exception are very timid and chary about facing up to. Already on 3 occasions after I had made the arrangements with the local cttees nothing has developed due to the cttees making no move ...', an attitude he attributed to 'the old antiquated idea still prevalent amongst the workers, that a woman's place is at the fireside'.[36] At Methil and Wellsgreen, the guilds were not progressing due to the 'neglect of the local UMS officials', while the Methilhill guild was making headway 'in spite of the local UMS officials who do nothing to assist them'.[37]

At a meeting of the Women's Guild Committee in July 1930, the UMS President admitted 'the lack of real life in the Guilds' and the 'turning of their attention inwardly instead of out towards work amongst the mass of working women'. It was reported that in East Fife, the guilds were 'retrogressing and were now in a bad position'.[38] The UMS Executive accepted that 'the Guilds were drifting away from the original objectives' and agreed a number of measures which would 'guide the Guilds into activity'.[39] However, a union commission in January 1931 continued to report 'a serious underestimation of the value of the women's guild organisation by the officials, organisers and local committeemen in the Union'. In September, the Executive endorsed a report on activity in East Fife which accepted that the guilds 'have been neglected and there has been a lack of coordinated activity'. Despite the injunction that every leading member of the union 'must take on the responsibility of helping to build the Guilds', a resolution the following year from the Methil UMS branch demanding more attention be directed to guild activity suggests these instructions were not fully implemented.[40]

The Secretary of the Cowdenbeath guild insisted that the guilds would 'break down the sex barriers which at present prevent the masses of working women from pulling their full weight in the mass struggle'. They were not 'like other women's guilds where they have a speaker and a cup of tea and go home ... The UMS guilds are out to educate women.' In practice, the guilds' activities were varied. At Methilhill, there were weekly discussions of an article in the *Daily Worker*; at Lochgelly, a male comrade gave a talk on the coal situation and the struggle of the unemployed to a well-attended meeting. Collections were organised for strikes. Protests at minor local issues such as changes in refuse collection times or the early wakening of hospital patients were also a feature.[41] In their support of the UMS, the guilds often reflected prevailing conceptions of appropriate gender roles. After the Sub-Executive decided that the UMS would supply a contingent of twenty on a 1930 hunger march to London, it was reported that the guilds 'were being drawn in to the work of helping to supply equipment and are also being asked to prepare banners for the marchers'.[42] Activities were sometimes social or welfarist rather than overtly political. The Methilhill guild had a 'Sketch Party' while its counterpart at Methil organised a Christmas treat for a hundred children in 1929; the Lochgelly guild enjoyed a 'splendid Christmas social' in 1930, hearing speeches from the UMS organisers 'after an entertainment by the Guild members'.[43]

The nineteen guilds known to have been established are listed in Table 7.2, and this compares unfavourably with the union's ninety branches in 1930. There are no comprehensive membership figures, only impressionistic reports: in Lochgelly a membership of 50 was claimed; in Lochore 37, although a miner's wife there reported that 'the previous winter the women were very apathetic'; in Leven, 31; Lumphinnans, 45.[44] Given these figures are drawn from the *Daily Worker*, they are not likely to underestimate the membership. But, with the heavy demands of domestic routine on miners' wives' leisure, such numbers are not unimpressive and suggest limited pockets of support. McArthur later admitted that:

> generally we did not entirely succeed, because we were in many cases merely duplicating the Co-operative Women's Guild of which most of the women were already members and it meant that we were hauling women out of their houses for another night of the week, or we were in competition with the Co-operative Women's Guild.[45]

Table 7.2 Formation of UMS Women's Guilds, 1929–32

Region	Guild	Approximate date of formation
Mid/East Lothian	Prestonpans	August 1929
Fife	Methilhill	September 1929
"	Wellsgreen	September 1929
"	Methil	January 1930
"	East Wemyss	December 1930
"	Lochore	By March 1930
"	Lumphinnans	December 1930
"	Kelty	December 1930
"	Cowdenbeath	By March 1930
"	Lochgelly	By March 1930
"	Clackmannan	By March 1930
Ayrshire	Auchinleck	April 1930
Lanarkshire	Bellshill	April 1930
"	Shotts	May 1930
Mid/East Lothian	Newcraighall	May 1930
Ayrshire	Springside	July 1930
Fife	Leven	December 1930
"	Denbeath	March 1932
Lanarkshire	Tannochside	By December 1932

Sources: MPL, Proudfoot Letters; MPL, UMS records; *Daily Worker*, 1930–5.

The UMS also attempted to develop wider cultural and sports activities. A UMS sports day and gala was held in Shotts in July 1930 involving five-a-side football, egg and spoon races and 'organised Russian mass games', as well as speeches by Allan and a YCL representative, followed by a dance in Shotts Public Hall. A British Workers' Sports Federation football team was also formed in the village.[46] In the Buckhaven area, a junior football team, the East Fife UMS, known locally as 'the ums', successfully competed in the junior football association.[47]

Novel though such social and cultural innovations were, it was by its membership and influence in the workplace that a revolutionary union must ultimately be judged. In the months after the foundation conference in April 1929, much progress was bruited in the Communist press. In May, it was claimed that eighteen branches had been established in Lanarkshire, including Shotts, Woodhall, Bedlay, Coalburn, Ponfeigh, Burnbank and Blantyre.[48] In August, 5,000 members were claimed in Lanarkshire compared with the

LMU's alleged membership of 3,000, although 20,000 were thought to remain unorganised; in West Lothian, only 300 were said to be in the county union; in Scotland as a whole, only 20,000 miners were organised out of 90,000: 'Fourteen to fifteen thousand of these were in the United Mineworkers of Scotland.'[49]

Such figures were wildly exaggerated. The following month Proudfoot, then a Fife UMS organiser (and a man of pessimistic temperament) confided:

> This is my second experience of assisting in building a new Union and I can assure you that there is a considerable difference in the attitude of many of those who were with us in building the R[eform] U[nion] to that which they are showing today in building the UMS. Out of the 17 Cttees we have in East Fife, only 3 have got down to the work as if they meant to build a Union ...

The situation in central and West Fife, was he claimed, even worse.[50]

Proudfoot's misgivings were borne out in the minutes of the county unions outside Fife which indicated that the new union was not only unable to extend beyond the previous boundaries of MM support but that these were contracting. The establishment of the UMS posed a difficult choice for a number of non-Communist, left-wing activists. In Ayrshire, George Gilmour and Dan Sim, both former prominent MM supporters, remained within the AMU although at Drongan, Springside and Hurlford – former islands of MM support – the bulk of the AMU members went over to the UMS. Hurlford's Communist delegate, Alex McLuskie, became a UMS organiser for Ayrshire.[51] In the MELMA, some difficulty was reported due to 'communist activities' at the Prestongrange branch but a resolution banning members of the CP, MM and UMS from holding any office in the association was overwhelmingly supported by the branches.[52] In the West Lothian Mineworkers' Union, only the Loganlea and Foulshiels branch delegates defected from the Executive, and new branches were soon re-established in these districts.[53] In the LMU, there were secessions to the UMS by the Thankerton, Milnwood, East Parkhead, Braidhurst, Rosehall, Hattonrigg, Bedlay, Priory and Douglas branches. Later ballots at Auchenraith Colliery, Blantyre, supported continued LMU membership by 234 to 109 and at Calderhead, Shotts, by a majority of 46.[54]

A clearer picture of the trend in UMS membership, and its

regional distribution, can be gained from Table 7.3. These estimates are calculated from the branch dues collected in 1929–30 and in each February from 1931 to 1934, and are based on the full contribution of six pence per week. The figures will underestimate the membership somewhat, since some paid less than the full rate: boys under 17 and surface workers paid three pence, unemployed members two pence.[55] Nevertheless, even allowing for such factors, it is manifest that the paid up membership of the union represented only a small proportion of the Scottish miners, probably less than five per cent. It is equally apparent that the union was increasingly concentrated in Fife, which contained four-fifths of the membership by 1934, and within Fife in the eastern and central districts. This was paralleled by the collapse of the union's presence in Lanarkshire. In 1930, the ten largest branches of the UMS included four in East Fife: Methil, Buckhaven, Gallatown and Leven; two in central Fife, at Cowdenbeath and Lumphinnans; as well as two in Lanarkshire, at Ponfeigh and Coalburn, and two in Ayrshire, at Auchinleck and Drongan. Two years later, the ten largest branches included only Ponfeigh and Hurlford outside of Fife.[56]

The decline of the union's membership was interrupted but not reversed by regular recruitment campaigns. These not only drained the energies of activists, they were hampered by the vicious circle of the union's constantly precarious financial position which in turn reflected the problem of declining membership.[57] In January 1930, for example, the union engaged in several contradictory initiatives. It embarked on an ambitious drive to recruit 5,000 new members. At the same time, it reduced its funeral benefits by 33 per cent, a move opposed by a significant minority of branches; sought to extend the voluntary principle among local officials, who were thus denied financial incentives to recruit; and suspended five full-time organisers because of lack of funds. Although the Executive claimed 1,100 new recruits – a figure which may be regarded with some scepticism – it accepted that 'insufficient progress was made with regard to activising the branches'.[58]

Membership is only one, albeit critical, indicator of a union's impact. The Executive reported to the second Annual Conference that the union's 'main weakness' remained the inability 'to close the gap between our influence and actual organisational strength'. In 1933, Pollitt reported to a meeting of the Comintern's Anglo-American Secretariat in similar terms: 'So far as the UMS is con-

Table 7.3 Estimated membership of the United Mineworkers of Scotland, 1930–4

	1930	1931	1932	1933	1934
East Fife	951	1,278	430	401	466
Central Fife	616	1,035	614	407	437
West Fife and Clackmannan	327	348	164	100	100
Total Fife	1,894	2,661	1,208	908	1,003
Lanarkshire	698	547	228	119	88
Ayrshire	405	357	215	128	130
West Lothian	162	137	37	6	3
Mid and East Lothian	211	184	103	50	39
Total	3,370	3,886	1,791	1,211	1,263
Fife as percentage of total	56	68	67	75	79

Sources: MPL, F122, Abstract of dues for period ending 27 September 1930; F123, Statement of Income for period 26 January to 21 February 1931; F132, Statement of Income for 4 weeks ending 27 February 1932; F137, Statement of Income for 4 weeks ending 25 February 1933; F148, Statement of Income for 4 weeks ending 24 February 1934.

Notes:
1. The membership has been calculated by dividing the total dues collected by the six pence per week paid by a full member. The figures for 1931–4 are based on the dues paid in February each year. The 1930 figures are calculated from a return giving the dues paid by each branch for the 'Year to 27th September'. It has been assumed that these refer to the twelve month period prior to the second UMS Annual Conference in October 1930 and have been divided by 26 shillings (equivalent to 52 weeks' dues).
2. In the 1930 document, only one branch out of 90 failed to return dues; in 1931, 12 branches out of a total listed of 75 made no return of any dues income; in 1932, this figure was 9 out of 65; in 1933, 7 out of 53; in 1934, 7 out of 46.
3. The 1930 total includes 53 members in Stirlingshire.

cerned, there is not a big increase in membership, but its influence is extending.'[59] Although the CPGB was forced, at least in private, to concede its failure to build the UMS membership, there remains the critical question of broader support among the miners. Explanations of the patterns of membership distribution and evaluation of the union's wider purchase must now be addressed.

A central problem for the UMS was the refusal of coal companies to recognise or negotiate with it. At Glencraig, management attempted to drown out UMS speakers by continuous blowing of the colliery horn.[60] During strikes organised by the UMS at Broomfield, Hassockrigg, Woodhall and Kenmuir collieries in Lanarkshire in 1930, its officials were refused an audience by the managers.[61] When under pressure to negotiate, managers often had the less unattractive option of dealing with the county unions. David Meek recalled the UMS attempt to organise Hamilton Palace colliery where union organisation had collapsed after the 1926 lockout. After a pithead meeting addressed by Abe Moffat, he had joined the UMS along with his stepfather and their drawer:

> ... and our [UMS branch] numbers were 6, 7, and 8 ... and it gathered and gathered until there were well over a hundred which got stronger every week, and the manager of the colliery was a Fifer, and he knew Abe Moffat, and past experience had told him what would happen if Moffat really got in here ... So he phoned up the LMU at Cadzow Street, Hamilton, and he asked Willie Small, the Secretary, if he would come out and organise the Lanarkshire Miners' Union at Hamilton Palace colliery, which he duly did and inside of a month, I would say that 75 per cent of the men were all back inside the Lanarkshire Miners' Union again ...[62]

Such testimony adds weight to the claims by a Lanarkshire Communist that: 'In Bardykes the manager allows LMU recruiting slips to be handed out in the pit bottom. In Viewpark, Earnock, Doctor, Priory [collieries], the management and the officials are very pally indeed, the managers acting as recruiters for the Lanarkshire Miners' Union.'[63] The situation was further complicated by continuing local breakaways from the county unions. At Irvine in Ayrshire in 1932, it was reported that there were four different unions in competition: two 'local scab unions' as well as the AMU and the UMS; at the Dardanelles Pit in West Lothian, the men broke away from the county association and 'formed a pit union of their own'.[64]

In parts of Fife, there was a sufficient body of support to force management to deal informally with UMS representatives, but even here the situation was highly uneven: 'The power to negotiate even unofficially at each pit was varied ...', recalled McArthur: 'It depended on the strength and the willingness of men in a given pit to make a stand ...'.[65] One such example occurred at Lumphinnans no. 11, 'Peeweep', pit, in 1929. Abe and Alex Moffat had been elected checkweighers there a few months before and several disputes had been successfully waged to defend conditions. In September 1929, a strike took place which was significant because it was not defensive but rather to enforce a new method of payment in the highly mechanised pits of the Fife Coal Company.

Companies increasingly sought to impose a 'yardage' rate in mechanised coal faces, based on the length rather than weight of coal stripped, which removed the need for checkweighers. The strike was to secure instead the 'cooperative tonnage' or 'common pool' system which remunerated the entire face team according to output. This had the advantages of eliminating the contracting system, cementing workgroup cohesion and retaining checkweighers. The strikes spread to other Fife Coal Company pits in the district but were called off after Adamson's FCKMU persuaded its members to return. The company then secured an interdict removing the Moffats as checkweighers, claiming they had incited the dispute.[66] If the strike was an early indication of the problems of dual unionism, it nevertheless suggested a policy for dealing with the employers' new drive to mechanise underground work and there were further attempts to introduce the cooperative system at Wellsgreen in East Fife, at the Klondyke pit, Newcraighall, and the Mary, Lochore.[67] At the Randolph Colliery, Gallatown, near West Wemyss, the UMS successfully led a strike under Proudfoot's direction over the introduction of new explosives, and consolidated the Gallatown branch into one of the largest of the union.[68]

Many local disputes in which the UMS was involved were waged with less tactical skill or strategic understanding, particularly in the strike-prone Lanarkshire coalfield.[69] Having been criticised prior to the formation of the UMS for their 'constitutionalism', CP miners in Lanarkshire swung towards an unrestrained militancy in the face of a collapsing coal industry. Third period rhetoric cloaked the discourse of militants in a sectarianism unlikely to win support beyond the party's committed cadre. For example, Small was described as 'the notorious social-fascist' during a strike at Shotts in January 1930. A meeting of strikers organised by the LMU was abandoned amid 'pandemonium' after Allan and other UMS organisers insisted on the right to speak. When the LMU called a strike in the district in May 1930, the UMS stated: 'The calling of the strike by the scab union has obviously been done in order to secure the leadership of the men for the purpose of betrayal.'[70]

The UMS Executive reported in 1930 that during the previous year the union had been 'continually engaged in a ding-dong struggle against the coalmasters and their trade union tools and allies ...', but nevertheless demanded the:

> complete elimination of the bad mistake of hurriedly calling for strike action without serious preparation and on issues which are in no way linked up to the grievances existing in the pit, etc. The blunders made at Blantyre in the latter part of 1929 in this connection should serve as an object lesson to every member of the Union. Here the mistake of mechanically bringing the men on strike on an issue entirely unrelated to the prevailing circumstances in the locality ... brought about a strike defeat that could have been avoided and did serious harm to Union organisation.[71]

Proudfoot was highly critical of the ultra-leftism of some Lanarkshire Communists. Upon being sent to Shotts in September 1930 he described the situation as 'one hell-of-a-mess', despite the 'many reassuring reports about big additions to the Party, YCL and UMS':

> The usual line of keeping us in the dark until everything has gone phut, then in a panic deciding that some 'Right-Winger', 'Social Democrat', 'Federalist', 'Pessimist' or 'Non-believer in the Radicalisation theory', etc, like myself is then pitchforked in to attempt in a few weeks to build up after clearing away the bloody mess created by the political purists who draft resolutions in the approved 10th plenum etc manner, without understanding what they are drafting or how to apply the decisions some of them are so glib at yapping about.[72]

He found that there were only five party members in Shotts: two unemployed men, two women and the UMS organiser. Because there were no party contacts in any of the seven working pits in the district, the UMS was 'exceptionally weak' with less than a hundred members, of whom half were unemployed. Fear of victimisation was widespread, even extending to the former UMS collector who refused to be seen entering the party rooms. In addition,

> There is also the bad heritage of the 'Strike', 'Strike', 'Strike' contin-

ually 'Strike' slogan of our Lanarkshire coms plus the impression created in Shotts by some of the romantic, stupid types of one-time Party members in this area. Party members seen with their pockets bulging with lit[erature], pamphlets, D[aily] W[orker] or leaflets are chaffed by the average worker about having 'another pocketful of bombs'.[73]

A strike took place at Broomfield Colliery, Stonehouse, a few weeks later which exemplified such tactics. A dismissed miner had struck the colliery manager during an interview for reinstatement and was arrested. The UMS checkweigher immediately called a strike, in contravention of UMS advice to first convene a meeting and send a deputation to the manager: 'The men, however, had been pulled out on strike without consultation, before they were aware of the facts in an issue which was not calculated to get support, with the result that they returned the next day.' Although the UMS Executive 'discountenance[d] such methods of conducting strikes' and the checkweigher was subsequently replaced, these ultra-left tactics help explain the diminution of the union's membership in Lanarkshire.[74]

In Fife, in contrast, there was significant support in December 1930 for UMS calls to wage a Scottish strike against general wage reductions and the introduction of the 'spreadover' system. The Coal Mines Act, 1930, stipulated a seven and half hour working day, although it permitted as an alternative an eight hour day on certain occasions so long as the total working hours spread over any fortnight did not exceed ninety. A meeting in Denbeath of 500 miners 'and a considerable number of women', was chaired by McArthur and addressed by Proudfoot; it elected a 'Central Strike Committee' of twenty-four strikers, four unemployed miners and five miners' wives. The audience of 800 marched to picket the large Wellesley colliery and were joined by a further 750 people. The attendance swelled each night until some 3,000 'congregated to see the sport'. Less than twenty of the colliery's 1,500 employees proceeded to work. The Central Strike Committee met daily while local strike committees were formed in every village. A motorcycle courier service was established with central Fife and telephone contact was maintained with the UMS head office in Glasgow. In Lumphinnans, pickets organised in 'eight companies, well disciplined and armed with pickshafts marched through the streets for three hours', following a rumour that strikebreakers would be imported from Lanarkshire.[75]

Although the NUSMW had also supported strike action, when it called off the dispute the UMS urged the miners to remain out. However, it was indicative of the union's restricted reach even in Fife that the Central Strike Committee was forced to recommend a return to work two days later to avoid isolation.[76] Convinced that 'a new wave of militancy [was] developing throughout the coalfields', a special national conference of the MMM in Sheffield a week later concluded that it was 'essential that the strike machinery built up during the recent conflict should remain in existence in order to conduct the local struggle and prepare for the bigger struggles under independent leadership'. As with the earlier campaign for 'committees of action', the tensions between building a union and exercising 'independent leadership' went unresolved, other than by formulaic exhortation: 'The local and district strike machinery should at the same time carry out systematic recruiting to the UMS.'[77] Lacking any clear purpose, the temporary strike organisation could not be sustained after the dispute ended. Proudfoot proudly claimed that the UMS emerged from the strike 'with added prestige in Fife but matters are different in the other areas ... In Lanarkshire many had not been out and others were solidly back by Saturday.' He went on to argue that a commission be established to investigate 'the entire Scottish situation during the strikes'.[78]

The Secretariat of the CPGB PB moved swiftly at a meeting on 23 December 1930 to replace Allan by Proudfoot as UMS General Secretary – a procedure examined in more detail below.[79] Upon his appointment, Proudfoot wrote that it was 'almost impossible to describe the chaos' at the union's Glasgow office.[80] A union commission was established and recommended a number of administrative reforms. It admitted that the union continued to function 'on a residential basis in nearly every branch. This form of organisation is basically wrong and does not permit ... the membership effectively [to be] used in a period of struggle.' A 'real campaign' to establish the organisation in the pits was demanded.[81] Such a move cut against the grain of union culture in Fife, where branches had traditionally been based on villages. Moreover, union reorganisation was hampered by the serious financial situation. Three organisers were paid off in January and this further increased the burden on those remaining.[82]

The UMS attempted to mobilise a further strike in March 1931 against a new wages agreement involving a temporary extension of the spreadover. Originally planned for 1 March, the CP national apparatus decided that the strike be postponed for two weeks, which Proudfoot considered a mistake. The strike was a dismal failure with support at only one or two collieries in East Fife and at the militant Peeweep Pit, Lumphinnans, with no stoppages outside the county. The strike highlighted tensions between Communist UMS members and other party functionaries and the difficulties of mounting industrial action to an externally formulated timetable. When Alex Moffat advised a mass meeting of the Peeweep miners to return to work, Comrade Cohen of the YCL urged the men to stay out, circumstances described by the CPGB PB as 'an extremely bad situation'. Moffat had displayed tactical commonsense and independence – insisting to the Scottish CP Secretariat that he would advise a resumption of work irrespective of its instructions – but was subsequently censured by the CP's Scottish District Party Committee (DPC) for action that was 'impermissible and demoralising'. Cohen, who had sought to implement the line of the DPC, was also condemned for his breach of party discipline in disobeying the decision of the Fife Local Committee.[83] The UMS Executive passed a self-critical resolution condemning its own tactics – 'committees elected by unrepresentative meetings of volunteers from the body of the hall can in no wise be regarded as genuine strike committees' – and admitting yet again 'the general failure to develop pit organisation and elementary forms of pit leadership'. It sought to launch a further campaign to address these failings, to enliven branch life and provide central classes for active members.[84]

There were renewed outbreaks of strikes in July against further proposed wage reductions. While the NUSMW continued negotiations with the owners, the UMS mobilised support beyond its own membership. The UMS claimed 15,000 were involved; the official figures estimated 10,500.[85] The strikes were clearly far from comprehensive. A detailed internal assessment by the UMS 'of the most important pits' indicated that four collieries in East Fife employing 3,800 men were partially on strike, while the Dubbie Pit with 600 workers was entirely out. West Fife was the most solid area, with six collieries struck, a further four partially. In Lanarkshire, only three Blantyre mines supported the strike. However, the participation of Annbank Colliery in Ayrshire along with four mines in Midlothian, including some men from Newbattle Colliery, Newtongrange, indicated that the UMS had caught a growing mood of militancy.[86] The agreement finally negotiated by the NUSMW – characterised by the UMS as a further 'betrayal' by the 'old gang' – involved only a four penny reduction on the minimum shift rate of 8s 4d, compared with the owners' original demand of 1s 4d. With some justification, the UMS claimed that the owners had been 'compelled to modify their wage-cut demands because of the solid strike stand made by Fife, Lothian, Burnbank and Blantyre miners ...'.[87] No sooner had work resumed than a fresh wave of strikes erupted a week later as the effects of the agreement became apparent. The number of strikers was again disputed, the official estimate being 9,000 while the CP claimed more than 20,000. Certainly the strikes had wider geographical support, Lanarkshire, Stirlingshire and West Lothian being more severely affected than the previous month. In the normally anti-Communist village of Larkhall, it was claimed that an 'incensed meeting' refused to listen to Small. The strikes dragged on in ragged fashion for a further three weeks as the county union officials urged a resumption of work.[88]

Despite this limited success, Proudfoot resigned his post and withdrew from all party activity in August.[89] Exhausted by his strenuous organising duties and recurrent bouts of malaria contracted during the First World War, Proudfoot found 'the almost unbelievable mess the UMS was in due to the previous maladministration' too much to bear. A further factor was what he regarded as the 'sabotage by leading Party UMS coms', and cited the example of Jimmy Stewart who had resigned as a UMS organiser in July complaining that he had received no wages for two weeks and had been forced to borrow money. It was symptomatic of Stewart's own disillusionment with the union that he concluded his letter of resignation with the invitation to use it 'from the PB up to Stalin if you like'. At the time of its receipt, Proudfoot had not received wages for three weeks and for the eight weeks prior to his decision to resign had received only £9.[90]

Proudfoot's successor was Abe Moffat, whose period of leadership of the UMS was notable for three developments. The first was the consolidation of the union's strength in Fife. This refers not only to the increasing percentage of membership concentrated in the coalfield, but also its serious contention with the FCKMU for leadership of the miners in key areas. In early May 1932, the union led a successful two-week strike of 5,000 miners employed by the Fife Coal Company in central Fife, at Bowhill, Lumphinnans and Kelty, against proposed reductions. At Lochore, members of the FCKMU joined the strike against Adamson's advice. However, Adamson issued circulars 'pointing out the futility of the men's conduct, as no negotiations for settlement would be entertained by the Coy. so long as the men remained out'. The dispute was eventually called off by the UMS 'Central Strike Committee' due to the miners 'being unable to extend the strike as a consequence of the strikebreaking work of the MFGB officials supported by the whole capitalist press ...', to allow negotiations. Nevertheless, the UMS made significant gains, securing a guarantee of no victimisation and, unusually, a written undertaking from the Fife Coal Company to negotiate at the affected collieries.[91] It was symptomatic of this refocusing of Communist energies towards more conventional union activity that Moffat informed the CC in 1933 that: 'In many cases I find our comrades do not know the first thing about workmen's compensation, conditions of employment, etc. To be able to talk on broad political issues, of course, is necessary, but it is an intimate knowledge of these other vital questions which will gain them the confidence of the workers ...'.[92]

The second, related development was an increased commitment to safety questions through the election of workmen's inspectors. Miners had a statutory entitlement under section 16 of the Coal Mines Act, 1911, to appoint 'any two persons' who had been 'practical working miners' with not less than five years experience of underground work, to carry out inspections of the workings at least every month. Managers were required to offer these inspectors 'every facility'. Although these provisions had been utilised by the LMU until the First World War, they had fallen into disuse during the 1920s.[93] In 1928, the Mines' Inspector for Scotland reported that only four reports had been received from workmen's inspectors during the year and 'regretted that workmen do not take more advantage of the facilities offered by section 16'.[94]

The challenge was soon taken up by the UMS. Abe and Alex Moffat, after being removed as checkweighers at the 'Peeweep' pit, successfully mounted a campaign to be elected workmen's inspectors. One union activist urged the extension of this strategy in November 1930 but the suggestion was not immediately followed: in 1932 the Mines' Inspector reported that inspections had only been carried out at four mines in Fife.[95] However, that year marked the beginning of a concerted campaign by the UMS to secure the election of its leading activists. At Bowhill, two UMS candidates, Jimmy Stewart and the 23 year old John Sutherland, were elected by a combined 1300 votes to 780. In 1933, there were ballots for inspectors at eight mines – six in Fife, Priory (Bothwell Castle, nos 3 and 4) in Lanarkshire and the Klondyke, Midlothian. The UMS candidates were elected at five pits in Fife, being narrowly defeated at the sixth amidst allegations of company intimidation, and the Klondyke; at the Priory, one UMS inspector was voted in alongside an LMU candidate. In addition, UMS inspectors were appointed without opposition at the large Michael Colliery in East Wemyss.[96]

These victories were of considerable significance in extending UMS influence beyond its membership. A total of 6,153 votes were cast for the UMS candidates, against 4,142 for their 'reformist' opponents. In 1934, UMS inspectors were successful in elections at 10 out of 12 pits, gaining 8,173 votes against 5,183 for their opponents.[97] While those voting were still a small fraction of the miners in Scotland, the ballots were indicative of the union's ability to extend its reach by addressing the real problems of safety associated with mechanisation and speed up. They also established the reputation of leading UMS activists as authoritative and competent champions of the miners. This standing was enhanced by management attempts at victimisation. At the Klondyke, for example, the Niddrie and Benhar Coal Company attempted to sack those connected with the campaign for workmen's inspectors and evict one of them from his company house. The UMS sent organisers to the district and a strike succeeded, albeit temporarily, in forcing the company to withdraw the threat.[98]

Some UMS leaders were inspectors at more than one pit: for example, Abe Moffat and Stewart were elected at both the Aitken Pit, Kelty, and Lumphinnans No. 1 in 1933. This not only raised their profile among the miners, but also developed their proficiency as inspectors. They carried out their duties rigorously. The Inspector of Mines reported 58 inspections lasting 214 days at 21 collieries in 1933; in 1934, this increased to 150 inspections occupying 376 days at 33 collieries. Although in the latter year he suggested the newly found 'great interest' in inspections was 'for reasons not altogether confined to safety', he paid tribute to some inspectors' reports which 'make them models well-worth copying by most colliery firemen whose daily reports are, as a rule, characterised by extreme terseness'. Thousands of copies of those by UMS inspectors were circulated among the miners.[99]

The final distinguishing feature of Moffat's leadership was the search for 'unity' in the Scots coalfields. In April 1933, the UMS made the first of a series of approaches to the NUSMW for joint action against fascism and against the current national wages agreement.[100] In January 1934, a further initiative suggested a common campaign against the agreement and excessive overtime, as well as for the appointment of workmen's inspectors at every pit.[101] By May, a total of five approaches had been made: all had been rejected without the courtesy of a reply.[102] In November, the UMS Executive agreed to recommend a joint conference with the NUSMW to consider wages, safety issues 'and the establishment of one union for the Scottish miners'.[103] In May 1935, the UMS issued a further unity appeal proposing a ballot vote of all Scottish miners under the supervision of the MFGB on the question of one Scottish union, an approach which was rejected by the NUSMW conference.[104] In October and November, the union again wrote to the NUSMW and MFGB with unity proposals which would involve 'the whole of our branches and members being taken over on the basis of full trade union rights and membership ... We don't even suggest the UMS officials be taken over as officials, but merely as rank and file members on the same basis of any other member.' A further letter in December from the UMS Executive asked again for its members to be admitted to the county unions. Receiving no response, a UMS delegate conference at the end of the month decided to 'take the most decisive step for achieving unity' and liquidate the union.[105]

While such repeated attempts to merge with their bitter rivals might convey a sense of mounting desperation from a UMS increasingly isolated from the rest of the Scottish coalfields in its Fife redoubt, the picture was considerably more complex. In order to fully understand it, we must return our attention towards the development of Communist policy.

The UMS, the CPGB and the Comintern

As the preceding chapter demonstrated, the leadership of the CPGB had taken a close interest in developments in the Scots coalfields since the mid-1920s. After the formation of the UMS, scrutiny of the union by the party and Comintern became even more intense and prescriptive. The memoirs of Margaret McCarthy, a young British Communist attached to the Anglo-American Section of the RILU, or 'Profintern', in 1931, provide some insight into the vigilance with which the Comintern (of which the RILU was essentially a satellite organisation) observed the UMS.[106] Her section prepared detailed evaluation reports on specific industries which normally concluded with 'propositions for action by the Profintern to guide the Communists in the industry concerned ...'. A 'typical example' of the work of her section concerned the 'Scottish Mineworkers' Union' which was, she claimed, 'entirely in the hands of the Party and was controlled from our Anglo-American Section' in Moscow:

> The detailed work was in the hands of the leading member of our section, a Polish-Jewish woman named Barishnik. Fritz Emmereich was officially head of the department, but in actual fact Barishnik led it, rather in the manner in which a senior permanent Civil Servant guides a minister. Barishnik was a beautiful, languorous, green-eyed woman of about forty-five. She was extremely clever, a brilliant linguist and of a wide western culture ... Barishnik was certainly the motivating spirit of our department and consequently responsible for the guidance of that most important sphere of Communist influence in the industrial life of Britain, the Scottish Mineworkers' Union.[107]

McCarthy's account, published during the Cold War, must be treated with caution: she left the CP, disillusioned by her sojourn in Moscow, and subsequently worked for the TUC. Her suggestion that this svelte cosmopolitan apparatchik could, from Moscow, direct events in Buckhaven and Blantyre seems like the confection of a John Le Carre novel. Yet an examination of the intricate workings of the Communist chain of command suggest that it contained a significant element of truth.

Soon after the general election in May 1929, the PB held a meeting with 'Comrade Bennett', the pseudonym of David Petrovsky, then Comintern representative in Britain, 'on the question of the future work of the Party'. Among the points decided, was a change in the organiser of the Fife Sub-District.[108] In July, Arthur Horner reported to the ECCI Political Secretariat (PS) that:

> Comrade Stewart has been ordered to Scotland to take charge of the

mining situation which is at a difficult stage. There we have undertaken the terrific task of building a new miners' union for the first
time in Britain; and we have decided to send a mature political
leader, Cde Stewart, who belongs to Scotland to direct this struggle
on behalf of the Central Committee.

Bob Stewart was a member of the party's PB and a former CPGB
representative to the Comintern who had been elected a candidate
member of the ECCI in 1924. His appointment to this task was
indicative of its importance to the party and no doubt was also
intended to reassure the Comintern that, after what were seen to be
unnecessary delays in the formation of the UMS, the union was
receiving the careful attention of the CPGB.

The CC elected at the Eleventh Congress in December 1929 also
contained members who were highly familiar with the Scottish coalfields. William Gallacher, also a member of the PB, had contested
the West Fife constituency at the 1929 general election and was well
known by political activists there. William Joss, the CP Scottish
Organiser was a member of the CC, as was George Allison, a miner
originally from Bowhill but who represented the Lothians on the
UMS Executive before he became an organiser for the MM. Allison
played a major role during the UMS strikes in December 1930 and
July 1931.[109] Jim Shields, a former YCL activist was a CC member
who had been given overall responsibility by the party Secretariat
for 'UMS work in Scotland' in December 1929. Allan was a
member of the CC from 1927 until 1935, as was Abe Moffat, then
a Fife UMS organiser, from December 1929.[110]

This was a far from coherent grouping. There was personal
antagonism between Allan and Moffat. When Moffat criticised
Allan for his conduct of the UMS at a meeting of the CC with a
Comintern emissary present, Allan angrily protested 'that Moffat
had not said these things in Scotland'. Leaving aside personal ambi-
tion, their antipathy may also have been rooted in the traditional
suspicion between Lanarkshire and Fife miners, as well as the
increasing domination of the UMS by Fife. In April 1930, Pollitt
revealed that Allan had informed him 'that the Fife miners are
saying that they are strong enough to stand on their own'.[111] In
June, the PB was informed of 'a very serious situation' in the UMS
due to 'a very serious difference between the leading comrades in
Fife, and leading comrades in other parts of the coalfield'.
Gallacher was despatched north to convene a fraction meeting of

CP members in the union to try and resolve the difficulties.[112] The following month, the PB approved a document to be discussed at the party's Scottish District Congress to 'intensify' the campaign to build the UMS. Its prescriptions included the need to place the UMS on a 'self-supporting basis' by campaigning for 'voluntary work in the union'; the need for party fraction meetings 'from top to bottom', as well as 'the ruthless exposure of the tendency to hide the face of the party'; and 'the strong combattal ... particularly [by] the Fife organisers of the secessionist tendencies in Fifeshire'.[113]

In addition, the Comintern targeted some organisational assistance to the UMS. In April 1930, the ECCI PS informed the CPGB Secretariat that the party required 'a rapid overcoming of its organisational weakness and a vigorous re-organisation'. Towards this end, the PS had organised 'four organisational instructional groups' among the British students graduating from the Comintern's 'secret' International Lenin School (ILS) in Moscow:

> The South Wales and Scotland groups will specialise on questions of Party activity and leadership of the mass struggle in the mining areas ... All groups are receiving suitable practical preparation for this purpose. The Polit-Secretariat considers the work of these groups of extra-ordinary importance in overcoming the organisational weakness of the CPGB.[114]

One of these students, Peter Kerrigan, was soon to replace the seriously-ill Joss as the CP's Scottish District Organiser, following reports that he was 'doing very well with the assistance of the group of Lenin students there'. Alex Moffat, who became Vice-President of the UMS, also attended the ILS in 1930.[115]

The 'mining situation' generally, and the position of the UMS, attracted a considerable amount of discussion at meetings of the PB and CC during 1930. The strategic relationship of the UMS to the other British mining unions was posed specifically by the expulsion of the Communist-dominated Mardy lodge from the South Wales Miners' Federation (SWMF) for supporting Horner as a CP candidate in the 1929 general election.[116] In March 1930, Gallacher introduced a thesis on the mining situation to the PB. He questioned why miners were not joining the CP and suggested this was due to a lack of an 'independent mining policy', of which the isolation of Mardy was merely a symptom. 'All our forces must be directed towards the UMS as the vanguard of the miners' revolutionary struggle ... The question must be faced. Is the UMS to be brought into the forefront of the fight of the miners?' Idris Cox, the South Wales District Organiser, supported Gallacher and spelled out the implications of his thesis: 'the UMS should be brought to the forefront of the fight for the national revolutionary miners' union'. Robin Page Arnot, then an alternate member of the ECCI Presidium, also supported Gallacher, arguing that the UMS was the 'beginning of the united mineworkers of Britain'. The meeting was attended by a RILU representative, 'Comrade Mills', whose circumlocutions supported the perspective of eventually building a new union – 'We see the new union here superseding the MFGB, and we say in the meantime we consolidate on a national basis in the Minority Movement.' When Gallacher interrupted him: 'Do you keep secret the fact of the new union?', Mills replied, 'Of course. How do you build new unions, by shouting about it?' Although the Minority Movement had published a detailed constitution for a 'British Mineworkers' Union' the previous year, drawn up by Horner and Nat Watkins, Secretary of the MMM, this was clearly intended as a merger of the existing unions affiliated to the MFGB. The policy of establishing a new 'revolutionary' British miners' union was a radical departure and other CC members were sceptical. Accordingly, Pollitt and Gallacher were instructed to draw up a new document.[117]

At the PB the following week, which 'Mills' also attended, Pollitt introduced a new resolution which raised the slogan of 'the United Mineworkers of Great Britain'. However, it emphasised 'that we see the perspective of the United Mineworkers' Union, and to this all organisation and agitation is directed, but it must be achieved out of actual struggle ...'. Discussion centred less on the validity of the perspective than on whether it was premature to raise it at that stage.[118] At the next CC, Pollitt addressed this point:

> We don't raise sharply the question of new unions tomorrow or even a month or two from now. New unions cannot come artificially. New unions artificially set up are no use to our Party. Therefore we give this perspective of a single miners' union not as a task for tomorrow but as a task for our comrades ... to create in a healthy way, out of the class struggle itself ...

This perspective appeared to have the imprimatur of Moscow. Watkins reported to the CC that the RILU had discussed 'the programme' and the Mardy situation. It was felt that the present line of fighting for the lodge's re-admission to the SWMF was 'incorrect' and that 'the position should be considered in the light of the creation of a new section of a new union in South Wales'. He added that after viewing the draft document, the Anglo-American Section of the RILU had submitted it to the Anglo-American Secretariat of the Comintern: 'we are of the opinion that the present line is not helpful to the Party ... We cannot say that the MFGB is a Social-Fascist organisation and then ask militant lodges to get the re-instatement of the Mardy lodge.'

Scepticism remained among other members of the PB and CC, including J.T. Murphy, who argued that to launch a new union in South Wales without a mass basis was 'putting the cart before the horse'. Allison asked: 'What have we in South Wales at the present time? Absolutely nothing! ... How many pit committees has the Minority Movement at the present time in South Wales? If we cannot form a pit committee in South Wales how can we form a new union?' For his part, Pollitt was anxious to avoid giving 'South Wales the perspective of a district union, we must give them the perspective of the united mineworkers of Britain, through their identification with the Minority Movement'. Despite these divisions, the resolution was referred back to the PB for final revision and publication.[119]

The following month the ECCI PS, having perused the mining resolution, sent a letter to the CPGB CC, commending 'the self-critical attitude towards the past opportunist mistakes of the Party in this sphere of activity'. Nevertheless, the slogan of a United Mineworkers' Union of Great Britain was regarded as 'a serious mistake and premature ...'. The PS 'requested' that the slogan be withdrawn and that the MM and UMS 'must organise a campaign for building up committees of action, accompanied by a strengthening of our work in the reformist unions, preparing the mobilisation of the organised and unorganised workers under Party leadership'. The approved, if hardly agitational, slogan to be used in this campaign was 'Down with the wage cutting arbitration board of the Labour government'.[120] The episode highlighted both the tensions between the more leftist leadership of the RILU under Losovsky and the growing caution of the Comintern against 'left sectarianism' – and the determining force of the latter – as well as the difficulties faced by the CPGB leadership in interpreting and applying the shifting nuances of Moscow policy.[121]

The PB was informed of the Comintern letter and the need to change the mining resolution by Allison, who had also received a letter from the Anglo-American Section of RILU, 'which included two points indicating confusion regarding the role of the UMS. Wires are being sent with a view to getting this matter cleared up.'[122] A revised resolution was brought before the CC in July but a minority, despite the Comintern's intervention, wished to pursue the policy of a revolutionary British miners' union with the UMS as its core. Gallacher insisted that 'we have got to accept the implications of the UMS ... we cannot avoid the question of new unions ...'. Allan, a previous opponent of the SLP's dual unionism and any premature establishment of the UMS, now argued in a way which reflected the union's weakness rather than his previous convictions: 'If the UMS exists seriously for us, then we must put the question of setting up its counterparts in other districts of the coalfields ... and so counter the feeling of isolation of the UMS.' The meeting was attended by a Comintern representative, 'Comrade Butler', who argued that the slogan of 'one miners' union' would be 'a substitute for the fight'. The task of the UMS was to 'show to the workers that it is actually and objectively guaranteeing the fight. It should attempt to get a strike in the whole of Scotland, from Scotland to other areas ...'. He went on to suggest that the slogan would provide ammunition to the 'bureaucrats' and allow them to say '... you are here to form One Big Union. You are here to disrupt this organisation.' The ECCI did 'not say that the perspective is wrong, but that it cannot be put forward at the present time'. The majority of the CC voted to accept the Comintern line.[123]

Nevertheless, at the English Commission of the Comintern's Anglo-American Secretariat the following month, both Gallacher and Pollitt (who had not been present at the CC) defended the perspective of one British miners' union. While Pollitt pointed out that no member of the CPGB leadership had been 'a more consistent opponent at [sic] the epidemic of new unionism' than himself, he emphasised the perspective was not of an immediate new union and stood firmly with Gallacher in his opposition to the Comintern line.

The chairman of the commission was William Weinstone, the Lithuanian-born representative of the CPUSA to the ECCI. He displayed considerable knowledge of the workings (and failings) of the UMS:

the situation is that in regard to the structure of the organisation, as some of the comrades have pointed out, our union is not a class union, not organised sufficiently upon the new forms indicated by the RILU, that the cadres are mainly old cadres, many branches have come over wholesale into our union, that we have been [un]able to reorganise them, that there are only 88 members of the Party that are miners in this organisation and that the fractions have not been functioning properly and they are making an attempt now to organise our fractions.

He was critical of the conduct of the strikes at Shotts, which he analysed in some detail, and the situation in Blantyre where 'everytime the UMS appeared there was a struggle, in consequence we have no local there ...'.

Weinstone went on to refer sarcastically to 'the wisdom that Comrade Pollitt gave us ... that a split exists among the miners in Great Britain ... What is this split? Our union has 1,000 members, the Miners' Federation of Great Britain has over 400,000 ...'. While he accepted that it would be impossible to capture the apparatus of the MFGB, and that 'we shall be compelled to split the organisation', that moment had not yet arrived: 'you have not yet discredited the officials of the MFGB ... you have not yet got the workers organised for struggle ...'. The role which the UMS was to play in this was:

> to make the Party the leadership of the economic struggles, to identify our union in Scotland with the miners. That is the first proposition to overcome such a situation as the Shotts strike and Blantyre, and really day in and day out not overnight to show the miners of Scotland and the miners throughout the country that they are fighting, to popularise its work so that the workers in the rest of the country will realise that if they had a leadership as the UMS they could solve their problems.[124]

This meant that the UMS was to play the role of revolutionary exemplar rather than the vanguard of the United Mineworkers of Great Britain.[125] While the perspective of a red miners' union for Britain was not formally abandoned, in his summing up, Weinstone noted 'the problem of one miners' union ... that by publishing its programme that we will facilitate the bureaucrats in isolating our people ...' .

Weinstone had also recommended that:

... the coming convention of the UMS, which is set for the end of September, I think we must postpone this convention, I think this convention should be a deciding convention to effect a change within, to get new cadres, to introduce the spirit of self criticism, to find out what these tasks are and to commence a recruiting campaign ...

That this edict concerning the body with nominally 'supreme authority' in the UMS was accepted, apparently without question, is perhaps the more remarkable given the past history of delayed conferences in the union's formation. Three weeks later, the CPGB Secretariat reported 'serious weakness in preparatory work' for the UMS conference to the PB, and it was agreed that the conference be postponed until October.[126]

This drawn out debate on the mining situation was indicative of the real mechanisms of Comintern control over the CPGB and UMS. In concluding his report to the CC on his somewhat humiliating experience before the English Commission, Pollitt warned these senior cadres: 'One last word, no beating the breast when you return to the Districts saying that the Party has been put right by Moscow', adding: 'The decisions arrived at have come out of the work of the Party itself.'[127] If we assume he was not being disingenuous, this remark provides a telling insight into the psychology of Stalinist functionaries.

The debate also pointed to the direction of Comintern policy towards the reformist unions. At the Fifth RILU Conference in August 1930, the MM was criticised for its 'isolation from the masses', but there was a shift in the tenor of the complaints. Not only were its well known 'right opportunist errors' such as 'trade union legalism' rehearsed again, there was also condemnation of its 'left sectarian errors', such as calling ill-prepared strikes. It was instructed 'to formulate a broad united front programme of action' in the form of a campaign for a 'Workers' Charter', to strengthen its work in reformist unions, as well as support the British red unions.[128] When Pollitt reported to the CC in September, he similarly argued: 'What we have to do is to make a sharp turn in another direction, that is, our trade union work ... We have to take a decisive turn to bring our comrades back into the trade unions.' The same meeting heard a report from Allison on the RILU conference which reflected this new turn and how it would apply to the UMS:

Therefore in Scotland we recruit the unorganised into the UMS. But as far as the reformist members are concerned, we get them round a pit committee and then when we are operating a united front tactic with a section of the reformist workers we don't recruit them individually into the red union out of the reformist union where we have a united front in operation with them. We are very careful how we decrease our strength in the reformist organisation. The big sphere of activity for the UMS so far as recruitment of members is concerned is the unorganised workers.[129]

The theme of the isolation of CP militants from members of the reformist unions was reinforced at the end of the month in a lengthy and critical resolution from the ECCI PS to the CPGB:

the independent leadership of economic struggles was very often taken to mean the abandonment of persistent organised work in the reformist unions (the practical absence of MM groups and Party fractions in the reformist trade unions, attempts at a premature formation of a Red Miners' Union ...) ... the MM must make a real turn towards systematic work in the reformist trade unions and must form a mass revolutionary opposition inside and outside the reformist trade unions ... The MM must try to win elected positions in the local unions, must put forward MM candidates for various posts in the trade unions ...[130]

By the autumn of 1930, the Comintern's policy had therefore created new parameters for CP members in the Scottish coalfields. Recruitment to the UMS was to be directed at non-unionised miners while the reformist county unions were once again seen as legitimate spheres of Communist activity.

Before this new strategy could be implemented, however, there were real problems within the UMS to be addressed, which had their roots in the earlier, ultra-leftist phase of the 'third period'. In October, the PB was informed by its secretariat of 'a very serious report' concerning the UMS which precisely reproduced Weinstone's concerns: 'the constant application of the "strike now" slogan had seriously undermined the influence of the union in areas where it had previously had a good hold, there was no life in the union and general opposition to the leadership in the central office'. Pollitt was appointed by the PB as the fraternal delegate from the MM to the UMS conference in an attempt 'to clear up the confusion', and it was recommended that Proudfoot should become the union's President in place of Alex Kirk of West Lothian, where the union had little base.[131] Illustrating the swiftness with which democratic centralism could on occasion operate, three days later the UMS Executive unanimously agreed to endorse to the Annual Conference (which was being held the following day) the recommendation of its Sub-Executive that Proudfoot should act as President to allow Kirk to concentrate on organising in the Lothians.[132]

Such changes were deemed insufficient, however. Just before Christmas, the PB concluded that there should be 'a decisive change in the leadership of the union', and that Allan be replaced by Proudfoot as General Secretary. Shields, who was described as 'the representative of the PB on the UMS', but who had been 'entirely subordinated to Allan and unable to play a decisive part', was also to be removed. It had been proposed to Allan 'that he should go to Moscow as MM representative for a period. At first he regarded this as political banishment, but after a careful discussion he accepted the proposals, and admitted that he had not produced the required results.' Pollitt was despatched to a fraction meeting of party members to implement these decisions. The changes may at least in part have been prompted by criticism from Moscow of the UMS calling off the strikes earlier that month, although the tactic was supported by the PB; the antagonism towards Allan by Fife Communists and the poor support for the strikes in Lanarkshire were more likely the predominant factors.[133] By the end of December, a commission consisting of Pollitt, Campbell, Allan, Proudfoot and Shields had reported to a meeting of UMS party cadres, analysing the role of the union in the strikes. Among their various recommendations was that Proudfoot should replace Allan.[134] At the UMS Executive on 10 January 1931, Allan dutifully resigned his position and moved Proudfoot as his successor. His proposal was unanimously supported and recommended to the branches for endorsement.[135]

The subsequent development of UMS strategy can be seen as conforming to the direction of Comintern policy. Thus the moves by the UMS to invigorate its organisation in April 1931 reflected the instruction of the RILU Executive to the MM that it must assist the union 'to reorganise itself on the basis of the pits and to carry through the necessary changes in order to develop the UMS into a mass organisation, concentrating in its methods above all upon winning the unorganised workers'.[136] However, the transmission of Moscow instructions did not always proceed smoothly. A RILU 'Comrade' arrived unexpectedly at a UMS conference at Falkirk in early July 1932 and insisted on changes being made to the main resolution. According to Gallacher:

> The line which Comrade was putting forward was contrary to that of the PB on the mining situation. Comrade had demanded to be allowed to make criticism before Conference, but Gallacher and others opposed this. The comrade also complained that translator did not understand Marxist-Leninist line and could not translate. All these events had had a bad effect on Conference, and his presence had only hindered the Conference.[137]

By the Twelfth Plenum of the ECCI in August 1932, when considering the alternative 'right' and 'left' dangers confronting the CPGB, the emphasis had moved decisively towards avoidance of the latter. One of the main causes of the 'insufficient mobilisation of the masses' was held to be 'the impermissibly weak revolutionary work carried on *inside the reformist trade unions*' [emphasis in original]. A 'ruthless struggle' was demanded against 'leftist sectarian elements' who had given up work in such unions.[138] This Comintern line was swiftly followed by leading sections within the CPGB, and in particular in the UMS. In October, following an aggregate meeting of CP miners, Ed Laughlin of Blantyre wrote self-critically in the *Daily Worker*, reflecting on the ultra-leftism of the early UMS: 'making wild calls for action ... In the process of our "Left" shouting we stigmatised all and sundry who were members of the reformist unions as people whom we could not associate with.' He went on to advocate building 'a strong pit unity committee, conducting agitation in the pit, among the Reformist Union members'.[139] Two months later, Abe Moffat also published an article prior to the UMS Fourth Annual Conference. In reviewing UMS strike activity in the previous two years, he acknowledged that 'there can be no united front of the Scottish miners without hard and consistent work in the ranks of the old county unions in Scotland'.[140] Moffat's address to the conference had a valedictory undertone, reviewing the union's achievements since its formation. He concluded on the need to 'win the unorganised miners' and 'build a united front of the miners in the reformist unions'.[141]

Faced with the growing threat of fascism after Hitler's accession to power in 1933, the Comintern increasingly urged its constituent parties to adopt such 'united front' policies. Accordingly, there were repeated attempts by the UMS to seek an accommodation with the NUSMW. It is significant that during discussions between the CP and ILP leaderships in 1933, both sides recognised the need for unity in Scotland and the CP did not attempt to get ILP support for the UMS. Rather, Gallacher advised: 'ILPers in Lanarkshire, when the question comes up, may feel that they can be advised to join the reformist union, but on the line of conducting a fight for unity in action', while Pollitt urged that 'our main drive, both in the ILP and the Party should be that of getting united action between the two unions'. Such moves were assisted by the later instruction of the ILP that all its members in the Scottish coalfields should 'work vigorously to end the present position and establish one union'.[142] At the Thirteenth Congress of the CPGB in February 1935, Pollitt praised the UMS for advocating 'the fusion of all unions in Scotland into one union for all Scottish mine workers'.[143] The following month, a coded radio message to the CPGB from Moscow drew attention to a recent approach by the RILU to the non-Communist, Amsterdam trade union international on the need to re-establish trade union unity: 'We attach extraordinary great importance to this ... Profintern letter must be discussed in all meetings of Party organisations and revolutionary trade unions ...'.[144] In May 1935, the UMS Executive issued new unity proposals to the NUSMW. At the Seventh Comintern Congress in 1935, the final break with the revolutionary goals of the third period and the adoption of the policy of the 'popular front against Fascism and war in all capitalist countries' were formalised.[145]

The logical conclusion of this move towards the popular front was the liquidation of the UMS, which increasingly resembled the baggage of a bygone, revolutionary phase. The PB, in September 1935, approved the decision of the UMS 'to immediately propose to the Scottish Reformist Unions and the MFGB the acceptance into the Scottish unions of the branches of the UMS ...'. The absence of any positive response by the NUSMW led in December to the PB accepting the 'proposals of Comrade Pollitt and Moffat regarding the UMS and its entry into the Reformist Miners' organisations in Scotland'.[146] At the next CC, Pollitt was enthusiastic about the initiative which he ascribed to Moffat:

As a result of this the split in the Scottish coalfields has gone. It means we shall soon have an early perspective of one Miners' union for Scotland. It means that comrades like Abe Moffat with influence in Fifeshire will, in my opinion, in the course of six months or so be playing a leading role in the MFGB ...[147]

While Pollitt was over-optimistic in his time-scale, his prognosis was essentially correct.

The county unions and the NUSMW

If the UMS deserves attention on account of its novelty and limited influence, the county unions affiliated to the NUSMW continued to function in much the same way as before, subject to the constraints of a diminished membership.[148] UMS claims that these unions had practically gone out of existence by 1929 were exaggerated. The numbers on which they affiliated to the NUSMW are given in Table 7.4. Unions may have inflated or deflated their affiliated membership to increase representation on the Executive or reduce affiliation fees. It is not suggested that these are accurate figures based on the actual, dues-paying membership as they are too obviously round and in some cases, such as the MELMA, unchanging. On the basis of dues income, Sime calculates that the FCKMU membership was 4,240 in 1930 and 6,303 in 1934 yet it affiliated to the NUSMW on the basis of 5,000 in both years.[149] The affiliation figures can therefore only be regarded as a very approximate indicator of membership trends.

Declining membership led the NUSMW to reduce the number of full-time agents from nineteen to fourteen in 1929. Despite such economies the expenditure on agents' wages and expenses, together with the cost of Executive meetings and delegations, increased from 56 per cent of NUSMW dues income in the period 1925–9 to 67 per cent in 1931.[150] Lanarkshire faced the most dramatic reduction in membership, reducing its NUSMW affiliation by almost two-thirds between 1929 and 1932. The scale of this decline necessitated economies in the LMU: the size of the Executive was reduced from twelve to eight, the General Secretary's salary halved to £25 and the office cleaner's wage cut by 7s 6d per week. As in the UMS, financial stringency hindered attempts to increase membership. Temporary agents could only be employed on a monthly basis to

Table 7.4 Affiliated memberships of the constituent county unions of the National Union of Scottish Mine Workers, 1929–38, expressed as a percentage of the total number employed.

	Lanark	Fife	Ayr	Stirling	West Lothian	Mid and East Lothian	NUSMW
1929	16,100	5,000	9,500	2,500	2,000	7,500	42,600
	42.4	21.1	83.6	35.4	24.7	54.0	41.1
1930	13,100	5,000	8,500	2,000	1,000	7,500	37,100
	36.2	20.6	78.9	28.6	12.6	52.6	37.0
1932	6,000	5,000	6,000	2,500	1,000	7,500	28,000
	21.8	24.8	58.1	39.7	14.3	58.2	32.8
1934	7,000	5,000	6,000	2,500	1,000	7,500	29,000
	25.1	23.7	59.1	42.1	13.6	58.3	33.6
1936	10,750	11,000	7,000	3,000	2,000	7,500	41,250
	37.4	48.4	59.5	52.8	25.2	57.7	45.9
1938	17,000	14,000	7,000	3,500	2,000	7,500	51,000
	55.9	60.1	56.2	62.3	24.4	62.4	54.5

Sources: Calculated from P. Long, 'The economic and social history of the Scottish coal industry, 1925–39, with particular reference to industrial relations', unpublished PhD thesis, University of Strathclyde, 1978, Tables 27, 28 and 31.

conduct recruitment campaigns and, despite their efforts, it was reported to the Council that:

> Additional members were being enrolled from week to week, but the unfortunate coincidence was that the monthly income did not reveal this increase. This was due to the fact that collieries and sections of collieries were being closed more rapidly than members were coming in. Another factor militating against the consolidation of the mineworkers was that contracting was on the increase, and most of the men employed thuswise were not paid at the colliery.[151]

In 1933, organisation in the LMU was reported as 'poor' at 21 branches, 'fair' at 17, and 'good' at only 15.[152]

Such straitened financial circumstances severely limited the organisational capacity of the NUSMW and its affiliates, and encouraged the pacific proclivities of union leaders who were reluctant to incur expenditure on official disputes. During the strikes in August 1931, the LMU advised a return to work, declaring that 'everyone regretted that they had to suffer a reduction in wages, but they had to remember what the alternative would have meant' – presumably a prolonged strike. That such sentiments had significant resonance within a sorely demoralised workforce was demonstrated by a membership ballot of 19,150 in favour of acceptance of the new agreement with 5,757 against.[153] Nevertheless, the strikes of that month indicated that the tide was slowly turning in support of a reawakened militancy and thereafter the incidence of industrial conflict accelerated, creating further problems for NUSMW affiliates. A special meeting of the FCKMU discussed recruitment and the difficulties facing the industry, and claimed that 'the trouble created by the repeated stoppages engineered by the Communists in past months made it extremely difficult for organising work to be successfully carried on in the county'.[154] In 1934, the NUSMW President complained of 'a spirit of anarchy ... none of us seeks to curb the natural desire of our members to resist and even fight against injustice and tyranny but we cannot and should not ignore the [negotiating] machinery set up ...'.[155]

This increase in the rate of strikes accompanied an upturn in union membership and there was renewed pressure for democratic reform within the county unions, with growing support for more militant policies. In 1932, the MFGB Conference had endorsed the desirability of a single Scottish affiliate and this call was echoed by militant branches of the LMU the following year. The Ponfeigh branch urged that the union withdraw from the NUSMW if a scheme for 'one union for the Scottish miners' was not swiftly brought into operation. The motion was lost by 33 votes to 2, but there were similar resolutions from the Kingshill and Cadzow branches later in the year. The Council also refused to receive a deputation from a 'Miners' Unity Committee'. In February 1934, the Dixon's, Blantyre, branch narrowly failed to win support for a unilateral reduction in the 'working policy' from six days per week to eleven days per fortnight. The following year, a resolution from the Gateside (Cambuslang) and Priory branches seeking to alter the union's rules to prevent union agents holding official positions – 'the Officials were their own bosses', stated the mover – was rejected by 30 votes to 12 at a special meeting of the LMU Council.[156]

Yet such moves were straws in the wind and the NUSMW shifted slowly in favour of one Scottish union, at least in principle, in the following years.[157] It is likely that these stirrings at the grassroots reflected the CP's re-orientation towards the county unions and there had been movement of some of its cadres back into these bodies. In 1932, Gallacher reported to the PB that in Lanarkshire the party was 'ensuring continued work in the old union branches', while Kerrigan stated that there had been 'careful consideration and working out of activity for the Party inside the reformist unions in West Fife'.[158] James McKendrick, who, despite having opposed the formation of the UMS, had been expelled from the LMU in 1929 and was initially a UMS Area Secretary, nevertheless rejoined the county union in the early 1930s.[159] In 1934, he stood unsuccessfully for the LMU Finance Committee, an action which may well have prompted the LMU Council to support the Larkhall delegate's motion 'that candidates for official positions in the union should conform to the constitution of the Labour Party'. By 1935, McKendrick was the Secretary of the LMU Area 5 (Blantyre) District Committee and also Secretary of the LMU Priory branch covering the Bothwell Castle nos 3 and 4 pits. An attempt by the colliery's owners, William Baird, to dismiss him after he had left the pit to fight another miner, was successfully countered by strike action by his members, for which the UMS in Lanarkshire held support meetings.[160] When the LMU Executive called a conference of labour movement bodies in February 1935 to protest against government changes in welfare relief, the Knowes branch proposed the inclusion of the UMS, a move ruled out of order by the LMU President. The Tannochside branch officers also attracted the President's reprimand for signing a CP resolution in favour of a united front against the new regulations, while the Priory branch unsuccessfully moved that industrial action be taken against the cuts.[161]

That year witnessed a growing militancy among Lanarkshire miners as the economic prospects of the industry improved: by December, the Scottish coal owners announced 'record profits'.[162] At Bardykes Colliery, Blantyre, the LMU branch officials were voted out of office and the branch waged a half-day token strike against non-unionism. At the nearby Earnock Colliery, a lightning strike forced the management to reinstate seven men sacked for filling dirt. In the Shotts district, three thousand struck successfully, but in defiance of the LMU leadership, in support of miners sacked by the Shotts Iron Company at its Castlehill Colliery near Carluke. According to the *Daily Worker*, the strikes at Priory and Shotts were a 'smashing reply' to the argument that strikes could not be won and a 'wholesale repudiation' of the advice of the LMU officials whose daily telegrams demanding a return to work 'were burned in the mass meetings of the men'.[163]

The formal dissolution of the UMS released a further wave of Communist militants into the county unions. William Pearson, a former UMS organiser and Executive member had been the UMS checkweigher at Broomfield Colliery since 1931, and was also a workmen's inspector. In January 1936, he was elected President of the LMU's Broomfield branch.[164] By May, Small was complaining that:

> Since the UMS was dissolved there has been an intensive campaign carried on within many of the Branches to capture the organisation on behalf of the Communist Party ... At a meeting in Motherwell held recently between representatives of the Shotts Disputes Committee and No. 5 Area Committee, the work of the Executive Committee and the affairs of the union were reviewed to its detriment ...

The Executive also reported that militant Area Committees, whose functions were formally limited to organising the branches and comparing working conditions, were instead 'usurping the powers which rightly belonged to the Executive Committee and Council'.[165] That same month the Scottish District of the CP reported to the PB in terms that mirrored Small's concerns: '... Party influence inside the Mining Unions since the dissolution of the UMS has considerably strengthened in Lanarkshire and particularly in Fifeshire ...'.[166]

In Fife, John Sutherland, the Bowhill workmen's inspector and checkweigher, attracted strong support when he stood for FCKMU agent, coming third in the first ballot and topping the second against two Adamson supporters.[167] However, other leading Communists and former UMS members, including the Moffats, Stewart and McArthur, were excluded from the FCKMU for some time on the grounds that they were unemployed, a stance supported by the NUSMW despite pressure from the MFGB that the union was 'under an obligation to accept all members of the disbanded organisation'.[168] At the well attended Fife Gala in June 1936, there were organised chants demanding that unemployed miners and workmen's inspectors be admitted to the union.[169] Abe Moffat eventually secured employment at a small mine in Clackmannanshire in 1938, which entitled him to rejoin the union and the following year was appointed the Lumphinnans branch delegate. That year McArthur was also re-employed and became Buckhaven branch delegate.[170]

The impact of such reinforcements was soon apparent. The Priory branch organised a ballot of its members to introduce the pool system and abolish contracting. The branch also secured a narrow majority of LMU branches in support of CP affiliation to the Labour Party.[171] In September, militants at the neighbouring Blantyre Colliery staged a dramatic stay-down strike. The tactic had been essayed tentatively at Bardykes Colliery three years earlier, when three drawers who were sacked for demanding equal pay with their workmates had refused to leave the pit and were reinstated after the rest of the workers in the section had downed tools for an hour. Added stimulus to the adoption of the tactic was given by a wave of stay-down strikes in South Wales against non-unionism.[172] After a strike over a wage demand was suspended to allow negotiations, the Blantyre miners in no. 2 pit declared their stay-down strike as soon as they descended the shaft on Thursday, 10 September, sending their elderly workmates home. The manager cut off the electricity and refused to allow food or water to be sent down, despite the plea of a local doctor that the pit water was unfit for human consumption. Claims were made that the management were manipulating the ventilation system to alternately 'freeze and roast' those underground.

These tactics generated considerable sympathy for the fifty-four strikers, several of whom were brought to the surface in a weakened state. Huge crowds gathered at the pithead, their emotions stirred by a note from the strikers declaiming that: 'We are perpaired [sic] to die down here until we get the agreement we want – [signed] The Boys'. Attempts to storm the colliery to send down food were defeated by a strong force of police surrounding the barricaded pithead. Five thousand miners in seven neighbouring pits in Blantyre and Cambuslang struck in sympathy the following day on the instructions of the Area Committee. When the stay-down miners ascended on Sunday evening after ninety hours underground: 'The news that the men were up travelled with amazing rapidity throughout the whole district and men, women and children rushed to the road beside the pit and cheered the men as they came out.' Such was the support generated by their dramatic gesture that the LMU Executive had been forced to call a county-wide, one-day strike, for 'humanitarian motives only', on the Monday. The ascent of the strikers late on Sunday meant this could not be cancelled and the strike was widely observed the following day.[173] The dispute was resolved following the involvement of NUSMW officials in negotiations with management. A Home Office report noted that the stay-down strike 'had not the approval of the county union though it may well have been engineered by the local branch'. The LMU Executive complained that the Blantyre Area Committee had acted beyond its powers, placing the Executive in an 'intolerable position', and instigated an NUSMW inquiry into Communist intervention in the dispute. A statement issued by Ed Laughlin on behalf of the Blantyre CP branch insisted that the strike occurred 'because of the adamant attitude of the coalowners', but did not deny that 'immediately the strike started the local communists did all they could to defeat the action of the coalowners'.[174] The NUSMW Report subsequently condemned the stay-in strike as 'an ill-advised venture' which had originated 'among a number of young men' who were LMU members, though 'not necessarily' branch officials: 'Yet, we cannot escape the conclusion that some of the Branch Officials, together with several members of No. 5 Area Committee, were not only conversant with what was being arranged ... and gave it the approval and authority of that Committee.'[175]

Despite the NUSMW recommendation that Area Committees be disbanded, this was insufficient to prevent militants continuing to harry the union leadership during the following year. The Shotts District Committee, described by Small as 'a body of no standing whatsoever in the organisation', assumed control of a strike at Northfield Colliery and spread it to seven other mines owned by the Shotts Iron Company.[176] Although a ballot vote of the NUSMW membership in December 1936 had narrowly accepted a new wages agreement with the Scottish owners, Lanarkshire was the only county union with a majority against acceptance.[177] Militants in the coalfield waged a successful campaign for a shorter working day on Saturdays. Miners at Bardykes Colliery unilaterally adopted a six and half hour Saturday at the beginning of the year in breach of the national agreement. When management refused to discuss any grievances until normal Saturday working resumed, the colliery struck work unofficially, defying the LMU Executive's recommendation to return. The growing strength of the militants was underlined when this recommendation was only narrowly endorsed by the Council by 25 votes to 23. The NUSMW Executive viewed 'with grave disapproval the refusal of the Bardykes workmen to recognise the authority of their own accredited representatives'. After a lengthy discussion of the unofficial strikes in the coalfield, the LMU Council was asked by its Chairman 'whether order was to be restored and constitutional practice resorted to?' The ensuing vote highlighted the difficulties which the LMU officials continued to face: 29 delegates voted 'in favour of constitutional practice' while a large minority of 22 voted against.[178] The NUSMW Executive discussed these 'spasmodic unofficial stoppages' and called for a return to work, its chairman declaring, 'he had no sympathy with the unofficial stoppages. He was prepared to exhaust all the machinery provided for negotiating disputes ...'.[179] However, militancy was proving increasingly effective as union membership expanded within the economically recuperating industry: the NUSMW grew by over 10,000 in the year to June 1937.[180] As more Lanarkshire and Fife miners unilaterally adopted the short Saturday and the threat of a Scottish strike on the issue loomed, the Scottish owners were forced to make concessions during negotiations on the issue.[181]

Age was rapidly catching up with the older generation of miners' leaders. Early in 1932, James Hood of the AMU and NUSMW Executive died at the age of 68. Hugh Murnin of West Lothian, a former NUSMW President and MP, died a few weeks later aged 70, as did James Doonan, then NUSMW President and also from West Lothian. 1935 saw the deaths of Robert Smith, Secretary of both the AMU and NUSMW; Charles Toner, the 55 year old FCKMU President; Joseph Sullivan, former MP and NUSMW Executive member, aged 69; and James Tonner, a 78 year old LMU agent, who had occupied his post since 1904. The following year, William Adamson died, aged 72. James Brown, an agent of the AMU since 1904 and Secretary of the NUSMW from 1917 to 1936, was a member of the NUSMW Executive until his death at the age of 76 in 1939. Robert Smillie, who had withdrawn from Scottish miners' affairs in 1928, died in 1940.[182]

They were steadily replaced by the generational cohort of militant activists against whom they had fought a bitter, rearguard action for two decades. In the election for LMU General Secretary in 1936, McKendrick was narrowly beaten by the 63 year old Small by only 0.7 per cent of the votes; the following year, McKendrick secured the post with over two-thirds of the vote in a straight contest against Small. While McKendrick's vote was strongest, at times overwhelmingly so, in the traditionally militant branches of his home district of Blantyre, as well as in Shotts, Coalburn and Ponfeigh, the breadth of his support was indicated by him securing a majority in 44 branches out of a total of 56. While it remained lowest in the traditionally non-militant Larkhall district – he secured only 12.4, 23.5 and 23.6 per cent respectively at the Ferniegair, Summerlee and Law branches – even here there were signs of change in the face of industrial dereliction. McKendrick won 40 per cent of the ballot in the Larkhall branch, 55 per cent at Quarter, 58 per cent at Netherburn and 80 per cent at Cornsilloch. He was elected an LMU agent and also to the NUSMW Executive the following year, and secured a crushing majority in his re-election for LMU Secretary in 1939. William Pearson was elected to the NUSMW Executive in 1936 at the age of 40; he mounted a strong challenge for LMU President in 1938 and was elected to the post in 1940; in 1942, following the death of the incumbent who had held the post for twenty-one years, he became NUSMW Treasurer with a huge majority, and was elected NUSMW Secretary the following year. From Fife, the 44 year old Abe Moffat was elected to the NUSMW Executive in 1940 and became the union's President two years later. In 1946, John McArthur became a full-time official of the newly-formed National Union of Mineworkers.[183] In West Lothian, Bill McLean, a former UMS organiser who had joined the CP in 1925 and been victimised in 1926, got a job in the pits in 1939; he was elected to the Armadale branch committee of the West Lothian county union in 1940 and represented the county on the NUSMW Executive that same year.[184]

This generational cohort was not monolithic, however. Some individuals dropped out from this onward march. Although David Proudfoot was perhaps the most significant loss to the party, there were a number of others. James MacDougall did not stay long in the CP, leaving after a visit to the Soviet union in 1926. Disillusioned by Stalinism, he joined the Liberals. At a meeting in 1928 in Ponfeigh, where he had campaigned for revolutionary socialism with John Maclean before the First World War, he denounced 'the new ruling class' in Russia and asked: 'What would their pit at Douglas Water be like under a Soviet system? There would be a "nucleus" of Communists and they would give orders to the whole village ...'. According to the press report, 'Heckling was active'. MacDougall stood as a Liberal at Rutherglen the following year, coming third in the poll above the young Alex Moffat, who came fourth and last as the CP candidate.[185] John Bird, Maclean's principal Fife protégé, never joined the UMS and appears to have left the CP by 1930; he resigned as checkweigher and became a tenant of the Bowhill Hotel.[186] William 'Mosie' Murray, a stalwart of the MRU, a member of the CP since 1922, arrested in 1926, and later a UMS Executive member, became alienated by Communist policies: he recalled that when Proudfoot was made General Secretary, fellow Communists 'started stabbing him in the back because Davey wanted to adopt different tactics as far as the UMS was concerned':

> ... We thought that as far as the Communist Party was concerned that they were nae working in the interests of the Scottish miners but they were working in their own interests in so much that they were nae so much concerned about building the miners but with building the Communist Party in Scotland, and it didnae work, frankly it didnae work. We were supposed to be representing the miners, fighting on behalf of the miners ...

Soon after Proudfoot resigned, he also left the CP.[187] Other nameless activists were forced out of the mines by victimisation and unemployment: about ninety CP members emigrated from the Scottish coalfields in 1928 alone.[188]

Conclusion

The UMS was a contradictory and, within the British coalfields, unique phenomenon. Its initial attempt to build 'revolutionary trade unionism' was predicated upon the misplaced optimism of the 'third period' and the belief that, in the economic crisis after 1929, the tendencies within trade unionism which posed a challenge to capital could be developed by the CP to overcome the competing pressures of accommodation with employers. Such a strategy woefully misread the available political opportunities and seriously underestimated the obstacles to recruitment as well as the heavy drag chains of union routinism. The UMS was perennially in financial difficulties, saddled with a cumbersome structure and staffed by over-burdened organisers. Its membership was never more than a small fraction of the Scottish mining workforce.

The union was never an independent organisation but manifestly an appendage of the CPGB which, in subordination to the Comintern, decided on its personnel and policies. In the face of Proudfoot's threat of resignation, the PB recognised, but could not resolve, this problem, other than by agreeing 'that the union should have a more independent life rather than be a propaganda reflex of the Party'.[189] Although a UMS commission on East Fife reported in the wake of Proudfoot's departure that there was 'a pronounced tendency for all leading Union work to be left in the hands of a small propaganda group which is also responsible for Communist activity in the area', it is telling that fifteen months later Gallacher continued to insist that 'a stop had to be put to the situation' whereby 'the UMS agent is also known as the Party organiser. UMS organisers must appear as UMS organisers and not as party organisers.'[190] Such exhortations could not change the essential principles of democratic centralism nor well-established perceptions of the personnel in a self-proclaimed 'red union'. Although fraction organisation of CP members within the union was inadequate by the rigorous standards of the Comintern, it nevertheless took place episodically, as Mosie Murray recalled:

> And before we had the Executive meeting we had to go to Communist Party headquarters [in Glasgow] to get our instructions. You had the agenda of business there and this is how you had to vote, whether right, wrong or reasonable ... We discussed it at this particular meeting and we were told how to vote when we went to the Executive meeting ...[191]

Communist influence on and within the organisation could not be concealed – the great majority of, if not all, the Sub-Executive Committee and UMS organisers were well-known party members – and any evidence of political vassalage was seized on by the NUSMW. For example, to the chagrin of Pollitt and Moffat, an inaccurate statement on the expenditure of the UMS by Pianitsky, a member of the ECCI PS and the RILU Executive, was published by the NUSMW as a four-page pamphlet and distributed at every pit in Scotland.[192] Allan accepted that 'the party label that is on the UMS is also hindering recruitment to the UMS'.[193] Yet such barriers were also imposed by the union's subservience to the dictates of Stalinist organisation: for example, during the strikes in December 1930, mass meetings were urged to pass motions demanding the death penalty for the 'Industrial Party plotters' then being tried in the Soviet Union.[194]

Nevertheless, the UMS made pioneering attempts to politically mobilise miners' wives and waged significant attempts to defend mineworkers' conditions, particularly after the shifts in Comintern policy allowed Abe Moffat the freedom denied his predecessors to organise on the basis of militant, rather than revolutionary, trade unionism. However, by then the union's base was largely confined to Fife. This can in part be attributed to the quality of the party's cadre in the Fife coalfield. Proudfoot complained that in Lanarkshire,

> they do not attempt ... to try and operate a policy but just attempt one thing, throw it aside, batter away on another without attempting to judge or make any analysis of the situation ... That appears to be the spirit animating many of them ... It is better to do nothing at times than to be continually doing 'something' which makes balls of the position.[195]

There are unfortunate echoes of the popular stereotype of the 'feckless Glasgow Irish' in McArthur's similarly critical appraisal of his Lanarkshire comrades, though it may contain an element of truth:

> Allan, in spite of his enormous ability, suffered from what I always felt was a weakness common to most people that I knew in the Lanarkshire movement. That was a lack of serious responsibility, a go-easy, devil-may-care, sometimes flippant and jocular attitude to organisational questions and the solving of problems ... In later years I found the approach of Jimmy McKendrick ... to be like Allan's.[196]

But of probably greater importance was the more favourable economic position in Fife, where, in contrast to the industrial devastation in Lanarkshire, the technically progressive, large mines were better able to weather the depression. This could also render them more vulnerable to pressure. In his analysis of the successful strike at the Randolph colliery in 1930, Proudfoot speculated that one factor explaining the uncharacteristic willingness of the Fife Coal

Company to negotiate before the men had returned to work was 'due to the delicate poise of mining in Scotland at present: the machine mining being very easily dislocated and therefore costs considerably increased by the slightest stoppage'.[197]

Ironically, the union's relative influence in Fife prolonged its existence. Its weakness elsewhere encouraged the re-integration of Communist cadres within the county unions where they increasingly exercised militant local leadership and were well-placed to exploit the improving economic circumstances throughout the Scottish coalfields. The translation of this industrial militancy into electoral success within the LMU and later the FCKMU and NUSMW underlined the ultimate sterility of the adventure into dual unionism. Had the Communists remained within the county unions in 1929, a war of attrition with the ageing and organisationally weary 'old gang' might have delivered these electoral victories sooner and enabled the reconstruction of the NUSMW as a fighting organisation. However, the meaning of Communist electoral success in the unions requires further interrogation. Support for CP candidates does not necessarily suggest popular endorsement of broader Communist policies; it is equally plausible that miners cast their votes for militants in the unions despite the political views of these candidates. An evaluation of party politics in the coalfields is the subject of the final chapter.

Notes

1. There is only brief treatment in Arnot, *History*, pp. 213–22, Branson, *History*, pp. 182–3, and Macintyre, *Little Moscows*, pp. 66–70; and merely passing references in Martin, *Communism*, pp. 128–9, and Fishman, *British Communist Party*, pp. 35, 89. There are valuable memoirs in MacDougall, *Militant Miners*, pp. 126–36, Moffat, *Life*, pp. 48–63, and Long, 'Abe Moffat'. There are short accounts in Long, thesis, pp. 429–40, and N. Fishman, 'Party coalmining strongholds: South Wales and Scotland', unpublished paper. An unpublished paper by Martin Sime, 'The United Mineworkers of Scotland' (c. 1978) provides a more detailed study, though it is primarily focused on Fife. I am grateful to both Nina Fishman and Martin Sime for allowing me sight of their unpublished work. None of these writers had access to the CP and Comintern records now available

and only Macintyre and Sime made any use of the extensive UMS material contained in the Proudfoot Papers.

2. J.R. Campbell, 'The new trade union situation', *Labour Monthly*, 11, 4, 1929, p. 213; MacDougall, *Militant Miners*, p. 127.

3. H. Pollitt, 'The future of revolutionary trade unionism', *Labour Monthly*, 11, 8, 1929, p. 491.

4. MPL F001, *United Mineworkers of Scotland: Constitution and Rules*.

5. PL, 8 November 1929 and accompanying document, 'Critical Situation for the Mineworkers'; MPL, UMS leaflet, dated 27 November 1929.

6. PL, 2, 10 January 1930. See vol. 1, chs 3 and 4.

7. PL, 2 January 1930.

8. Ibid.

9. NMLH CI 1, CC, 19/20 July 1930.

10. PL, 8 February 1930.

11. PL, 28 February 1930. The UMS constitution declared full-time officials ineligible for nomination to the Executive (*UMS Constitution and Rules*, section 9.2).

12. NMLH CI 1, CC, 11/12 January 1930.

13. *Daily Worker*, 23 January 1930. For such practices in the county unions, see chapter one of this volume.

14. MPL F023, UMS Circular, 1 July 1929.

15. MPL F035, *UMS Information Bulletin*, no. 7, 11 July 1930.

16. *Daily Worker*, 18 August 1930.

17. *Daily Worker*, 23 September 1930.

18. *Daily Worker*, 14 October 1930.

19. PL, 14 February 1931.

20. MPL FO33, Report of Union Commission, January 1931.

21. Calculated from MPL F122, Abstract of dues collected ... for period ending 27 September 1930; F123, Statement of Income for period 26 January to 21 February 1931; F148, Statement of Income for 4 weeks ending 24 February 1934.

22. MPL F008, Executive Committee Report submitted to Second Annual Conference, claimed sales of 250 to 450 (p. 15); Mary Docherty, a Communist activist in Cowdenbeath, recalled selling between twenty and forty dozen of the various pit papers (M. Docherty, Autobiographical talk delivered to Scottish Labour History Society Conference on 'Scotland and the Russian Revolution', 31 October 1987). In September 1930, Proudfoot wrote that the *Spark*'s production of 35 dozen had sold out and that it was planned to raise the print run to 50 dozen (PL, 13 September 1930).

23. But see Raphael Samuel's aside that the CP's factory papers constituted 'one of the most striking of the Party's literary inventions and a mine of information on workplace life' (R. Samuel, 'Staying power:

the lost world of British communism, part two', *New Left Review*,
156, 1986, p. 85n). The most comprehensive listing is E. and R. Frow,
*Pit and Factory Papers Issued by the Communist Party of Great
Britain, 1927–1934* (Salford, 1996).

24. J. Barrowman, *A Glossary of Scotch Mining Terms* (Hamilton, 1886).
25. Interview with Rab Smith, Lumphinnans, by Suzanne Najam, 24
February 1986. I am grateful to Dr Najam for sight of her transcript.
26. *Fan*, no. 3, 17 July 1931; *Headlamp*, no. 8, 14 July 1933.
27. Selkirk, *Life*, p. 21; Najam interview, Rab Smith. Hugh Sloan, a
Denbeath miner with some artistic skills who acted as cartoonist on
the Methil *Spark*, recalled how appalled he was at the restricted
nature of stencil reproduction (Interview with Hugh Sloan, 6 August
1986).
28. NMLH CI 1, 'Report of International Agit-Prop Conference', CC,
21 July 1931; H. Wilde, 'The factory newspaper, a mighty weapon for
communism', *Communist Review*, 3, 4, 1931.
29. *Worker*, 19 April 1929. For the NUR Guilds see P. Bagwell, *The
Railwaymen: the history of the National Union of Railwaymen* (1963),
pp. 227–8. In 1927, the *Sunday Worker* advocated trade union guilds
'embracing the adult women relatives of trade unionists ... to ensure
that like miners' wives, the wives of all other workers will stand
solidly behind their men in struggle' (*Sunday Worker*, 15 May 1927).
30. MPL F227, UMS Sub-Organising Committee, 18 September 1929.
31. MPL F294, Women's Guild Committee, 21 December 1929.
32. PL, 8 February 1930.
33. MPL F296, Report of the UMS Trade Union Women's Guild
Conference, Kirkcaldy, 2 March 1930.
34. MPL F273, UMS Executive, 20 August 1932.
35. See vol. 1, ch. 5, for gender relations in the coalfields.
36. PL, 2 September 1929.
37. PL, 28 February 1930; see also the criticism of the failure of local
committees 'to understand the important role of women in the fight
by their neglect to work in conjunction with the Guilds', by the UMS
Executive (MPL F008, Executive Committee Report to Second
Annual Conference, 12 October 1930, pp. 8–9).
38. MPL F297, Women's Guild Committee, 3 July 1930.
39. MPL F188, No. 1 Area Committee, 13 July 1930.
40. MPL FO33, Report of Union Commission, January 1931; F044,
Report of the Commission on East Fife; F267, UMS Executive, 5
March 1932.
41. *Daily Worker*, 23 January, 5 March 1930, 8, 22 January 1931.
42. *Daily Worker*, 26 March 1930.
43. MPL F294, Women's Guild Committee, 21 December 1929; *Daily
Worker*, 1, 6 January 1930, 2 January 1931.

44. *Daily Worker*, 16, 17, 20, 23 December 1930, 22 January 1931.
45. MacDougall, *Militant Miners*, p. 127.
46. *Daily Worker*, 19 July, 18 September 1930. For a recent review of CP attempts to foster a network of Communist cultural organisations and activities at this time, see Worley, thesis, ch. 6.
47. MacDougall, *Militant Miners*, pp. 127–8. In the 1935–6 season, after 'noted captures' of players from other local teams, the UMS reached the fifth round of the Scottish Juvenile Cup (*Daily Worker*, 6 August, 24 December 1935).
48. *Workers' Life*, 17 May 1929.
49. *Workers' Life*, 9 August 1929. Moffat later claimed that 'at one time we had over 20,000 members ...', a figure which Long rightly views as 'most unlikely' (Long, 'Abe Moffat', pp. 12, 18).
50. PL, 2 September 1929.
51. NLS Dep. 258/1, AMU Delegate Meetings, 27 April, 1, 29 June, 7 December 1929; MPL F013, Report of Fourth Annual Conference, 1932; Long, 'Abe Moffat', p. 16.
52. NLS Acc. 4312/13, MELMA Board, 11 May, 29 June 1929, Executive 19 May, 7, 19 June 1929.
53. NLS Acc. 4312/3, West Lothian Mineworkers' Union Executive, 17 April, 5 June, 10 July, 22 September 1929.
54. NLS Dep. 227/45, LMU Council, 3 April, 7 August, 4 September 1929; Dep. 227/71, LMU Executive, 5, 8 April, 16 August, 10 September, 11 October 1929.
55. MPL F001, *UMS Constitution and Rules*, para. 15.4.
56. MPL F122, Abstract of dues collected ... for the period ending 27 September 1930; F132, Statement of income for four weeks ending 27 February 1932.
57. For example, see the references to the union's 'critical financial position' and 'the very critical condition' in 1931 and 1932 (MPL F041, 'Position of coal industry', 8 June 1931; F236, Sub-Executive, 13 July 1932).
58. MPL F008, Executive Committee Report to Second Annual Conference, 12 October 1930.
59. Ibid.; NMLH CI 32C, Anglo-American Secretariat, 31 May 1933.
60. *Daily Worker*, 1 July 1930. See also Moffat, *Life*, p. 54, and MacDougall, *Militant Miners*, p. 131.
61. *Daily Worker*, 17 February 1930; NLS Dep. 227/71, LMU Executive, 23 August, 10 September 1930.
62. Interview with David Meek, Motherwell, 25 July 1984. See also *Daily Worker*, 10 February 1933; NLS Dep. 227/45A, LMU Council, 8 March 1933.
63. *Daily Worker*, 10 February 1933.
64. *Daily Worker*, 18 February, 8 March 1932.

65. MacDougall, *Militant Miners*, p. 132.
66. PL, 4 October 1929; *Workers' Life*, 20 September, 4, 18 October 1929; Moffat, *Life*, p. 49; Arnot, *History*, p. 196; Macintyre, *Little Moscows*, pp. 68–9.
67. *Daily Worker*, 1 February 1930, 16 January, 20 September 1932.
68. For Proudfoot's analysis of the strike, see MPL I010, Strike at Randolph Colliery, 24 March 1930.
69. See vol. 1, ch. 3.
70. *Daily Worker*, 25, 27 January, 13 May 1930; *Hamilton Advertiser*, 25 January 1930.
71. MPL F008, Executive Committee Report. The events in Blantyre which the report refers to are obscure, but they may be reflected in the miners at Auchenraith Colliery, Blantyre, voting by a large majority to return to the LMU. The UMS also brought out the workforce at Bothwell Castle, nos 3 and 4 pits, over the relatively minor issue of management's refusal to erect a union box for its collector (NLS Dep. 227/71, LMU Executive, 10, 24 September 1930).
72. PL, 27 September 1930. See the claims that the UMS had recruited 84 members in Shotts following the January strike (*Daily Worker*, 15 March 1930) and that the party had 32 members operating in eight pit cells (*Daily Worker*, 11 June 1930).
73. PL, 11 October 1930. McArthur was similarly critical of his Lanarkshire comrades: 'It seemed to me that far too much emphasis was laid on getting a pit idle, that a strike had taken place on a given date, rather than that the benefits had been secured for the men ... In Lanarkshire any kind of issue, real or imaginary, was good enough in some cases for the local UMS leaders to get the men to walk home, so that they could report that a strike had taken place' (MacDougall, *Militant Miners*, p. 133).
74. MPL F255, UMS Executive, 20 December 1930; F257, UMS Executive, 7 March 1931.
75. *Daily Worker*, 8 December 1930; *Leven Advertiser and Wemyss Gazette*, 2 December 1930.
76. *Daily Worker*, 1, 8, 9 December 1930.
77. Modern Records Centre, University of Warwick, Mss. 88/3/1/4i, Special National Miners' Conference, 14 December 1930.
78. PL, 10 December 1930.
79. NMLH CI 11, PB, 23 December 1930.
80. PL, 14 February 1931; see also PL, 10 April 1931. The danger of maladministration by his SLC protégés, who included Allan, had been recognised by John Maclean, and he had sent them to business training classes in 1920. These were markedly unpopular with the students, who sent 'deputation after deputation' to him in protest, but he insisted that 'if we were to be trained as trade union officials

of the future we must have business knowledge' (MacDougall, *Militant Miners*, p. 34). The Comintern representative, Petrovsky, perceived a similar need upon Allan's election in 1927: 'There was a danger that the new officials elected in the mining and other areas would be a failure from a business point of view, unless something was done in the form of a school, lectures, etc, to prepare them for this union work' (NMLH CI 32, Anglo-American Secretariat, 10 August 1927).

81. MPL FO33, Report of Union Commission, January 1931.
82. For example, see McArthur's account of his organising duties in MPL I012, McArthur to Proudfoot, 27 October 1930; see also MacDougall, *Militant Miners*, p. 128.
83. NMLH CI 12, PB, 26 March, 9 April 1931.
84. *Daily Worker*, 6, 7 April 1931.
85. *Daily Worker*, 8, 10, 14, 15, 28, 30, 31 July 1931; A. Moffatt [*sic*], 'Successes in the Scottish miners' struggles', *Labour Monthly*, 16, 1934, p. 165; PRO LAB 34/48, Board of Trade Disputes Book, 1931.
86. MPL I013, untitled report on support for strikes; *Leven and Wemyss Gazette*, 28 July 1931.
87. *Daily Worker*, 29 July, 4 August 1931.
88. PRO LAB 34/48, Board of Trade Disputes Book, 1931; *Daily Worker*, 10–21 August 1931.
89. MPL F262, UMS Executive, 22 August 1931. Proudfoot had previously threatened resignation in April due to the serious financial situation and considered that he had been 'left with the baby to hold' (NMLH CI 12, PB, 9 April 1931).
90. PL, 13 September 1931, and accompanying copy of letter from James Stewart, 4 July 1931.
91. PRO LAB 34/48, Trade Disputes Book, 1932; Moffat, 'Successes', pp. 165–6; *Daily Worker*, 4–17 May 1932; NLS Acc. 4311, FCKMU Sub-Executive Committee, 29 April, 5 May 1932; FCKMU Executive Board, 14 May 1932; Long, 'Abe Moffat', p. 16; Moffat, *Life*, p. 53.
92. NMLH CI 4, CC, 10 September 1933.
93. Home Office, *The Law relating to Mines under the Coal Mines Act, 1911* (1914), pp. 27–8. David Gilmour, a former LMU Secretary, claimed that 'we took full advantage of the law' concerning inspections during his long period of office which ended in 1918 (*Glasgow Herald*, 5 August 1926).
94. *Report of H.M. Inspector of Mines, Scotland, for 1928* (1929), p. 44.
95. Moffat, *Life*, p. 50; *Daily Worker*, 14 November 1930; *Report of H.M. Inspector of Mines, Scotland, for 1932* (1933), p. 46.
96. *Daily Worker*, 12 September 1932; Moffat, 'Successes', pp. 167–8; MPL F013, Report of Fourth Annual Conference, 17–18 December

1932; F111, UMS Progress, 1933. Biographical information on Sutherland is in NMLH CP/CENT/PERS/07/02.

97. Moffat, 'Successes', p. 168; *Daily Worker*, 4 June 1934.

98. *Daily Worker*, 14, 21 December 1933; MacDougall, *Militant Miners*, pp. 128–9, 133.

99. *Report of H.M. Inspector of Mines, Scotland, for 1933* (1934), p. 53; ibid., *1934* (1935), pp. 58–9; Moffat, 'Successes', p. 168.

100. *Daily Worker*, 10 April 1933.

101. Ibid., 15 January 1934.

102. Ibid., 20 March, 16 April, 16 May 1934.

103. Ibid., 17 November 1934.

104. Ibid., 29 May, 29 August 1935.

105. Ibid., 17 October, 23 November, 16, 31 December 1935.

106. For an account of the Comintern's relationship with the RILU, see A. Kuusinen, *Before and After Stalin* (1974), pp. 43–4. Aino Kuusinen was a Comintern agent, married to Otto Kuusinen, an influential member of the Comintern Secretariat.

107. McCarthy, *Generation*, pp. 165–9.

108. NMLH CP/CENT/PC/01/15, 'Report of voting in Executive Committee and Political Bureau from 10th to 11th Congress'. For Petrovsky, see B. Lazitch and M. D. Drachkovitch (eds), *Biographical Dictionary of the Comintern* (Stanford, Ca., 1973), p. 310.

109. *Worker*, 19 April 1929; Martin, *Communism*, p. 124; *Daily Worker*, 9 December 1931.

110. NMLH CI 28, PS ECCI, 11 July 1929; for Stewart, see Lazitch and Drachkovitch, *Biographical Dictionary*, p. 386, and V. Kahan, 'The Communist International, 1919–43: the personnel of its highest bodies', *International Review of Social History*, 21, 1976, p. 165; for Allan and Moffat see Branson, *History*, pp. 339–41; for Shields' appointment to UMS work, see NMLH, un-numbered reel of microfilm deposited by Monty Johnstone, 1995, containing Minutes of Secretariat, 8 December 1929. An article in the *Daily Worker*, 12 May 1930, carried the by-line, 'J. Shields, UMS', but there is no evidence that Shields was ever a miner: he came from Greenock, outwith the coalfields, and his obituary by Kerrigan merely referred to him playing 'an active part in supporting the fight of the militant miners ...' (*World News and Views*, 17, 1949, p. 201).

111. NMLH CI 1, CC, 11/12 January, 5/6 April 1930. A 'German Comrade', who made authoritative and critical remarks, was present at the January CC. This was possibly Walter Ulbricht who had been sent to Britain in late 1929 to assist the party in overhauling its apparatus (Morgan, *Pollitt*, p. 70).

112. NMLH CI 11, PB, 12 June 1930. McArthur, James Stewart and Abe

Moffat wrote a highly critical report on the failings of the UMS and CP in regard to the union's Fife gala which 'fell flat and was almost farcical'. Allan, one of the main speakers, came in for particular criticism for failing to treat the event sufficiently seriously. Unlike Fife, where galas were a well-established element in the miners' union culture, there was no similar tradition in Lanarkshire (MPL F032, Fife Miners' Gala, 12 June 1930).

113. NMLH CI 11, PB, 10 July 1930.
114. NMLH CI 30, 'To the Secretariat of the CPGB, Confidential, 8 April 1930'. There were ten British Communists sent in January 1928 to the two year course at the International Lenin School (NMLH CP/CENT/CONG/02/06, *The New Line: documents of the 10th Congress of the Communist Party of Great Britain held at Bermondsey, London, on January 19th–22nd 1929*, p. 54) The graduates returned to Britain in May 1930 (PB, 3 April 1930).
115. NMLH CI 1, CC, 21 July 1930. In 1935, Pollitt reported that the minutes of the UMS were the basis of study on the British situation by ILS students (CI 15, 'Meeting 17 January'). Kerrigan was appointed to the CC in 1932. Moffat left the School early, though it is not clear why. I am grateful to Dr Barry McLoughlin, Vienna, for information on Moffat based on his researches on the ILS in Moscow.
116. For the Mardy episode, see H. Francis and D. Smith, *The Fed: a history of the South Wales Miners in the twentieth century* (1980), pp. 165–9, and Macintyre, *Little Moscows*, pp. 37–9. An article on the UMS in the *Communist International* had already drawn attention 'to serious errors in connection with the failure of the EC of the Party and the leadership of the MM to carry through a supporting campaign in the English districts' (E.H. Brown, 'The struggle in the Scottish coalfields: the Communist Party and the new miners' union', *Communist International*, 6, 29, 1929, p. 739).
117. NMLH CI 11, PB, 27 March 1930; NMM, *British Mineworkers' Union* (n.d., 1929).
118. Ibid., PB, 3 April 1930.
119. NMLH CI 1, CC, 5/6 April 1930. The party subsequently published a pamphlet, *The Fight of the Miners: the position of the British coal industry*, with an introduction signed by the CC which contained the call 'to bring forward the UMS, its role and great importance, to bring forward the Miners' Minority Movement as the centre through which we shall ultimately unite the whole of the revolutionary miners' forces in the One United Mineworkers' Union of Britain' (p. 9).
120. NMLH CI 31, PS ECCI to CC CPGB, 24 May 1930.

121. Worley, thesis, pp. 183–4.
122. NMLH CI 11, PB 12 June 1930.
123. NMLH CI 11, PB, 3, 17, 18 July 1930; CI 1, CC 19, 20 July 1930. Gallacher later complained that the Comintern representative had used 'the most demagogic methods to get the Party executive members to swing and vote for the CI' (CI 32, Anglo-American Secretariat, 11 August 1930). See also the comments by Pollitt on the subject to the same meeting. It is possible that the Comintern representative referred to was Sergei Ivanovich Gusev: see Cox's oblique reference to 'Comrade Gussiev' at the PB of 3 July 1930. An old Bolshevik and supporter of Stalin, Gusev was elected a member of the Presidium of the ECCI in 1930, having previously been the leader of the CI secretariat for central Europe and a Comintern representative to the United States (Lazitch and Drachkovitch, *Biographical Dictionary*, pp. 136–7; Wicks, *Keeping My Head*, pp. 105–6).
124. NMLH CI 32, Anglo-American Secretariat, 11, 12 August 1930.
125. For example, see Pollitt's report to the PB in 1932 in which he stated that 'the whole aim of the Party should be to make the UMS a model union which we must speak of in the rest of the country, in order to strengthen our work in the existing reformist trade unions' (NMLH CI 13, PB, 9 January 1932).
126. NMLH CI 11, PB, 4 September 1930.
127. NMLH CI 1, CC, 13 September 1930.
128. E.H. Carr, *Twilight of the Comintern, 1930–35* (New York, 1982), p. 209.
129. NMLH CI 1, CC, 13 September 1930.
130. NMLH CI 29, Resolution of PS ECCI on the situation and tasks of the CPGB, 30 September 1930.
131. NMLH CI 11, PB, 8 October 1930.
132. MPL F253, UMS Executive, 11 October 1930.
133. NMLH CI 11, PB, 23 December 1930.
134. NMLH, Klugmann papers, 'Report on sitn in UMS by HP, 31/12/30'. Proudfoot later claimed that party members in the UMS had only accepted his appointment because it was presented by Pollitt, but that it was not popular (PL, 13 September 1931). This may explain why he was first installed as President in October rather than General Secretary.
135. MPL F256, UMS Executive, 10 January 1931. Proudfoot later reported that Shields had been 'taken off payroll' (PL, 14 February 1931).
136. *Daily Worker*, 6, 7, 11 April 1931.
137. NMLH CI 13, PB, 9 July 1932; *Daily Worker*, 4 July 1932.
138. Carr, *Twilight*, p. 221; J. Degras (ed.), *The Communist International, 1919–43: Documents, vol. 3, 1929–43* (1971), pp. 234–5.

139. *Daily Worker*, 12 October 1932.
140. Ibid., 10 December 1932.
141. Ibid., 19 December 1932.
142. NMLH CI 4, Discussion between ILP and CP, 21 September 1933; Annual Report of the NAC submitted to the ILP Annual Conference, April 1935, Appendix 4, Report of the sub-committee on dual unionism especially as it related to Scottish coal fields. I am grateful to Gidon Cohen for supplying me with the latter reference.
143. Quoted in Carr, *Twilight*, p. 236.
144. PRO HW 17/18, Decrypted radio message from Moscow to London, 9 March 1935.
145. McDermott and Agnew, *Comintern*, pp. 130–2; Carr, *Twilight*, ch. 8; Branson, *History*, ch. 9.
146. NMLH CI 15, PB, 20 September, 21 December 1935. Andre Marty, who chaired a Comintern secretariat on 'the English question' the following year, roundly condemned this PB minute as a serious breach of party security – 'If this is found it is easy to say that the United Mineworkers of Scotland are directed by the PB of the British Party' – which laid the CPGB open to the charge that 'the whole British Party is directed from Moscow' (NMLH CI 33, Meeting of Secretariat of Comrade Marty, 22 February 1936).
147. NMLH CI 7, CC, 4 January 1936.
148. The most detailed account of their activities is Long, thesis, ch. 10.
149. Sime, 'United Mineworkers', Appendix 2.
150. Calculated from NLS Dep. 227/88, NUSMW Statement of Accounts for the four years ended 31 July 1929; Dep. 227/89, NUSMW Statement of Accounts for year ended 31 July 1931.
151. NLS Dep. 227/45A, LMU Council, 4 May 1932.
152. NLS Dep. 227/45A, LMU Council, 3 February 1932, 11 January 1933.
153. NLS Dep. 227/45A, 12 August 1931; Arnot, *History*, pp. 208–9.
154. NLS Acc. 4311/1, FCKMU Special Committee Meeting, 24 June 1932.
155. NLS Dep. 227/90, NUSMW Annual Conference Proceedings, 1934. For strike incidence, see Table 3.3 and the accompanying discussion in vol. 1, ch. 3.
156. NLS Dep. 227/45A, LMU Council, 11 January, 19 June, 1 November 1933, 7 February, 7 March 1934, 21 November 1935.
157. Long, thesis, pp. 339–41.
158. NMLH CI 13, PB, 6 February, 29 December 1932.
159. McKendrick is listed as an Area Secretary of the 'New Scottish Union' in MPL M124, *UMS Information Bulletin*, no. 1, March 1929; Long, 'Abe Moffat', p. 16.

160. NLS Dep. 227/45A, LMU Council, 4 July, 5 September 1934; NLS PDL 45/7, NUSMW Executive, 29 July, 2, 12 August 1935; *Daily Worker*, 3, 5 August 1935, 20 January 1936. Such activities may have prompted the discussion on the NUSMW Executive on the tactics of the UMS 'in certain districts in Lanarkshire' (NLS Dep. 227/90, NUSMW Executive, 29 May 1935).
161. NLS Dep. 227/45A, LMU Council, 8 February 1935.
162. *Colliery Guardian*, 7 February 1936.
163. *Daily Worker*, 14 August 1935.
164. MPL F257, UMS Executive, 7 March 1931; *Daily Worker*, 23 January, 17 August 1936.
165. NLS Dep. 227/45A, LMU Council, 13 May 1936.
166. NMLH CI 16, PB, 7 May 1936.
167. *Daily Worker*, 7, 17 August 1936.
168. NLS PDL 45/7, NUSMW Executive, 7 December 1936.
169. *Daily Worker*, 2 June 1936; Moffat, *Life*, p. 64.
170. Moffat, *Life*, p. 66; MacDougall, *Militant Miners*, pp. 165–7.
171. NLS Dep. 227/45A, LMU Council, 3 June, 1 July 1936.
172. *Daily Worker*, 10 February 1933; Smith and Francis, *The Fed*, pp. 280–98.
173. *Daily Worker*, 11, 12, 14, 15, 19, 22 September 1936; *Hamilton Advertiser*, 12, 19 September 1936.
174. PRO POWE 20/41, undated memorandum, 'Stay-in Strikes'; *Daily Worker*, 22 September 1936; *Hamilton Advertiser*, 26 September 1936; NLS Dep. 227/45A, LMU Special Conference, 14 September 1936.
175. NLS PDL 45/7, NUSMW Executive, 5 April 1937.
176. NLS Dep. 227/45A, LMU Council, 3 March 1937.
177. *Daily Worker*, 17 December 1936.
178. NLS Dep. 227/45, LMU Council, 3 March 1937. McKendrick's challenge to this formulation in the minutes at the following meeting was narrowly defeated by two votes (ibid., 7 April 1937).
179. NLS PDL 45/7, NUSMW Executive, 1 March 1937.
180. Ibid., NUSMW Annual Conference, 24–26 June 1937.
181. *Daily Worker*, 14, 18 January, 10, 15, 17, 20 February, 1, 3, 23 March 1937.
182. Arnot, *History*, p. 210; Knox, *Labour Leaders*, pp. 58–61, 70, 221–2; NLS Dep. 227/45A, LMU Council, 6 March, 3 April 1935; Saville and Bellamy, *Dictionary of Labour Biography*, *3*, pp. 165–71; *Lochgelly Times*, 10 April 1935.
183. NLS Dep. 227/45A, LMU Council, 5 August, 2 December 1936, 7 July 1937; Dep. 227/46, LMU Council, 4 May, 6 July 1938, 12 July 1939, 3 July 1940; Arnot, *History*, pp. 236–7, 250–1; Moffat, *Life*, p. 66; MacDougall, *Militant Miners*, p. 167.

184. NMLH CP/CENT/PERS/4/7; Arnot, *History*, p. 245.
185. *Hamilton Advertiser*, 10 November 1928; Knox, *Labour Leaders*, p. 174; F.W.S. Craig, *British Parliamentary Election Results, 1918–49* (Glasgow, 1969), p. 636.
186. The *Daily Worker* reported that Bird had 'transferred' from the ranks of the militants to the 'reformists' in 1930 (*Daily Worker*, 22 March 1930); MacDougall, *Militant Miners*, pp. 37, 169–70.
187. Sime/Gilby interview with Mosie Murray, Leven.
188. NMLH, Klugmann Papers, CC, 28–30 April 1928, Organisation Reports 1930.
189. NMLH CI 12, PB, 27 August 1931. See also McArthur's reflection that 'a serious mistake' of the UMS was 'the mechanical acceptance of directives ... that were not applicable to the situation in Scotland' (MacDougall, *Militant Miners*, p. 134).
190. MPL F044, Report of the Commission on East Fife; NMLH CI 13, PB, 29 December 1932.
191. Sime/Gilby interview, Mosie Murray.
192. NMLH CI 5, CC, 14 December 1934.
193. NMLH CI 13, PB, 3 September 1932.
194. *Daily Worker*, 2 December 1930. For the 'Industrial Party' trial, see A. Vaksberg, *The Prosecutor and the Prey: Vyshinsky and the 1930s Moscow show trials* (1990), pp. 51–3.
195. PL, 2 August 1928.
196. MacDougall, *Militant Miners*, pp. 133–4.
197. MPL I010, Strike Randolph Colliery; see also vol. 1, ch. 1.

CHAPTER EIGHT

Party politics, 1918–39

Introduction

The electoral efforts of the Labour Party (LP) in the Scottish coal-fields before 1914 were unimpressive, with William Adamson the sole representative of a mining constituency at Westminster. Labour's performance in the 1918 general election scarcely represented a breakthrough: the only new Labour Members were the LMU's Duncan Graham at Hamilton and James Brown, AMU Secretary, in Ayrshire-South. Labour performed significantly better in 1922, winning all but two of the Scottish constituencies where over 20 per cent of the male working population were employed in mining. For Christopher Harvie, 'the breakthrough in the mining areas was inevitable ... with the return of ex-servicemen to the pits and the failure of the Lloyd George coalition to do anything about the crisis-ridden industry, even after the radical Sankey Report of 1919, a shift to the left could scarcely be stopped'.[1] Yet the situation in the Scottish coalfields was more complex than this. Labour's forward march had not reached journey's end by 1922.

The first aim of this chapter is therefore to analyse Labour's uneven electoral performance in the light of previous discussion of the miners' communities. The second is more conjectural, to explore the degree to which the conflicts between the militant miner and bureaucratic reformism in the miners' unions were translated into the political arena. For there were limited left-wing successes: the election of Communist MPs J.T. Walton Newbold at Motherwell and Wishaw in 1922 and Willie Gallacher at West Fife in 1935, while Jennie Lee of the ILP drove the Labour candidate into a poor third place at Lanark in 1935. In particular, the chapter acknowledges Knox and McKinlay's analysis of Scottish Labour's reorganisation and ideological redefinition after the disaffiliation of the ILP in 1932; it suggests a greater fluidity than Harvie allows and points

to the lost possibilities of a more radical electoral politics. In conclusion, through case studies of Motherwell and West Fife, it indicates the circumstances under which such politics could, on occasion, manifest themselves.[2]

The rise of Labour

Table 8.1 summarises Labour's electoral performance in Scottish
'mining' constituencies during the inter-war general elections. Of
the fourteen constituencies listed, only Hamilton was consistently a
Labour seat from 1922 to 1935. Labour's uneven advance was
obstructed by significant 'technical' problems, even after the extension of the parliamentary franchise in 1918. The most important
remained the composition of the constituencies. Only one seat in
Scotland – West Fife – had a majority of miners in 1921, compared
with 19 in England and 8 in South Wales.[3] In some county constituencies, such as Ayrshire-South and Lanark, mining villages like
Annbank or Coalburn, Douglas and Ponfeigh, were diluted by agri-
cultural workers, even at the level of individual wards.[4] Elsewhere,
concentrations of miners in the Fife villages of Buckhaven and
Methil were aggregated with geographically separate settlements
outwith the coalfield, such as Burntisland and Kinghorn, to form
the Kirkcaldy District of Burghs, while Cowdenbeath and
Lochgelly, largely populated by miners, were included with the
larger town of Dunfermline in the Dunfermline Burghs. In
Lanarkshire, minorities of miners also lived in towns such as
Coatbridge and Motherwell, while the mining villages of Blantyre
were aggregated with the industrially diverse town of Rutherglen.[5]

Ethnicity also influenced Labour's performance. The United
Irish League supported most Labour candidates in 1918, but this in
itself was insufficient to guarantee victory in a year when turnout
was generally low before the return to peacetime normality. In only
three mining constituencies did Catholics constitute more than 20
per cent of the electorate: Hamilton, Lanark-North and
Rutherglen.[6] Nevertheless, the establishment of the Irish Free State
allowed 'the Irish Catholic community to accept its class identity'.[7]
The permanent shift in allegiance of this minority ethnic bloc was
an important accession of strength to Labour, for the party's victories in the coalfields in 1922 were often marginal ones. Table 8.2

Table 8.1 Labour electoral performance (%) in Scottish mining constituencies, 1918–35

Constituency	Percentage Miners, 1921	1918	1922	1923	1924	1929	1931	1935
Fife-West	51.9	**72.6**	Unop	**65.4**	**70.9**	**60.0**	35.8	35.7
Bothwell	48.2	49.1	**57.0**	**60.2**	**56.3**	**55.2**	43.5	**60.3**
Hamilton	46.0	**42.1**	**57.6**	**58.4**	**60.8**	**67.1**	53.9	**65.7**
Ayrshire-South	40.2	37.3	**55.6**	**55.9**	**50.4**	**58.1**	45.2	**57.6**
Lanark-North	37.3	34.1	**47.3**	**50.5**	46.1	**55.9**	44.7	37.3
Lanark	36.8	31.0	45.0	**50.5**	43.5	**48.7**	36.4	35.0
Linlithgowshire	32.4	40.3	**46.4**	**50.9**	48.9	**51.6**	45.3	**54.1**
Dunfermline	32.3	32.8	**50.4**	**53.6**	**57.9**	**58.5**	42.1	**52.3**
Rutherglen	32.9	40.9	**55.1**	**54.5**	**52.1**	**52.2**	43.2	49.3
Midlothian-North	31.7	-	38.3	**45.3**	44.8	37.5	27.7	37.1
Stirling-West	30.1	28.7	**52.4**	**51.9**	49.3	**56.7**	46.7	**55.1**
Midlothian-South	29.0	39.4	**36.0**	**43.0**	40.8	**45.5**	34.5	47.2
Kirkcaldy	26.4	-	48.6	**54.4**	**52.7**	**59.6**	43.1	**56.3**
Stirling-East	23.8	32.8	**42.0**	**51.1**	**52.6**	**53.2**	40.1	**42.1**

Sources: M. Kinnear, *The British Voter: an atlas and survey since 1885* (1981); F.W.S. Craig, *British Parliamentary Election Results, 1918–49* (Glasgow, 1969).

Notes
1. A 'mining constituency' is defined as having more than 20 per cent of the male population over the age of 12 in 1921.
2. Where no Labour candidate stood, ILP and Cooperative candidates have been treated as Labour proxies.
3. Figures in **bold** indicate a Labour victory.

indicates that the percentage of Catholic electors was often greater than Labour's victory margin in a number of mining seats in 1922, and the party cultivated this constituency through support for Catholic schools and the Catholic Relief Bills of 1925 and 1926.[8]

The 'Orange vote' is less easy to identify and allocate. At the Bothwell by-election in 1919, Labour's candidate, NUSMW President John Robertson, focused on nationalisation and housing. As a Protestant and former war-patriot, he might have been expected to have some appeal to the constituency's Orange electorate, estimated at 5,000. However, the District Master of the Orange Order was confident that miners would support Robertson's opponent, a Coalition Liberal and a coalmaster: 'between nationalisation and the interests of Ulster ... Ulster would come first'. He

Table 8.2 Estimated influence of Roman Catholic voting strength in electoral outcomes in Scottish mining constituencies, 1922

Constituency [Percentage mineworkers]	Percentage Catholic vote	Percentage Labour victory
Ayrshire – South [40.2]	3.9	5.0
Lanark – Bothwell [48.2]	16.7	14.0
Lanark – Hamilton [46.0]	22.5	15.2
Lanark [36.8]	3.8	Labour lose
Lanark – Northern [37.3]	21.3	10.9
Lanark – Rutherglen [32.9]	30.8	10.2
Linlithgow [36.4]	7.5	13.4
Stirling – East [23.8]	3.5	12.0
Stirling – West [30.1]	11.6	4.8
Fife – West [51.9]	3.2	Labour unopposed
Dunfermline District [32.3]	11.2	0.8
Kirkcaldy District [26.4]	5.9	Labour lose
Midlothian – North [31.7]	9.5	Labour lose
Midlothian – South and Peebles [29.0]	2.6	2.3

Sources: As for Table 8.1.

was proved wrong when Robertson won a crushing victory with 68.8 per cent of the vote in a constituency comprising 48 per cent miners. Although the UIL supported Robertson, Catholics only comprised 16.7 per cent of the electorate and it seems likely that some Orangemen voted for their union leader.[9] Nevertheless,

Conservative victories at Lanark in five out of the seven inter-war general elections, at Rutherglen in 1931 and 1935, at Motherwell in 1923 and 1931, at Lanark-North in 1924, 1931 and 1935, and in Linlithgowshire in 1924 and 1931, all suggest that significant numbers of Orangemen among the miners continued to vote for Unionist candidates.[10] But it is also probable that an increasing number voted Labour out of a perceived class interest in the face of falling wages and unemployment. *Forward* may have exaggerated when it claimed in 1923 that there were 'literally thousands of Orangemen who are members of the Labour Party', but the paper made some attempt to woo Orangemen in the early 1920s and the Larkhall ILP organised a debate with an Orange speaker in 1921.[11]

Labour's electoral success ultimately depended upon its political organisation and the party only slowly developed an effective local machine. Labour's new constitution of 1918 preserved its federal structure of union and ILP affiliation at local and national level, as well as providing for individual membership in local parties.[12] Yet Labour never became a mass party in the Scottish coalfields during the inter-war period. Individual LP membership in Scotland as a whole was only 9,200 in 1930, compared with a British membership of 277,211; by 1939 it had increased to 29,000, but the British membership had grown to over 400,000 and the average Scottish constituency party was much smaller than in England.[13] Even these figures are probably inflated. Of the 57 Scottish constituency parties for which affiliated membership was given in the Labour Party's *Annual Report for 1930*, 30 (including many in the coalfields) claimed to represent the maximum of 180 members which the minimum affiliation fee of £1 10s entitled them to. Their actual memberships were probably lower.[14]

Within the party's skeletal framework, local organisation in the coalfields remained based on the miners' unions and ILP branches. The unions operated 'like a party within a party', claiming the right to automatically appoint miners' candidates in mining constituencies through the deployment of considerable funds; see Table 8.3.[15] In Dunfermline in 1918, the local ILP and Labour Party did not put forward a Labour candidate, instead supporting the candidature of the anti-war, left-Liberal MP, Arthur Ponsonby. The FKCMA held a meeting and decided to nominate William Watson, an NUSMW political organiser, who stood as an 'Independent Labour' candidate. A Coalition Liberal was elected after Watson attracted over

Table 8.3 Expenditure on NUSMW candidates in Scottish county seats, 1922

Constituency	Expenditure £	Legal maximum £
South Ayrshire	925	889
Bothwell	742	909
Hamilton	647	799
North Lanark	794	885
North Midlothian	735	727
South Midlothian	684	777

Source: R. McKibbin, *The Evolution of the Labour Party, 1910–24* (Oxford, 1974), p. 148.

5,000 votes. According to a contemporary observer: 'The miners must have voted solidly for [Watson], even though many did not approve of his candidature. They are very highly organised and put loyalty to the union before all other considerations.'[16] Ten years later, it was claimed that in West Fife 'the local union committees in that constituency function as local Labour Parties'.[17] At South Midlothian and Peebles, the Labour Party was founded at a meeting dominated by miners in 1919. Joe Westwood, NUSMW Political Organiser in Fife, was the sole nominee to contest the seat which he held from 1922. At South Ayrshire, eleven miners sat on the nineteen-strong Executive Committee of the Divisional Labour Party (DLP).[18]

The surviving records of the Hamilton DLP, in the LMU's heartland, provide more detail on how the miners' unions operated locally. At a meeting soon after its establishment, following discussion 'regarding the most suitable candidate for the division, it was agreed to await finding of Miners' EC'. The same gathering was also addressed by Westwood. At a meeting the following week, 19 delegates from 11 LMU branches formed a large minority of the 48 delegates. After a member of the LMU Executive opened the meeting by stating the union's position, an LMU agent then proposed the LMU's General Secretary, Duncan Graham, as parliamentary candidate, seconded by an LMU branch delegate. Speeches were made in support of Graham – the only nominee – by Small and Alex Hunter, both LMU officials, and Ben Shaw, Scottish Secretary of the Labour Party.[19]

While the miners and ILP might amicably agree to divide responsibility for seats – as in 1918 where the ILP supported AMU nominations for the mining constituencies of North and South Ayrshire and the union supported ILP candidates in two other contests – there was occasionally friction between them.[20] The death of John Robertson in 1926 caused a by-election in his Bothwell seat. A deputation from the Scottish Council of the Labour Party (SCLP) to the NUSMW Executive pointed out 'that this is a miners' seat and expected that the miners would contest same'. The Executive remitted the matter to the LMU, along with power to nominate the candidate. After a ballot of LMU branches had chosen a nominee, the DLP nevertheless endorsed an ILP candidate, to the LMU's fury. Pressure from the LMU and NUSMW led the LP National Executive to accept that Bothwell was a miners' seat, and the ILP candidate subsequently withdrew. A meeting of the NUSMW Political Committee, attended by Shaw, demanded and was granted a full enquiry 'into the conduct and method of the ILP and local Labour Party'.[21] The NUSMW representative on the SCLP Executive insisted that 'the Miners had an unchallengeable right in constituencies in which they had previously expended large resources'. In considering the NUSMW's claim to an 'indefeasible right' to the constituency, the SCLP Executive's Bothwell Enquiry Report only accepted that the miners 'had an indefeasible claim ... of a moral character which it was anticipated would be respected, but it was equally made clear that other affiliated bodies had an equal right to make nominations, if so disposed'.[22] Three years later, another attempt by the ILP to nominate a candidate against the sitting MP, the LMU's Joseph Sullivan, led to further protests from the miners' unions. The NUSMW Political Committee notified Shaw 'that the ILP nominee should be withdrawn' and Sullivan was later adopted unanimously.[23]

If the miners' unions brooked few incursions into what they regarded as their sovereign territory, their political machine was largely immune from internal challenge. The NUSMW Political Committee was a sub-committee of the Executive, and dominated by miners' MPs, former MPs or aspiring MPs. For example, in 1929, its membership included five sitting MPs and one ex-MP, while its Secretary was a former parliamentary candidate. By the 1920s, the NUSMW employed four 'political agents' as organisers, and the Political Committee oversaw their work, which largely involved campaigning for the Committee's parliamentary members. Shaw was also regularly invited to attend. The Committee's recommendations to the NUSMW Executive were usually formally accepted.

The thirteen Scottish miners' officials who stood for parliament in the inter-war years are listed in Table 8.4, and it can be seen that on several occasions when an MP lost a mining seat, he was subsequently re-allocated to another. This relatively small, oligarchical group of MPs and parliamentary candidates were thus able to deploy the diminishing resources of the NUSMW not only to secure the miners a political voice but also in support of their own parliamentary careers. For example, when the Committee discussed a

Table 8.4 Scottish miners' union officials who stood in parliamentary elections, 1918–1935

William Adamson	West Fife: **1918, 1922, 1923, 1924, 1929,** 1931, 1935
James Brown	South Ayrshire and Bute: **1918, 1922, 1923, 1924, 1929,** 1931, **1935**
Andrew Clarke	North Midlothian: 1922, **1923,** 1924, **(1929),** 1929, 1931
Duncan Graham	Hamilton: **1918, 1922, 1923, 1924, 1929, 1931, 1935**
Hugh Murnin	Stirling and Falkirk Burghs: **1922,** 1923, **1924, 1929,** 1931
D.J. Pryde	South Midlothian: 1935
John Robertson	Bothwell: 1918, **(1919), 1922, 1923, 1924**
Alexander Sloan	North Ayrshire and Bute: 1929, 1931; South Ayrshire and Bute: **(1939)**
Robert Smith	North Ayrshire and Bute: 1918
Joseph Sullivan	North Lanarkshire: 1918, **1922, 1923,** 1924; Bothwell: **(1926), 1929,** 1931
William Watson	Dunfermline Burghs: 1918, **1922, 1923, 1924, 1929,** 1931, **1935**
James C. Welsh	Lanark: 1918; Coatbridge: **1922, 1923, 1924, 1929,** 1931; Bothwell: **1935**
Joseph Westwood	South Midlothian: **1922, 1923, 1924, 1929,** 1931; Stirling and Falkirk Burghs: **1935**

Source: F.W.S. Craig, *British Parliamentary Election Results, 1918–1949* (Glasgow, 1969).

Notes: Dates in **bold** indicate the candidate was elected; dates in brackets indicate a by-election.

pending by-election in North Midlothian in December 1928, it was agreed 'we adopt Mr Andrew Clarke as the candidate ... the Political Agents to carry out the work of the election. The selection conference to be held on 5 January 1929.' This was endorsed by the Executive the following week, and Clarke, a member of the Political Committee, was subsequently adopted and elected.[24] The Committee also agreed to fund a temporary political agent in Ayrshire to support another of its members, James Brown of the AMU, in his election campaign in 1929.[25] The Committee could also share the allocation of funds for parliamentary candidates from the MFGB amongst themselves. Such funding was allocated to MFGB affiliates on a quota proportional to membership. Thus in 1929, when the MFGB funded three seats in Scotland, the ÑUSMW Executive agreed that the salaries and expenses be pooled among all successful miners' candidates in Scotland.[26]

Despite the unevenness of support for Labour in the mining constituencies, miners' officials took little risk in standing for parliament. Some, such as Adamson, retained their union post while in parliament, and union agents were usually guaranteed reinstatement if they lost a subsequent election. The defeat of six out of seven NUSMW-sponsored candidates in the disastrous 1931 general election caused some difficulty in the LMU where Sullivan and Welsh were formerly agents. The LMU agreed that they should return to these positions, their replacements being given one month's notice and retained on a month to month basis for organising campaigns.[27]

If bureaucratic control of the NUSMW and county union executives largely insulated miners' MPs from political challenge, the more formally democratic procedures of the LMU did allow some pressure from the left. It was a measure of William Allan's support among union activists that he was able to secure the LMU's nomination for North Lanark in 1927 with a financial vote of £1,371, more than twice that of his nearest rival and comfortably more than the combined total of his three opponents, who included John Fotheringham, an NUSMW political agent. Allan had declared himself a member of the CP the previous year (when he was runner up for LMU nomination for the Bothwell by-election) and the NUSMW Executive refused to accept his nomination. The LMU Executive therefore recommended to the union's Council that a new, non-Communist candidate be selected, a recommendation rejected by a financial vote of £1,682 to £1,140. The NUSMW, supported by the Scottish and national Labour Party, refused to accept Allan's name going forward to a selection conference. A ballot of the LMU's membership nevertheless supported Allan by 5,083 to 4,447, but the selection conference refused to accept his nomination. Fotheringham was nominated by the Shotts Labour Party and secured the candidacy, although he did not stand at the next election.[28]

The candidate eventually selected at North Lanark, in the 'face of competition from powerful trade union nominees who offered to pay all election expenses', was the ILP's Jennie Lee, the university-educated grand-daughter of an FKCMA agent.[29] Her victory in a by-election in 1929 and successful defence in that year's general election, directs attention to the second significant element within the Scottish Labour Party, the ILP. David Howell has cautioned against uncritical characterisation of the ILP as a 'left opposition' within the Labour Party; its membership remained 'politically heterogenous' and many MP's retained their membership with wide degrees of commitment and varieties of rhetoric.[30] Knox and McKinlay also stress the party's diverse composition and weak structure: 'The Scottish ILP was as much an association as it was political party. It was based on a network of loosely controlled branches composed of individual members whose first allegiance was "fighting capitalism" rather than to the party as an institution.'[31] Even this is probably too constraining a definition since Adamson allegedly joined the ILP in 1928.[32]

While the surge in membership at the end of the First World War had moved the Scottish ILP to the left, it lost members of its Marxist wing to the CP after 1920. The numbers are unknown, and may have been small, but certainly contained some leading cadres, such as Newbold and Helen Crawfurd, a vice-president of the Scottish ILP who joined the CPGB Executive, as well as experienced local activists. For example, Alex Ritchie, a miner from Bridgeton in Glasgow, a reform movement activist and Chair of the CP's Scottish Central Committee in 1922, was a former ILP member; in Coatbridge, all three Communists elected in municipal elections in 1923 were former ILPers and included an LMU checkweigher who was Secretary of the Trades Council; the nucleus of the CP in Motherwell and Wishaw were ex-ILP members, including John Donnelly, later a Communist councillor and unemployed activist.[33] During the 1920s, the ILP was divided over the question of CP affiliation to the LP, but increasingly the Scottish ILP endorsed the LP leadership's firm opposition to Communist activity within the party. For example, when a short-lived Buckhaven ILP branch was attempted in 1927 with twenty-five members, most were 'well-known local Anti-Communists'.[34] As it sought to differentiate itself from the CP, the ILP eschewed involvement in the MM or NUWM, and increasingly became more 'self-contained'. While ILP branches threw themselves into support for the miners through the long months of 1926, raising funds and contributing to soup kitchens, these efforts appear to have generated few new members and in the aftermath many branches in the coalfields were depleted.[35] Nevertheless, within the coalfields, ILP membership remained stable in the later 1920s compared with a diminishing CP: see Table 8.5. But the continuing weakness of the ILP in Fife is also significant, for it allowed political space into which the CP could consolidate its influence in the 1930s. In East Fife, there was no permanent branch of the ILP in the 1920s and the CP's main left-wing opponents were 'a few old die-hards of the SDF who still cling together in the name of a branch' affiliated to the Labour Party.[36]

The existence of ILP branches with some tradition, if to very varying degrees, of political debate and activity acted as an obstacle to individual sections of the LP. Some insight into LP/ILP relations, and ILP branch life generally, in coalfield communities can be gained from the records of the Bo'ness branch. The branch effectively absorbed two LP Women's sections in the district in 1927 and four women were elected to the general committee of the ILP branch. Attendance at branch meetings was generally low – a vote disapproving of the Cook-Maxton manifesto (which called for 'unceasing war against capitalism') was passed 9 – 2. While the minutes often discuss the routine organisational business of fund-raising and booking rooms, there were Sunday evening political debates and discussion of reports from the DLP and Trades and Labour Council (TLC). ILP delegates to the TLC succeeded in convening a conference 'of all the members of organised Labour Bodies and the Labour members of all local bodies ... to preserve contact between the rank and file of the local Labour Movement and the Public Representatives'.[37] The branch voted against disaffiliation from the LP and reconstituted itself a branch of the Scottish Socialist Party which remained affiliated. Meetings became less frequent,

Table 8.5 ILP and CP membership in the Scottish coalfields, 1928 and 1930

	1928		1930	
	ILP	*CP*	*ILP*	*CP*
Coalfield				
West Central				
Lanarkshire	559	191	528	78
West Lothian	148		147	14
Stirlingshire	125	50	166	23
Dunbartonshire	14		23	
Ayrshire	358	50	343	26
Fife	194	157	197	68
Clackmannan	80		106	
Mid and East Lothian	49	54	44	14
Total	1,527	502	1,554	223

Sources: Report of ILP Annual Conference, 1928 and 1930; NMLH, CPBG Archive, Klugmann Papers; NMLH, CI 12, PB, 9 April 1931, Scottish District Organisation Report.

Notes: ILP membership has been estimated on the basis of branch affiliation fees at the the rate of 2d per month per member. Only those ILP branches within the geological boundaries of the coalfields have been included in this table, including the large branches at Ayr and Kilmarnock in Ayrshire, and Kirkcaldy and Dunfermline in Fife. It is not suggested that all, or even a majority, of the ILP members within these boundaries were miners. The CP figures for 1928 were only available at the level of counties; those for 1930 were given for individual towns and villages. Again, it is not suggested that all, or even a majority, of the CP members in these branches were miners.

sometimes because of lack of members, and the terse minutes convey little sense of vigorous branch life.[38]

If the ILP had some semblance of political activity, the life of the DLPs was sporadic and geared towards electoral activity. Arthur Woodburn, Shaw's successor as Scottish Secretary of the LP, pointed to this contrast: 'The main power of the Labour Party is therefore exercised by delegates who only have a periodic association and little possibility of permanent or social association. The ILP was small and intimate. The Labour Party by its very size could not have this advantage.'[39] Fraser similarly summarises the activities of the Hamilton DLP:

Essentially the Divisional Labour Party was a machine for coordinating and approving election activities in national, municipal,

county and education authority elections. What signs of political
debate there are seem to indicate that the executive was generally on
the right of the movement.[40]

Local LP sections for individual members were only established
with considerable difficulty and their political focus was electoral.
The episodic efforts of the Bo'ness TLC to establish an individual
membership section in 1935 were unsuccessful.[41] The minutes for
1935 of the Dalkeith Local Labour Party, established a decade
earlier, are largely concerned with the minutiae of organising fund
raising activities, such as whist drives, sales of work and picnics, by
the small group of less than twenty active members. For example,
there was considerable debate on selling the party's carpet bowls –
'after a great deal of discussion it was decided to do nothing in the
meantime' – and a vote of 9–7 in favour of refunding the three-
pences paid for tickets to a cancelled picnic. 'Politics', in so far as
they intruded, were largely defined by the municipal elections when
a 'propaganda meeting' with Labour councillors and a 'victory
social' after the party won control of town council for the first time
were held.[42]

Only in 1939 were two members of the women's section co-opted
on to the Dalkeith party committee.[43] Yet recent research by Savage
and others has pointed to the importance of women voters' support
for welfare policies as a factor in Labour's inter-war advance.[44]
Although some of the Scottish mining constituencies had very high
rates of female registration among eligible women – 93.3 per cent in
Hamilton, for example, where women constituted 40.6 per cent of
voters – this must be viewed within the context of miners' wives'
political deference to their husbands, evidenced previously.[45]
Numerically, there was some growth of LP Women's Sections in the
coalfields in the 1920s: they were established at Bothwell,
Coatbridge, Hamilton, Stirling, Kilmarnock, Dunfermline, and
Kirkcaldy by 1923; at Bothwellhaugh, Leven and West Calder in
1924; at Dalkeith in 1925; at Kilsyth and Gorebridge in 1926.[46]

Few records of LP Women's Sections remain, but those for
Larkhall for the 1920s permit insight into women's activities in a village which by then had a significant Labour tradition. The picture
they portray is of a small circle of members, among whom Smillie's
daughter played a leading part, whose activities were as much social
as political: meetings included poetry recitals (such as the self-

composed 'My ain wee hoose') and songs, and sometimes took the form of rural outings. Numbers attending the regular meetings ranged from thirteen to thirty-two. Meetings were often preceded by refreshments – references to 'a good tea', 'a nice tea', 'tea and dumpling', 'tea and a good spread', appear in the minutes – for which a charge of a shilling was made to raise funds.[47] In 1926, the General Strike and lockout impinged regularly on the section's activities: on 6 May, Miss Smillie read from *Forward* and also a letter 'asking the women to be ready to do anything if it be asked of them'. The following week, after a report on the LP's meeting with the Council of Action, the Secretary read from the *Scottish Worker*. Two weeks later, Duncan Graham, MP, addressed an open air meeting on 'The coal crisis and the miner's wife'. In June, Miss Smillie spoke on 'what this strike meant to mother and child'. These meetings were interspersed with picnics and rambles, and meetings over the summer were abandoned. In October, at the winter's 'opening social', the President referred to the depressing circumstances of the lockout with a cheery stoicism: 'but no doubt all would be well sometime. Tea was afterwards served ... a nice, big rich dumpling was served all round', before Miss Smillie talked again on the coal crisis.[48]

Such activities doubtless sustained and consoled the section's membership during the harrowing months of 1926, but the women appear as a small group of observers rather than actors, well aware that their primary political function was to raise election funds through raffles, socials and Burns Suppers, and to act as auxiliaries in the next election campaign. Pamela Graves has criticised 'the male definition' of fund-raising activities as not 'real' politics. Yet important though such activities are to all political organisations, any redefinition of tea-making as empowering is perhaps to retreat unduly before contemporary notions of gender relations. If the attempts by the UMS and CP to build women's guilds were generally unsuccessful, they at least endeavoured, however haltingly and imperfectly, to challenge such conceptions.[49]

But if women activists were often segregated within Labour's electoral machine, this does not mean that 'welfarist' policies were of little significance. The poverty and unemployment experienced in 1926 and the following decade placed a considerable electoral premium on welfare policies at the national and local levels. The achievements of the 1929–31 Labour government in Scotland –

modest job creation, the 1930 Housing Act, reform of the Poor Law, the provision of free milk to Lanarkshire schoolchildren – though limited, were nevertheless significant by contemporary criteria.[50] The opportunities such legislation provided required Labour support at municipal and county level – particularly in the field of housing, where the Scottish coalfields benefited greatly from the 1930 Act.[51] By 1936, Labour controlled Hamilton, Motherwell and Wishaw, Cumnock and Cowdenbeath burgh councils, and were neck and neck with their opposition at Airdrie, Rutherglen and Bo'ness.[52] But such success was neither uniform nor the result of an unproblematic 'forward march'. As Knox and McKinlay point out, the 're-making' of Scottish Labour, abandoning class analysis and embracing 'a form of state interventionism and improved welfare provision' occurred only in the 1930s under the catalytic impact of economic depression.[53] Alternative strategies were propounded to the left of Labour, primarily by the CP. It is to an assessment of its political impact that we now turn.

CP organisation

The unification of left groupings into the CPGB which culminated in January 1921 could scarcely have occurred at a more unpropitious time in the Scottish coalfields. The fledgling party struggled to survive in the coalfields following the three-month lockout later that year. At Galston in Ayrshire, it was reported that prior to the dispute, there had been an 'ardent group' of Communist supporters 'who owing to victimisation have been scattered or unemployed'. The Secretary of the Buckhaven CP branch reported in 1922 that 'the communist branches in this district has [sic] had a gradual falling off of members since the defeat of the miners ...'. There were four Communists in Methil, ten in Buckhaven, while East Wemyss had three active members and five or six 'who can hardly be draged [sic] to their own branch meetings'.[54] A new CP group was formed in East Fife in September 1923 but by the end of the year, its 'strength was now only eight'; its Secretary, David Proudfoot, described it 'as about as dead as the dodo' in 1924. The pressures on the group were epitomised by the pit manager informing its 'newsagent' that 'if he was seen with a *Workers' Weekly* in his possession on the pit head he would be dismissed. As he has physical disabilities and has to support his parents, who are old, he has decided to resign from the party.'[55] By 1924, there were CP locals within the coalfields at Blantyre, Hamilton, Coatbridge and Airdrie, and Motherwell in Lanarkshire, Kilmarnock and Kilmaurs in Ayrshire, Stoneyburn in West Lothian, and Methil, Leven, East Wemyss, Kirkcaldy, Bowhill and Cowdenbeath in Fife, though their memberships were often small. At Hurlford, there were only three Communists in 1924.[56]

The resurgence of union organisation in 1925 and the impending coal crisis led to a quickening in party recruitment. Proudfoot reported a revival in Methil and a new group was formed in West Wemyss. In East Lothian, a local was set up at Musselburgh. In Lanarkshire, the first meeting of the Burnbank local recruited nineteen members, the second a further eighteen; at the small pit village of Tannochside, the new local had a membership of twenty; another was established at nearby Uddingston.[57] During the 1926 lockout, miners and their wives flocked to join the party in Fife: Proudfoot reported a total of eighty-four new recruits in Methil on two consecutive days in May, but reflected realistically: 'Of course many of them will be shed but it demonstrates how things are going here.' A week later, the membership in Methil approached 200 and by July was claimed to be 421. At Lochgelly, CP membership quadrupled.[58] Membership growth elsewhere was significant if less dramatic: locals were formed at Kilsyth in Stirlingshire (36 members), at Crossgates (18), Leslie (46), Lochore and Glencraig in Fife, at Lesmahagow (30) in Lanarkshire, and at Dalkeith (35) in Midlothian. The membership at Dalkeith included groups in the mining villages of Newtongrange, Rosewell, Gorebridge and Arniston. A new local was also established at Prestonpans by the end of the year.[59]

While membership in Lanarkshire increased by 250 per cent between May and October, the party Secretary, James McKendrick, reported there was 'no attempt to disguise the weaknesses existing in the Sub-District' given that the 'bulk of members are new to the Party'. The following year, eight party training class with 94 students were run in the county to develop this new membership.[60] However, reports to a Lanarkshire Sub-DPC conference indicated the problems the party faced: at Bellshill, 'many members ... had recently fallen away'; Lesmahagow had 'consolidated' an active membership of twenty-one; Burnbank 'could do with raising the percentage of active members'; Motherwell needed 'special attention as some of its groups were weakening'; Blantyre claimed its large new membership 'was presenting many problems, but 40 of these were now participating in party work'.[61] Such publicly claimed figures should be treated circumspectly, but the tenor of the reports accurately reflected an inevitable decline in membership in the post-lockout period. Proudfoot complained that:

> At present the Party in Fife is practically an unemployed Party, very few members have been restarted and the result is that some have left the Party and others are failing to put in an appearance at Party meetings due to the bright and handy idea that membership of the Party is the reason for them not being employed. The new Party membership is certainly being tested now, and events are proving that we have picked up a good number of 'strike Communists'.

The local was 'going to pieces ... since asking for subs many kent faces have had to be posted as missing', and only fourteen members attended a branch aggregate meeting.[62] In an effort to revitalise the Methil local it was divided into three groups at Methil, Denbeath and Buckhaven which would each meet weekly for training classes. The attempt was unsuccessful: 'The local here is now a joke, the splitting into groups being the tombstone of our efforts as far as the crowd who "wandered in" during last year's scrap is concerned.'[63] At the CP Scottish District Congress in 1928, a decline in registered membership was held to represent those who had never been properly drawn into party work.[64]

Although the UMS struggles generated some new recruits to the party – Proudfoot reported 'fairly good gains' after the 1930 strike in Fife, and the Methil local increased to almost thirty members – CP membership in the Scottish coalfields remained low in the early 1930s.[65] See Table 8.6. These figures were compiled from membership of branches within the coalfield boundaries. It is not suggested that all the members of these branches were miners. In April 1931, 50 per cent of the Scottish membership was unemployed, and the percentage in the coalfields was very probably higher: only fifty-five party members were employed in the mines that month. The following year, the Scottish District Committee admitted 'we are largely a Party of unemployed workers'.[66]

Work among the unemployed in the coalfields was a major area of CP activity in the early 1930s and, according to police estimates,

Table 8.6 CP membership in the Scottish coalfields, 1928–32

	1928	1930	1931	1932
Coalfield				
West Central				
Lanarkshire	191	78	71	104
West Lothian		14	12	9
Stirlingshire	50	23	13	12
Ayrshire	50	26	33	59
Fife	157	68	89	147
Mid and East Lothian	54	14	12	35
Total	502	223	230	366
Total Scottish membership	910	524	503	1,314

Sources: NMLH, CPBG Archive, Klugmann Papers; CI 12, PB, 9 April 1931, Scottish District Organisation Report.

support for the CP-led National Unemployed Workers' Movement (NUWM) demonstrations was considerable. In Motherwell, there were regular NUWM protests against the Means Test. In October 1931, for example, there were three demonstrations: the first amounted to about 5,000 people by the time it reached the Council Chambers; on the second, a contingent of 150 from Motherwell were joined by a further 100 from Flemington and about 800 from Wishaw and Craigneuk; the third involved a demonstration of about 250, mainly from Craigneuk, to the Public Assistance Committee (PAC) offices. In early November, 600, the bulk from Craigneuk, supported a deputation to the Town Council. In April 1932, a 1200-strong NUWM demonstration included 400 from Coatbridge, 500 from Bellshill, 150 from Rutherglen and Blantyre, 90 from Wishaw and Craigneuk, and 50 from Motherwell, each contingent accompanied by a flute band; speeches were made by the CP's Ed Laughlin from Blantyre and John Donnelly from Craigneuk.[67] A Lanarkshire NUWM demonstration at Bellshill in October 1932 was estimated by police to number 8,000.[68] In Coatbridge, NUWM protests numbering 2,000–3,000 took place.[69] On occasion these demonstrations had some effect, as at Kilbirnie in January 1932, when the NUWM successfully protested in support of a man whose benefit had been wrongly reduced.[70] The demonstrations were closely monitored by the police who variously categorised the participants as mainly 'irresponsible youths', 'young hooligans about 18 years of age', 'youths about 20 years of age, all the hooligan type and mostly Roman Catholics of Irish parentage', 'young men of from 18 to 25 years of age, and many of an apparently undesirable type'.[71]

The failure to build CP organisation in the Scottish coalfields despite the party's increasing influence among the miners and unemployed youth was a constant theme in the upper echelons of the party apparatus in the 1930s. At the CC in January 1930, Jim Shields asked why, 'where the UMS has grown up in a particular county, the Party has gone out of existence?'; at the meeting in April, Pollitt accepted that despite having a revolutionary union, 'we have no Party in Fife'.[72] The Young Communist League fared little better. In Lanarkshire, there were only two or three YCL members in 1930, while in Fife there was 'no League whatsoever ... The decline of the Party there and its partial collapse has meant that it could give no assistance to the League.'[73] In 1932, Pollitt welcomed victories in the pits, but complained that 'the Party fraction does not use these victories for the purpose of getting the Scottish miners into our Party'.[74] Two years later, Gallacher reiterated that:

> There is a situation in Lanark, Lothians and Fifeshire, a better situation than exists anywhere, and there is no party ... In Fife, it used to be the easiest thing to have a couple of thousand members and now we have 50 members in the Communist Party.[75]

Even after Gallacher's election in 1935, there was only a limited increase in Party membership. Arnot claimed that whereas there had been only 70 members in Fife before the election, there were 250 a few months later. This increase appears short lived. Moffat reported in 1937 that despite 'the tremendous influence' of the party in Fife, there had only been a net gain of fifty members in the recent past.[76]

In addition to the real barriers of victimisation and unemployment, there were a number of internal, political causes of the CP's failure to build a larger membership in what it saw as 'objectively favourable' conditions. The first was a blurring of the division between trade union militancy and party politics. McArthur later admitted that most CP activity focused on the miners' union:

> and it was difficult to tell where trade union activity ended and Party
> activity commenced. This was one of the factors in all probability
> that militated against the building of organised Communist Party
> branches. The generally haphazard approach in the Fife coalfield to
> Party organisation was really due to us seeming to think that trade
> union branch activity was the same as Communist Party branch
> activity.[77]

This was particularly the case during strikes when the demands on
party organisers' time were greatest. Arnot complained in 1931 of:

> The fact that in strike after strike, as soon as a strike begins the Party
> ends and only resumes again when the strike is finished ... in West
> Fife one of the things you could not help noticing was that whereas
> the Union [i.e. UMS] leaders had real contact with the masses in sev-
> eral villages, this was more as individuals and not as members of the
> Party and in all of the activities the Party took a very small place ...
> In West Fife the Party did not meet for three months ... The Party
> disintegrates, splits up and becomes a series of individual active
> strikers ...[78]

Gallacher reported the following year that while the UMS was leading strikes in West Fife, 'in regard to the Party it has not been functioning in Fife at all'.[79] Pollitt noted that Moffat's speech to the
UMS conference in 1932 'was a good statement from a miner, but
not a political statement from the Party', while Kerrigan, the
Scottish Organiser, complained of 'the submerging of the Party to
the UMS'.[80]

A second element was the inconsistency of CP policy, with the
shift from united front activity in the early 1920s to the increasing
sectarianism after 1926 and the approach of the 'third period'. The
ultra-leftism of Bob Selkirk and others in Central Fife in 1928–9
was reviewed in chapter six of this volume. Selkirk and William
O'Neill, a fellow Cowdenbeath Communist of militaristic views,
were expelled from the party in 1930; they accused the CPGB of
'opportunism' and attempted to set up a new local loyal to
Comintern.[81] Later that year, Pollitt admitted that 'the incorrect
application of the new line had led to sectarian mistakes'.[82] Squires'
revisionist argument that CP membership increased as a consequence of the 'new line' is only tenable if one accepts his periodisation of the years 1930 to 1933.[83] Yet the evidence in chapters six and

seven of this volume suggests the amelioration of the worst sectarian excesses by 1930. The membership data in Table 8.6, with a halving of the membership in branches within the coalfields between 1928 and 1930 and a revival only in 1932, confirm the conventional analysis that the 'new line' had a disastrous impact on party numbers. The dramatic swing towards the opposite policy of the popular front by 1935 may have had a similarly negative effect on membership as the CP subordinated itself to the Labour Party's election campaign. According to Arnot, many CP members 'forgot' they were Communists during the general election: 'they acted as members of the Labour Party and of Labour Party only'. Following the liquidation of the UMS, some party members fully expected 'the liquidation of the CP as the further stage in carrying out the line of the Seventh [Comintern] Congress'.[84]

Such shifts in policy were dictated by the Comintern. A related factor in limiting the appeal of the CPGB to potential members was the Bolshevisation of the party demanded by the CI, which imposed a rigid and bureaucratic structure upon its tiny membership. McArthur recalled: 'When we started to read documents coming out from the Communist International we were learning a new language. They were talking in terms of bourgeoisie, proletariat, lumpenproletariat, nuclei, fractions. It was like going back to school.'[85] Some British Communists did go 'back to school', to the ILS in Moscow, and a number became leading cadres on their return. Yet Pollitt was critical of the 'education' they received:

Most of our best comrades and best district organisers have been through the schools. [sic] We can make many criticisms against the school. The main one is that the comrades come back with an education that fits them to function in Soviet Union where socialism is established.[86]

Kerrigan was described by a fellow ILS graduate as being 'the most Stalinist of Stalinists,' and Harry McShane, then a member of the Scottish DPC was withering in his critique of the 'Stalin-worship' by ILS students who were allocated to Scotland: 'they were utterly impossible when they came back. They would come up to Glasgow and lecture us on every little thing that should be done ... all they knew was what had been taught to them at the Lenin School – they had never thought anything through for themselves.'[87]

The party's close identification with the Soviet Union was

regarded by its members as an inspiration and advantage, yet the connection was at best ambivalent in terms of building the membership. There were a significant number of mining activists who visited Russia and gave favourable reports on their return. Jas Miller from Methil went as a Young Pioneer to Moscow in 1927 where Stalin presented him with a badge to award to 'the best comrade' when he returned; Bob Selkirk was a delegate to the Sixth Comintern Congress in 1928; Mary Docherty, from Cowdenbeath, travelled to the Soviet Union as youth delegate from August 1929 to May 1930, and spoke at numerous meetings on her return. Such visits were not unusual and Docherty estimated that about one person a year went to Russia from Cowdenbeath. Mrs Pettigrew, a UMS Women's Guild Delegate who visited Russia in 1932 addressed a meeting of 500 miners and their wives in Leven upon her return, painting a glowing picture of pithead baths and miners' food rations. A Fife miner working the Donbas coalfield wrote home in similar terms.[88] But while the support for the Soviet Union sustained CP activists, its broader appeal is uncertain, not only because of the hostility of the popular press but also the anti-Stalinism rooted in the instinctive anti-authoritarianism of many British workers.[89]

Finally, the CP's small membership created a vicious circle by the demands imposed on leading party activists which both exhausted them and acted as a disincentive to potential members. The Buckhaven CP Secretary reported that 'on the united front question we have not been able to do very much as we are few and our duties are so numerous ... every active member has his hands full, being on committees of all sorts'.[90] Proudfoot adumbrated his many responsibilities in 1925:

> 1. Group leader and representative on District Party Committee; 2. Group trainer (oh, hell); 3. Chief literature distributor ...; 4. Delegate for Union Branch to local Trades and Labour Council; 5. Delegate for Trades and Labour Council to Divisional Executive; 6. Collector of subscriptions for Communist Book Club; 7. Doormat for local industrial disputes; 8. Checkweighman in spare time.[91]

Such hyper-activism could also be seen as a substitute for building a broader party organisation. It was felt that cadres such as Proudfoot and Moffat 'are doing so much that workers simply regard them as all sufficient'.[92] Kerrigan wrote in 1935 of the need to break down 'the conception that exists among many Party workers ... that Party membership means giving up entirely their previous mode of life, maybe even their friends, and also working day and night'.[93] Given the Party's small cadre, the expansion of work in one area meant abandoning another. In 1936, Finlay Hart, then CP Scottish Organiser, complained that: 'Many of the unemployed comrades have taken up work for the *Daily Worker* to the neglect of unemployed work ...':

> Our comrades are going into the County Unions. We thought that this would release the party functionaries and that they would be able to carry on party work in the other sense of the term. But the opposite has been the case. Their work has broadened out and their work in the County Unions has taken a considerable amount of their time and they are now doing less propaganda work for us than before.[94]

But if CP membership remained stubbornly low, the party was not wholly without local electoral success. In 1928, the Scottish party counted twelve parish councillors, six town councillors and four county councillors, including Alex Moffat in Fife, as its elected representatives.[95] In Lochgelly, the Communists numbered five out of the twelve strong School Management Committee.[96] By 1933, there were pockets of Communist support in the municipal elections: Jimmy Stewart won a seat in Lochgelly while the reinstated Selkirk secured 932 votes compared with the ILP candidate's 1,026. In Methil and West Wemyss, McArthur and Jimmy Hope also won seats. In Hamilton's fifth ward, the Communist polled 995 against Labour's 1,716; in Rutherglen's Castle and Shawfield wards, the comparable figures were 410 – 684 and 212 – 383. In Musselburgh's third ward, the Communist candidate pushed Labour into third place.[97] In 1935, three Communists were elected to Lanarkshire County Council, including Barney McCourt, an NUWM activist from Bellshill, and James Beecroft, an unemployed Blantyre miner who had led the Lanarkshire contingent on the previous year's Hunger March to London. Blantyre's Ed Laughlin was among the six Lanarkshire Communists elected to district councils.[98] By 1936, the Party had twenty-six councillors in Scotland, and in the new found spirit of the popular front were able on occasion to work with Labour and ILP councillors.[99]

These results suggest there was some scope for translating the local prestige and persistent agitation of its leading militants into electoral success. However, this more consistent work in the localities was not echoed in the party's parliamentary interventions in the coalfields. Table 8.7 records the limited and generally poor performance of CP candidates in the Scottish 'mining' constituencies. Shifting policies towards the Labour Party precluded any sustained electoral activity, except in 1929 when its strident sectarianism was at its most unappealing. Moreover, according to Gallacher, while three seats were contested in Scotland in connection with the mining situation, 'only one would have been chosen from the point of view of Party strength and influence'. These others were contested purely for 'political reasons', possibly at the behest of the Comintern.[100] The party's choice of candidate's in 1929 also failed to capitalise upon its electoral successes in the miners' unions. In Bothwell, the candidate was Helen Crawfurd; in Hamilton, the relatively obscure Motherwell activist, Frank Moore; at Dunfermline, the Glaswegian Jack Leckie, who was not a miner; at Rutherglen, Fife's Alex Moffat, who was totally unknown in the Lanarkshire coalfield at that time. Although the PB decided in December 1930 that Allan, then UMS General Secretary, should be the party's candidate for Bothwell, in the 1931 general election the party put forward Barney McCourt who made little impact in this mining seat.[101] Allan was instead selected as the CP candidate in the Rutherglen by-election that year, but was unable to raise the deposit.[102] Only in West Fife, where Gallacher was the candidate in 1929, 1931 and 1935, was there consistent parliamentary activity, to which we shortly return.

Table 8.7 Communist electoral performance (%) in Scottish mining constituencies, 1922–35

	1922	1923	1924	1929	1931	1935
Fife-West	-	-	-	20.5	22.1	42.1
Bothwell	-	-	-	5.5	6.5	-
Hamilton	-	-	-	1.6	-	-
Dunfermline	-	-	-	6.5	-	-
Rutherglen	-	-	-	2.5	-	-

Sources: See Table 8.1.

Conclusion: two vignettes

Neither Labour nor the CP built a mass membership in the Scottish coalfields before 1939. While it was Labour which dominated the mining constituencies, its presence was not hegemonic. If the process of increasing working-class parliamentary representation in the inter-war years was 'inevitable', the form it took was not. Two concluding case studies suggest first, the openness of labour politics in the 1920s, and second, the potential for translating trade union militancy into a more radical politics in parts of the coalfields.

Motherwell, 1922

At the general election of 1922, Walton Newbold was returned for Motherwell and Wishaw as a Communist MP. In 1918, when still a member of the ILP, Newbold had stood for the constituency on the uncompromising slogan of 'Complete and unconditional surrender of capital and all power to the working class'. He came third with 23 per cent of the votes on a programme of support for the Bolshevik revolution and militant industrial unionism. Developments between 1918 and 1922 in the constituency have been analysed elsewhere.[103] Here we need only note the agitation by Newbold's supporters on housing and rents, and the one-day sympathy stoppage on the issue by the LMU in 1920; Newbold's advocacy of militant support for the miners in 1921; large demonstrations of the unemployed organised by Communist activists; and Newbold's vigorous campaigning at street corner meetings and in the local press.[104] Newbold's candidature after he left the ILP to join the CP was a matter of intense controversy and his ultimate selection as the sole left-wing candidate a complex and drawn out affair in the face of hostility from the Labour and ILP leaderships. Despite such opposition, after his adoption he was aided by a closing of ranks in a united front of the local labour movement. At Newbold's numerous meetings, miners' Labour candidates from neighbouring constituencies rubbed shoulders with prominent Communists. For example, James Welsh rallied 'a crowded and enthusiastic meeting in the town hall' with an endorsement of 'Comrade Newbold', promising 'were they united they could capture the legislative machine'. Newbold then spoke passionately and analytically on the unemployment affecting the local coal and steel industries and poor housing, urging the dispossession of the landowners to let them live on the dole: 'they could have a chance at Cowie's Square of Berryhill Rows (laughter). When he heard of the prestige of the British empire, he felt like asking if they had ever heard of the prestige of Craigneuk ...'.[105]

The CP claimed that: 'Craigneuk is our stronghold. The housing conditions in the locality are atrocious and the poverty of its inhabitants simply appalling.'[106] In addition to poor housing, the high percentage of Catholics there points to a further source of Newbold's support. Newbold described Craigneuk as 'the dreariest of slums ... inhabited by the Irish labourers at the Lanarkshire and adjacent steel-works and coal-pits' who had been deeply moved at the death of the Mayor of Cork after a hunger strike. The appearance of Newbold in the front rank of the Irish Transport Workers in the memorial procession through Dublin was only one of his activities in the republican cause which helped win their support.[107]

Newbold's election in 1922 was on exactly a third of the vote. His characteristically flamboyant telegram to the Kremlin – 'have won Motherwell in Scotland for Communism' – was over-optimistic. The Secretary of the Trades Council warned against taking the telegram literally and pointed to the complexities of the result, including, crucially, a divided opposition and 'a united front amongst the various sections of the Labour and Socialist bodies'. He also pointed to divisions based on generation: 'The majority of the young men gave their votes to the Communist candidate because they are suffering more from unemployment than the married men, and a desire to see a change in the old order.' Such aspirations were vague – 'only in a dim and hazy way do they understand the meaning of the words "Socialism" and "Communism"'. In contrast, 'the older people' were 'alarmed and frightened' by talk of atheism and free love.[108]

Nor had divisions based on religion been dissolved. While Newbold claimed to have 'the solid force of the Catholic Irish' and some of the younger priests behind him in 1922, religious opposition intensified in the following year's general election: 'The wire-pullers who control Catholic opinion to a very large extent did their best to get Newbold out, and the burgh was flooded with lies about "persecution of Catholics" in Russia.'[109] Newbold marginally increased both his vote and share of the vote, but was defeated in a three-cornered context by the Conservative, Hugh Ferguson, a former miner and fundamentalist Protestant. In 1924, Ferguson was himself defeated by a Labour candidate, the Reverend James Barr, a moderate ILPer who attracted 4,000 more votes than Newbold in 1923. Newbold had grown increasingly disenchanted with the CP, especially the 'fatuous' discussions he witnessed at the ECCI and the Comintern's attitude to workers in Western Europe in 1923. He formally resigned from the party in September 1924:

> I have wished to see the CP dominating the LP, in the same way as the ILP has come to do, never as replacing the LP after disintegrating it ... But I am, perhaps, too English in outlook and in thought, too grounded in insularity and tradition to be a good Communist.[110]

The events in Motherwell in the post-war years were testimony to the 'ideological openness of the ILP among the socialist community of an extended Clydeside ... before the "double closure" of Labour and Communist alignment' and the potential of a united labour movement under radical, campaigning leadership.[111] For McKibbin, they demonstrated that:

> ... the Communist Party was electorally strong only when it worked within the traditional Labour organisation. Although Communists could gain influence by their own ingenuity, perseverance, plain hard work, a skilful and decisive exploitation of local grievances, and by the inertness or complaisance of others, once they were excluded from that organisation they were ineffective.[112]

While in general this conclusion carries much persuasive weight, the electoral contest in West Fife thirteen years later suggested that the generation of post-war Communist militants had been able to extend their base in the mining communities there to successfully challenge Labour.

West Fife, 1935

West Fife was the one constituency in the Scottish coalfields where the CP pursued a consistent parliamentary strategy. Willie Gallacher had been a regular speaker to miners' gatherings since the First World War and was the CP's parliamentary candidate in each election after 1929. In that year, he took second place to Adamson with 20 per cent of the vote. In 1931, he came third, though increasing his vote and share of the vote sufficiently to allow a Conservative victory over Adamson.[113] Prior to the election, Proudfoot sketched the political complexion of the constituency, from which the large mining centres of Cowdenbeath, Lochgelly, Methil and Buckhaven were excluded and which contained a mixture of CP citadels such as Lumphinnans and Glencraig as well as the 'Adamson strongholds' of Kinglassie, where the UMS branch was 'defunct', and Lassodie and Kincardine, where there were neither UMS branches nor party organisation. In the Culross district at Blairhall, there was only a 'weak UMS branch due to fear of victimisation', while at neighbouring Valleyfield, Proudfoot detected a 'growing UMS influence and active new Cttee. Should be good possibilities here for Gallacher.'[114] Events proved Proudfoot's political antennae to be sensitively attuned to political shifts in the Culross district as miners migrated there from Hamilton and Blantyre in Lanarkshire and there was a subsequent growth in industrial militancy.[115]

Gallacher appreciated the importance of the consistent, conventional campaigning which had been largely absent from the CP's other parliamentary interventions. In 1934, he argued before the PB: 'So we have got to make a party campaign and try and get national speakers involved in it, to put the party line in the mining industry and drive in these areas ... If we make a big attack on Lanark and Fife we can capture the situation.' By January 1935, the PB decided that Gallacher should be largely resident in Scotland to engage in such propaganda.[116] His campaign in the general election of that year was given additional impetus by strikes at Blairhall Colliery over a wage dispute and at Valleyfield over the introduction of a new 'dirt scale' of deductions for 'foreign' material in the coal. By mid-October, 1,700 men were on strike at the two mines.[117] While the Blairhall dispute was soon settled, at Valleyfield the FCKMU recommended an immediate return to work pending negotiations. This advice was rejected and the men's defiance of their union, as well as the FCKMU's refusal to issue strike pay, allowed the UMS space to organise support. Alex Moffat took responsibility for applications to the PAC for relief for the strikers' families while Abe Moffat's wife, Helen, helped run a feeding centre. The UMS organised collections for the strikers throughout Fife and made a series of donations to the strike fund. Faced with the hostility of Adamson and the union leadership after they reaffirmed their determination to remain out, the Valleyfield branch of the FCKMU collaborated closely with the UMS in a dispute that dragged on for twelve weeks.[118]

The Valleyfield dispute provided a backdrop to the election campaign. Abe Moffat made an early and tactically shrewd approach to Adamson for a single united front candidate to be selected by representatives of all workers' organisations in the constituency, pointing out that the CP were supporting the Labour candidate in every other mining constituency in Scotland.[119] Following the inevitable rejection of this offer, an elderly and recently-widowed Adamson was harried and heckled by his opponent's supporters. He defensively confined his speeches to the main points of Labour's national manifesto: at Kelty, the chairman of his election meeting refused to allow questions on the Valleyfield strike as it was a 'political meeting'. At Lumphinnans, 'on account of the time lost through interruptions, Mr Adamson was unable to allow a period for questions and the meeting ended on an unsatisfactory note'. His attempt to address a meeting of 500 electors in High Valleyfield received a particularly hostile reception when he refused to answer questions and, amid prolonged disorder, the meeting was abandoned. As Adamson was driven away amid boos and catcalls, a young Valleyfield miner, Patrick McGurk, punched his fist through the car window, slightly injuring the driver.[120]

Gallacher's campaign was conducted with some élan. As one of only two CP candidates standing in the general election, the party was able to devote personnel, resources and national speakers to the constituency. Gallacher's close identification with the UMS was strongly projected: Abe Moffat spoke prominently at his meetings and regular collections were taken at them for the Valleyfield strikers. Gallacher forcefully contrasted Adamson's 'relations with the coalowners' with the work conducted by UMS workmen's inspectors.[121] His manifesto spoke to the concerns of mineworkers and included the pledge to introduce a four clause Bill into parliament, covering a seven hour day, a guaranteed wage, a commission on safety and the appointment of workmen's inspectors, and a commission on rebuilding the mining villages.[122]

In a review of the party's campaign to the PB following Gallacher's victory, Bob McIlhone highlighted the significance of the Valleyfield strike. In one of the few areas of Fife with a significant Catholic population, the absence of sectarian division was also important:

> There was tense feeling on the Sunday morning as to what the priest would say and it was with a feeling of great relief that during the sermon not a single word was said about the election. They had word on the Saturday that the Orange lodges had met and given them [their members] a free vote ...

Gallacher reinforced both these points in his own report to the PB:

> The big important thing was that Catholics and Orangemen were united in the support of the campaign. At Valleyfield one of the women of the Orange [lodge] came with 2–3 others at the big dance that was held and there was unity of the Catholics and the Orange people.

This unity, he argued, had been achieved as a result of the successful campaigns by CP members for workmen's inspectors and the unification of the miners' unions: 'but undoubtedly the Valleyfield strike and the handling of the strike by the local officials played considerable part in strengthening this movement'.[123]

Gallacher's exceptional victory showed how consistent campaigning by an experienced and able Communist leader might build on the industrial militancy channelled through the UMS, even in a constituency whose boundaries did not encompass all the main areas of UMS influence. That the CP failed to do so elsewhere in its pockets of support in the Scots coalfields suggests the debilitating impact of Comintern policies, the lack of a coherent electoral strategy, continuing sectarian divisions and the dilute industrial composition of the other 'mining' constituencies. Gallacher's campaign also pointed to the generational exhaustion afflicting the general staff of bureaucratic reformism, particularly in Fife: Adamson died a few months after his defeat, aged 72.

Notes

1.   C. Harvie, 'Before the breakthrough, 1886–1922', in I. Donnachie. C. Harvie and I.S. Wood (eds), *Forward: Labour politics in Scotland,*

1888–1988 (Edinburgh, 1989), pp. 26–7. For a critique of such assumptions, not only as applied to Scotland, see D. Tanner, 'The Labour Party and electoral politics in the coalfields', in Campbell, Fishman and Howell, *Miners, Unions and Politics.*

2.   W. Knox and A. McKinlay, 'The re-making of Scottish Labour in the 1930s', *Twentieth Century British History*, 6, 2, 1995; see also Price's earlier argument about the fluidity of LP politics in Britain until the 1920s (R. Price, *Labour in British Society*, 1986, p. 137).

3.   M. Kinnear, *The British Voter: an atlas and survey since 1885* (1981), p. 117

4.   Tanner, 'Electoral politics', p. 87, n. 21.

5.   *Report of the Boundary Commission (Scotland)*, PP 1917–18, XIV, 89, 104.

6.   G. Brown, 'The Labour Party and political change in Scotland, 1918–29: the politics of five elections', unpublished PhD thesis, University of Edinburgh, 1981, p. 42. See vol. 1, ch. 7, Table 7.4.

7.   Hutchison, *Political History*, p. 287.

8.   I.S. Wood, 'Hope deferred: Labour in Scotland in the 1920s', in Donnachie, Harvie and Wood, *Forward!*, p. 33. For the shift in Catholic support to Labour in Glasgow, see T. Gallagher, *Glasgow, the uneasy peace* (Manchester, 1987), ch. 5; McLean, *Legend*, ch. 14.

9.   Brown, thesis, pp. 128–9; *Glasgow Herald*, 9 July 1919; F.W.S. Craig, *British Parliamentary Election Results, 1918–1949* (Edinburgh, 1969), p. 630.

10.   See also Dyer, *Capable Citizens*, p. 152.

11.   See vol. 1, ch. 7; G. Walker, 'The Orange Order in Scotland between the wars', *International Review of Social History*, 37, 1992, pp. 188–94; W.S. Marshall, *The Billy Boys: a concise history of Orangeism in Scotland* (Edinburgh, 1996), pp. 138–42; Hutchison, *Political History*, p. 288; *Forward*, 29 October 1921.

12.   See R. McKibbin, *The Evolution of the Labour Party, 1910–1924* (Oxford, 1974), ch. 7.

13.   Donnachie, 'The 1930s', p. 59; Knox and McKinlay, 'Re-making', p. 175; H. Pelling, *A Short History of the Labour Party* (2nd edn, 1965), pp. 134–5.

14.   NMLH, *Labour Party Annual Report for 1930*, pp. 144–8.

15.   Brown, thesis, p. 393; McKibbin, *Labour Party*, p. 148.

16.   Quoted in Hutchison, *Political History*, p. 283.

17.   *Workers' Life*, 3 February 1928.

18.   Hutchison, *Political History*, p. 298.

19.   Elections Committee Minute Book, 16 November, 22 November 1918 (Reel 1 of Hamilton Labour Party records in E.P. Microform series).

20. Brown, thesis, p. 61.

21. NLS NUSMW Executive, 22 February 1926, Political Committee, 8 March; Dep. 227/42, LMU Council 25 February, 3 March 1926; Brown, thesis, p. 394.

22. NMLH, SCLP Executive, 12 April 1926; SCLP, *Report of the Twelfth Annual Conference*, 5 March 1927; Annual Meeting of the Scottish Council, 1927.

23. NLS Dep. 227/88, NUSMW Political Committee, 2 April 1929, Executive, 12 April 1929.

24. NLS Dep. 227/88, NUSMW Political Committee, 28 December 1928, Executive, 4 January 1929.

25. NLS Dep. 227/88, NUSMW Political Committee, 2 April 1929.

26. NLS Dep. 227/88, NUSMW Executive, 29 April 1929.

27. NLS Dep. 227/45A, LMU Council, 2 December 1931, 6 January 1932; PL, 5 April 1932.

28. NLS Dep. 227/43, LMU Council, 5 January, 1 June 1927; Long, thesis, pp. 408–9.

29. J. Lee, *My Life with Nye* (Harmondsworth, 1981), p. 71. She recalled that after her election she met considerable hostility from the Scottish miners' MPs whose 'faces curdled up like a bowl of sour milk' whenever they met her at Westminster (Lee, *Great Journey*, p. 99).

30. D. Howell, 'Traditions, myths and legacies: the ILP and the Labour left', in McKinlay and Morris, *ILP on Clydeside*, pp. 207, 210, 212; see also Hutchison, *Political History*, pp. 279–80.

31. Knox and McKinlay, 'Re-making', p. 177.

32. *Workers' Life*, 19 October 1928.

33. NMLH Unnumbered reel of CI microfilm, document 495/33/239a; *Workers' Weekly*, 16 November 1923; R. Duncan, '"Motherwell for Moscow": Walton Newbold, revolutionary politics and the labour movement in a Lanarkshire constituency, 1918–1922', *Scottish Labour History Society Journal*, 28, 1993, p. 58. Kendall suggests only a few hundred left the ILP to join the CP (*Revolutionary Movement*, p. 276).

34. The LP's increasing prescription of Communists is analysed in E. Shaw, *Discipline and Discord in the Labour Party* (Manchester, 1988), pp. 4–15. PL, 14 November 1927; the Buckhaven branch is not listed as existing in 1928 or 1929 (*ILP Conference Reports*, 1928 and 1929).

35. W. Knox, '"Ours is not an ordinary Parliamentary movement": 1922–1926', in McKinlay and Morris, *ILP on Clydeside*, p. 167; A. McKinlay and J.J. Smyth, 'The end of "the agitator workman": 1926–32', in ibid., pp. 178–81; Hutchison, *Political History*, p. 279.

36. NMLH Unnumbered CI microfilm, R. Thompson to CPGB

Executive, 5 October 1922. For the ILP's weakness in Fife before 1914, see ch. 2 in this volume.

37. NLS Acc. 11087/2 and 3, 'Notes from ILP Bo'ness Branch Minutes: summary and extracts', 7 December 1927, 3 February 1932, and *passim*;

38. NLS Acc. 11087/3, Bo'ness SSP, 11 September 1932, 5 April 1933, 5 June, 3 July 1935, 5 June 1936, 7 July 1937.

39. Quoted in Knox and McKinlay, 'The re-making', p. 177.

40. W.H. Fraser, 'Introduction', Hamilton Labour Party (1981), p. 4.

41. NLS Acc. 11087/3, Bo'ness SSP, 5 June, 3 July 1935, 7 July 1937.

42. NLS Dep. 200, Dalkeith Local Labour Party, 4 August, 8, 12 September, 13 October, 24 November 1935. The AGM was attended by twenty-seven members (13 December 1935).

43. Ibid., 11 January 1939.

44. M. Savage, 'Urban politics and the rise of the Labour Party, 1919–39', in L. Jamieson and H. Corr (eds), *State, Private Life and Political Choice* (1990); J. Mark-Lawson, M. Savage and A. Warde, 'Gender and local politics: struggles over welfare, 1918–39', in L. Murgatroyd et al. (eds), *Localities, Class and Gender* (1985).

45. See vol. 1, ch. 5.

46. NMLH, SCLP Executive, 1924–7.

47. Minute Books, Women's Section, Larkhall Labour Party, 3 July, 7 August 1924, 15 April, 17 June 1926 (reel 2 of Hamilton Labour Party records in E.P. Microform series).

48. Ibid., 6, 12, 31 May, 3, 7 June, 3 July, 24 July, 16 September, 14 October 1926.

49. P.M. Graves, *Labour Women: women in British working-class politics, 1918–39* (Cambridge, 1994), pp. 157–67. Cf S. Bruley, 'Socialism and feminism in the Communist Party of Great Britain, 1920–39', unpublished PhD thesis, London School of Economics, 1980, pp. 92–125.

50. I. Donnachie, 'Scottish Labour in the depression: the 1930s', in Donnachie, Harvie and Wood, *Forward!*, p. 52.

51. See vol. 1, ch. 6, Table 6.4.

52. Donnachie, 'Scottish Labour', p. 59.

53. Knox and McKinlay, 'The re-making', p. 192.

54. NMLH Unnumbered CI microfilm, R. Thompson to CPGB Executive, 5 October 1922.

55. *Workers' Weekly*, 21 September 1923, 11 July 1924; MPL G032, Letter Book, 25 December 1923; MacDougall, *Militant Miners*, pp. 188, 214.

56. *Workers' Weekly*, 11, 25 July, 26 September, 3, 31 October 1924.

57. MacDougall, *Militant Miners*, p. 221; *Workers' Weekly*, 2 January, 24, 31 July 1925.

58. MacDougall, *Militant Miners*, pp. 281, 285; SRO HH 56/22, P.J. Rose to J.W. Peck, 23 July 1926; *Workers' Weekly*, 13 August 1926.
59. *Workers' Weekly*, 9 July, 13 August, 3 September 1926, 7 January 1927.
60. *Workers' Weekly*, 24 September 1926; *Workers' Life*, 23 December 1927.
61. *Workers' Life*, 25 March 1927.
62. PL, 27 January, 10 March, 11 May 1927.
63. PL, 31 March, 4 May 1927.
64. *Workers' Life*, 2 March 1928.
65. PL, 8 January 1931.
66. NMLH CI 12, PB, 9 April 1931; *Daily Worker*, 11 March 1932.
67. SRO HH 55/666, Reports to Chief Constable of Motherwell and Wishaw from Inspector Thompson, 12 October 1931, DC Murray, 21, 30 October 1931, DC Harris, 8 November 1931, DS Murray, 6 April 1932.
68. SRO HH 56/671, Chief Constable of Lanarkshire to Under-Secretary of State, Scottish Office, 28 October 1932.
69. SRO HH 55/681, Reports by Chief Constable, Coatbridge, to Under-Secretary of State, 1931–32.
70. SRO HH 55/695, Chief Constable of Ayrshire to Sheriff of Ayr, 11 February 1932.
71. SRO HH 55/666, Reports to Chief Constable, Motherwell and Wishaw, by DC Murray, 21 October 1931, DS Murray, 6 April 1932; HH 55/667, Report to Chief Constable, Motherwell and Wishaw, by DS Murray, 2 May 1933; HH 55/702, Chief Constable of Ayr to Under-Secretary of State, 1 February 1933.
72. NMLH CI 1, CC, 11–12 January, 5 April 1930.
73. NMLH CI 11, PB, 24 July 1930.
74. NMLH CI 3, CC, 4 June 1932.
75. NMLH CI 15, PB, 6 April 1934.
76. NMLH CI 33, Marty Secretariat, 20 February 1936; CI 8, CC, 3–4 December 1937.
77. MacDougall, *Militant Miners*, p. 139.
78. NMLH CI 2, CC, 19–20 September 1931.
79. NMLH CI 13, PB, 14 May 1932.
80. NMLH CI 13, PB, 29 December 1932.
81. NMLH CI 11, PB, 12 June 1930; *Daily Worker*, 26 June 1930. O'Neill had advocated the formation of Workers' Defence Corps at the first UMS conference (*Workers' Life*, 4 October 1929). It is not known when Selkirk rejoined the CP. His memoirs do not mention his expulsion, although when discussing 'class against class' he admits, 'we could not truthfully be accused of being to the right of that line' (Selkirk, *Life*, p. 26).

82. NMLH CI 1, CC, 13 September 1930.
83. Squires, 'CPGB', pp. 7–10.
84. NMLH CI 33, Marty Secretariat, 20 February 1936.
85. MacDougall, *Militant Miners*, p. 138.
86. NMLH CI 15, PB, 17 January 1934.
87. Wicks, *Keeping My Head*, p. 127; H. McShane and J. Smith, *No Mean Fighter* (1978), pp. 211–12.
88. Kay interview, Jimmy Miller; Macintyre, *Little Moscows*, p. 185; M. Docherty, *A Miners' Lass* (Cowdenbeath, 1992), pp. 66–81; *Daily Worker*, 2 May, 20 December 1932; interview with Mary Docherty, Cowdenbeath, 21 August 1989.
89. Cf Macintyre, *Little Moscows*, pp. 186–7.
90. NMLH Unnumbered CI microfilm, R. Thompson to CPGB Executive, 5 October 1922.
91. MacDougall, *Militant Miners*, p. 200; see also PL, 15 July 1928, 28 February 1930.
92. NMLH CI 13, PB, 29 December 1932.
93. Quoted in Bruley, thesis, p. 233.
94. NMLH CI 7, CC, 4 January 1936.
95. *Workers' Weekly*, 2 March 1928.
96. *Workers' Life*, 25 May 1928.
97. *Daily Worker*, 9 November 1933.
98. SRO HH 55/667, Report of DS Murray, 21 January 1934; *Daily Worker*, 5 December 1935
99. NMLH CI 6, CC, 4 January 1936; MacDougall, *Militant Miners*, p. 147.
100. NMLH CI 28, 'To Members of the Politsecretariat' (submitted by the British members of the ECCI), and Politsecretariat, 1 July 1929.
101. NMLH CI 11, PB, 12 December 1930.
102. *Daily Worker*, 30 April, 14 May 1931.
103. *Motherwell Times*, 30 December 1921; Duncan, 'Motherwell', p. 50. Duncan's essay provides a valuable and detailed analysis of the constituency and election. For a more institutional account, see McKibbin, *Labour Party*, pp. 196–204.
104. *Motherwell Times*, 6 August, 17 September 1920, 22 April, 16 September 1921.
105. *Communist*, 11 November 1922; *Motherwell Times*, 3 November, 1922. For Cowie's Square and Craigneuk, and for housing conditions in Motherwell generally, see vol. 1, chs 4 and 5.
106. *Communist*, 11 November 1922.
107. John Rylands Library, Manchester, Newbold papers, 'Autobiographical materials relating to Newbold's political life'.
108. *Motherwell Times*, 24 November 1922.

109. John Rylands Library, 'Autobiographical material'; *Workers' Weekly*, 14 December 1923.
110. John Rylands Library, 'Autobiographical material'; NMLH, microfilm deposited 1995, Newbold to Inkpin, 8 September 1924.
111. Duncan, 'Motherwell for Moscow', p. 50.
112. KcKibbin, *Labour Party*, p. 204.
113. MacDougall, *Militant Miners*, pp. 17, 21, 86; Gallacher, *Last Memoirs*, pp. 184–6; Craig, *Election Results, 1918–1949*, p. 624.
114. PL, 14 February 1931.
115. See vol. 1, chs 3 and 4.
116. NMLH CI 15, PB, 6 April 1934, 31 January 1935.
117. *Lochgelly Times*, 9, 16 October 1935; *Dunfermline Press*, 5, 19 October 1935.
118. *Daily Worker*, 28, 29, 31 October, 5, 6, 14 November 1935; Moffat, *Life*, pp. 55–6. The UMS had gained support earlier that year through successfully taking the case of a young Valleyfield miner to the House of Lords. The Lords ruled that the Fife Coal Company's practice of deducting rent from the wages of the sons of miners who became unemployed was illegal (*Daily Worker*, 4 July 1935).
119. *Daily Worker*, 22 October 1935; *Lochgelly Times*, 16, 23 October 1935.
120. *Dunfermline Press*, 9, 16 November 1935.
121. *Dunfermline Press*, 9 November 1935; *Daily Worker*, 5, 9 November 1935.
122. *Daily Worker*, 9 November 1935.
123. NMLH CI 15, PB, 21 November 1935.

Conclusion

In 1945, the Scottish coalfields voted solidly for the Labour Party. Of the fourteen mining constituencies listed above in Table 8.1, Labour was victorious in all except North Midlothian and West Fife, where Gallacher increased his share of the ballot and raised his majority over Labour to 2,000 votes. Labour's victories were often decisive: the party secured 74 per cent of the vote in Hamilton, and over 60 per cent in seven other seats. For many historians and political scientists, this psephological pattern appears so natural a class reflex as to be beyond curiosity, the culmination of Labour's 'magnificent journey' which requires no further interrogation.

Yet as David Howell observes, 'it is an insensitive history which by telling it as it was, implies that that was how it had to be'.[1] For if we take as our vantage point the year 1920, a little more than two-thirds of the way through the period covered by these volumes, the future seemed less clear cut than such a teleology allows. In that year, the number of Scottish mineworkers reached their peak of 147,000 after the coal industry's long expansion, their economic importance underlined by the recent experiences of war, their bargaining power and confidence as yet not undermined by unemployment. If real differences endured between the four mining regions, these had nevertheless been significantly eroded since 1874 and, as the companion volume demonstrated, a more homogeneous workforce was to be forged in the following two decades through the ongoing effects of mechanisation and industrial concentration, endogamy and migration.

Labour had performed disappointingly in the mining areas in the general election two years before, while substantial votes for Marxist candidates in other parts of Scotland held out the prospect of greater influence for the left than had ever been achieved before 1914. John Maclean, standing as a member of the BSP and official Labour candidate for the Gorbals, and despite commencing his campaign in prison, secured the support of Irish organisations in the constituency and won 7,436 votes against over 14,000 cast for his Coalition opponent, the ex-Labour MP and government minister, George Barnes. At Motherwell, Newbold stood on an uncompromisingly revolutionary platform and gained 23 per cent of the vote.[2] The Scottish ILP had moved significantly to the left while the formation of the Communist Party of Great Britain in July 1920 and the subsequent unity negotiations with other left-wing elements appeared to offer the hope of a regroupment which might transcend the sectarianism of the pre-war years.

If the trade union leadership remained in firm control of the bureaucratic organisations which they had laboriously and painfully constructed in the preceding thirty years, their command was nevertheless under growing challenge from an insurgent reform movement with the support of the militant minority among a still youthful membership: 35 per cent of mineworkers were under twenty-five in 1921. The vote to dismiss the LMU General Secretary, David Gilmour, in 1918 was a portent of how this constituency might be mobilised. Moreover, union leaders such as Smillie and John Robertson were induced to voice the rhetoric of direct action as a result of this threat on their left flank. If the Sankey Award of 1919 had checked the immediate post-war militancy, the strong support for the short national coal strike in October 1920 which secured a temporary wages agreement demonstrated that that militancy had not yet been broken.

Yet 1920 also marked the beginning of a series of closures to any optimistic prognosis for the development of left alternatives to Labour. In August, the CPGB made the first of its applications for affiliation to the Labour Party; it received the first of its rejections the following month. Rather than function as a left opposition inside the Labour Party as Newbold had hoped, the CP was to follow a very different trajectory, in the coalfields as elsewhere. The Second Congress of the Comintern in Moscow in July 1920 laid down the twenty-one conditions for admission which imposed a hitherto unknown democratic centralism upon its British affiliate. As Kendall argues: 'It was here, rather than at the coincident London Communist Unity Convention, that the ideology and organisation of the CPGB was decided.'[3] This transformation did not come about overnight – indeed the slowness of the CPGB's 'bolshevisation' was a matter for constant criticism by the Comintern – but the mechanisms of Stalinist control which were in place by the formation of the UMS in 1929 were sufficient to preclude any semblance of organisational independence for that union. The large subsidies to the CPGB from Moscow – in 1922 alone, the fledgling party received five 'allocations' totalling £18,500 compared with a mere £866 collected in dues from its members – were only one of the control devices by which the indigenous left was suborned.[4] As the 1920s proceeded, the CPGB occupied the political space to the left of Labour and suppressed any potential alternatives. Although the full history of the ILP after its disaffiliation from the Labour Party in 1932 is only now being fully researched, the scope for a non-Stalinist left by the 1930s was heavily circumscribed by the presence of the CPGB.

The year 1921 saw a further closure with the collapse of the Triple Alliance and the failure of the trade union leadership to deliver support for the miners in the lockout. If the government had planned for such a contingency, and chosen the timing of the crisis strategically, its emergency organisation was nevertheless untried, its resolve untested. Although the coal industry was confronted with long term economic problems, the sinews of its still combative workforce, and those of other workers, had not yet been wasted by unemployment. By the next major conflict in 1926, the world had changed: weakened union organisations confronted a government determined and well equipped to impose the insistent demands of the coalowners and other sections of the ruling class.

By 1922, unemployment was biting deeply into Scottish mining communities, and continued to do so for fully fifteen years. In that year, Labour's electoral breakthrough narrowed further any hopes of developing political alternatives to its restricted ambitions. Although the party's hold on some Scottish mining seats remained tenuous, subject to potential challenges from the left or from right-wing sectarianism, a timid and cautious gradualism rather than political radicalism became the pervasive and dominant tradition. Writing in the 1960s, Hugh McDiarmid succinctly summarised the then prevailing ethos of bureaucratic reformism:

> The working-class movement in Scotland today is full of ... a lot of honest folk somewhat small minded and devoted to the cult of the petty virtues, if possible non-drinkers and good fathers of their families, 'afraid above all to go too far'. Striving not for social equality, but for the betterment of the workers, their 'leaders' (saving the mark) love the retail, the precedent and the routine. Punctilious administration is their main strength. Almost all of them have been workers. They have ... been educated 'not in the class struggle but in

administrative patience'. They were, and remain, afraid of John
Maclean.[5]

There were forceful and rational reasons for such an approach.
Unemployment corroded the aspiration that a better society might
be created in the post-1918 world. In the squalid housing conditions
of the Scottish mining communities, a flushing toilet or an indoor
water supply were, indeed, significant reforms for their recipients. In
the absence of any reformist solutions to the problems of the coal
industry, at least until after 1945, and in the context of union weakness and leadership caution, miners were forced to rely on pit
politics to defend working conditions. Here the Communist Party's
militants found sufficient space to exert some leverage and win
influence as the champions of working miners as well as their unemployed neighbours.

Yet translating this influence into party political support was an
enormous struggle. As well as working-class hostility to Stalinism
and the oscillating demands of Comintern policy, employer victimisation and state repression were a recurring hazard to militants.
The ruthlessness of Scottish coalowners in their dealings with union
activists has been documented in the preceding pages, even in
'paternalistic' villages such as Newtongrange where the threat of
eviction persisted into the 1930s. Nor was the application of state
violence exclusively a feature of the major mining conflicts. When
the NUWM successfully won an increase for an unemployed man
in the north Ayrshire village of Kilbirnie in 1932, the Chief
Constable reported that: 'The Communists were somewhat elated
by their victory ... They got the idea they were top dog ...'. His force
brutally baton charged the next NUWM demonstration of 2,000
people, which had been mounted, claimed the Chief Constable in
justification for the assault upon it by his men, 'in this spirit of "We
are the masters"...'. Despite widespread protests from the local
labour movement, he insisted 'that the touch of the baton they got
has done no harm'.[6] The truncheons of the state continued to keep
'hotheads' in their place so that voting Labour might well appear a
less painful alternative than a broken head.

Despite such barriers, the Communist Party was able to exert
leadership in some communities, notably in central and east Fife,
which escaped the scale of industrial devastation that afflicted
Lanarkshire and north Ayrshire. A cadre of local leaders was estab-

lished by the 1930s whose representation of workplace and community concerns won them popular political support.[7]

It was this generation of Communists who were trusted to lead the Scottish miners industrially once the long fought for goal of transforming the federal NUSMW into a single union was achieved in 1944 after a massive vote in favour by 50,570 to 3,011.[8] Yet it was an irony of history that the primary role of this generational unit and its successors was to oversee the 'rationalisation' and dismantling of the coal industry in Scotland under nationalisation. The nationalised coal industry marked the zenith of the industrial ambitions of bureaucratic reformism, but it exhibited the flaws predicted by Robert Small of the SDF in 1911 when he characterised nationalisation as state capitalism not socialism. Robin Page Arnot could justifiably end his *History of the Scottish Miners* in 1955 with proud hopes for the industry and its workers; in that year fifteen new sinkings were planned in the Scottish coalfields.[9] Looking back over the pit closures of the subsequent decades and the sustained state assault on the miners in 1984–5, such optimism was, alas, to prove unjustified.

Electorally, the Scottish miners became a significant reservoir of support for the Labour Party's 'one party state' north of the border. How the fruits of this political strategy are evaluated perhaps ultimately depends on one's view of the quality of life which came to be visited upon the former mining communities in what Christopher Harvie appropriately termed the 'unlovely third Scotland'.[10] In the years covered by this volume and its companion, Scottish miners and their families endured much, both above and below ground, as their industry expanded, rationalised and contracted: one cannot but conclude that they deserved a better future than the one they received.

Notes

1. Howell, *Lost Left*, p. 219.
2. Ibid., p. 193; Craig, *British Parliamentary Elections, 1918–1949*, p. 634.
3. Hessel, *Theses*, pp. 92–7, especially conditions 12 and 16; Kendall, *Revolutionary Movement*, p. 296.
4. NMLH Unnumbered reel of microfilm deposited 1995, 495/100/63, CPGB Statement of Income for the year ending December 31st 1922.

Kendall's arguments concerning the financial influence exerted by Moscow (Kendall, *Revolutionary Movement*, pp. 250ff) have been confirmed by recent archival openings. In 1933, for example, substantial subventions of £2,800 per month were being sent to the British party (PRO HW 17/19, GCHQ Decrypts of Comintern Messages, London to Moscow, 19 August, 30 October 1935).

5.   H. MacDiarmid, *The Company I've Kept* (1966), pp. 140–1.

6.   SRO HH 55/695, Chief Constable of Ayrshire to Sheriff of Ayr, 11 February 1932.

7.   Although Gallacher lost his parliamentary seat in 1950 at the height of the Cold War, the enduring tradition of communism in Fife was evidenced by continuing support for CP candidates in local elections. In 1971, 30 per cent of votes in Cowdenbeath were cast for the party and two Communist councillors sat on the twelve-strong town council. The party branch claimed a membership of 145 (A. Maxwell, 'Are Cowdenbeath folk different?', *Comment*, 6 February 1971).

8.   Arnot, *History*, pp. 263–4.

9.   R.S. Halliday, *The Disappearing Scottish Colliery* (Edinburgh, 1990), p. 45.

10.   C. Harvie, *No Gods and Precious Few Heroes: Scotland, 1914–1980* (1981), p. 66.

Index